NEOLIBERALISM AND YOUNG ADULT FICTION

Children's Literature Association Series

NEOLIBERALISM AND YOUNG ADULT FICTION

Exceptionalism, Exploitation, and Erasure

Sean P. Connors and
Roberta Seelinger Trites

University Press of Mississippi / Jackson

www.upress.state.ms.us

The University Press of Mississippi is a member
of the Association of University Presses.

Copyright © 2025 by University Press of Mississippi
All rights reserved
∞

Cover art by Dylan Hale

Portions of chapter 1 appear in the *ALAN Review* (NCTE) and
Engaging with Young Adult Literature in the Secondary Classroom
(© 2019, Routledge/Taylor & Francis: Reproduced by permission of
Taylor and Francis Group, LLC, a division of Informa plc.)

Portions of chapter 2 appear in *SIGNAL* and the
Journal of Children's Literature (NCTE).

Portions of chapter 6 and 7 appear in *English Journal* (NCTE) as
"Critiquing Neoliberalism and Postrace Discourse in Narratives for Young People"
and in *Race in Young Adult Speculative Fiction*, edited by Meghan Gilbert Hickey
and Miranda A. Green-Barteet (University Press of Mississippi, 2021).

Portions of chapter 8 appear in *FRAME: A Literary Journal*:
https://www.frameliteraryjournal.com/34-1-literature-and-activism
/34-1-sean-p-connors-and-roberta-seelinger-trites/.

Library of Congress Cataloging-in-Publication Data

Names: Connors, Sean P., author. | Trites, Roberta Seelinger, 1962– author.
Title: Neoliberalism and young adult fiction : exceptionalism, exploitation, and erasure / Sean P. Connors, Roberta Seelinger Trites.
Other titles: Children's Literature Association series.
Description: Jackson : University Press of Mississippi, 2025. | Series: Children's literature association series | Includes bibliographical references and index.
Identifiers: LCCN 2024052587 (print) | LCCN 2024052588 (ebook) | ISBN 9781496855794 (hardback) | ISBN 9781496855800 (trade paperback) | ISBN 9781496855817 (epub) | ISBN 9781496855824 (epub) | ISBN 9781496855831 (pdf) | ISBN 9781496855848 (pdf)
Subjects: LCSH: Young adult fiction, American—21st century—History and criticism. | Neoliberalism in literature. | Dystopias in literature. | Racism in literature. | Sexism in literature.
Classification: LCC PS374.Y57 C65 2025 (print) | LCC PS374.Y57 (ebook) | DDC 813.009/9283—dc23/eng/20241217
LC record available at https://lccn.loc.gov/2024052587
LC ebook record available at https://lccn.loc.gov/2024052588

We dedicate this work to our students and to those scholars who encouraged us to pursue this topic—you know who you are.

CONTENTS

Preface ix

Introduction 3

Chapter 1: Self-Enclosed Individualism and the Neoliberal Tradition . . 23

Chapter 2: Neoliberalism's Logic of Exploitation 55

Chapter 3: US Neoliberalism and Its Racist Origins 83

Chapter 4: Racism in Our Neoliberal Era 105

Chapter 5: Resisting Postfeminist Thinking 128

Chapter 6: Biopolitics and Neoliberal Erasure 161

Chapter 7: Knowledge Production and Neoliberalism 186

Chapter 8: Youth Activism as a Response to Neoliberalism 209

Notes 229

Works Cited 235

Index 253

PREFACE

> You have provided a spark that, left unattended,
> may grow to an inferno.
>
> —Suzanne Collins, *Catching Fire* (23)

Because the coauthorship of this book started unexpectedly, we regard its presence in the world as a testament to the serendipitous turn that life sometimes takes. The first author, Sean, reached out to Roberta in 2015 to tell her about a young adult (YA) dystopian novel undergraduates were reading in an elective he was teaching: "The Hunger Games and YA Dystopian Fiction" (Connors, "Orleans"). Sean recommended Sherri L. Smith's *Orleans* to Roberta because he knew she would appreciate how it rejects what was then a prevalent trope of a talented, purportedly feminist protagonist (who is almost always white, cis, heterosexual) using her femininity to dismantle unjust systems of power so as to liberate her society from dystopian oppression. Smith's 2013 novel rejects that pattern by depicting a teen protagonist who sets aside her individualism to work toward the common good with other people. At the end of the novel, her survival is an open question. Not long after Sean emailed Roberta about *Orleans* in 2015, we began writing our first scholarly article together.

In the days, weeks, and months of drafting and redrafting that article, we found ourselves exchanging many questions about dystopian fiction for teenagers. For example, what are the social implications of the genre repeatedly depicting talented individuals, rather than governments, solving complex social problems? Why are so many dystopian narratives for the young set in a future that purports to be color-blind or gender-blind, and do readers come to understand how that futuristic US society has managed to escape its own history of racism and sexism? Likewise, recognizing that YA dystopias are often set in societies ravaged by global warming and other climate-related disasters, we wondered: to what extent do these stories connect those problems to economically motivated exploitation of the environment? As we contemplated related questions, we began to ask whether the aforementioned issues are germane only to dystopian fiction or whether they also permeate other YA genres, including realism.

More broadly, we found ourselves investigating how neoliberal practices reflect—and even shape—YA narratives and their ideological apparatuses. Our deep dive into the scholarship on neoliberal exploitation of peoples and the environment, as well as our studying neoliberalism's resistance to government regulations and institutions, confirmed our theoretical speculations, leading us to also recognize that we only had the bandwidth to analyze this econo-political ideology as it manifests itself in the US. Even just an initial review of relevant scholarship indicated that examining the effects of global neoliberalism on YA literature would take volumes.

Proponents of neoliberalism in the US advocate for the following: weakening government regulations (including those that favor environmental protection over profitability); defunding social safety-net programs that provide a lifeline for vulnerable peoples; undermining unions and collective bargaining agreements that benefit workers; eroding institutions such as public education, the judiciary, and the postal system, all of which the nation's founders considered imperative to its survival; implementing austerity budgets; privatizing public goods and services; and conceptualizing nearly all domains of human life (from child care to retirement) as markets in which people ought to be made to compete. But individuals are not poised to correct widescale human error, discrimination, economic downturns, wastefulness, pollution, or corporate and bureaucratic corruption. Only governments have the material resources to create regulations and fund projects to reverse that which threatens the future welfare of humans, nonhuman animals, plants and vegetation, and the very Earth itself.

Furthermore, as we worked on this book, we became even more acutely aware of how insidiously the neoliberal econo-political system depends on exploiting the environment and people of color. Neoliberalism upholds and perpetuates systemic racism, sexism, classism, and anthropocentrism, even while it masks the form these insidious constructs take. Having witnessed President Trump's prioritization of the economy over people's health during the COVID-19 pandemic and the police murder of George Floyd in the summer of 2020, we wondered how the country we both love so much had arrived at such a dismal, dark, and dangerous place.

If the picture we paint of US neoliberalism appears unnecessarily bleak, we wish to emphasize that we paint this portrait so starkly because we worry about the impediments these massive problems pose for our students and their futures. As teachers and scholars of YA literature, we have seen neoliberalism's fingerprints all over the texts we've studied and taught. For example, after working on *Orleans*, we discovered that another popular YA dystopia our students often recommended, *Cinder*, diametrically opposes the former's ideology in its valuation of economic individualism. From there, the neoliberal influences on the Hunger Games trilogy were easy to connect to this project. We then began to examine the prevalence of neoliberalism in genres other than dystopia. The Harry Potter series convinced us that fantasy novels can also be neoliberal, especially when they emphasize exceptionality and competitiveness. *The Disreputable History of Frankie Landau-Banks* proved to us that neoliberalism influences realism, too, whereas *Marcelo in the Real World* surprised us in its critique of hypercompetitiveness. We increasingly found ourselves wondering about the ideological spectrum along which texts for teenagers could be placed, depending on the extent to which they reproduce or resist neoliberalism.

We eventually realized that teen fiction ranges from that which is fully neoliberal, even when unintentionally so, to that which rejects neoliberalism altogether. Most YA literature falls somewhere between the two poles of that spectrum. And by the time we were writing the final chapters of this book, we came to understand that neoliberalism influences nonfiction, too—especially when youth activists write memoirs rejecting neoliberal environmentalism. Despite the gravity of the social and political issues our study has led us to confront, it paradoxically culminates in our feeling some hope for the future because we observe many young people questioning, or rejecting altogether, neoliberalism's ethos of unchecked greed and hyperindividualism.

As our recounting of this book's evolution suggests, we approached this project as an inductive study of neoliberalism in YA fiction from the beginning. As early as 2015, when we were reading YA books—often during the process of syllabi formation, but more often for pleasure—we would communicate with one another about the degree to which various novels reflected or rejected neoliberal ideologies. As we read more widely, we identified recurring issues in those texts and gradually began to outline this book. Interestingly, on the short drive to work one day, Roberta realized that our core topics were "economics, embodiment, and ecocriticism." Not long after, Sean's reading led him to propose that we examine the relationship between postracialism, postfeminism, and neoliberalism. Still later, as our study began to ripen, we modified the list to generate more specific categories: *exceptionalism* (and competition), *exploitation* of people and the Earth, and *erasure* based on race, gender identity, sexual orientation, or ability. Nevertheless, our interrogation of YA literature published in the US was not without hope, especially once we became aware of how such books as *The Hate U Give* and *A Snake Falls to Earth* depict teenagers resisting neoliberal exploitation of their communities through engaging in activism. Building on prior research Sean had already undertaken, we developed an appreciation of YA narratives' potential to inspire some teens to activism (Connors, "Becoming Mockingjays" 18–29).

When we have talked about these issues with our college students, especially traditionally aged undergraduates, we find them to be surprisingly receptive, in part because their generation cares so much about social justice and the climate, regardless of political affiliation. For example, the in-service and pre-service teachers Sean works with in Arkansas report observing high schoolers becoming especially animated about the concept of competition and individualism, since they themselves have been harmed by these attitudes. In Illinois, the English education majors Roberta teaches report observing high school students' strong responses to nonfiction, such as Marc Aronson's YA nonfiction book *Race*, which traces the long history of racism and anti-Semitism in so-called "western" countries. Sometimes these high school freshmen react positively; sometimes they reject the book outright, but they always engage in a rich conversation. This is also the case when students in Sean's YA literature class read *Stamped* by Jason Reynolds and Ibram X. Kendi. Why? Because while high school and college students may not be familiar with such academic concepts as "neoliberalism," "biopolitics," "neoliberal environmentalism," and "postracialism," they likely understand intuitively how these forces (if not necessarily the specific terms used to describe them) operate in their own lives.

Our initial concern with helping college and high school students, as well as those who teach them, to identify the neoliberal ideologies that teenagers consume in YA literature and popular culture informed how we approached writing this book. Early in the project, we decided we wanted to write a book aimed at multiple audiences: scholars of YA literature; teacher educators; practicing teachers and pre-service teachers; librarians and information scientists; and graduate and undergraduate students interested in literature.

One might imagine that living with a topic such as neoliberalism and its negative societal effects for years on end could prove dispiriting. That was not our experience, however. What started when Sean thought to reach out to Roberta with a book recommendation evolved into a productive writing partnership, and eventually, a close and mutually valued friendship that has only grown stronger with time. For that, we are both grateful.

Our gratitude does not end there, however. We wish to acknowledge the many colleagues and scholars whose work has inspired us and who have generously shared their feedback, encouraging us to persist with this project, even when we questioned the wisdom of doing so. We would thus like to thank the following for their support, insights, feedback, and many kindnesses: Michelle Abate, Ed Bentgson, Molly Blackburn, Susan Burt, Mike Cadden, Sarah Park Dahlen, Sara K. Day, Victor Devinatz, Toby Emert, Neda Farnia, Steve Field, Meghan Gilbert-Hickey, Ricki Ginsberg, Wendy Glenn, Chris Goering, Miranda A. Green-Barteet, Libby Gruner, Dylan Hale, Roxanne Harde, Betsy Hearne, Sarah Hentges, Crag Hill, Maude Hines, Billie Jarvis-Freeman, Jeremy Johnston, Kenneth Kidd, Amber Majors Ladipo, Amy and Allen Lewis, Greta Little, Margaret Mackey, Victor Malo-Juvera, Rose Marshack, Richard F. Martin, Mary Jeanette Moran, Megan Musgrave, Phil Nel, Terry Noel, Sally Parry, Anne Phillips, Amy E. Robillard, Joseph Rodriguez, Joe Sutliff Sanders, Anna O. Soter, Jim Stanlaw, Susan L. Stewart, Lissette Lopez Szwydky, Paul Thomas, Rick Valentin, Mark West, Scott Williams, and the late Vivian Yenika-Agbaw. Katie Keene, Katie Turner, and the whole team at the University Press of Mississippi—including our copyeditor, Peter Tonguette—also deserve our praise and appreciation.

We must also thank our families for their patience, love, and support. For Sean, this includes his mother, brother, and sisters. For Roberta, this includes her husband, sons, daughter, sisters, twin brother, and his wife. The University of Arkansas and Illinois State University provided us with sabbaticals that gave us time we both needed for research and writing. The Children's Literature Association and the International Research Society for Children's Literature gave us intellectual spaces to commune with scholars who share our interests. And last, but certainly not least, we wish to thank Arthur Smalls, Sean's black lab and faithful writing companion, who begrudgingly passed up walks to help bring this book to fruition. When we found ourselves immersed too deeply in economics and politics, simply talking about him brought a smile to both our faces.

NEOLIBERALISM AND YOUNG ADULT FICTION

INTRODUCTION

At times, the list of concerns facing the US in the second decade of this century feels overwhelming. From our vantage point in the middle of the 2020s, this list includes persistent problems caused by systemic racism, as evidenced by the continued brutalization of people of color at the hands of the police; a once-in-a-century pandemic that, at the time of this writing, has claimed the lives of over seven million people worldwide; massive economic inequality and corporate corruption that is reminiscent of the Gilded Age in the US; seemingly irreconcilable political and ideological divisions leading to increasingly divisive factionalism; the unfolding of a sixth great extinction that scientists attribute to human activity; and climate change, the threat of which imperils the future of many species, including humans, due to the latter's dependency on fossil fuels. Wars rage in Ukraine and the Middle East, generating animosity among groups who regard these violent conflicts from differing perspectives. Indeed, the institutions of democracy seem to be under threat from authoritarianism across the globe (Freedom House). In the face of these calamities and cataclysms, many people feel powerless, even hopeless. Our decision to write a book that examines the presence of neoliberalism and its attendant discourses and ideologies in literature for teenagers was motivated in part by our desire *not* to give in to feelings of despair, *not* to remain silent in the face of the many problems that beset our society in the first quarter of the twenty-first century.

But why a book about neoliberalism? And why a book about neoliberalism in young adult (YA) literature? To answer those questions, we would like to examine some of the aforementioned problems in closer detail by looking closely at the first year of this decade: 2020.

HOW DID WE GET HERE?

We assume that most readers will agree that 2020 was a historic year. In February, as a novel coronavirus spread, crossing national borders and forcing governments around the world to close schools and businesses and order their citizens to stay at home, its economic impact was felt internationally. In the US, record layoffs and bankruptcies led nearly a fifth of the American workforce to file for unemployment (Tappe). At the same time, some elected officials expressed concern about the long-term impact social distancing measures would have on the national economy (Wise). While their concerns were warranted, in some cases, they led to a worrisome privileging of the economy at the cost of human health.

For example, in March 2020, Dan Patrick, the acting lieutenant governor of Texas, appeared on the Fox News network, where he shared his concerns about the pandemic's impact on the economy with then-host Tucker Carlson. In the course of his remarks, Patrick, who was sixty-nine years old at the time, argued that out of concern for their children and grandchildren, elderly people ought to be willing to sacrifice themselves to protect what had been, until that point in time, a robust economy. When a visibly surprised Carlson, hardly a liberal commentator, asked whether Patrick meant to say there are worse things than dying, Patrick responded in the affirmative. A month later, in April, he returned to Carlson's program where, rather than walking back or qualifying his earlier remarks, he instead doubled down on them, reiterating his contention that "there are more important things than living" (Madani).

Shocking though Patrick's comments were at the time, he was not alone in his concern for the welfare of the US economy. Although health officials and some political leaders insisted on the imperative of keeping people home until businesses and schools were prepared to implement measures to protect those they serve from the coronavirus, others, like Trey Hollingsworth, a Republican congressman from the state of Indiana, advocated for reopening the economy as quickly as possible so that people could return to work and school. Characterizing the latter option as the lesser of two evils, Hollingsworth argued, "it is always the American government's position to say, in the choice between the loss of our way of life as Americans and the loss of life of American lives, we have to always choose the latter" (Zhao). Even Larry Kudlow, then the White House National Economic Council chairman, cautioned against allowing the "cure to be worse than the disease" (Wise).

President Donald Trump, ever mindful of what a poor economy would mean for both his reelection prospects and his business interests, was among the most vocal advocates for reopening the economy quickly. That Americans risked losing their lives in the process appeared to mean little to Trump, who likened them to military combatants when he told reporters in early May while the number of coronavirus cases in the US continued to grow: "I'm viewing our great citizens of this country to a certain extent and to a large extent as warriors. They're warriors. We can't keep our country closed. We have to open our country." He continued, "Will some people be affected badly? Yes. But we have to get our country open and we have to get it open soon" (Goldschlag and Janison). Faced with the prospect of a damaged economy on the one hand and a loss of human life on the other, Trump, like Hollingsworth, understood the latter as the lesser of two evils.

Although Trump neglected to comment on *who* might perish so that the economy could reopen, the risk was not distributed evenly throughout society. Communities of color were found to experience the effects of COVID-19 disproportionately. On the Navajo Nation reservation, for example, where food deserts are a persistent problem, many people had no alternative but to leave home and travel long distances to shop for groceries and other household necessities. Infrastructural inequalities, such as limited access to running water and the internet, made it hard for many of the Navajo to comply with health department guidelines and wash their hands frequently or even stay abreast of the most current health-related information (Morales). As a result, the virus spread rapidly, and in May 2020 the Navajo Nation surpassed New York and New Jersey in reporting the highest number of COVID-19 cases per capita in the US (Silverman et al.).

African Americans, Latinx, and Indigenous peoples were found to suffer disproportionately from COVID-19 as well, prompting Dr. Jerome Adams, the acting US surgeon general at the time, to recommend that they curb their use of tobacco, alcohol, and drugs so as to lessen their vulnerability to the disease, a victim-blaming injunction that the African American surgeon general had offered to no other groups (Papenfuss). Instead, Adams's comments masked the role that structural problems, such as poverty, racism, lack of access to health care, high unemployment, and poor air and water quality, play in causing people of color to experience comorbidities. After Trump contracted the coronavirus himself, he tweeted, "Don't be afraid of Covid. Don't let it dominate your life," ignoring the fact that he had the best medical care available in the world, while also implying that those who had already died chose to let the disease kill them (Kolata and Rabin). Racism, economic opportunism, incompetent leadership, and a blatant disregard for human lives were all factors implicated in worsening the number of deaths attributable to COVID-19 in a country that was one of the hardest hit in 2020: the United States of America.

As if a hundred-year pandemic and unprecedented economic problems weren't enough, in late May 2020, the country fractured further when four police officers in Minneapolis, Minnesota, murdered George Floyd, an African American man who was unemployed because of the pandemic, and who was accused of having purchased cigarettes at a local convenience store with a fake twenty-dollar bill. In a cell phone video that subsequently went viral, a white police officer, Derek Chauvin, was shown holding his knee against the back of Floyd's neck for nearly nine minutes, despite Floyd's repeated protests that he was unable to breathe and despite the fact that he had proven to be physically incapable of resisting arrest. In the weeks that followed, massive protests engulfed cities throughout the US. Even though the protests were overwhelmingly peaceful, in some cases they devolved into chaos after night fell, when angry people clashed with the police, torched buildings and cars, and looted local businesses. In Portland, Oregon, President Trump deployed federal agents (untrained in how to respond to protestors) from Customs and Border Protection, Immigration and Customs Enforcement, the Transportation Security Administration, and the Coast Guard to support the (trained) Federal Protective Service (Olmos, Baker, Kanno-Youngs). Since Martin Luther King's assassination in 1968, only four times has a sitting US president called for federal agents to engage with civilians: Richard Nixon (1970), George H. W. Bush (1989 and 1992), and Donald Trump (2020) (Berlin and Rumore). Trump also used the National Guard to quell civil unrest following George Floyd's death (Rogers). Events seemed to come full circle when, amidst reports that the unemployment rate had also fallen, Trump callously drew a direct line between the economy and George Floyd's death, stating, "Hopefully George is looking down and saying this is a great thing that's happening for our country. (It's) a great day for him. It's a great day for everybody" (Vazquez).

What do these conditions and historical events have in common? In each instance, they are the result of some form of exploitation: exploitation of the economy by political leaders for their own political gain; exploitation by CEOs and Wall Street trading companies intent on amassing vulgar fortunes; the exploitation of African Americans still living with the structural racism that is the wicked legacy of enslavement; exploitation on many levels of immigrants, too many of whom have had children caged at the border of Mexico; exploitation of the Earth that has led to floods and fires and famine. Indeed, scientists speculated in 2020 that the coronavirus likely emerged in Wuhan from human interaction with bats, whose natural habitat once provided a buffer between them and humans, but which has since been encroached upon and developed to accommodate the city's growing population (Friedman). Not coincidentally, the working-class laborers who were deemed "essential" during the initial phase of the 2020 coronavirus quarantine in the US were those earning minimum wage, driven to keep their jobs or face unemployment. Exploitation is both the fundamental and the necessary condition for neoliberalism's existence.

NEOLIBERALISM: FROM INDIVIDUALISM TO SOLIPSISM

From political leaders prioritizing the economy over human life, to a higher mortality rate for COVID-19 patients in communities of color, to the murder of George Floyd (and Philando Castile, Breonna Taylor, Ahmaud Arbery, Michael Brown, and Tamir Rice, to name but a few of those whose lives have been taken by the police) at the hands of the state, the aforementioned events are not unrelated. Rather, they bear the imprint of neoliberalism, a set of economic, political, social, and cultural forces founded on a belief in the inviolability of the free market and the supremacy of competition as the engine of progress. Central to neoliberalism is a belief that all of society benefits when individual actors, including both people and corporations, are free to maximize their talents in the service of responding to social needs and problems. In contrast to eighteenth- and nineteenth-century classical *laissez-faire liberalism*, which opposed government intervention in the economic sphere but recognized a need for government to protect the rights of its citizens in the public sphere, neoliberalism does not distinguish between these two realms of human life.[1] Instead, it is hostile to government intervention and regulation, and it advocates limiting the role of government to promoting competition, opening up new economic markets, and protecting existing ones. In this way, "neoliberal theory and practice aim to free human beings from excessive state control in order to pursue their own lives through market competition" (Braedley and Luxton 12).

According to Wendy Brown, "neoliberal rationality disseminates the *model of the market* to all domains and activities—even where money is not at issue—and configures human beings exhaustively as market actors" (31, emphasis in the original). In the twenty-first century, the influence of neoliberalism resonates through all domains of human life and well beyond the marketplace, from the privatization of education and health care to the deregulation of air travel, telecommunications, and the fossil fuel industries. Everything is affected, from child care to social media, from Big Pharma (which is a public good in many countries) to the widespread availability of assault weapons that enable mass murderers. In many cases, deregulation has been a result of a movement toward privatization. For example, whereas in the past education was regarded as a public good, today, many state legislatures are less willing to support public education, with the result that charter schools, virtual schools, and for-profit colleges compete for taxpayer dollars with traditional public schools, colleges, and universities. Homeless shelters and food banks, once the purview of local municipalities, have increasingly been privatized, as have prisons. Neoliberalism has even changed how wars are fought at a time when governments turn over responsibility for conducting military operations to private security forces, as was the case with Blackwater, a private American military company, during the second US war in Iraq.

In a society where competition reigns supreme and where success is predicated on the degree to which individual entrepreneurs are able to leverage their skills and talents, individual people's relationship to themselves is fundamentally changed. As Julie A. Wilson explains:

> Neoliberal individuals are selves who think of and relate to themselves as an investment, that is, as subjects who are constantly working to *appreciate* the self and its value over time.... Freedom and success are not guaranteed by one's status as a citizen; instead, they depend on making good choices and the right investments across all of the increasingly marketized contexts of everyday life. (*Neoliberalism* 65, emphasis in the original)

The responsibility for one's choices and investments can become untenable, especially for those who are not succeeding in this neoliberal economy.

Whereas in the past, a middle-class union worker, or even a nonunion worker, might have expected to stay in a secure job with benefits for the long term, in today's gig economy, flexibility and adaptability are valued and rewarded. Therefore, a growing number of Americans are faced with the reality of having to move frequently between short-term jobs. To maintain their competitive edge, people are expected to assume responsibility for continually expanding their knowledge and skill set, lest they lose ground to competitors. High school and college students compete for grades, internships, and other resume-building opportunities to bolster their competitiveness in an otherwise tight job market. In an age of social media, people are expected to act as their own self-agents, using Instagram, LinkedIn, the platform formerly known as Twitter, and other such sites to promote their own personal "brand." In such a climate, is it any wonder that a growing number of people report feeling more stress, anxiety, and exhaustion?[2]

Underlying neoliberalism's emphasis on competition is an unwavering, long-term faith in American meritocracy. Neoliberalism, influenced as it is by libertarian thought, denies that such social constructs as race, gender, and class influence people's life chances. In turn, this blinkered thinking then allows for the dismissal of structural problems like racism and sexism and classism. At the same time, neoliberalism creates an atmosphere in which social programs that were meant to ensure that members of domestic minorities have access to equal opportunities—for instance, affirmative action—can be maligned for somehow providing beneficiaries of social programs an undue advantage, thus undermining their competitive spirit. For example, a conservative-leaning Supreme Court struck down the consideration of affirmative action in college admissions in the 2023 case *Students for Fair Admission v. Harvard and UNC*. In such instances, neoliberalism depends on discourses such as the labels "postracialism" and "postfeminism," which presuppose the pernicious idea that society has progressed to a point at which race or gender no longer advantage or disadvantage people. These presumptions are belied, of course, by a body of data that attests to women earning lower wages than men; higher rates of unemployment for people of color; unequal pay for Black, Indigenous, and Latinx workers; substandard support for education in majority-minority communities; and insufficient health care for people of color. To delegitimize socioeconomic concerns about racial stratification, however, proponents of neoliberalism resort to "power-evasive strategies such as blaming minorities of class and color for not working hard enough" (Giroux 193). Within the logic of neoliberal thought, *structural* problems—for example, racism and poverty—are recast as *individual* problems. In a neoliberal social order, when people experience poverty, that is ostensibly attributable only to their own individual failures.

Although capitalism has always privileged some groups of people at the expense of others, in neoliberalism, even more people seem to be potentially disposable. Consider, for example, the case of the 2008 Great Recession, when millions of Americans suddenly found themselves unemployed, some for years, in spite of their education and prior accomplishments. This was the case again twelve years later when the novel coronavirus wrought havoc on the US economy, producing unemployment levels not seen since the Great Depression. In her book *State of Insecurity: Government of the Precarious*, Isabell Lorey argues that a concern with maintaining acceptable levels of social precarity is in fact central to neoliberal governance: "Contrary to the old rule of a domination that demands obedience in exchange for protection, neoliberal governing proceeds primarily through social insecurity, through regulating the minimum of assurance while simultaneously increasing instability"

(2). In a society founded on the precept of competition, most people cannot be allowed to rest on their laurels or bask in feelings of security. Instead, they are expected to hustle to get ahead. This is why staunch neoliberals perceive social safety-net programs such as Social Security, Medicare, and Medicaid as breeding reliance on the government. We agree, however, with Julie Wilson: no one, no matter how talented or competitive they might be, is entirely in control of their fate when they live within complex socioeconomic systems (*Neoliberalism* 4).

Neoliberalism's hyperemphasis on competition and individualism privileges independence at the expense of *interdependence*, which Dan Goodley and Mark Rapley define in terms of people working together toward the shared goals of their community (137–38). In doing so, neoliberalism conveniently papers over the reality that our fates are in fact connected. This was evident in the remarks of political leaders who callously acknowledged that reopening the national economy in the midst of a 100-year pandemic necessitated sacrificing some people so that others might return to school and work. And as the protests over George Floyd's death also made clear, peace is not possible in a society that values some lives more than others.

In extolling individualism, neoliberalism precludes people in the US from recognizing that our ability to address the pressing problems that divide and weaken us as a nation necessitates collective action, not a retreat into solipsism. As Julie Wilson notes, "living in competition paradoxically undercuts what enables our lives—that is, our social connections and infrastructures—while telling us to assume more and more responsibility through self-enclosed individualism, thereby squashing our capacities for coming together, trusting and caring for each other, and organizing for social change" (*Neoliberalism* 5). In short, incessant competition breeds social isolation.

NEOLIBERALISM AND YA LITERATURE

In *A Brief History of Neoliberalism*, David Harvey argues, "For any way of thought to become dominant, a conceptual apparatus has to be advanced that appeals to our intuitions and instincts, to our values and desires, as well as to the possibilities inherent in the social world we inhabit. If successful, this conceptual apparatus becomes so embedded in common sense as to be taken for granted and not open to question" (5). In this book, we argue that YA literature, a category of literature that Trites has argued socializes teenagers to accept their place in the extant power structure, can normalize neoliberalism in precisely the way that Harvey envisions (Trites, *Disturbing* 20). As early as

1988, Peter Hollindale led the field of children's and adolescent literature to understand the importance of Louis Althusser's work "Lenin and Philosophy," which demonstrates how people are interpellated by ideology. According to Althusser, "Ideology represents the imaginary relationship of individuals to their real conditions of existence" (109); moreover, "the reproduction of labour power requires not only a reproduction of its skills, but also, at the same time, a reproduction of its submission to the rules of the established order" (89). Althusser defines school as being chief among the "Ideological State Apparatuses" that provide children with their early immersion into the culture's system of beliefs (88–89). Writing about literature for the young as an ideological apparatus, Hollindale characterizes the concept of ideology as "a climate of belief" that permeates any given text (19). In his 1992 work, John Stephens emphasizes Althusser's investment in the discursive basis of ideology, arguing: "Ideology is formulated in and by language; meanings within language are socially determined, and narratives are constructed out of language" (Stephens 8). Althusserian examinations of ideology have proven to be one of the most important long-term developments in the study of literature for youth. This book continues that line of intellectual inquiry with a specific focus on neoliberalism as a political, economic, and social theory that slowly began to permeate YA literature in approximately the middle of the 1960s and has crescendoed since the 1980s.

Hollindale and Stephens have inspired many scholars to explore the ideological nature of literature for the young, examining its influential use as a political tool within historical contexts. Among these are, for example, Lynne Vallone (1995), who explores the concept of "virtue" as it was used to indoctrinate girls into femininity in the eighteenth and nineteenth centuries. Also writing about gender, Kenneth Kidd (2004) examines how the concept of the American boy was framed within the concept of "boyology"—the study of boyhood—that emerged in the late portion of the nineteenth century. In 2006, Kate Capshaw (Smith) demonstrates how fully the literature written for youth during the Harlem Renaissance served to knit together Black communities throughout the US. Also in 2006, Julia Mickenberg describes in intricate detail how the Radical Left of the first half of the twentieth century relied on literature for youth to appeal to children and teenagers. Trites (2007) situates the US tendency to value adolescent reform-oriented literature within the ideological reform legacies left by Louisa May Alcott and Mark Twain. Sara L. Schwebel (2011) identifies misinformation in historical children's novels that are canonically taught in US classrooms, pointing out particularly the problematic whitewashing of America's racial history. Joe Sutliff Sanders (2011) analyzes the role of discipline as it was historically used in fiction to socialize girls via the genre of the orphan tale. Ebony Elizabeth Thomas (2019) examines the "Dark Fantastic" as a pattern in which Black girls in fantastic genres are displaced by white characters, reflecting the violence endured by Black and brown people to ensure white supremacy; she also observes how readers of color reimagine fantasy worlds in ways that reflect their own lived experiences. All of these critical volumes acknowledge the discursive power of ideology in shaping youth culture in the US. We see our project as following in the same vein of culturally situated ideological interrogation, specifically in the way we examine neoliberal ideologies in YA literature.

As scholars, we believe that YA literature is best understood by those trained to read it within its sociohistorical context. A generation of students has grown up with inadequate knowledge of the role that economic and political forces have played in shaping the social conditions they confront, largely as a result of the No Child Left Behind laws of 2000 that lined the neoliberal pockets of standardized testing companies and that ultimately prioritized math, reading, and writing over other subjects, such as social studies and history in the K-12 curriculum. Throughout this book, we thus provide social and political contextualizations that we hope will help readers understand the long-term social and political developments that gave way to neoliberalism. With its invitation to focus on the self and future competition, neoliberalism detracts attention away from historical, economic, and social forces at work in YA novels. Teenagers may enjoy reading fiction like the Harry Potter series (1997–2007) or *Thirteen Reasons Why* (2007) or the Hunger Games trilogy (2008–2010) or *The Hate U Give* (2017) or *The Children of Blood and Bone* (2018), but all of these novels participate in—and result from—neoliberal influences, while only *The Hate U Give* provides readers with full explanations of the historical context in which its tensions are set.[3]

ONE EXAMPLE OF NEOLIBERALISM IN YA LITERATURE

A preadolescent boy, marked at birth and possessed of exceptional powers, joins a world of tightly class-controlled beings who compete—sometimes even brutally—with each other to win power. Some people in this culture hold slaves; the class-controlled groups rarely intermarry, and among those who are human, race is little more than a cosmetic factor, so that racial disparities and discriminations are effectively hidden, erased, or depicted as obsolete, despite the twentieth-century setting in western Europe.

Welcome to Hogwarts.

Harry Potter's powers allow him to succeed where many grown-ups have failed. He is the truly unique individual—the individual we refer to as "super-special" when we are writing about *exceptionalism*. Neoliberalism depends on the concept of exceptionalism: ostensibly, exceptional entrepreneurs succeed in a neoliberal economy because they are more talented than others (rather than because they have had superior resources, such as access to better education or loans). The concept of exceptionalism is therefore foundational to our argument.

Neoliberal advocacy of exceptionalism stems from its valuation of entrepreneurship, which is on display everywhere in the Harry Potter world, from Diagon Alley to Hogsmeade, and which has also made the Wizarding World of Harry Potter theme park in Orlando, Florida, lucrative for Universal Studios, which, like the Disney Corporation, is always happy to find a way to sell the ideas elaborated in its media franchises to children and their parents. Jack Zipes refers to this as the *commodification of children*, that is, the transformation of an idea, such as a literary character from a children's film, into a commodity to be purchased for play or fun (Zipes 22). This includes merchandise such as Harry Potter-branded action figures or video games or earrings or pajamas—or the replica of a wand that is nothing more than a costly plastic stick.

Within the Harry Potter novels, Fred and George Weasley are successful entrepreneurs, given their creation of a successful joke shop that appears to have no other form of competition. Like Ollivanders' Wand Shop, which also has no competition, the Weasleys' shop produces *commodities*, which means they work in an economic process known as *material production* (that is, producing material goods). Hogwarts, itself, however, produces an intangible good: the knowledge its students gain there. The production of intangible goods, such as education, is known as *immaterial production*. Professor Trelawney's prophecies are yet another form of immaterial production. But have the goblins of Gringotts or Mr. Ollivander ever had competition in the form of either material or immaterial production? Or are both enterprises so successful that they either absorbed all competition or drove the others bankrupt, like the immaterial tech producers associated with neoliberalism in the twenty-first century, such as Google and Facebook, or the material and immaterial tech producer Apple?

Competition is fundamental to exceptionalism: only the most simultaneously efficient and effective entrepreneurs or individuals or companies or even nations can succeed in a neoliberal economy. And competition, of course, helps readers understand Harry Potter's exceptionalism. He is remarkable in his competition as a Quidditch player, not least because of his superb athletic abilities flying on a broom. He passes his O.W.L. levels with a score of "Outstanding" in Defense Against the Dark Arts, and he "Exceeds Expectations" in the Care of Magical Creatures, Charms, Herbology, Potions, and Transfiguration (*Half-Blood Prince* 102). He wins the Triwizard Tournament by being more competitive than the other (older) characters in terms of his heightened abilities of logical deduction, intuition, courage, and honor. Almost every time he competes with Voldemort in a confrontation, Harry gains some form of advantage. He is by far the character with the greatest competitive advantage in the series, which results directly from his exceptionalism.

As we have mentioned, neoliberalism is hostile to institutions that seek to regulate or control exceptional individuals since this might prevent them from exercising their full talents. Thus, although Hogwarts empowers students by deepening their knowledge of magic, the school is also an oppressive force in their lives. For example, when Dolores Umbridge, a government bureaucrat, replaces Dumbledore as head of the school, she enacts a government-authorized curriculum that prepares students for standardized tests but fails to equip them with practical knowledge and skills they can apply in their lives outside of school. Likewise, even though a wealth of evidence suggests that Voldemort has returned, the Ministry of Magic, as the government of the wizarding world is called, refuses to act, so its citizens are exposed to great risk. In both cases, Harry and his talented friends avert disaster only because they resist the control of two institutions: their school and their governing body. In the first instance, they form Dumbledore's Army and teach each other how to combat dark magic, and in the second, they take it upon themselves to confront Voldemort rather than wait for the Ministry of Magic to act. This is one more way the series implies that talented individuals, rather than institutions such as governments, are best positioned to solve social problems.

Another concept essential to our argument is *exploitation*, whether that involves exploitation of the environment, animals, or people—such as squibs in the wizarding world, who are exploited because they are nonmagical. Animals, too, are often exploited in the series, most notably when Voldemort exploits the snake Nagini's venom to heal himself, or when he uses her body to store a horcrux, or when he drinks the blood of dead unicorns to strengthen himself. *Harry Potter and the Half-Blood Prince* even opens with the Death Eaters' deliberate destruction of the environment—both in terms of physically destroyed civil structures and changed weather patterns, including what Muggles believe to be an unprecedented "freak hurricane" (2). To be fair, most of the exploitation of animals and the environment is conducted in the name of evil, so readers are meant to understand how wrong exploitation is; nevertheless, the house elves continue to be an exploited group even as the series ends. While Hermione objects to the inherent evil of slavery when she strives to free the house elves, few other characters embrace her mission. This understandably frustrates Hermione, but the cause of freeing slaves is, in this case, a very unfortunately lost one.

We also deal herein with the related concept of *erasure*, whether this involves erasing entire groups of beings or whether this entails attempted efforts to pretend that damaging ideologies, such as racism and feminism, no longer exist. The "Pureblood" war on "Mudbloods" in the Harry Potter series is a thinly veiled reference to the horrors of the Holocaust. The series firmly establishes that genocide is wrong. Nevertheless, the Aurors themselves have attempted to obliterate giants in the First Wizarding War, which underscores the genocidal tendencies of the wizarding world.

Related to the concept of *erasure* is the idea of *biopolitics*, which Michel Foucault describes as "the attempt, starting from the eighteenth century, to rationalize the problems posed to governmental practice by phenomena characteristic of a set of living beings forming a population: health, hygiene, life expectancy, race" (*Birth* 317). In the Harry Potter books, the Ministry of Magic serves as the biopolitical regulating agency for the beasts, beings, and spirits of the wizarding world. Genocide is the most extreme negative aspect of biopolitics, but intermarriage regulations also create another form of biopolitics, as occurred in the US up until 1967, before which African Americans could not legally marry Euro-Americans. In the Harry Potter series, Muggles and wizards can breed with each other—just as giants and Veelas can breed with humans—but goblins and elves and trolls can't or don't, even though they are humanoid in form. While the narrative clearly criticizes the notion of bloodlines, condemning those "pureblood" elites who refer to wizards with Muggle ancestry as "Mudbloods," the series nevertheless gives very little attention to how wizards who are entirely "Mudblood" must face disadvantages that wizards from older wizarding families don't experience.

Many social institutions in the wizarding world also have unexplained discrepancies that can be traced to the economics of biopolitics. Are social institutions filled with humans—such as the prison Azkaban, the hospital St. Mungo's, and the school Hogwarts—socialist entities supported by a government? If so, how are they paid for? By sales taxes or garnished wages or income taxation? That does not make sense, of course, because no one in the wizarding world appears to draw a paycheck, but that being the case, how is social mobility possible? And if social institutions are paid for by magic, why are some families richer than others; that is, if the Ministry of Magic can support its social institutions by magically created income, why can't the Weasleys magically create more income? Ron Weasley may be financially poor, but on the other hand, he has inherited stores of immaterial production in the form of information about the wizarding world that Hermione has had to teach herself from the hard work of conducting her own research. How does that disadvantage someone in a similar position? And how is it that Hermione is *not* poor, while Ron *is*?

Similarly, to which form of government can we assign the Ministry of Magic? It seems to have something between imperialistic, oligarchic, and parliamentarian powers, but if the latter, how and when do elections occur? Who is enfranchised? Do the nonhuman or nonhumanoid creatures in the magical world get a vote? And what about the judiciary arm of the Ministry of Magic, the Wizengamot? How are judges and jurors selected? While it is admittedly not incumbent upon J. K. Rowling to provide a complete socioeconomic political theory of a magical world, we cannot help but wonder why British socialism is not more pronounced in the novel. For example, criminally insane people are sent to Azkaban, as are people who were not insane before they become prisoners, but who are driven mad by their prison guards, the Dementors; on the other hand, the noncriminally insane are sent to St. Mungo's—yet several characters seem like they could benefit from psychosocial medical help they are not getting, including Luna Lovegood and Sybil Trelawney. Is there universal health care or socialized medicine in the wizarding world? The point seems trivial to contemplate, until we consider the implications of how thoroughly this series steeps young readers in the necessity of wealth, privilege, individual entrepreneurship, competition, exploitation (at least of house elves), and, above all else, *success*.

Furthermore, the sense of entitlement and privilege associated with the 1 percent in the UK and US when these novels were being written is largely reflected by the attitudes of the ambitious Slytherins, for whom ambition—their predominant house trait—is often conflated with greed for power. The Lestrange family, the Black family, and the Malfoys are wealthy and have historically been associated with Slytherin, albeit with notable exceptions, such as the renegade exceptional individual Sirius Black. While Rowling's novels are vehemently opposed to the idea that anything can be "pure-blood" and therefore worth preserving for that simple fact alone, the novels certainly do go to great lengths to valorize the prestige of being wealthy, as James Potter's family is, for example.

Classism also abounds throughout these novels. Certain magical creatures—centaurs, for example—appear to be more noble and esoteric than others, like deceptive sirens or, even worse, annoying boggarts. Wealthy

Gryffindors are positioned as morally superior to rich Slytherins, but what about poor Slytherins? (There don't seem to be any poor Ravenclaws, either; the Hufflepuffs are not influential enough for their income to make much difference, apparently.) Racism based on ethnic identity among humans, however, is ideologically erased, suggesting that the wizarding world is a *postrace* society.[4] The Asian British characters Cho Chang and the Parvati twins, along with the Afro-British Angelina Johnson and Quidditch commentator Dean Thomas, are all initially described as people of color within the original text of the series. None of them is subject to discrimination; none of them ever seems to have been. Scholar Ebony Elizabeth Thomas "found it odd that the Black witches and wizards had British surnames. [She] didn't understand how that could be possible. How could anyone subject a magical person in Rowling's legendarium to chattel slavery? Wouldn't their magic prevent it?" (*Dark Fantastic* 145). She observes with clarity how problematic it is for the Afro-British to be depicted without any acknowledgment that they are likely descendants of enslaved peoples (*Dark Fantastic* 145).

Yet when the actress Noma Dumezweni, born in South Africa but raised in the UK from the age of eight, appeared in *Harry Potter and the Cursed Child* (2016), Rowling professed to being annoyed by the "racists" who protested Dumezweni's casting as Hermione in the West End play (Ratcliffe). At least one blogger, however, deconstructs Rowling's protestations, noting that "aside from her bushy brown hair, large teeth, and shrill voice, J. K. Rowling didn't really describe the rest of Hermione's physical appearance," so it therefore seems inaccurate for Rowling to assert that Hermione *could* be Black, when she has introduced every other character of color with racialized commentary and Hermione goes "white" when she is frightened and appears "tanned" after one summer vacation (Diary).[5]

Ultimately, however, the Harry Potter series does espouse one antineoliberal sentiment that redeems the series in some ways. Voldemort's individualistic crusade to conquer death can only be defeated when an entire community works together to stand up to him. The very premise of Hogwarts is predicated on placing people into one of four living communities, even a community of ambitious people, such as the Slytherins. This privileging of the work of a community or a collective whole over the most successful individual(s) is known as *collectivity* or *collectivism*. Fortunately, the characters in the Harry Potter series ultimately succeed in their mission because they embrace collectivism, rather than advocating for its rejection. Dumbledore's Army, along with centaurs, a giant, citizens of Hogsmeade, and the Hogwarts community, ultimately defeat Voldemort's Death Eaters and Voldemort himself. Indeed, the Chosen One proves not to be the hero expected to vanquish the would-be tyrant; rather, humble Neville Longbottom defeats the necrophobic Voldemort—but Neville can only do so with the help of many others who have found all of the necessary horcruxes, including Harry himself. For all the neoliberal economic trappings of the wizarding world, collectivism ultimately saves the day and redeems this series from teetering on the edge of being a neoliberal rejection of post-World War II policies in the UK, which was a time when citizens embraced the idea that government had both the power and the obligation to strengthen social safety-net programs and educate the poor, while simultaneously providing citizens with medical support and childcare in order to help improve social conditions for all citizens.

Our discussion of the Harry Potter series, coupled with our experience working with college and high school students, suggests to us that readers can be taught to interrogate the issues of neoliberalism that inform any YA novel with socioeconomic ideologies both overpowering and simultaneously understated. Critical readers know how to identify racism, classism, and sexism, as well as neoliberal exaltations of individualism, exceptionalism, and entrepreneurial competition in a rejection of collectivist social institutions. Critical readers are also able to place any novel in its historical context. For example, J. K. Rowling wrote the Harry Potter series just as the UK was ending its second extended period of poverty in the twentieth century. According to the UK's Joseph Rowntree Foundation, twentieth-century poverty lines in the UK reached 20 percent or more in only two eras: during the Great Depression in the years 1930–1933, and beginning again in the 1980s through the turn of the century, in the era following Thatcherism's neoliberal policies that defunded social support systems throughout the UK (Glennerster et al. 44–46).

NEOLIBERALISM AND YOUNG ADULT FICTION: CHAPTER OUTLINE

This book is concerned with explaining the cultural work that YA literature does in reproducing and resisting a neoliberal social order.[6] As the writings of children's literature scholars from Lynne Vallone to Ebony Elizabeth Thomas, whom we cited above, have shown, performing cultural criticism invites a different way of reading and thinking about literature than traditional close reading offers. Literary texts are not merely works of art that explore timeless themes, as some pedagogues imply. Nor are they apolitical. Rather, as Jane Tompkins argues, literary texts represent a writer's efforts to remake the social order. From this perspective, "novels and stories should be studied not because they manage to escape the limitations of their particular time and place, but because they offer powerful examples of the way a culture thinks about itself, articulating and proposing solutions for the problems that shape a particular historical moment" (Tompkins xi). We also find it important to acknowledge that texts shape readers. In *Letting Stories Breathe: A Socio-Narratology*, Arthur Frank examines how stories can both expand and constrain the possibilities that people recognize as available to them: "Stories work with people, for people, and always stories work *on* people," he argues, "affecting what [they] are able to see as real, as possible, and as worth doing or best avoided" (3, emphasis in the original). While stories can be transformative, they can also naturalize ways of understanding the world that are problematic, destructive even. They "have the capacity to make one truth seem inevitable," so that "people become caught up in that truth and act on it" (Frank 148–49). We argue that neoliberalism constitutes one such "truth."

Books for teenagers have received considerable critical attention in the past few decades, but their potential to reproduce a neoliberal social order has not yet received enough attention from scholars. That this should be the case is perhaps not surprising. As Clare Bradford and her colleagues argue, "It is often the case in the field of children's literature that texts for children lead in new directions while the existing critical paradigms lag considerably" (7).[7] With that in mind, in this book we examine how some YA literature naturalizes neoliberalism by interpellating teenagers as self-enclosed, competitive individuals who are willing to accept personal responsibility for their social and economic standing in life. At the same time, however, we recognize YA literature as a potential site of resistance, one that acknowledges teenagers' agency to reject neoliberalism's destructive impulses and encourages them to take action and work for social justice and equality through collective action.

As we have indicated in the preface to this volume, our interest in neoliberalism and, more specifically, in how literature for adolescents reproduces and resists this set of economic, political, and social forces initially grew out of our shared work on dystopian YA fiction. Although dystopias are typically set in the future, they are ultimately concerned with interrogating the long-term consequences of contemporary social and political practices that, followed to their logical extreme, have the potential to prove destructive.[8] In many YA dystopias, an exceptional teenager is drawn into a conflict with the government. Relying on their prodigious talents, such characters fight for transformative change in their respective societies, eventually emerging as leaders in the fight for social justice and equality. An emphasis on the exceptional individual is not unique to dystopian YA fiction, however. As our brief analysis of Harry Potter demonstrates, it crosses genres, from fantasy to dystopia, from historical fiction to contemporary realism. With that in mind, in chapter 1, we examine the trope of the exceptional individual in various genres.

In chapter 2, we move to an analysis of how the concept of exceptionalism encourages business enterprises to expand economic production by moving into new territories, which necessarily creates environmental tensions (Pellizzoni and Ylönen 4). Because neoliberalism operates according to a logic of exploitation, not only people but also the land and the environment become resources to be exploited in the name of economic progress. The fallacy of exploitation is reflected in a growing number of books for teenagers that examine issues that range from the effects of climate change to the consequences of our exhausting finite natural resources, and from endangered species to the interconnectedness of all life. In chapter 2, we thus examine how books for adolescents imagine the relationship between neoliberalism and the environment.

By emphasizing competition and individualism, and by erasing the role that social constructs such as race, gender, and class play in privileging some groups of people and oppressing others, neoliberalism naturalizes a meritocratic worldview. In doing so, it creates the impression that anyone can experience social mobility provided they are willing to work hard, compete, and exercise their talents. One particular manifestation of this discourse is *postracialism*, which spuriously asserts that US society has progressed to a point that race no longer affects a person's life chances. Postrace discourse alleges that racism is a relic of history in the US and dismisses the color hierarchy that shapes the lived experiences of people of color in this country. This falsely conceptualizes racism as an individual, as opposed to a systemic, problem. In chapter 3, we examine these historical machinations of systemic racism in the US. In chapter 4, we build on that discussion by critiquing neoliberalism's reliance on the concept of postracialism and analyzing how neoliberalism is critiqued in YA novels by authors of color.

In a similar vein, *postfeminism* assumes that in a world where men and women ostensibly compete on a level playing field, feminism is no longer necessary. In chapter 5, we thus interrogate postfeminist discourse in books for teenagers that depict strong female characters, especially the supersmart, exceptional girls who rise above their social conditions; then we move on to contrast postfeminist thinking with the important feminist work of nuancing gender, having gender-inclusive groups work together, interrogating motherhood, and affirming ecofeminism.

Because neoliberalism erases the roles that race, gender, and social class play in advantaging some people and disadvantaging others, the extent to which people can leverage their individual talents in the service of competing against others becomes neoliberalism's ultimate arbiter of success. As Julie Wilson argues, "neoliberal biopolitics holds individuals, and individuals alone, personally responsible for their lives. It is up to each individual to maintain and optimize their bodies, mind, health, and well-being in the market" (151). People who experience success are perceived as having worked hard. This logic cuts both ways, however, with the result that people are held accountable for their own personal struggles. In a neoliberal social order, those who do not contribute to the economy—or who are unable to do so—are cast aside. Therefore, in chapter 6, we ask how YA literature participates in those neoliberal biopolitics that imply an inherently genocidal logic. We then interrogate sociopolitical indifference to the humanity of the systemically poor, immigrants, and those who are seriously ill. Related to the issue of biopolitics is the concept of immaterial production, such as the generating of ideas and information. In chapter 7, we consequently analyze YA novels that address knowledge and knowledge production as epistemological issues that can help to enhance or hinder collectivism.

As we have explained, although stories can naturalize a particular worldview, they can also expose readers to alternative ways of being in the world. With that in mind, in chapter 8, we examine YA literature as a possible site of resistance, one that has the potential to lay bare neoliberalism's destructive impulses and open up what Harvey calls "spaces of hope" for teenage readers. Nicole Aschoff argues that in a neoliberal social order, "The way we are told to get through it all and realize our dreams is always to adapt ourselves to the changing world, not to change the world we live in. We demand little or nothing from the system, from the collective apparatus of powerful people and institutions. We only make demands of ourselves" (105–6). There is cause for hope, however. In recent years, many books for teenagers have underscored the importance of teens working together for systemic change, highlighting the transformative power of youth activism and collective action. In chapter 8, we demonstrate how books for young readers are accomplishing this.

CONCLUSION

By atomizing society and reducing human life to an infinite series of competitions, neoliberalism forecloses our ability to recognize that many of the problems we find ourselves facing in fact share a common source: social affordances for exploitation. Once we understand this, we can begin to address the social conditions that are responsible for producing the feelings of anxiety, stress, and despair that so many people experience. Today, YA literature is read by adults and teenagers alike, but relatively few readers are prepared to investigate the genre's neoliberal econo-politics critically. In writing this book, we hope to equip readers with conceptual and critical tools they can use to do so. In some cases, the YA novels we examine are problematic insofar as they participate in neoliberal discourses that are injurious to people. Others stand out for offering readers a vision of a more just and compassionate society, one that is founded on principles of equality, collective action, and a shared sense of respect for the common good. As the subtitle to this book indicates, we believe that when trained readers explore neoliberal problems surrounding exceptionalism, exploitation, and erasure, they can help create a society that respects all peoples, the Earth, and its environment alike.

Chapter 1

SELF-ENCLOSED INDIVIDUALISM AND THE NEOLIBERAL TRADITION

> Meritocracy is corrosive of the common good.
>
> —Michael J. Sandel (TED2020)

The reality television show *Keeping Up with the Kardashians* (2007–2021) transformed the Kardashian-Jenner clan into household names, so much so that the Kardashian-Jenner sisters became in many ways the ideal standard-bearers for neoliberalism. They were young then and still are wealthy, beautiful, successful, independent women who have profited tremendously from promoting their hypercapitalist, hyperconsumerist lifestyle. In the early years of their television show, audiences followed Kim, Kourtney, and Khloé Kardashian as they endeavored to launch and develop a boutique chain that sold their own brand of clothing and accessories. As the show progressed over the years, however, the sisters became a brand in their own right, trading on the recognizability of their famous last name to sell a seemingly endless array of consumer products: everything from nail polish, makeup, perfume, and jewelry to beauty masks, books, digital apps, and sneakers. Subsequently, the sisters have been celebrated as shrewd businesswomen who leveraged their work ethic, entrepreneurial spirit, and financial acumen to build a successful business empire while at the same time amassing tremendous personal fortunes. Seen from this perspective, the Kardashian-Jenner sisters appear to emblemize American meritocracy.

This characterization of the Kardashian-Jenners as ideal neoliberal subjects is typified by a 2019 *Forbes* article that noted that Kylie Jenner, the half-sister of Kourtney, Kim, and Khloé, had, at age twenty-one, unseated Facebook founder Mark Zuckerberg as "the youngest-ever self-made billionaire" (Robehmed). In the article, Jenner, who had recently entered into a lucrative business deal with Ulta after the beauty supply retailer agreed to carry her line of Kylie Cosmetics, reflected on her success, noting, "I work really hard." She also conceded that, although she hadn't sought the recognition, the knowledge that she was then the youngest self-made billionaire was "a nice pat on the back" (Robehmed). In insisting that she has succeeded based on working "really hard," Kylie Jenner affirms the myth of American *meritocracy* that underlies neoliberal thinking. According to Harvard political philosopher Michael Sandel, the "heart of the meritocratic ideal" is the belief that "if everyone has an equal chance, the winners deserve their winnings" (TED2020). The problem, of course, lies in the hypothetical clause starting with "if": not everyone does have an equal chance in the globalized economy. Furthermore, as Sandel explains, the logic of meritocracy is tyrannical: if "winners deserve their winnings," then it stands to reason that people who struggle to succeed in the system deserve their fate, too (TED2020).

When one of the authors of this book, Sean, has shared the aforementioned *Forbes* story about Kylie Jenner with undergraduates in his YA literature courses, it has stirred debate. The majority of Sean's predominantly white, middle-class, southern students—who are near Jenner's age—embrace a meritocratic worldview. They are persuaded by cultural narratives that valorize rugged individualism and fair play, and many of them are quick to defend the idea that the Kardashian-Jenners' financial and personal success is indeed attributable to their own hard work and talent. These students note, for example, that the sisters maintained a busy schedule filming a popular reality television show while also juggling their considerable business obligations. They also point out that the sisters are still masterful at leveraging social media, the result of which allows them to promote their brand to large audiences and attests to their entrepreneurial skills. However, another (always smaller) group of students will typically object to the article's characterization of Jenner as a "self-made" billionaire, noting that she is a beneficiary of opportunities her older sisters created for her, as well as her family's wealth and the many business connections she has been able to make while appearing on a popular television show that is distributed internationally. Ironically, in spite of patting herself on the back for her own hard work, Jenner appears to contradict the idea that she is a self-made success when she acknowledges her popularity on social media with having advantaged her. "It's the power of social media," she explains in the article. "*I had such a strong reach before I was able to start anything*" (Robehmed, emphasis added). With this self-observation, Jenner undercuts the assumption that merit alone leads to success.

NEOLIBERALISM: HISTORY AND DEFINITION

In the nineteenth century, economic "liberalism" was equated with industrialists' desire for governmental laissez-faire in the US and the UK, which then became a political position that industrialists invoked to forestall government regulation. However, starting in the 1880s and continuing into the 1970s, US progressives pushed for laws that would regulate industries and improve social support systems, including such reforms as the Sherman Anti-Trust Act (1890), the Meat Inspection Act and Pure Food and Drug Act (1906), the Federal Trade Commission (1914), the enfranchisement of women voters (1920), the Social Security Act (1935), the desegregation of the US Armed Forces (1948) and public schools (1954), the Civil Rights Act (1964), the Voting Rights Act (1965), Medicare (1966), and the founding of both the Environmental Protection Agency (1970) and the Consumer Product Safety Commission (1972). During the 1980s, however, both US President Ronald Reagan and UK Prime Minister Margaret Thatcher began rolling back progressive regulations by embracing what they thought of as a new form of nineteenth-century economic "liberalism," one that shares its forebear's preference for small government and that led to the deregulation of major industries, such as telecommunications, the airline industry, and public utility companies. Although they didn't coin the term, Reaganites called this movement "neoliberalism," even though the ideas weren't new at all; it was simply a "new" form of the old laissez-faire liberalism. Despite all evidence to the contrary (Leonhardt 2), advocates of neoliberalism promote the idea that individual entrepreneurs, rather than large governments, are best positioned to stimulate economic growth when they are made to compete to deliver goods and services (Harvey, *Brief* 2). Those who succeed are rewarded for their efforts, and those who do not are ostensibly motivated to work harder. Today, neoliberalism's emphasis on individual exceptionalism and competition shapes virtually all domains of human life in the US, and so the twinned discourses of exceptionalism and competition are naturalized in much of this country's popular culture.

Neoliberalism places a strong emphasis on rugged individualism. In prioritizing individual freedom, it also opposes government regulation, not only of economic markets, but of almost all areas of life: education, health care, commerce, air travel, social media—even the delivery of utilities and public services, such as community recycling. Neoliberalism also prioritizes competition—whether between people, organizations, businesses, or nation states—as the economic engine that drives all progress. For this same reason, neoliberalism is hostile to government assistance programs, including welfare, federally funded nutrition assistance for women and children, unemployment, and universal health care, as these are all perceived as fostering dependence rather than self-reliance. Ronald Reagan, who embraced neoliberal policies as a way to address the economic downturn his administration inherited in 1981, depicted government as antagonistic to individual freedom when he famously asserted that "government is not the solution to our problem; *government is the problem*" (quoted in Wilson 37, emphasis added). In the same decade, on the other side of the Atlantic, Margaret Thatcher championed the merits of rugged individualism and self-reliance when she argued that that there is "*no such thing as society*"; there are only "*individual men and women* and there are families and no government can do anything except through people and people look to themselves first" (Keay, emphasis added).

Consistent with its emphasis on the triumvirate of competition, self-reliance, and meritocracy, at the center of neoliberalism is a belief in individual *exceptionalism*. As we use the term in this book, an exceptional individual is a talented person with the ability to maximize their potential to its fullest extent in the service of accomplishing their goals and ambitions. In the face of adversity, exceptional individuals don't despair or give up; instead, they "pick themselves up by the bootstraps" and persevere, exemplifying a "can do" spirit. In the popular imagination, they are innovative entrepreneurs, and as such, they continually search out, and capitalize on, opportunities to advantage themselves. Unlike "lesser" humans, exceptional individuals aren't complacent. Instead, they reinvent themselves in order to gain a leg up on their competition. They are also flexible and thus able to accommodate to changing conditions around them. Inspired by their exceptionalism, other people may look to the exceptional individual as a leader. Although the latter may not aspire to that role, they might still take it on, driven by a strong sense of fair play. Implicit in Sean's students' impassioned defense of Kylie Jenner as a self-made billionaire is a tacit acknowledgement of her exceptionalism.

As we will argue elsewhere in this book, however, neoliberalism's emphasis on individual exceptionalism and its insistence that people take responsibility for their situation in life ignores that not all people have access to the same opportunities and resources, and so they may require government protection and assistance. Likewise, we argue that a system that pits people against each other and that forces them to compete tirelessly in all areas of life is damaging to everyone because only focusing on competitiveness impedes our ability to recognize our interconnectedness and prevents us from working together toward the common good. Worse, such a system sets up a cruel social ledger: on one side are exceptional individuals, the winners who figure out how to succeed in life, and on the other are the losers whose alleged lack of work ethic or talent renders them a drag on society. A neoliberal economy renders those in the latter group disposable.

In this chapter, we investigate how YA literature participates in, and resists, neoliberal discourses of individual exceptionalism and entrepreneurial self-reliance. Recognizing that literary texts can participate in the construction and transmission of cultural narratives that naturalize individualism and self-reliance, we begin by considering how these themes have recurred historically throughout canonical American literature. We then turn to an examination of the connection between individualism and neoliberalism. In doing so, we argue that the latter advocates for an extreme form of individualism, one that imagines the self as wholly enclosed and detached from the collective. Next, we contrast attitudes toward individual exceptionalism in two YA novels: *Legend* (2011) by Marie Lu and *Marcelo in the Real World* (2009) by Francisco X. Stork, and we conclude with a critically inflected reading of neoliberalism in the Hunger Games trilogy (2008, 2009, 2010). Ultimately, we demonstrate how fiction for teenagers can fall on a continuum that ranges between valuing self-enclosed individualism and/or valuing collectivism.

THE INDIVIDUAL AND INDIVIDUALISM IN EARLY US LITERATURE

We, the authors, find it unsurprising that contemporary YA literature should address themes of individualism and self-reliance, since both have a long tradition in US literature.[1] The white colonial men who wrote most of the literature that would become the young country's first canon often valued the same spirit of individualism and independence echoed in the Declaration of Independence, with its argument that governments are "instituted among Men" and only have power over citizens inasmuch as it stems "from the consent of the governed." The idea was an emerging one during the long eighteenth century of the Enlightenment: individuals create government, rather than royalty dictating to their subjects as the spokesperson for the Christian God. Thomas Jefferson, and the later framers of the US Constitution, distrusted democratic government precisely because it was an institution created by—and exploitable by—individuals, which is why the Constitution depends on so many checks and balances over individual leaders or group power.

Early US literature is replete with images that value the individual (usually male, usually white) in intersecting strands of theology and political theory.

Jonathan Edwards, for example, in the sermon commonly known as "Sinners in the Hands of an Angry God" (1741), lays eternal salvation not at the feet of a whole congregation, but at the feet of each individual: "let every one that is out of Christ, now awake and fly from the Wrath to come." Distancing himself from the more Protestant-inflected arguments of philosophers such as John Locke, Thomas Paine based *Common Sense* (1776) on the understanding that government is a "necessary evil" that is required given "the inability of moral virtue to govern the world." By the time he writes *Declaration of the Rights of Man* (1789), Paine extends Locke's argument in his *Second Treatise on Government* (1689) about man's "inalienable rights," which are "life, liberty, and property," to argue that "the aid of all political association is the preservation of the natural and imprescriptible rights of man. These rights are liberty, property, security, and resistance to oppression." By "man," Paine means "individual white males." Meanwhile, Benjamin Franklin's *Autobiography* (1793) is downright self-congratulatory about the author's ability to succeed as an individual despite the vicissitudes of his early life. In extolling traits such as temperance, order, resolution, industry, sincerity, and humility, he articulates a clear concept of Americans as a group of individuals with shared values that privilege self-reliance.

Perhaps the tipping point in US ideas about the role of the individual in society being formed by a relationship to the divine first appeared in Ralph Waldo Emerson's "Divinity School Address" (1838), in which Emerson denied the divinity of Jesus, calling him a "true man" and arguing, "He saw that God incarnates himself in man, and evermore goes forth to take possession of his world." God, in Emerson's construction, is a positive force that flows within all human beings: "If a man is at heart just, then in so far is he God; the safety of God, the immortality of God, the majesty of God do enter into that man with justice." Indeed, as Walt Whitman wrote in his 1855 "Song of Myself," "I celebrate myself, and sing myself." With joy, Emerson praised Whitman in an 1855 letter for "your free and brave thought . . . which large perception only can inspire" (Emerson, "Letter").

In and around Emerson's and Whitman's lifetimes, various novelists celebrated the individual, especially as a man (and, occasionally, woman) of action: James Fenimore Cooper's Hawkeye in *The Leatherstocking Tales* (1827–1841); Hester Prynne, isolated and persecuted in no small part because of her individualism, in *The Scarlet Letter* (1850); Herman Melville's Captain Ahab in *Moby-Dick* (1851), standing alone against the sea and a whale in a tale Ishmael later narrates while also standing alone; Uncle Tom seeking individual salvation in Harriet Beecher Stowe's *Uncle Tom's Cabin* (1852); Thoreau marching to the beat of a different drummer (*Walden*, 1854); Mark

Twain's Huckleberry Finn, "light[ing] out for the Territory ahead of the rest" in the 1885 novel (362); Stephen Crane's protagonist in *The Red Badge of Courage* (1895) emerging into manhood after battle: "He felt a quiet manhood, nonassertive but of sturdy and strong blood. . . . He had been to touch the great death, and found that, after all, it was but the great death. He was a man" (99). Although his maturation involves the clash between two large armies, he thinks of his manhood entirely in terms of himself alone.

THE HISTORY OF INDIVIDUALISM IN US LITERARY CRITICISM

The study of the individual was solidly entrenched as a norm in US literary criticism by the twentieth century. T. S. Eliot wrote about "Tradition and the Individual Talent" (1919), while in *Green Hills of Africa* (1935), Ernest Hemingway claimed "all modern American literature comes from one book by Mark Twain called *Huckleberry Finn*" (29). In this attribution, Hemingway acknowledges the importance of writers like Crane and Henry James, who depict individualistic characters; Hemingway also discourses on the importance of isolation to any writer: "writers should all write alone" (28).

With *Understanding Fiction* (1943), Cleanth Brooks and Robert Penn Warren inspired dozens of textbook authors to teach students to think about "man vs. man" conflicts—or "man vs. self" or "man vs. society" or "man vs. nature." In every case, the idea of one individual—one "man"—in conflict serves as the starting point for the rising action of a plot.[2] Their brand of New Criticism, focusing solely on the text, was admittedly a reaction to Freudian critics focusing too much on authors' psychological motivations; nevertheless, Brooks and Warren's refusal to allow any attention to the author's life or other historical contexts elevated further the importance of the individual protagonist as studied in the canons of American literary history, while simultaneously downplaying social conditions, such as structural racism and poverty, xenophobia, anti-Semitism, ableism, homophobia, and systemic sexism.

That said, other critics have decried the myth of the individual by celebrating novels that ideologically value the community. For example, Edmund Wilson, publishing in 1938, excoriates the aesthetic overreach of authors and critics focused more on the individual than society itself. He praises Flaubert's concept of "the triple thinker," which he claims George Bernard Shaw also displayed: at the foundation of Shaw's writing "is a commonsense sphere of practical considerations"; "above this" is a concern for the "anticipated reorganization of society in the interest of ideal values," and on the third level, above that, the author exists in the "poet-philosopher's ether," from which he contemplates humanity in light of eternity, "where the poet allows himself many doubts which neither the socialist nor the bourgeois citizen can admit" (179). In other words, Edmund Wilson values the literary artist who recognizes and puts into tension the everyday individual with current sociopolitical awareness and a long-term sense of the human spirit and its potential. Scholars such as Wilson—and those he influenced, including Irving Howe and Lionel Trilling—created the antithesis of New Critical thinking, precisely because it refused to focus solely on either the individual work removed from its historical context or the idea of the individual "man" always and only in conflict with himself or others or his environment.

Howe, active in the Democratic Socialist Party and cofounder of the radical journal *Dissent*, was one of the leftist New York intellectuals of the 1950s. He wrote *Politics and the Novel* (1957), calling attention away from the veneration of the "psychological novel," in which "the typical hero . . . was profoundly involved in testing himself, and thereby his values, against both the remnants of aristocratic resistance and the gross symbols of the new world that offended his sensibility" (18). He points to how the "best of these" novels evolved into "the novel of private sensibility" (18). But according to Howe, "the political novel" is "the kind in which the *idea* of society, as distinct from the mere unquestioned workings of society, has penetrated the consciousness of the characters. . . . They now think in terms of supporting or opposing society as such; they rally to one or another embattled segment of society; and they do so in the name of, and under prompting from, an ideology" (19, emphasis in the original). In our minds, the American obsession with individualism leaves young people vulnerable to ideologies that promote the needs and desires of the individual over those of the community or—as we sometimes refer to it in this book—the *collective* whole, especially when that ideology has implications that are harmful to the functioning of a healthy society.

Between the 1940s and the 1980s, at least three proto-neoliberal authors wrote novels that are still beloved by many teenagers and that continue to be taught in secondary schools: Ayn Rand, Robert A. Heinlein, and Orson Scott Card, most notably in his YA novel *Ender's Game*. Rand called her version of exceptionalism "Objectivism," a philosophy that venerated the "Great Man," that is, the great artist who shakes the foundations of a culture and whose primary objective is to fulfill his own happiness. That man is invariably something of a superman (or in Nietzschean terms, an *Übermensch*). Robert A. Heinlein also venerates the exceptional individual with characters such as the

Christ-like Valentine Michael Smith in *Stranger in a Strange Land* (1961), who self-sacrifices himself to nourish humans. Heinlein's character Lazarus Long (e.g., *Methuselah's Children*, 1958), a genetically modified human destined to live for millennia, is supersmart, cantankerous, and hyperindependent. He embodies the libertarianism Heinlein not so subtly embeds in his novels. Orson Scott Card, writing for a teenage audience, has a similarly superspecial character, Ender, the eponymous hero of *Ender's Game* (1985), who has been groomed to become the superhero who destroys Earth's enemies, the Buggers, all while thinking he is only playing video games. He is ruthless in his competition with others, and he need never make a moral decision about genocide because his commanders have never revealed the truth of his actions to him. Thus, between 1941, when Heinlein first published the serialized version of the novel he later revised, *Methuselah's Children*, and 1985, with the publication of the Hugo Award-winning *Ender's Game*, these authors created self-reliant characters who would also influence the literary concept of the neoliberal exceptional individual.

PROBLEMATIZING INDIVIDUALISM IN EARLY YA LITERATURE IN THE US

Significantly, some of the earliest YA literature criticized the idea of the exceptional individual as a hero. The characters in S. E. Hinton's *The Outsiders* (1967) value their fellow gang members as a collective: Dallas Winston almost kills himself to save Johnny Cade from a fire, and when Johnny dies, Dally commits suicide-by-cop. Ponyboy is left, like Ishmael, to tell their story, but he still lives in a virtual commune with his two brothers. On a surface level, the book clearly values collectivity. Nevertheless, it is also possible to read *The Outsiders* as reproducing the myth of rugged individualism and American meritocracy. Whereas other Greasers put little effort into school and break the law for the fun of it, Ponyboy and his brothers are eager to improve their situation in life, and they are willing to work within the system to accomplish that goal. Compared to other Greasers, they are also exceptional individuals. Describing Darry, his oldest brother, Ponyboy explains, "Living the way we do would only make him more determined to get somewhere. *That's why he's better than the rest of us*, I thought. He's going somewhere. And I was going to be like him. I wasn't going to live in a lousy neighborhood all my life (138, emphasis added). Ponyboy earns "good grades and [has] a high IQ" (4), unlike other Greasers who "never learned anything" in school and "just went for kicks" (10). At the novel's conclusion, Ponyboy sits down to tell his story in an essay he is assigned to write for his English class, suggesting that he will one day lift himself and his brothers out of their working-class conditions by capitalizing on his intellect and applying himself in school. In contrast, he assumes that "Curly Shepard and the Brumly boys and the other guys [he] knew [will] die [violently] someday" (154). Curly and the Brumly boys are the undeserving poor who serve as foils to the Curtis brothers with their upwardly mobile potential.

Robert Cormier's *The Chocolate War* (1974) critiques the violence of a culture that persecutes an individualist for daring to "disturb the universe" (129). After being pummeled and while he is possibly dying, the protagonist, Jerry Renault, talks to his best friend, Goober, in an unarticulated interior monologue: "Don't disturb the universe. . . . Otherwise, they murder you" (259). Significantly, Jerry does not voice these words aloud, so Goober walks away without knowing his friend has given up. Has Goober learned to value individualism? Or has he learned to fear the force of a corrupt collective? Either way, the text is relying on that ironic tension to inform readers that they themselves *must* disturb the universe, lest corruption subsume the whole culture.[3]

Both of these early novels were written in the milieu of 1960s and early 1970s social protests, especially in terms of the civil rights movement and anti-Vietnam War activism. By 1993, however, in the wake of Reagan's eight-year presidency, Lois Lowry won a Newbery award for creating a dystopia, *The Giver*, in which individualism is so suppressed that the superspecial hero, Jonah, rejecting his culture's conformity, kidnaps a baby and sleds away with him to light out for the territory, ahead of the rest, as it were. Ewan Morrison argues that books like *The Giver* and the countless other YA dystopias it has inspired "propose a laissez-faire existence, with heroic individuals who are guided by the innate forces of human nature against evil social planners." Morrison examines the neoliberal trend in twenty-first-century YA dystopian literature as follows:

> What marks these dystopias out from previous ones is that, almost without exception, the bad guys are not the corporations but the state and those well-meaning liberal leftists who want to make the world a better place. Books such as *The Giver*, *Divergent* and the *Hunger Games* trilogy are, whether intentionally or not, substantial attacks on many of the foundational projects and aims of the left: big government, the welfare state, progress, social planning and equality. They support one of the key ideologies that the left has been battling against for a century: the idea that human nature, rather than nurture, determines how we act and live.

In other words, despite modeling how social activism can be deployed, some YA dystopias are themselves inevitably steeped in the political and economic theory of neoliberalism. As we will demonstrate elsewhere in this book, however, the pattern Morrison describes is not limited to dystopian fiction; it is discernible in other genres of YA fiction as well.

As our discussion above suggests, the exceptional individual is nothing new in US literature or even in YA literature published in the US. The neoliberal superspecial, exceptional character is instead the culmination of centuries of an intellectual tradition in the US that valorizes individualism. However, as we argue in the sections that follow, neoliberalism, as an ideology, actively promotes an extreme form of individualism in the YA novel. We hope that readers trained to be aware of this self-enclosed individualism will recognize the potential damage it stands to inflict on teen readers' sense of existing in a society that was originally based on the recognition that "*we*, the people" must work together "to form a more perfect Union, establish Justice, insure domestic Tranquility . . . [and] promote the *general Welfare*," as the preamble to the US Constitution contends. In the next section, we thus turn to a discussion of the difference between individualism and the extreme form of hyperindividualism aggrandized by neoliberalism.

SELF-ENCLOSED INDIVIDUALISM
AND THE NEOLIBERAL "CULT OF SELF"

Individualism and autonomy may have a long intellectual history in American literature, but the form of individualism on which neoliberalism depends, and which we the coauthors have come to recognize in a growing number of books for teenagers, is a particularly extreme version. Noted economic geographer David Harvey argues, in fact, that neoliberalism is premised on an assumption that individuals who are unfettered by social institutions are most likely to thrive (2). Following Julie Wilson, whose insightful discussion of neoliberalism draws on the work of feminist scholar AnaLouise Keating, we refer to this extreme form of individualism using the term "self-enclosed individualism."

In her book *Transformation Now! Toward a Post-Oppositional Politics of Change*, Keating contrasts self-enclosed individualism with more positive forms of individualism: for example, "personal agency, integrity, and relational forms of autonomy" (171). Her use of the term "self-enclosed" is meant to emphasize this brand of individualism's "inflexible boundaries dividing self from other, its absolute isolation, and its intense focus on the particular individual human being" (171). In her discussion, Keating traces the origins of self-enclosed individualism to the Enlightenment era, arguing that it is premised "on a dichotomous framework that positions the individual in opposition to all other human and nonhuman beings" (171). Because self-enclosed individualism invites us to understand ourselves as wholly separate from other people, it "restricts our worldviews, fostering what [Keating] call[s] 'Me consciousness': an adversarial framework that valorizes and naturalizes competition and self-aggrandizement" (172). This worldview asserts that in order to compete against others effectively, we must constantly evaluate our performance, monitor our choices, assess our advantages and vulnerabilities, calculate our tolerance for risk. In doing so, self-enclosed individuals ask questions such as: "*'What's in it for me?' 'How can I succeed?' 'How will this event, this situation, affect me?' 'What can you do for me?' 'What can I take from you?'*" (171, emphasis in the original). How our interests intersect with those of other people, or how they align with the common good, is unimportant to those who adhere to this mindset.

As an example of how self-enclosed individualism is implicated in American culture, consider an incident that occurred during the 2012 US presidential race when Barack Obama, appearing at a campaign event in Roanoke, Virginia, (in)famously argued: "If you've got a business—you didn't build that" (Kiely). In the context of his speech, Obama's point was that people who achieve success in life don't do so alone; all of us, in some form or another, depend on other people and government support for help. Speaking to this point, Obama argued, "There was a great teacher somewhere in your life. . . . Somebody invested in roads and bridges. If you've got a business—you didn't build that. Somebody else made that happen."

In the days that followed, a plethora of politicians and media pundits angrily construed Obama's remarks as an assault on American meritocracy. In an opinion piece that appeared in the *Wall Street Journal*, for example, James Taranto criticized Obama for having leveled "a direct attack on the principle of individual responsibility, the foundation of American freedom." Mitt Romney, the Republican nominee for president at the time, argued, "To say that Steve Jobs didn't build Apple, that Henry Ford didn't build Ford Motors, that Papa John didn't build Papa John's Pizza . . . [is] not just foolishness. It's insulting to every entrepreneur, every innovator in America" (Blake). However, Romney's argument conveniently overlooks the many ways in which Jobs, Ford, and Papa John (John Schnatter) *did* rely on other people for help.

For example, the buildings and infrastructure that companies such as Apple, Ford Motors, and Papa John's Pizza rely on to carry out their businesses were built by construction workers, compensated for their physical labor and covered by state-based worker's compensation plans. On a daily basis, these companies rely on cultural tools (e.g., microchips, computers, robots, pizza ovens, food regulations, etc.) and whole bodies of knowledge (e.g., computer science, engineering, food science) that humans have developed and refined over time. Even our ability to read and use a menu to order our favorite pizza is contingent on our having access to language, which we inherited from the culture to which we belong, and literacy, which is shaped by culture and which most people learn in public, state-supported schools. In arguing that "you didn't build that," Obama's point is not that hard work and determination are unimportant. Rather, it's that those things *alone* can only get us so far in life. All of us, in some form or another, depend on other people for help. At the risk of stating the obvious, how many of us would have survived infancy had another person not fed and cared for us?

Self-enclosed individualism also ignores the point that "individuals alone cannot control their fates in a global, complex, capitalist society, no matter how well they compete" (J. Wilson 4). In the wake of the Great Recession of 2008, millions of educated, highly experienced professionals unexpectedly found themselves out of work, in some cases for years, as corporations sought to cut costs by laying off employees. At the same time, many newly minted college graduates—eager to join the workforce, contribute their expertise, and pay down their student loans—struggled to find employment, not due to a lack of effort or will, but rather because of a dearth of jobs. A decade later, many of the same people experienced this nightmare for a second time when a coronavirus first detected in 2019, COVID-19, became a pandemic that temporarily closed the economy. In both of these instances, the dire economic situations that people confronted were attributable to complex problems, and as such, they required complex solutions. Hard work, determination, and an entrepreneurial spirit alone were insufficient to address them.

On a related note, neoliberalism's emphasis on self-enclosed individualism also ignores that people do not all start from the same place in life. A wealth of evidence suggests that children who are born into poverty are likely to remain poor later in life. Conversely, wealthy families, like the Kardashian-Jenners, are able to leverage their resources and connections to create opportunities for their children that are not available to other people. Focusing exclusively on the self also leads us to ignore the structural inequalities that characterize schools, the workplace, the judicial system, health care, and so on. Hard work and determination are not alone sufficient for people to overcome social barriers created by poverty, racism, sexism, ableism, and other forms of discrimination. Many people fail to appreciate that point when they focus exclusively on the self. Faced with adversity, those confronting economic distress wonder what *they* can do differently or how *they* can change. Instead, we ought to ask how we can improve unjust systems that produce disparate life outcomes for different groups of people.

Self-enclosed individualism is also injurious because it is antithetical to democracy. As an institution, democracy is premised on an assumption that well-informed citizens will understand that, in spite of their differences, they are united by a set of common interests and concerns, as the preamble to the Constitution states clearly. Confronted with a consequential decision, citizens are meant to act for the benefit of the common good. Self-enclosed individualism, on the other hand, limits people's focus, causing them to fixate on their personal interests with little, if any, concern for the common good. As an example, during the COVID-19 pandemic, some people cast wearing protective masks as a matter of personal choice, never mind that electing *not* to cover one's mouth and nose risked exposing other people to a potentially deadly illness. When concern for self exists at the expense of concern for others, the result is a fractured society.

Finally, neoliberalism's emphasis on self-enclosed individualism is damaging because it invites us to imagine ourselves as existing in a state of perpetual competition with other people. We are expected to compete not only for jobs, but for access to important services, such as child care, schooling, and even health care. Those who manage to succeed—the so-called "exceptional" individuals—are perceived as winners, and by the same logic, those who fall short of their aspirations are losers, resulting, as Sandel argues, in the tyranny of meritocracy: "the smug conviction of those who land on top that they deserve their fate, and that those on the bottom deserve theirs, too," which ultimately "diminishes our capacity to see ourselves as sharing a common fate" (Sandel 25). As an antidote to self-enclosed individualism, we might instead focus on our interconnectedness—that is, on the many ways in which our fates intersect. Alongside independence, we can also value *interdependence*, a term that Goodley and Rapley use to refer to the strength that people possess when they work together to advance their shared interests (137–38).

Neoliberalism's incessant championing of individualism and self-reliance gives rise to the creation of a cult of self. In a world where people always exist in competition with other people, they are only ever able to focus on *their* needs, *their* desires, and *their* social futures. They therefore have little time to consider how they might partner with other people to work toward collective goals and projects. It doesn't, however, have to be this way. It is well within our power, and the power of writers and other creatives, to imagine more humane forms of social organization, more advanced ways of living together.

And although our cultural values can certainly include individualism, the potential also exists for literature to light our path at those crossroads where individuals work together for the common good.

With that in mind, in the following sections, we examine two works of YA fiction to demonstrate how literature for teenagers can reproduce as well as resist neoliberalism's emphasis on self-enclosed individualism. To focus our analysis, we examine in particular the attitude these novels take towards the exceptional individual, specifically, the self-enclosed individualists who are able to bend the systems that structure their society to their own ends in order to accomplish their goals. Exceptional individuals, however, only become exceptional in the ways that they are positioned as having transcended the groups into which sociopolitical institutions sort them; in addition, exceptional individuals are also more likely to display characteristics of competitiveness, rather than cooperation. We thus focus our analysis on *institutions* and *exceptionalism*. The institutions in Marie Lu's YA dystopia *Legend* give us an opportunity to further explore problems with genetic determinism, while *Marcelo in the Real World*, a work of realist fiction by Francisco X. Stork, invites us to contrast neoliberal values of *independence* with its opposite: *interdependence*.

INSTITUTIONS AND EXCEPTIONALISM IN MARIE LU'S *LEGEND*

Marie Lu's *Legend*, the first novel in a dystopian series of the same name, takes place in the distant future and is set in Los Angeles, California, now part of the Republic of America. Due to rising sea levels brought on by climate change, the city is periodically inundated by floodwaters, although its poor populations, relegated to slums along the shoreline, experience the consequences most severely. A government edict requires that all children, once they turn ten, take the Trial, a standardized test that determines their opportunities in life. Children who score between 1450 and 1500 attend one of the Republic's four elite universities upon completing high school. Those with a score between 1250 and 1449 are permitted to attend high school and are later assigned to a college. A score between 1000 and 1249 prohibits people from attending high school; instead, they are assigned undesirable (and often dangerous) jobs and are condemned to "join the poor" (7). The government's official narrative claims that children who fail the Trial are sent to labor camps, but readers soon learn that these children are in fact put to death in a genocide meant to "cull the population of weak genes" (246).

Narrated in the first-person, *Legend* employs two focalizers: Day, a fifteen-year-old prodigy from an impoverished family who escapes death after seeming to fail the Trial and thereafter engages in a campaign of subversion against the Republic; and June, a fifteen-year-old prodigy from a wealthy family who, upon completing her military training, is assigned to bring Day to justice after he allegedly murders her brother, Metias. June succeeds in doing so only to learn that the military murdered Metias once he discovered that the Republic was secretly exposing people in economically disadvantaged neighborhoods to strands of the plague to assess their effectiveness as bioweapons for use in the Republic's war against its enemy, the Colonies. At the novel's conclusion, June helps Day escape from prison, and the two embark on a journey to Las Vegas, where they plan to seek help from the Patriots, an underground resistance group.

In *Legend*, government and school represent two of the institutions that shape Day and June, and both institutions are depicted as hostile to individual freedoms; to wit, both characters' fates in life are determined by the Trial. Although the test is supposedly used to identify talented individuals, the government in fact uses it to reproduce the status quo and preserve its grip on power. Day earns a perfect score on his Trial, but the government, having recognized "something dangerous in him. Some defiant spark, the same rebellious spirit he has now" (202), falsifies his test score and fails him. Because he has been identified as an exceptional individual who is not easily controlled and because his production as a worker would be intellectual work, rather than the production of material goods, Day's energies are not easily commodified by the government, so he is subsequently subjected to medical experiments conducted by military doctors and left for dead. The text thus openly critiques authoritarian governments, but it also positions institutions, such as schools, as little more than training grounds for people to be transformed into government-manipulated pawns.

June also earns a perfect score on her Trial, but because she comes from an upper-class background, the government does not perceive her as a threat to the social order. Unlike Day, June is permitted to attend school—an Institutional State Apparatus, as Althusser would have it—that exists to produce conformity by immersing students in official government propaganda. Far from learning to think critically, June is instead taught to accept ideologies to which those in positions of power expose her without ever questioning them. She parrots her professors, for example, when she reiterates their argument that "better genes make for better soldiers make for better chance of victory against the Colonies" (13). Unlike Day, she is ignorant of the fate that awaits children who are sent to the government's labor camps; like Day, however, she is also a self-enclosed individual.

The institution of school is depicted as hostile to the individual in other ways. Although she is assigned to the Republic's premier university to be groomed for a future as an officer in the military, June's coursework fails to challenge her. When she formulates her own challenges to test her abilities, she draws the ire of her instructors. Bored with drills that require her to climb walls while carrying weapons, for example, June leaves campus and instead "scale[s] the side of a nineteen-story building with a XM-621 gun strapped to [her] back" (13). This results in her being sent to the dean's office, where she is reprimanded for her actions and warned that her noncompliant behavior will not be tolerated when she is assigned to a platoon. In contrast, a friend of hers, Thomas, who is considerably less capable yet willing to conform, manages to climb up in the ranks of the military as a result of his willingness to comply mindlessly with expectations his superiors impose on him. In *Legend*, then, institutions such as government and school do not exist to empower people; to the contrary, they impede people's ability to capitalize on their potential, reproducing the neoliberal view of public institutions as hostile to exceptional individuals.

In the novel, the government, with its IQ tests in particular, is the institution that positions both June and Day as exceptional individuals because the government creates the categories that allow them to be compared to others and thus prove to be superior to them, especially in their rule breaking. This institutional positioning makes it possible to read June and Day as examples of self-enclosed individuals. June has emerged as exceptional after earning a perfect score on her Trial, an accomplishment that results in her attending "the country's top university at twelve, four years ahead of schedule," and graduating early after she skipped her sophomore year and earned perfect grades (12–13). Likewise, though the Republic has tried to murder Day, he eventually survives to wage a sabotage campaign against the Republic. With self-enclosed panache, by himself, he steals large sums of money from Republic banks (167); by himself, he vandalizes the Department of Intra-Defense (168); and by himself, he sets fire to fighter jets intended for the warfront (168). In these ways, Day is the antithesis of his older brother, John, who conforms to the expectations his society establishes for him, and who has once instructed Day, "*You never fight back. Ever*" (275, emphasis in the original). Day and June both refuse to comply with their society's conformist expectations, and the text positions readers to respect them as a result.

June and Day represent the exceptional individual that Shauna Pomerantz and Rebecca Raby argue has arisen in popular culture in response to neoliberalism (238). As evidenced by their perfect scores on the Trial, both characters are supersmart, and their individual accomplishments mark them as superspecial in their society. Despite this, neither June nor Day fully acknowledges the role that social systems play in supporting them. June, for example, recognizes that Day "doesn't act like a desperate street kid," and she wonders whether "he has always lived in [the] poor sectors" (130), yet she is largely unaware of how her own social positioning as a member of the upper class privileges her. Rather than acknowledge how the opportunity to attend an elite high school and university might have advantaged her, June instead insists that her intellectual and physical attributes are innate, a result of "what the Republic considers good genes" (13).

In much the same way, Day's lower socioeconomic background poses few (if any obstacles) for him in the novel. He and his family may be considered poor, but his exceptional intellect and talents allow him to come into large sums of money whenever he needs it, whether through criminal activities or otherwise. Although the military's access to weapons and technology permits it to oppress people who inhabit the city's slums (252), these same resources pose few (if any) obstacles for Day, who succeeds in spite of them. In much the same way, the character of Thomas, who grew up in poverty, attributes his rising through the ranks of the military to his own hard work. As he tells Day, "*I'm* from a poor sector too. But I followed the rules. I worked my way up. *I earned my country's respect.* The rest of you people just sit around and complain and blame the state for your bad luck" (218–19, emphasis in the original). His assessment fails to acknowledge, however, that Metias, June's brother and an officer in the military, "had been the one to recommend Thomas (who had a high Trial score) to be assigned to the prestigious city patrols, despite his humble background" (40). In these ways and others, the social class system in the storyworld that Lu imagines neither advantages nor disadvantages characters. Instead, consistent with a neoliberal worldview, their accomplishments are presented as attributable to their unique talents and perseverance, with the result that June and Day are able to understand themselves as "the same person born into two different worlds" (304).

Significantly, the novel positions the reader to empathize with people who toil under the Republic's oppressive class system, but it never meaningfully interrogates the capitalist system that is responsible for (re)producing social inequity. Indeed, the text occasionally invites readers to envy June for her material comforts. For example, when she attends a military ball with Thomas, June explains, "I ended up choosing a corseted sapphire dress lined with tiny diamonds. One of my shoulders is covered in lace, and the other is hidden behind a long curtain of silk" (175). Thomas's "cheeks turn rosy" when he catches sight of her, but June is unable to understand "what the big deal is," given that she has "worn nicer dresses before" (175). True, June appreciates that her ability to wear such a dress is emblematic of her privilege; it occurs to her, for example, that the "dress could've bought a kid in the slum sectors several months of food" (175). Later, when she drinks out of an antique glass "imported from the Republic's islands of South America," she reflects: "Someone could've bought a plague cure with the money spent on this glass that I use to drink water out of" (251). She subsequently "hurl[s] it against the wall" so that it "shatters into a thousand glittering pieces" (251). She wants to reject her own materialism but does not think about how to transform her anger into a productive action that helps others. While June appreciates the injustice of an economic system that privileges some people and oppresses others, her critique of it is only symbolic and hence superficial: shattering an expensive glass that can be replaced, or feeling guilty about wearing fine clothes yet all the while continuing to participate in an unjust system, does little to disrupt the social structures that permit poverty.

In much the same way, Day boasts about having used money he got from robbing a bank to purchase "a nice pair of boots" on the black market, along with "an entire outfit, brand-new shirts and shoes and pants" for Tess, a young girl he protects (71). Upon seeing June dressed in her military regalia (just moments before he is scheduled to be executed), Day is struck by the "shining, luxurious epaulettes draping from each of her shoulders. A thick full-length coat made from some sort of rich velvet. Scarlet waistcoat and elaborate, belted boots" (284). In these ways, the text celebrates the materialistic aspects of capitalism, even while seeming to critique it. Although June and Day have experienced intense grief, having lost both of their parents and a brother each to a regime bent on preserving a rigid class system, Day is nonetheless able to assert that "money is the most important thing in the world, you know. Money can buy you happiness, and I don't care what anyone else thinks. It'll buy you relief, status, friends, safety . . . all sorts of things" (136, ellipses in the original). At no point does the novel critique or problematize that assertion and the materialism it implies. Instead, it allows it to stand as fact, thus perpetuating the neoliberal assumption that amassing financial resources matters far more than maintaining personal relationships or demonstrating social responsibility.

While we explore the topic in greater depth in chapter 6, we find it pertinent here to acknowledge how biological phenomena are used to organize people in novels, and so we ask: to what extent do they determine a person's worth to society? In regard to this question, we argue that *Legend* is critical of neoliberalism's tendency to view humans, nonhuman animals, and the environment as fodder for consumption by governments and corporations. In this novel, eugenics offers the government a rationale for using biological phenomena to engineer a socially stratified society.

People in the dystopia Lu envisions are placed into social castes according to the perceived quality of their genes, an assessment that is made via the Republic's administration of the Trial. Following the death of those who fail the Trial, government scientists autopsy their remains for the purpose of studying their imperfections and improving the genetic quality of society, so a person's worth is determined according to his or her perceived usefulness to government and industry, a fact that Day makes clear when he explains, "An inferior child with bad genes is no use to the country" (8).

The government's use of biological phenomena to organize and control society takes a second, even more insidious form in *Legend*, however, as the reader learns about the plague the Republic is secretly targeting toward families in working-class and poor neighborhoods, enabling military scientists to cultivate and weaponize these germs in government laboratories. By using the plague as a bioweapon, the Republic is able "to cull the population of weak genes, the same way the Trials pick out the strongest" (246).

June learns the truth about the Republic's eugenics program when she reads a series of journal entries her older brother, Metias, left for her online before he was assassinated by the military. In addition to discovering the truth about the plague, June comes to understand that her parents were murdered after her father, a scientist for the military, discovered the truth about the government's intentions. For her, the plague comes to serve as a metaphor for the government. She explains: "The plague has gotten its claws around all of us, in one way or another. The plague murdered my parents. The plague infected Day's brother. It killed Metias for uncovering the truth of it all. It took from me the people I love. And behind the plague is the Republic itself. The country I used to be proud of. The country that experiments on and kills children who fail the Trial" (250). June is horrified at the government's casual attitude towards genocide, so she decides to align herself with Day and the Patriots, a small band of freedom fighters dedicated to overthrowing the Republic's leadership. Especially in its emphasis on eugenics, *Legend* is a thinly veiled allegory for the genocidal thinking that led to the Holocaust. As with the Harry Potter series, the text makes clear that no government has the right to murder its citizens or, specific to *Legend*, to use them for biological experimentation. *Legend* frequently exhibits, as we have argued, neoliberal tendencies, so with this ideology, the novel promotes an ethos that governments govern best when they protect citizens, rather than harm them.

While we read *Legend* as criticizing the practice of using biological phenomena to arrange people in hierarchical relationships, and although we regard it as simultaneously condemning a neoliberalist assumption that regards people as human capital to be exploited by those in positions of power, we note that the novel nevertheless also invites the reader to identify with characters who are themselves biophysically exceptional people. That is, the novel does not position the reader to understand events from the perspective of characters who are less physically and intellectually capable. Instead, it positions the reader to identify with characters who stand out in their society as exceptional people, reifying, even if unwittingly, the neoliberal assumption that exceptional individuals, rather than institutions or the collective, are best positioned to combat oppression and injustice. A deconstructive tension thus lies at the center of *Legend*: on one hand, the text wants to argue that genocide is wrong, but on the other, it asserts that some people simply are biologically superior to other people, and as such, are positioned to be natural leaders. Unfortunately, we fear that any biopolitical system that asserts that some lives (in this case, June's and Day's) are more exceptional than others ultimately becomes vulnerable to something of a genocidal logic by which exceptional people are positioned to have more power and more rights than putatively inferior peoples.

Ultimately, despite offering some challenges to neoliberal thinking, Lu's novel undermines some of its intended critique of fascism with its emphasis on the exceptional, entrepreneurial hero as the only real savior, the only possible solution to the overreach of a corrupt federal government. In doing so, *Legend* ignores that groups of people are capable of working together, as a collective, to identify and address social injustices and advance their shared interests. Although this novel contains some social critique of a corrupt government, its neoliberal bias ultimately undermines that critique, offering instead glittering, self-enclosed individuals as those who are biologically destined by their superior brainpower to save society from itself.

MARCELO IN THE REAL WORLD AS A CRITIQUE OF NEOLIBERAL INDIVIDUALISM

In stark contrast, Francisco X. Stork's *Marcelo in the Real World* places the self-enclosed, neoliberally influenced individual in direct conflict with the sense of collectivity emphasized in the US Constitution in order to deconstruct the tyranny of merit. In this novel, the eponymous protagonist is a seventeen-year-old Mexican American boy experiencing symptoms he likens to those associated with Asperger syndrome. Marcelo is compelled by his father, a successful corporate attorney, to enter into the following arrangement: provided Marcelo is able to satisfactorily perform a summer job in the mailroom at the law firm where his father, Arturo, is a partner, thereby demonstrating Marcelo's ability to function in what Arturo calls the "real world," the teenager will be permitted to return to Paterson, a school for students with special needs, for his senior year of high school. In the event that Marcelo is unsuccessful, he must attend Oak Ridge, a public high school that Arturo believes will prepare his son to navigate the world in competition with neurotypical people.

At the law firm, Marcelo becomes interested in a lawsuit involving a teenage girl, Ixtel, whose face has been disfigured when the windshield of a car she was traveling in shattered during a minor traffic accident. He eventually learns that the maker of the windshield knew its design was faulty, but continued to manufacture the windshield anyway, reasoning that the cost involved in halting production was prohibitive. When Marcelo learns that his father's law firm chose to withhold this information during court proceedings, he decides to share the information with Ixtel's lawyer, which places his father's firm in jeopardy. Ultimately, an angry Arturo pronounces his son's experience at the law firm a failure and informs him that he will attend Oak Ridge. Marcelo accepts Arturo's decision, but he begins to plan for his future, deciding that after graduation, he will attend college in Vermont to pursue a degree in nursing so that he can one day work with children with disabilities.

As we did with *Legend* in the previous section, our first analytical process will be to examine the institutions that shape Marcelo's world, specifically how they empower and/or disempower him. We focus on two institutions in the novel: the law firm, which prioritizes self-enclosed individualism, and Paterson, where students learn to value collectivism. The law firm where Arturo works is a competitive environment in which the profit margin is emphasized over the needs of employees and the victims of crimes (such as Ixtel, the girl disfigured by a faulty windshield). Conversely, Paterson, the school for students with special needs, is a collectivist institution that accepts all students for their strengths and limitations alike. Moreover, the therapy horses that Marcelo works with at Paterson represent the importance of caring and sharing in the formation and sustenance of a communal, interdependent group. Because of his experiences at Paterson, Marcelo plans to spend his future with his girlfriend in Vermont in a similarly community-oriented environment.

Given its valorization of competition and self-enclosed individualism, and its "winner take all" ethos, the members of the law firm embody neoliberalism. In Arturo's words, "a law firm is not like Paterson. In a law firm the environment is competitive" (43). Emphasizing the connection between competition and the neoliberal self-enclosed individual, he instructs Marcelo, "Competition is good for all involved. The harder Stephen [a colleague] works, the harder and better I work. The more the associates work, the better the whole firm does" (43). Arturo also informs Marcelo, "Every day I come to work, I tell myself, I'm a warrior and this is a battle. I put on my war face" (46). Extending this metaphor, he likens his position at the law firm to "a war, where some will win and some will lose," prompting Marcelo to reflect, "*The real world*" (46, emphasis in the original). Despite Arturo's insistence on the value of competition, the novel positions the reader to question the desirability of living in an endlessly competitive world where individuals undermine others to advance themselves and where personal profit takes precedence over the health and welfare of other people.

In contrast to the law firm, the narrative depicts Paterson as a more desirable environment precisely because it is collectivist rather than individualistic and competitive. As a teenager on the spectrum, Marcelo understands how the accommodations that teachers at Paterson make for him empower him. He arrives at school each day with the feeling "that here at last is a place where I will not be hurried" (12). He understands that while "explanations about my condition are based on the assumption that there is something wrong with the way I am, . . . at Paterson I have learned through the years that it is not helpful to view myself or the other kids there that way" (55). Paterson provides a space that allows individuals to thrive because they are accepted within a larger community supporting and empowering them. In other words, the school rejects the self-enclosed individualism required to be "exceptional."

Pomerantz and Raby directly link neoliberalism's emphasis on individual exceptionalism to YA literature when they examine the trope of the "post-nerd smart girl" ("Reading" 287), a figure who is intelligent, beautiful, athletic, and popular, and who accomplishes whatever she wants to. They note, however, that these girls' "struggles are never connected to sexism, racism, heterosexism, and other social inequities" (303). Instead, the trope of the post-nerd smart girl fosters the illusion that individuals compete on a level playing field and succeed because of their own talents and abilities, thus perpetuating the neoliberal deception that we live in a postfeminist, postrace society, topics that we will examine in more detail later in this book.

Unlike *Legend*, which erases the intellectual effects of social class, *Marcelo in the Real World* resists neoliberalism's tendency to celebrate the exceptional individual while downplaying the role that identity politics play in privileging some people over others. As such, the novel reflects Keating's observation that self-enclosed individualism ignores that not everyone starts with the same economic advantage(s) and privilege(s). For example, whereas Wendell, the Harvard-educated son of the law firm's other major partner, Stephen Holmes, slanders Marcelo's father in private by referring to him to as a "minority hire"—a term that Wendell uses to refer to a person "whose skin is darker than the majority of folks, someone not born lily-white" (127–28)—he fails to interrogate his own privilege as a white, college-educated male from an upper-class family that traces its "lineage all the way to the folks that arrived on the *Mayflower*" (127). Marcelo, however, acknowledges the role his own socioeconomic status plays in privileging him when he reflects that "without the money Arturo earns from [the windshield company], we may not be able to afford Paterson" (212). Ixtel, on the other hand, lacks either the economic resources or the social capital needed to pay for cosmetic surgery and so is left to live with her disfigurement.

Stork's novel also implies that the emphasis neoliberalism places on meritocracy may, in keeping with the values of self-enclosed individualism, disadvantage oppressed peoples still further by pitting them against one another in a competitive tyranny of merit, thus preventing them from forming alliances that could lead to social gains. As an example, when Marcelo visits Jerry Garcia, a Mexican American lawyer who represents struggling people, including Ixtel, in a Hispanic section of Boston, he is surprised to learn that Garcia was a classmate of Arturo's at Harvard. According to Garcia, the seven Mexican American students in the law program met on a weekly basis to play poker. Rather than forge alliances, however, the students instead competed viciously, leading them to "openly envy and insult each other" (189). Garcia explains, "I could tell that people were really pissed when one got an A and the others didn't or when one got a job offer with a bigger law firm" (190). In contrast, his classmates could not understand why Garcia was motivated to open "a solo practice in a poor neighborhood," which suggests that their drive for personal profit overshadowed any obligation they felt to serve others. This is why, as Sandel argues, meritocracy is tyrannical: by pitting people against each other, especially people who share similar disadvantages, this ideology dissuades them from working together to address what are in fact shared sociopolitical problems, seducing them into surrendering their collective power with the result that they unwittingly participate in either their own oppression or the oppression of people who share their demographics.

In Stork's novel, Marcelo's relationship with a female rabbi, Rabbi Heschel, provides him with a strong argument for the importance of interdependence.

She critiques members of her congregation for being "worried about upgrading your Mercedes.... You think [God is] asking you to be a big success in whatever it is you're ambitious about, and that's not what he wants from you at all" (276). Rabbi Heschel clarifies that God wants for us "our longing for Him, the big longing," which too often in her view "gets confused with a hundred little longings, some of them okay, some of them not.... Buried under a mountain of silliness and selfishness" (276). In contrast, at the law firm, the principles that Rabbi Heschel advocates are perversely inverted. When Marcelo, quoting scripture, tells Arturo, "The first will be last," his father replies, with considerable "Me-consciousness": "In the world of work, the first are first and will be first and the last are last and will be last" (44). When a lawyer at the firm, having questioned the advisability of not compensating people for their injuries in the same windshield case that disfigured Ixtel, is fired for being "too soft" (173), the law firm is differentiating between winners and losers, with the former consisting of people who contribute to the firm's economy. Those who are not regarded as having something to contribute are disposable.

The novel also highlights the destructive role that self-enclosed individualism can play in restricting one's social vision, thus impeding one's ability to empathize with others. When Arturo angrily confronts Marcelo for having made public the role his law firm played in covering up the facts of Ixtel's case, Arturo is exclusively concerned with the damage he believes his son has inflicted on *him*. He insists, "Dammit, Marcelo! The world is not all black and white. There are rules you know nothing about. Rules *I* need to follow in order to *survive*. Those are the rules of this game *I play*. The system *I live by*! The system that puts food on the table and lets you ... go to a special private school" (289, emphasis added). Arturo's comments position neoliberalism as a "system" that shapes a person's experiences in the world, perpetually pitting them against others. Marcelo, on the other hand, is more concerned with the common good, specifically, the suffering that Ixtel and people like her will endure as a result of the windshield manufacturer's negligence. As such, he rejects the neoliberal rules his father has chosen to live by. Speaking about himself in the third person, as he often does, Marcelo tells Arturo, "I knew what could happen *to all of us*. Marcelo did not succeed in following the rules of the real world.... He knew that would happen before he talked to Jerry García. He thought it all through. All that would happen. And still he did it. And still he would do it again" (289, emphasis added). The novel positions the reader to admire Marcelo precisely because he is concerned about the welfare of other people, as opposed to focusing exclusively on his own needs and interests.

If neoliberalism emphasizes independence over interdependence, Rabbi Heschel's mentorship counter-instructs Marcelo that acting toward the common good creates more benefit than protecting certain individuals because they are superspecial. As we have noted, he is angry with his father's law firm for covering up the windshield case, reasoning that helping Ixtel "is something [Arturo] should do, we should all do" (205). Marcelo reflects, "For all the pain I saw at Paterson, it is nothing compared to the pain that people inflict upon each other in the real world. All I can think of now is that it is not right for me to be unaware of that pain, including the pain that I inflict on others" (302). It is perhaps not surprising, then, that at the novel's conclusion, Marcelo decides that he wants to pursue a career in nursing, a profession that involves caring for others, and in his case, children like him who have developmental differences. In settling on this career path, Marcelo chooses interdependence as a more humane and compassionate way of living in the world than the self-enclosed individualism in which his father has chosen to live.

IN BETWEEN: INSTITUTIONS AND EXCEPTIONALISM IN SUZANNE COLLINS'S HUNGER GAMES TRILOGY

Existing somewhere on the continuum between advocating neoliberalism and critiquing it, the Hunger Games trilogy promotes exceptionalism at times and interdependency at others. Set in the dystopic country Panem, the story is narrated by sixteen-year-old Katniss Everdeen, a skilled hunter who volunteers to take her younger sister's place in the Hunger Games, a reality television competition that pits twenty-four teenagers (a male and female from each of Panem's twelve districts) against each other in combat, and which permits just one victor—who is that year's truly exceptional teenager. Published in September 2008, the series' eponymous first book was released in the wake of accounting scandals at firms such as Enron, the implosion of the US housing market, and the onset of the worst economic collapse since the Great Depression, all of which were byproducts of neoliberal policies that sought to undo government regulation of the country's financial sector.

On the one hand, it is possible to read the Hunger Games series as reproducing certain neoliberal assumptions. Like *Legend*, Collins's novels also critique a government that is antagonistic to individual freedom. The twelve districts are ruled by the authoritarian Capitol, which governs through violence and fear. Katniss acknowledges that she "could be shot on a daily basis for hunting" (*Hunger* 17) because weapons are forbidden to the citizens of the districts, and she recalls that her father, who made his own bow and arrows for the same purpose, risked being caught and "executed for inciting a rebellion" (*Hunger* 5). Rue, from agricultural District 11, tells Katniss that in her district, people are tortured for holding back scraps of food they harvest (*Hunger* 202). Later, when Katniss arrives at District 13, she is surprised to discover that its government "is even more controlling than the Capitol" (*Mockingjay* 36). Like the Capitol, which commodifies the bodies of teenagers to further its own political agenda, leaders in District 13 commodify the bodies of people who seek refuge there, treating them as "breeding stock" to account for an epidemic that left a significant percentage of its population sterile (*Mockingjay* 8). Given its antigovernment sentiment, the trilogy teaches teenage readers "never to trust *any* government" (Trites, "Some Walks" 26, emphasis in the original). Should they do so, Trites argues, they will, like the neoliberal hero, "still ultimately have to save themselves from the greed and corruption of the adults who comprise the government" (26).

To a lesser extent than in *Legend*, the Hunger Games trilogy also reproduces neoliberalism's valuing of self-enclosed individualism. As Fritz observes, from the novel's start, Katniss is portrayed "as a survivor, an intelligent and independent individual who daily confronts the tyranny of her country's oppressive and opulent Capitol" (22). As a hunter capable of providing for her mother and sister following her father's death, Katniss is self-reliant, and her survivalist skills and knowledge of nature further advantage her self-sufficiency in the arena once the Games begin. After she arrives in the Capitol, she establishes herself as a formidable competitor, earning the highest training score of any tribute, male or female. In addition to her athleticism, the series also positions Katniss as exceptional due to her sexual desirability to heterosexual males, as evidenced by the fact that Gale, her hunting companion, and Peeta, her fellow tribute from District 12, both compete for her attention. She is a favorite of the Capitol audience as well, because they also recognize her exceptionalism, even though her stylists try to disguise her competence with conventionally fragile feminine beauty.

Beyond her exceptionalism, however, Katniss is initially concerned primarily with her needs and the needs of those in her immediate social sphere. She worries about her sister, Prim, whom she regards as "the only person in the world I'm certain I love" (*Hunger* 101). While Rue's death awakens Katniss's social conscience, it does not transform her into a social activist. Her decision to use the berries against the Gamemakers towards the end of the first book is neither attributable to a desire on her part to challenge the Capitol's authority nor to spark a revolution. Rather, her goal is to ensure that she and Peeta survive the arena and return to District 12, in part because she selfishly understands that her life there "would be unlivable if I let that boy die" (*Catching* 117). Later, in *Catching Fire* (2009), after Snow threatens the safety of her family and friends, Katniss briefly contemplates running away with Gale and their families, changing her mind only after Gale shames her, stating, "Don't you see? It can't be about just saving *us* anymore" (100, emphasis in the original).

We can also interpret the Hunger Games as sometimes valuing social practices that are antagonistic to neoliberalism. For instance, although Katniss is an exceptional individual, the series frequently connects her ability to survive to support she receives from other people, suggesting that care and coalition-building are preferable to self-reliance and rugged individualism. Katniss's knowledge of the woods and her skill as a hunter are attributable to childhood outings with her father, who taught her where to look for food, how to identify edible plants, and how to survive on her own. In the wake of her father's death, she is able to fend off starvation only because Peeta takes pity on her and gives her bread, thus allowing her to get back on her feet and figure out how to provide for her family. In their first Games, she is able to keep Peeta alive in part because of her familiarity with medicinal plants, which she acquired from her mother. She survives an encounter with the male tribute from District 11, Thresh, only because he shows her mercy and spares her life, appreciating how she has cared for Rue in her death. Even more, the series positions readers to admire Katniss because she is selfless: she volunteers to take her younger sister's spot in the Hunger Games, and in *Catching Fire*, she forms alliances with tributes others reject as weak. In the final book of the trilogy, *Mockingjay* (2010), she acknowledges her limitations as an individual, conceding, "Alone, I can't be the Mockingjay" (73). After the rebels take the Capitol, Beetee insists that the only hope for the future is that people will acknowledge that "unity is essential for our survival" (*Mockingjay* 370). In all of these instances, the Hunger Games trilogy emphasizes care for others as an antidote to selfish self-reliance, and in doing so, it suggests that people are stronger when they set aside their own individual interests and work together toward a common good.

Equally important, the Hunger Games series critiques neoliberalism as a tyrannical system that distinguishes between winners and losers, and which subsequently disposes of those who aren't perceived as contributing to the economy—unless, of course, they are a gaudily clad citizen of the Capitol. Katniss notes that the system by which teenagers are selected to compete in the Games "is unfair, with the poor getting the worst of it" (*Hunger* 13). From the time their names are drawn, tributes are positioned as self-entrepreneurs.

Prior to entering the arena, they must display their athletic prowess and abilities for the Gamemakers, who award them a score predicated on their perceived competitiveness. They also participate in television interviews, where they have the opportunity to compete for audience support. Those who are adept at self-promotion can win the support of sponsors. Additionally, tributes are permitted to form alliances once the Games begin, but they do so only for strategic, short-term purposes, disbanding when the situation dictates it. In contrast, toward the end of the first novel, Katniss and Peeta leverage their power as a coalition when they threaten to consume poison berries to protest a rule change that permits only one victor to survive. Recognizing that ending this competition without a victor would prove disastrous, the Gamemakers have no choice but to capitulate and declare them both winners.

The Hunger Games also critiques neoliberalism by calling attention to the role that social structures play in privileging some people and oppressing others. Although the novel diminishes how race and gender pose social obstacles for Katniss and other characters in the series, Panem's social class system does play a role in producing and maintaining inequality. In *The Hunger Games*, when Katniss encounters the other tributes she and Peeta will compete against in the arena, she notes that several of them are suffering from malnutrition, explaining, "You can see it in their bones, their skin, the hollow look in their eyes"; in contrast, "kids from the wealthier districts" are identifiable because they have "been fed and trained [to compete in the Games] throughout their lives," which leaves them with a physical advantage over other tributes (94). Compounding matters, because they are stronger and healthier, tributes from more affluent districts are more likely to earn support from sponsors, the result of which advantages them still further. Tributes from District 12, which is among the poorest districts in Panem, "never stand a chance" (*Hunger* 56).

Consistent with Julie Wilson's observation that in a neoliberal economy, "*we're all potentially disposable*: we exist and matter only insofar that we are deemed worthy of investment by the state or a corporate firm" (119, emphasis added), we find it also worth noting that even in the Capitol, people are subject to social insecurity. As an integral part of the annual Hunger Games festivities, stylists have the potential to reap considerable wealth and fame, and they circulate among the upper echelons of society. Nevertheless, Tigris's fate serves as a reminder that no one is secure in a system that values people only so long as they are able to contribute to the economy. Once a revered stylist, Tigris has fallen out of favor with President Snow (who is her cousin) for having had too many cosmetic alterations. As a consequence, her value to the state is depreciated. When Katniss encounters her, Tigris lives tucked away on a backstreet of the Capitol, where she runs a small business selling fur-lined undergarments. Her disposability to the Capitol is underscored by Katniss, who remarks, "So this is where stylists go when they've outlived their use" (*Mockingjay* 319).

Finally, it is worth noting how Collins's trilogy implicitly critiques neoliberalism's emphasis on self-enclosed individualism through its negative portrayal of President Snow, who is positioned as the ultimate self-enclosed individualist in the series. Snow is a shrewd competitor and consummate survivor whose loyalties extend only to himself. He is willing to destroy a hospital sheltering wounded men, women, and children because, as Gale reasons, he regards their lives as "expendable" (*Mockingjay* 98). In *Mockingjay*, the same logic compels him to use children from the Capitol as a human shield. Snow is also a shrewd entrepreneur who profits from commodifying human life; in *The Hunger Games* and *Catching Fire*, he sacrifices teenagers in the Hunger Games for political purposes, and in *Mockingjay*, Finnick reveals that Snow has long sold victors in the sex trafficking trade. In all of these ways, Snow exemplifies what it means to live a life devoted solely to the cult of self. He is a master tactician who is willing to advance his own interests by using other people as pawns. As he tells Katniss, "We both know I'm not above killing children, but I'm not wasteful. I take life for very specific reasons" (*Mockingjay* 356).

As our interpretation of the Hunger Games trilogy suggests, although the series is like *Legend* in reproducing neoliberalism's antigovernment sentiment and its valuing of the exceptional individual, it also, like *Marcelo in the Real World*, calls attention to social practices that can serve as an antidote to neoliberalism. Foremost among these is the books' emphasis on care and coalition building as alternatives to neoliberalism's ethos of rugged individualism and self-reliance.

CONCLUSION

While individualism is a character trait valued in America even before the United States came into existence, the self-enclosed individualism of neoliberalism results in an egocentric, competitive, undemocratic sense of solipsism that ignores the fact that no one controls their social status at birth and no one can control the fate of complex global systems, ecological disasters, pandemics, or international relationships among countries. Thus, we find it suspect when YA authors position teenagers as the exceptional individual, the entrepreneurial hero who alone can save the world.

Unlike June and Day, whose intellectual, athletic, and moral exceptionalism permit them to bend complex systems to their ends, Katniss cannot control the poverty in District 12 any more than she can change the competitive nature of the Hunger Games. She can, however, foster collaborations, as she does with Rue in the Hunger Games arena, and as the districts do later in the series when they come together to rebel against the Capitol's oppressive policies. Katniss only reluctantly agrees to become the Mockingjay in the third book in the trilogy because of her lack of "Me-Consciousness"; she doesn't do so without the self-interest of keeping her family, Peeta, and her stylists alive, however. She is a collaborator, as our discussion of the book indicates, but she is also fearsome in her competitiveness. She is an individual who has been made to appear superspecial when measured against criteria established by the institution of the Panem government and its Hunger Games. She helps bring down that government and the corrupt one about to replace it when she kills the unambiguously named President Coin, rather than President Snow, reasoning that because "collective thinking is usually short-lived," the future holds no promise for continued peace (*Mockingjay* 379).

The Hunger Games trilogy is mixed in its neoliberal and anti-neoliberal ideologies: Collins wants to have her cynicism and eat it, too. Ultimately, however, the cultural implications of the series cannot be ignored: only the machinations of a superspecial, exceptional individual—and a girl at that—can even temporarily save the world from itself. The many neoliberal, world-saving, exceptional, self-enclosed heroes this series engenders, as with those in *Legend*, are a strong testimony to the seductive nature of meritocracy in fiction.

In contrast, books like *Marcelo in the Real World* call teenage readers' attention to meritocracy's tyrannical potential by positioning them to consider the destructive aspects of neoliberalism's ceaseless championing of individualism and competition. Stork's novel suggests that a system that only ever pits people against each other in competition, including for basic resources, is destined to sow seeds of distrust and division. Such a system is devoid of concern for others, a point that Katniss also emphasizes when, critiquing her ancestors for bequeathing her and her family a dystopia, she reflects, "Clearly, they didn't care about what would happen to the people who came after them" (*Mockingjay* 84).

Based on our arguments about neoliberal exceptionalism, we turn in the next chapter to an examination of neoliberal exploitation. As we will argue, neoliberalism's privileging of exceptionalism leads inexorably to exploitation of peoples and the environment. Likewise, it champions a type of environmentalism—*neoliberal environmentalism*—that holds individuals, rather than governments and corporations, responsible for addressing threats to the future of all species, including humans.

Chapter 2

NEOLIBERALISM'S LOGIC OF EXPLOITATION

> They needed to believe we were animals. To justify the way they used us.
>
> —Laini Taylor, *Daughter of Smoke and Bone* (404)

Sitting on the Colorado Plateau in northern Arizona, the land of the western Navajo Nation, with its sweeping sandstone cliffs, majestic canyons, and unending blue sky, is a place of great natural beauty. For many of the tribal people, including children and teenagers, it is also a place characterized by economic hardships that affect opportunities, including educational access. According to a report compiled by the Arizona Rural Policy Institute, the median household income for the Navajo Nation in 2010 was $27,389, and more than a third of tribal members (38 percent) were classified as "severely poor" (38). Apart from jobs in smaller communities, such as Tuba City and Kayenta, the western Navajo Nation's local economy is, for the most part, dependent on subsistence farming and sheep and cattle grazing, although some people work in local mines.

Since the late 1960s, Peabody Energy (formerly Peabody Western Coal Company) has owned and operated two strip mines on Black Mesa, a land formation so named because of its rich coal deposits. One of the mines relied on train cars to transport extracted coal to other parts of the US, but the other, which closed in 2005, transported coal over more than 270 miles via a slurry pipeline that stretched from Black Mesa to a power plant in southern Nevada, where the coal was burned to generate electricity for parts of southern Arizona, California, and Nevada (but notably, not the Navajo Nation). To facilitate this process, each year Peabody Energy pumped approximately 1.3 billion gallons of pristine water, estimated to be between 10,000 and 35,000 years old, from the N-Aquifer (Glennon 157). In his book *Water Follies: Groundwater Pumping and the Fate of America's Fresh Waters*, Robert Glennon describes how this practice has lowered the water table in the region over time, causing once reliable springs to run dry and threatening people's access to potable water. In addition to depleting the local water supply and scarring the land, the strip-mining operations at Black Mesa are also thought to have contributed to an increase in air and water pollution (Wong).

The disproportionate impact of environmental degradation on First Nations' peoples and on other communities of color is not new. At the time of this writing, the predominantly Black city of Flint, Michigan, is still without clean water more than ten years after lead poisoned the local water supply, negatively affecting children because of their susceptibility to developmental delays and other health-related issues. In Nevada, the federal government has plans to store high-level radioactive waste at Yucca Mountain despite opposition from members of the Western Shoshone Nation, some of whom own homes in the area and fear the waste will contaminate the land that is sacred to them (Sadler). In Puerto Rico, where people continue to recover from the damage that Hurricanes Irma, Maria, and Fiona inflicted on the island, human suffering has been prolonged by the federal government's slow response to the storms. As these examples indicate, Indigenous peoples, Black people, and other marginalized communities experience the consequences of environmental degradation disproportionately, telling us that environmental justice and social justice are not unrelated topics.

In chapter 1, we examined how YA literature can reproduce as well as resist neoliberalism's emphasis on the meritocracy-based notion of individual exceptionalism. In this chapter, we argue that the concept of exploitation depends on oppositional binaries that privilege one term (e.g., white, male, heterosexual) over another (e.g., Black, female, queer). Indeed, the concept of exceptionalism itself requires oppositional binaries: one cannot be better than others without such a juxtaposition. Both exploitation and exceptionalism thus rely on basic power dynamics that too often justify unscrupulous treatment of lands, peoples, species, and all of nature itself. Neoliberal exploitation of the environment requires binaristic thinking to rationalize the exploitation of the land; because oppositional binaries support hierarchical thinking, they are an impediment to social justice. Building on our discussion in chapter 1, in this chapter we argue that neoliberalism encourages the exploitation of people and the environment in part *because* it emphasizes exceptionalism. *Intersectional environmentalism* emerges from an awareness that ecological environmentalism is tragically intertwined with intersectionality, including the intersections of race, social class, and gender. When readers examine literary texts through a lens of intersectional environmentalism, however, they are better prepared to critique oppositional binaries of the sort that authorize neoliberal exploitation of people, animals, and the environment.

In the discussion that follows, we examine how intersectional environmentalism builds on assumptions that are associated with *ecofeminism*, a branch of feminism arguing that the same ideology that is behind the rationalization of environmental degradation is also behind the oppression of women, people of color, people experiencing poverty, and the Earth itself. We then identify sociopolitical assumptions that lead literary texts to participate in neoliberal rhetorics about the environment that constitute what we refer to as *neoliberal environmentalism*. Having done so, we read Laini Taylor's Daughter of Smoke and Bone trilogy (2011, 2012, 2014) through the lens of those assumptions to demonstrate how this work of speculative fiction inadvertently rationalizes the exploitation of people, animals, and the environment. Next, we examine Eliot Schrefer's *Endangered* (2012), a work of YA realist fiction, through a lens of intersectional environmentalism to demonstrate how the text resists neoliberalism's logic of exploitation. Finally, to exemplify a work that emphasizes ethical caring—for people, animals, and the environment—as an antidote to neoliberalism's narrow focus on hyperindividualism, we examine Darcy Little Badger's *A Snake Falls to Earth* (2021).

INTERSECTIONAL ENVIRONMENTALISM

Following Leah Thomas and her colleagues' definitions on the website *Intersectional Environmentalist*, we use the term *intersectional environmentalism* to mean "an inclusive version of environmentalism that advocates for both the protection of people and the planet" and that is concerned with explaining how "injustices happening to marginalized communities and the Earth are interconnected." As a critical perspective, intersectional environmentalism is indebted to Kimberlé Crenshaw's work on *intersectionality*, which suggests that social categories such as race, gender, class, sexuality, and dis/ability do not exist independent of each other, but instead intersect in ways that compound the effects of discrimination. Consequently, some people (for example, a disabled and transgender Black woman) experience multiple forms of oppression. Building on this understanding, intersectional environmentalism acknowledges that communities of color, Indigenous communities, economically disadvantaged communities, and youth are more likely to experience the effects of environmental degradation than adult members of affluent white communities.

Intersectional environmentalism is related to critical multicultural analysis (CMA) in the attention that both forms of critique pay to issues of power. As Bothelho and Rudman explain in *Critical Multicultural Analysis of Children's Literature*, this interrogation of power begins with the following questions: "Who is represented, underrepresented, misrepresented, and/or invisible? How is power exercised?"; they continue: "race, class, and gender matter. Critical multicultural analysis brings socioeconomic class into the conversations about race and gender, so we can better understand how these systems of oppression intersect" (xiv). Bothelho and Rudman advocate for teaching "the reader to deconstruct dominant ideologies of US society (e.g., race, class, gender, and individualism) which privilege those whose interests, values, and beliefs are represented by these worldviews" (xiv). CMA also invites readers to question thought systems that privilege Eurocentric (usually cis-male) humans, especially in the ways that these systems were advanced as if ever since the Renaissance Euro-white cis males constituted the entirety of the world encompassed in the study of "the Humanities" (Braidotti 2). The fifteenth-century roots of the term "humanism" clearly prioritize white cis-males as the "humans" under interpretation.

As a result, intersectional environmentalism relies on *posthumanism*, which is the logical rejection of damaging long-term Eurocentric humanism, especially its tendency to center (white) humans as being of prime cultural importance. Posthumanism can thus be thought of as "post-*humanism*" rather than "post-*human beings*." Posthumanism values all humans and the world as it sustains us, including nonhuman animals, the environment, and even technology. The core values of posthumanism share the core values of CMA and intersectional environmentalism: living beings and nonliving entities—such as water tables, polar ice caps, technology, and the electric grid—are interconnected, so it is wrong to privilege one group or entity, such as white people, above any other.

Intersectional environmentalism disrupts false binaries of the sort that posthumanism critiques and examines issues of power similar to those that Bothelho and Rudman identify. In doing so, it invites questions such as: How do gender or race shape a child's relationship to environmentalism, especially, for example, if the child is a Navajo girl living in poverty? How does environmental degradation contribute to disability in childhood or later in life? How does socioeconomic status increase the health risks of a child who lives in a polluted environment or drinks water laced with toxins? Or, to be less abstract, would the cost-saving measure of switching from the Detroit Water and Sewage Department's water supply to relying solely on treating the water of the Flint River at the Flint Water Service Center have occurred if the citizens of Flint, Michigan, were largely white and upper middle class? And would the initial medical concerns a pediatrician raised about lead levels in Flint's water have been met with more careful scrutiny? In this situation, those with power—the city's government—had the capacity to affect the long-term health of humans occupying at least three intersectional positions: they are children; their parents belong to the working class or they live in poverty; and a great many are African American.

Although the concept of intersectional environmentalism is relatively recent as of this writing, it owes a debt to the work of ecofeminist scholars who, since the 1970s, have argued that the same ideology that authorizes human exceptionalism by elevating human culture over nature is also behind other forms of oppression, including sexism, classism, racism, heterosexism, ableism, and speciesism. Our review of scholarship on intersectional environmentalism and ecofeminism, coupled with our close reading of books for young adult readers that address environmental and conservation topics, has led us to identify several assumptions that we argue inform intersectional environmentalism. In the next section, we examine each of these assumptions separately. We use them as the basis for critiquing environmentally themed literary texts for the young to examine how they depict the relationship between environmental justice and social justice.

OPPOSITIONAL BINARIES SUPPORT SYSTEMIC OPPRESSION

Our theoretical framework for examining environmentally themed literature through a lens of intersectional environmentalism begins with interrogating oppositional binaries—for example, culture/nature; human/animal; male/female; rich/poor; white/Black—that support systems of oppression. Bruno Latour refers to oppositional binaries of this type as "Great Divides" because they benefit the oppressor at a cost to the oppressed, creating a chasmic power differential in the process (97–100). Donna Haraway considers Latour's insight into binaristic hierarchies to be a fundamental aspect of posthumanist thinking (9). She argues that scholars must understand the power dynamics inherent in these "Great Divides" before they can reject the oppression inherent in hierarchical binaries, such as white/Black or male/female or rich/poor or human/animal (9–10). N. Katherine Hayles, the first scholar to demonstrate usefully the efficacy of posthumanism in an in-depth exploration of literary studies, deconstructs the very sort of oppositional binaries that allow humans to imagine themselves as superior to nonhuman animals. She argues: "The posthuman subject is an amalgam, a collection of heterogeneous components, a material-informational entity whose boundaries undergo continuous construction and reconstruction" (3). For Hayles the literary critic—and for Haraway, the biologist and scholar of feminist studies—posthumanism decenters hierarchical notions of the supremacy of some beings over others.

In her book *Ecofeminist Philosophy: A Western Perspective on What It Is and Why It Matters,* Karen Warren critiques the role of oppositional binaries in producing and maintaining oppression. She argues that the oppression of people based on gender is authorized by a conceptual framework that consists of the following features: "Up-Down thinking, oppositional value dualisms, conceptions of power and privilege that systematically advantage Ups over Downs, and a logic of domination" (62). According to Warren, the same conceptual framework that is behind "the domination of humans by race/ethnicity, class, age, affectional orientation, ability, religion, marital status, geographic location, or nationality" also makes affordances for "the domination of nonhuman nature (and/or animals) by humans" (62). In each instance, one term in an oppositional binary is elevated above the other, the result of which gives rise to a hierarchical worldview. Moreover, aware of the oppositional binary "Global North/Global South" when she is writing about literature for youth, Australian critic Victoria Flanagan identifies not only such dualities as "man/woman" and "nature/culture" (36), but also falsely binarized dichotomies between adult/child (33) and "inorganic and organic, human and animal" (23). In other words, Flanagan demonstrates quite well the compatibility between the study of posthumanism and intersectional environmentalism in children's and YA literature.

By using false dichotomies to elevate humans (a type of animal) over nonhuman animals, the human/animal binary emphasizes human exceptionalism. This logic is evident in many stories, including the creation myth found in the first chapter of Genesis, which depicts God as giving humans "dominion over the fish of the sea, and over the fowl of the air, and over every living thing that moveth upon the Earth" (1:28 KJV). This is no small point, as in European and Anglophone cultures, the human/animal binary offers a rationale for humans to consume animals as food, to exploit them for their labor, to house them in zoos, and to use them as test subjects for household and beauty products. Similarly, in the Genesis creation myth, God is also said to have created woman from man, setting up another hierarchy that has too often been offered as a rationale for patriarchy over the millennia, as observed by, among others, feminist philosopher Elizabeth Grosz.

In contrast, the writer Thomas King juxtaposes the hierarchical nature of the Genesis creation myth with a Native American creation myth that emphasizes the interconnectedness of humans and nonhuman animals. Although King himself identifies as Cherokee, the creation myth to which he refers is about Skywoman—who falls from the heavens and then works cooperatively with animals of the land and sea to create the Earth. The story is usually associated with First Nation Peoples of the most easterly tribes of the Iroquois Confederacy in present-day Canada and the northeastern US; these Indigenous peoples include the Oneida, the Kanien'kehaka, and the Tyendinaga (Niro, George, and Brant). In preferring the more cooperative creation myth of the Skywoman over the Genesis myth, King argues that the difference between the competing worldviews these stories offer is not inconsequential. Indeed, it is the difference between understanding the universe as a place "governed by a series of hierarchies" and one that is "governed by a series of co-operations ... that celebrate equality and balance" (23–24). By calling readers' attention to false binaries of this type, intersectional environmentalism positions them to reject a logic that centers some beings as more important, or more deserving of protections, than others.

Like ecofeminism, intersectional environmentalism also assumes that women, Indigenous peoples, other peoples of color, and people living in poverty experience the effects of environmental degradation disproportionately. This assumption is attested to by research suggesting that women and people of color are often among the first to experience the effects of climate change. Bill McKibben, for example, notes that in Bangladesh, rising sea levels have caused ocean water to move further inland, polluting the freshwater sources that are available to people. As a consequence, in a culture where females are responsible for domestic chores, women and girls increasingly have to walk longer distances to retrieve potable water. Similarly, Amy Elizabeth Kings demonstrates how climate change and environmental degradation have adversely impacted women and girls in rural parts of the Global South. Citing a United Nations report, she notes that women and girls face a "higher risk of reproductive/fertility health issues caused by drinking from a contaminated water supply," and they are also "more likely to die in an ecological disaster than their male counterparts" (73). Other research suggests that people of color and people experiencing poverty are statistically more likely to live in polluted environments.[1]

As we argued in chapter 1, YA dystopian novels that celebrate exceptional, self-enclosed individuals single-handedly overcoming all obstacles to achieve their goals and rescue their society from an oppressive government are problematic insofar as they reproduce the worst aspects of the American myth of rugged individualism and meritocracy. In doing so, these books imply that large-scale environmental problems such as climate change are best addressed by individuals, not governments. However, these are complex problems that need to be addressed on a societal level, rather than individually. As Marek Oziewicz and Lara Saguisag write, "While industries . . . are rarely held accountable for the ecocide they enact on a planetary scale, individuals are urged to exercise personal responsibility by becoming eco-conscious consumers. This displacement of blame through the manufacturing of climate guilt is central to the operations of ecocidal neoliberalism" (vi). Despite neoliberal environmentalism's insistence on individual accountability as an antidote to global warming and other climate-related catastrophes, no one person has the power, let alone the resources, needed to tackle these vast problems. However, as evidenced by social media campaigns such as the youth-led #StudentsStrike4Climate movement, young people can leverage their collective power to pressure governments to employ their considerable resources to address these problems, as we discuss in chapter 8. That said, we now turn to examining how Laini Taylor's Daughter of Smoke and Bone trilogy employs oppositional binaries and so inadvertently participates in neoliberal rhetorics that rationalize the exploitation of people, animals, and the environment.

NEOLIBERAL EXPLOITATION IN THE DAUGHTER OF SMOKE AND BONE SERIES

The Daughter of Smoke and Bones trilogy is a work of speculative fiction that draws inspiration from John Milton's *Paradise Lost* and that imagines a centuries-old war waged between angels and demons that one day spills over into the human realm. Seventeen-year-old Karou, an art student living in Prague, is presented as an orphaned teenage girl. However, in the absence of human parents, she has been raised by chimaera (as demons are called in the series), and she assists her adoptive father figure, Brimstone, in collecting human and animal teeth that he in turn uses—initially unbeknownst to her—to resurrect the souls of chimaera soldiers who are killed in battle. After Brimstone is murdered by angels, Karou learns that, in a previous life, she was a chimaera named Madrigal who was put to death for falling in love with the angel Akiva. When in her reincarnated form, she and Akiva unexpectedly encounter each other in the human world, he recognizes Karou as Madrigal, and he helps her to remember her previous life. The two later embark on a journey to end the war between the angels and chimaera and fulfill their dream of initiating a "new way of living" together in peace (*Daughter* 171). The series takes its title from the fact that Karou, having apprenticed under Brimstone, will take her mentor's place as the resurrectionist for the chimaera, a position that requires her to place the souls of the dead, which are collected as "smoke," in bodies she fashions for them out of the "bone" of human and animal teeth.

On its surface, the Daughter of Smoke and Bone series appears to examine postcolonial themes. In particular, it aspires to critique the role that hierarchical thinking plays in producing (and supporting) structural oppression and social injustice. To do so, the series highlights several oppositional binaries that, in the context of the story, provide characters with a logic for exploiting people and the environment. The most prominent of these binaries distinguishes between angels, who, with the exception of having fiery wings, look like human beings, and chimaera, who queer the binary in that they are typically embodied as part-human and part-animal. In the story, the angels' hatred of the chimaera is motivated by their belief in their own racial superiority. Whereas the angels pride themselves on having built an empire replete with crystal cities, they regard the chimaera as "barbarians in mud villages" who ought to be grateful to their oppressors for bringing them gifts such as "light, engineering, [and] the written word" (*Daughter* 225). Karou, on the other hand, understands that the angels' oppression of the chimaera people is rooted in a far simpler logic: "the seraphim want to rule the world, the chimaera don't want to be ruled, and that makes them evil" (*Daughter* 225). Because the chimaera refuse to submit to the angels' sanctimonious authority, the angels wage a colonialist, genocidal war against them in an effort to rid the empire of them.

To justify their oppression of the chimaera, the angels invoke a binary that privileges the human form over any animal or animal form. As Brimstone tells Karou, "[The angels] needed to believe we were animals. To justify the way they used us" (*Daughter* 404). The angels "told themselves [the chimaera] were dumb beasts, as if that made it all right" (*Daughter* 405). The binary is thus a product of language: the book notes that the term *chimaera* is an angel construct, which "essentially meant nothing more specific than 'creature of mixed aspect, creature *not seraph*.' It was a term that took in every species with language and higher function that lived in these lands and was not an angel" (*Dreams* 80, emphasis in the original).[2] In this way, the series suggests that language (as a source of binaries) plays an integral role in allowing the angels to strip the chimaera people of their humanity, and to murder and enslave them without ever acknowledging the horror of their crimes against an entire group of people.

In addition to critiquing the connection between language, colonialism, hierarchical thinking, and racism, the series also demonstrates how oppositional binaries can offer a logic for the oppression of people within the same social and cultural group. For example, under the Emperor Joram, the angel military is divided into three distinct castes. At the top of the hierarchy is Dominion, which draws its soldiers from society's "elite, aristocratic" classes, which will presumably "fight to protect the privilege they were born to" (*Dreams* 297). Below Dominion is the Second Legion, which is made up of conscripted soldiers. At the bottom of the social caste are the Misbegotten: angels who are respected for their ferocity in battle, but who are socially marginalized because they are known to be bastards born of Joram's trysts with concubines. Because of their low social status, the Misbegotten serve a utilitarian function in angel society: they are "raised to be weapons of the realm" (*Days* 14), and as such, the powerful exploit them as a wartime resource that is "expendable, endlessly renewable" (*Days* 359). Toward that end, Joram's "secretaries kept a list of his progeny in two columns, girls and boys. Babies were always being added, and as they grew up and died on the battlefield, they were stricken unceremoniously off" (*Daughter* 171).

Chimaera society is less stratified than angel society; nevertheless, its leaders also objectify people and exploit them as a resource. When chimaera soldiers are killed in battle, for example, their souls are collected and preserved in thuribles until a time when the resurrectionist—first Brimstone and later Karou—is able to place them in newly fashioned bodies. The practice of resurrection thus advantages the chimaera in their war with the angels, as it permits Thiago, the commander of the military and the chimaera emperor's son, to send wave after wave of soldiers to attack angel strongholds without depleting their ranks. In this way, the series positions readers to acknowledge resurrection as a cruel practice that exploits people by allowing them to die horrible deaths time and time again for the benefit of the powerful. Taylor's Daughter of Smoke and Bone series is thus clear in its ideological position: any system of thinking that values the lives of one group over another inevitably leads to exploitation.

If the Daughter of Smoke and Bone trilogy critiques the role that oppositional binaries play in privileging some groups of people over others, the series also reproduces binaries that undercut its otherwise progressive, postcolonialist ideology. Although the angels refer to the chimaera as "animals" (*Days* 289), "beasts" (*Days* 186), and "monsters" (*Daughter* 210), the chimaera people themselves employ a similar logic when they evince a preference for chimaera whose aspect is "high-human" (or predominantly human) over those who are primarily animal, or "high-creature." For example, after

Madrigal's foster sister, Chiro, is killed in battle, Madrigal, whose aspect is high-human, takes great care to fashion a body for her sister that resembles her original high-creature aspect. In her mind, Madrigal does this as an act of love. She is therefore surprised when Chiro accuses Madrigal of selfishly giving her a predominantly animal body to protect her own status as the more desirable of the two sisters. Chiro's suspicions appear to be validated when Thiago—for whom Chiro has feelings, and who is also of high-human aspect—expresses a preference for Madrigal. At no point does the series ever problematize Chiro's assumption that a high-human aspect is preferable to a high-creature aspect. Instead, this assumption is left to stand as self-evident.

The series also reproduces the misleading, hierarchical human/animal binary through its depiction of the chimaera's treatment of animals (that is, animals devoid of any human embodiment). Even though the chimaera are part-human and part-animal, they nonetheless exploit animals as "beasts of burden" (*Dreams* 594), harnessing their labor to rebuild cities devastated in their war with the angels. They further exploit animals by using their teeth to create bodies for resurrected chimaera, a point we will examine in more detail shortly. The chimaera can use human teeth for the same purpose, but Karou only ever collects animal teeth, suggesting that this practice is somehow less odious than harvesting something from human skulls. In all of these ways, the series implies that the angels' treatment of chimaera as "beasts" is abhorrent, while the chimaera's treatment of animals as "beasts" is understandable and natural.

Moreover, the trilogy is characterized by contradictions in its attitude toward the exploitation of nature and the exploitation of people. On its surface, the Daughter of Smoke and Bone books appear to condemn neoliberalism's rapacious consumption of natural resources and its lack of concern for the environment. For example, the third book, *Dreams of Gods and Monsters* (2014), introduces readers to Esther, a wealthy older woman who has regularly harvested animal and human teeth for Brimstone in exchange for wishes, which she has subsequently used to attain wealth and immortality. Esther also agrees to serve as Karou's unofficial guardian, a position that requires her, among other things, to enroll Karou in school, supply her with forged identification cards, and set up bank accounts on her ward's behalf. When the angels, led by Joram's brother, Jael, visit the Vatican in hopes of persuading humans to supply them with weapons they can use against the chimaera, Esther recognizes an opportunity to advance her own selfish economic interests. In exchange for supplying Jael with "arms, ammunition, technology, even personnel" and turning over Karou and Akiva to him, Esther expects to obtain "mining rights. To an entire world. An entire undeveloped world with a slave population already in place, and an army to guard her interests" (*Dreams* 483). Esther's entrepreneurial scheme demonstrates how the exploitation of people is connected to the exploitation of the environment—and how evil both forms of exploitation are.

This connection is further reinforced by the economic system of magic that operates in the series. In this economy, pain and suffering constitute the primary currency that one must tithe in order to practice magic. For instance, at one point in time, chimaera practitioners of magic harvested their own pain. As time passed, however, they discovered a cheat: by extracting human and animal teeth, they could pass the requisite pain on to others. As a consequence, those in power sadistically exploit people and animals alike in order to achieve their goals. Karou reminds Brimstone of this point when she admonishes him: "You do business with killers, and you don't even have to see the corpses they leave behind. . . . But I've seen them, piles of dead creatures with bloody mouths. Those *girls* with their bloody mouths; I'll never forget as long as I live" (*Daughter* 38, emphasis in the original).

Nevertheless, the series also downplays and even erases the connection between the exploitation of the environment and the exploitation of people. For example, when, in a flashback scene, Madrigal/Karou laments the suffering that animals endure in order for Brimstone to practice magic, Issa, a chimaera woman who helps care for her, angrily responds, "Perhaps you would prefer to torture slaves" (*Daughter* 333), implying that animal suffering is somehow less abhorrent than human suffering. Likewise, although Karou occasionally experiences guilt for the role she plays in collecting animal teeth for Brimstone, she is able to compartmentalize her feelings. After she retrieves an elephant's tusks at auction, Karou is initially sickened by the animal's death and her complicity in what she acknowledges is a "blood trade"; almost immediately, however, she "shut the thought away in a dark room in her mind" so as "not to think about it" (*Daughter* 44). Throughout the series, Karou continues to participate in the trafficking of animal teeth, even frequenting a natural museum in Rome "to replenish her store of teeth" prior to confronting Jael and his army of angels at the Vatican (*Dreams* 418). At the series' conclusion, Karou involves even her human friends, Zuzana and Mik, in the collection of animal teeth that Karou can use in the service of resurrecting chimaera revenants.

Taylor's Smoke and Bone trilogy is thus ambivalent in the stance it takes toward environmental and social justice. On the one hand, it criticizes an economy premised on the suffering of others, be it humans or nonhuman animals. It also criticizes how oppositional binaries construct hierarchies that privilege the interests of some groups over others. On the other hand, there are occasions when the series reproduces oppositional binaries, as when it implies that animal suffering is preferable to human suffering, thus positioning animals as a means that humans are justified in using to advance their own self-interests. In the next section, we examine a work of realist YA fiction that deconstructs the human/animal binary and critiques neoliberal commodification of nature through a lens of intersectional environmentalism.

INTERSECTIONAL ENVIRONMENTALISM IN *ENDANGERED*

The Ape Quartet is a series written by Eliot Schrefer, a Euro-American man whose empathetic environmentalism has motivated his advocacy for endangered great apes. Each of the four books that comprise the quartet focuses on a different type of great ape: bonobos in *Endangered*; chimpanzees in *Threatened* (2014); orangutans in *Rescued* (2016); and gorillas in *Orphaned* (2018). The books are thematically related, but their narratives do not build on or reference each other.

Even though it was a finalist for the National Book Award for Young People's Literature, *Endangered* is not without problems. For example, a review of the book on *Africa Access*, a website concerned with representations of Africa in books for young readers, notes that this novel is "filled with troubling tropes and stereotypes excoriating humans (Congolese, that is)" (Gondola). It also smacks of an "American white savior complex" because the protagonist, whose mother is Congolese, has a white American father. While acknowledging this novel's flaws, especially its colonialist attitudes, we still perceive how the book advances ideologies critiquing the dualistic thinking that rationalizes the oppression of any group of humans and/or nonhuman animals and/or the Earth itself. In that regard, our decision to examine *Endangered* through a lens of intersectional environmentalism is motivated by our belief that the text exemplifies how this critical lens can work in offering young readers another way to understand their relationship with the natural world that moves beyond oppositional binaries.

Endangered is the story of fourteen-year-old Sophie Biyoya-Ciardulli, a privileged multiracial Congolese American teenager who travels from Miami, Florida, where she lives with her Euro-American father, to the Democratic Republic of the Congo, where she intends to spend the summer with her mother, a Congolese conservationist who operates a sanctuary for rescued bonobos. Modeled after Claudine André, the founder of the Democratic Republic of the Congo's first bonobo sanctuary, Sophie's mother is a woman whom bonobos adore; indeed, "everything she came across adored her" (13). The text later explains that bonobos are a matriarchal society, which is why they are so much more tolerant of Sophie and her mother than they would be of any male, and which also explains why this particular story could only be narrated by a female character.

In the first chapter, while traveling from the airport to her mother's sanctuary, Sophie encounters a bush trader selling a young male bonobo. Against the advice of her chaperone, she purchases the ape, whom she names Otto, and from that point on she becomes its surrogate mother. Toward the end of her visit, Sophie's mother and a team of assistants leave the sanctuary to reintroduce a group of mature bonobos to the wild. Not long after, Sophie and the remaining staff learn that an army of Rwandan mercenaries has assassinated Congo's president and captured Kinshasa, the capital city, causing the country to fall into a violent civil war. As an American, Sophie has the opportunity to evacuate. When UN peacekeepers arrive at the sanctuary to escort her to the airport, however, she runs away and hides in the bonobo enclosure, hoping to stay and care for Otto. After enemy soldiers capture the sanctuary and kill the remaining staff, Sophie has no choice but to embark on a dangerous survivalist journey with Otto to reunite with her mother at the release site. This is where the story becomes one that must be told by both a girl (whom bonobos can trust) and a multiracial Congolese American girl, too: were she white, Sophie would not be tolerated by the rebels, and were she a Black Congolese person, she would not receive preferential treatment from UN military personnel.

Significantly, *Endangered* calls attention to the problem of wealth inequality and class oppression in Congo by contrasting people who have money with those who are experiencing poverty, which emphasizes the power differentials that exist between these groups. The novel thus insists that readers grapple with the exact type of power dynamic that critical multicultural analysis exposes. Juxtaposing Congo with the US, Sophie likens visiting the country to "descending into the muggy and dangerous back of nowhere" (2). When her American friends ask her to describe Congo, she notes that she can do so using a single word: "poor" (5). She is cognizant of her own privilege and of the role that wealth inequality has historically played in producing social instability in Congo, especially in the way that war subjects local populations to violence and suffering. In the capital city of Kinshasa, where her mother maintains a home, Sophie notes with disapproval that "residents with money lived like colonists in a hostile land, shuttered into manor houses with guards stationed in front" (28). Money and power are inevitably linked to war and violence in this novel. Indeed, in a country that is characterized by extreme wealth inequality, Sophie struggles to reconcile the money her mother invests in caring for orphaned bonobos with the knowledge that "people all over Congo were dying in poverty" (23). The book's critique of economic oppression is especially evident in the scene in which Sophie purchases Otto from the bush trader. When she first encounters the man, she instantly interprets "his crippled foot and greasy ragged tunic tied closely with woven palm frond" as evidence that he "was close to starvation" (4). Defending his decision to engage in animal trafficking, the man justifies his actions by telling Sophie that if she purchases Otto from him, she can help him and his family to avoid starvation. A primary oppositional binary here is the clear critique of a hierarchy that distinguishes between "haves" and "have-nots," leading some people to suffer while others live comfortably and complacently within their power structures.

A second oppositional binary that *Endangered* calls attention to juxtaposes white people with people of color. In doing so, the book critiques Congo's long history of racial oppression due, among other factors and in no small part, to colonialism. Although Sophie is multiracial, she notes that when she first moved to the US with her father, her status as "the only African girl in the whole school" (5) caused her predominantly white classmates to regard her as an object of exoticism: "I'd gotten plenty of looks, with my plastic slippers and hair whose kinkiness I hadn't decided whether to embrace or fight" (5). In Congo, however, her lighter skin color results in her being mistaken for Caucasian, as evidenced by the fact that people she encounters frequently refer to her using the term *mundele*, which Sophie connects to Belgium's colonization of Congo in the twentieth century. Throughout the book, Sophie is depicted as benefiting from her status as a *mundele*. For example, when a UN van arrives at the sanctuary to take her to the airport, she notices that her Black coworkers look upon her with a mixture of "relief and envy and fatigue," a result of their understanding that "some people got rescued, and most didn't" (62). Exactly who the UN rescues is clarified moments later when Sophie climbs into the van and discovers that it is "full of scared white people" (64).

The book emphasizes the problem of racial stratification in Congo again later when Sophie and Otto encounter a group of Congolese refugees traveling to the airport where they hope to find protection from the war. One woman, a mother accompanied by three young girls, gestures at the skin on Sophie's arm and exclaims, "Look at you! The UN is here. They can get you out!" She continues, "The blue helmets have abandoned the capital, but they made a base near here to help the *mundeles*" (148). She instructs Sophie, "They don't want to see us.... But go ahead. The blue helmets will take care of you" (149). When Sophie finally arrives at the UN encampment, she is surprised when the first soldier she meets refuses to help her, but she gains admission to the base by leveraging her status as an American citizen, which causes her to think, "If I'd had purely black skin, he would have said no. But I was half-white" (170). While she does not have white privilege in the US, Sophie recognizes that she does in Congo, and while the power that privilege confers on her saddens her, she is also willing to use it to her advantage.

A third oppositional binary in *Endangered*—human/animal—calls attention to the oppression of nonhuman animals and establishes anthropocentrism as a topic of critique in the novel. Throughout the story, Sophie struggles with the question of whether human suffering takes precedence over nonhuman animal suffering. For example, when she is escaping the sanctuary and an elderly school principal lets her use a motorized bicycle, she lets Otto ride on her back, but the man reprimands her, exclaiming, "*People first*, Sophie. *People first*. Then you can help Otto" (142, emphasis added). She ignores him and rides on. Thus, *Endangered* positions readers to understand how oppositional binaries give rise to hierarchies that support classism, racism, and anthropocentrism.

Read through a lens of intersectional environmentalism, *Endangered* also exemplifies ecofeminism's assumption that the same ideology authorizing the oppression of nature also motivates the oppression of people. Sophie speaks directly to this assumption when she reflects, "It had always been my mom's philosophy that *the way we treat animals goes hand in hand with the way we treat people*" (2, emphasis added). This becomes painfully clear after Sophie arrives at the UN encampment and is surprised to learn that peacekeepers have recently confiscated two young bonobos from a bush trader and then released the little apes into the jungle behind one of the buildings, oblivious to the fact that they were unlikely to survive in the absence of caregivers. When Sophie finally finds them, they are dead, "curled up, one inside the arms of the other, impossibly small" (160). Still more horrifying, the smaller of the two apes has died clutching the end of a nylon rope his captor had wrapped around his waist, and which the UN peacekeepers callously neglected to remove prior to releasing the animals. Overcome by guilt and shame, Sophie acknowledges that the moment she consented to purchase Otto, she became "part of a system, as permanent and complex as war itself, made a dozen small choices that had led to these dead creatures with their wide faces and chapped lips" (160). She connects the human suffering she witnesses in Congo to the same oppressive system when she catches herself thinking "not only about these two bonobos but of the stream of homeless refugees, of my dead friends in the sanctuary, of the larger and yet-unknown tragedies elsewhere in the country, in the world" (161). In this way, the novel positions readers to understand environmental justice and social justice as related topics.

Over the course of the story, Sophie develops as a character, transitioning from thinking with oppositional binaries to acknowledging the role that hierarchical thinking plays in condoning the oppression of people and the environment. To accomplish this, the novel actively calls attention to the ethics of oppositional binaries. For example, Sophie grapples with the question of whether human suffering supersedes animal suffering, as other characters suggest it does. Surrounded by human suffering brought on by poverty, war, government corruption, and corporate greed, she worries that the concern she feels for Otto is not justifiable, let alone moral. Her self-doubt is compounded by the fact that many of the people she meets on her journey to reunite with her mother at the bonobo release site chastise her for losing sight of the fact that Otto is "just an animal" (64). When Sophie insists on taking Otto with her on an evacuation helicopter, the UN officer who arranged the flight bewilderedly exclaims, "Help a monkey? No. I've got my men doing tours to stop as many *people* as we can from being shot" (155, emphasis in the original). Moments later, he scolds Sophie for her loyalty to Otto, reminding her, "There are millions of *people* suffering. Do yourself a favor and worry about them instead" (158, emphasis in the original). Sophie initially embraces a similar logic. When she encounters a young Congolese girl traveling with her mother and a group of displaced refugees, she thinks, "I could just as well be taking her with me as a bonobo. Wouldn't that be the *better* thing to do? Wasn't it my duty to protect *my own kind* first?" (173, emphasis added). Over the course of the story, however, she comes to question the latter assumption.

In her role as caretaker for Otto, Sophie is unable to escape the thought that "the prevention of his misery, was the answer that defied all logic" (161). Acknowledging the legitimacy of her feelings for him, she thinks, "The moment he'd come under my care, it hadn't been a question how much I would do for him" (173). In turn, she questions the possibility of hierarchizing suffering, concluding in the novel's most ideologically firm stance: "Though I knew there was human suffering out there, it wasn't like there was a tragedy scale where some things outranked others, or that care given to a bonobo meant less left for people" (173). Instead, she concludes that a logic that prioritizes human suffering over nonhuman animal suffering, and that advocates for protecting only one's "own kind," is ultimately destructive for all beings and for the environment (173).

At the story's conclusion, Sophie, having grown older and graduated from college with a degree in international politics and development, returns to Congo to help her mother run the bonobo sanctuary. This time, however, she has a plan she devised to help the country's people and animals by "mak[ing] Congo accessible to tourists" (242). Sophie and her mother want these people with wealth and power to recognize the interconnectedness of humanity, nonhuman animals, and the environment. It is worth noting that in positioning ecotourism as a solution to environmental problems that are attributable to capitalism, the book reproduces neoliberalism's faith in free market competition as the sole engine that drives remedies for social problems. In so doing, it demonstrates the difficulty of stepping outside of capitalist ideology, even when an author such as Schrefer aims to critique it. At the same time, however, by explicitly linking human well-being to the well-being of the environment, and by calling attention to the impossibility of hierarchizing suffering, *Endangered* also advocates for a world where care, compassion, and respect are extended to the totality of all the Earth. The novel thus rejects hierarchical thinking as an impediment to social justice and environmental justice.

ETHICAL CARING AS RESISTANCE IN *A SNAKE FALLS TO EARTH*

Abaki Beck defines Indigenous Futurism first by asking this question: "What would the world look like if tribal supernatural entities ruled?" That question, among others she poses, then leads into her formal definition: "Indigenous futurism is an artistic movement . . . that explore[s] questions like these to reimagine what Indigenous people lived like in the past and consider an unlimited future."[3] Darcie Little Badger's YA novel *A Snake Falls to Earth* is a work of Indigenous Futurism that is told from the perspective of two teenagers who live in separate but interconnected worlds. Nina, a teenage Lipan Apache girl, lives in southern Texas with her father, a bookstore owner, and mother, a translator who is seldom home. Notably, the book connects Nina's mother's absence in her life to the economy: unable to live on the income their small business generates, her mother takes a second job working on international research expeditions during which scientists study the impact of global warming on the climate. In her mother's absence, Nina develops a close relationship with her grandmother, who lives on the same land her ancestors have occupied for generations. Meanwhile, in the Reflecting World, a fifteen-year-old Cottonmouth person named Oli takes up residence on the banks of a bottomless lake after his mother insists that he leave home and find his way in the world. Like other inhabitants of the Reflecting World,

Oli is an animal person, a race of beings that once lived peacefully alongside humans during the period known as the "joined era," but who were subsequently driven into a parallel world after a series of wars left one human spirit—the Nightmare King—in power (49).

Two years after moving away from his mother, Oli recognizes that his closest friend, Ami—an animal person of the species referred to in the novel as a "Dallas toad"—has become comatose, falling terribly ill after a hurricane decimates his species' population on Earth. Oli and three other animal people (two coyote sisters, Reign and Risk, and a Cooper's hawk named Brightest) embark on a journey to restore balance to the environment of Earth and its Reflecting World. Eventually, this group of animal people meets Nina, and together, they work to resuscitate the remaining Dallas toad population.

Even more clearly than in *Endangered* and the Daughter of Smoke and Bone trilogy, *A Snake Falls to Earth* deconstructs binaries that support systemic oppression. The animal people themselves are perhaps the best example of this novel's queering of binaries. Some animal people, like Ami, live primarily as animals, seldom talking or changing form. Others, like those who work in the Reflecting World as scribes, find their human form more useful because only in that form do they have hands with fingers for holding writing utensils and turning the pages of the books they are translating. Other animal people are even more amorphous. For example, animal people who are mockingbirds can take on the shape of any living thing, not just their dualistic bird or prescribed human form; one mockingbird in the story alternately appears as a hawk, a bear, and a coyote, as well as in varied human forms. Only her eye color remains constant throughout all of these transitions. The way animal people think about their own transformations epitomizes posthuman thinking: when animal people assume their human embodiment, they refer to this as their "false form," while their animal embodiment is their "true form" (8). This "ontological mutability," as the children's literary critic Zoe Jaques would have it, positions these beings well within the values of posthumanism (5).

Gender identities and sexual orientation are also fluid in this novel, especially among the various animal people. For example, a coyote couple from the pack's mythical lineage is unapologetically a married lesbian couple; Nina's grandmother has neighbors who are "off-the-grid married women" who prove to be mindful of the animal people when they come to Earth from the Reflecting World (47, 231–32). Nothing about how either couple is portrayed depicts them as "different" than any other married couple. Additionally, some animal people identify as male, using "he/him/his" pronouns; some identify as female, using "she/her/hers"; but Brightest, the hawk person, consistently uses "they/them/theirs" pronouns. Oli identifies as male. When he first meets Brightest, however, he knows without being told that the hawk uses nonbinary pronouns. As Nina explains, "the Lipan language doesn't use gendered pronouns. There is no *he hunted* or *she hunted*. There's only, like, '*they—singular-hunted*,'" but the language does include "pronouns that indicate whether the plural version of *they* means two people or more than two people" (193–94, emphasis in the original).

Not only does the novel queer gendered binaries, it also queers the Earth via the mechanism of the Reflecting World. Animal people see only a reflection of the sun in their sky, so it does not harm their skin. Tree people can also take human form, although "even in their false forms, plant people must remain rooted, their legs or torsos sprouting directly from the ground" (11). The Reflecting World has several access points to Earth, including through the deepest depths of a freshwater lake and from the highest peak of the tallest mountain, a mechanism by which the novel eschews the type of binaristic thinking that suggests there is only one way to get from "here" to "there" and that further emphasizes Earth and the Reflecting World's intricate interconnectedness. This interconnectedness is integral to the story's valuing of community, posthumanism, and environmentalism. All beings within both worlds thrive only when all aspects of life are respected and valued.

For example, prior to the arrival of white developers, Nina's great-great-grandmother, Rosita, did little to manage the ancestral land on which she lived. Instead, "she'd allowed most of her property to grow unimpeded; beyond a well-trimmed backyard and a fenced-in patch of longhorn grazing land, the Earth sprouted thick tangles of brush, mesquite trees, and allthorn plants with leaves shaped like green porcupines" (46). Under these conditions, life in the area thrived: "Every morning, the chachalacas cheered. Every night, the screech owls cooed" (46). However, after an era of unchecked suburban sprawl metastasizes near Rosita's fifteen acres, the local government declared her property "too wild, too ugly" (46). To avoid financial penalties, she has had a stone wall built around her property to conceal it from view.

When Nina's father finds the date 1894 written on the back of a sepia-toned photograph of Rosita that was taken in her youth, the family is left to reconcile themselves to the fact that she was approximately 150 years old when she died, a seeming impossibility. However, Nina eventually learns that her great-great-grandmother is descended from human spirits, and her longevity, as with Nina's grandmother's, is attributable to magic that permeates the land they live on, a result of its being a portal to the Reflecting World. So long as these women stay close to home, their health is robust. The further they venture away from the land, however, the more their health flags.

A corresponding connection exists between life in the Reflecting World and life on Earth, as evidenced by a story Oli recalls his great-grandmother telling him about visiting the city of the Bison people when she was a girl. "There, farmers tended fields of maize: the bright, jewellike kernels brought living rainbows to the land every harvest season.... It was the most prosperous city in the central continent, a hub of agricultural trade and art" (71). One day, however, the Bison people inexplicably fell ill, and their once thriving city collapsed. When a team of animal people later visited Earth to discern what had happened, they learned that a group of humans "known as *colonizer*" had slaughtered millions of bison because these oppressors "desired to annihilate another group of humans. Indigenous peoples. They knew that the Indigenous ones relied on bison. So the bison had to go" (72, emphasis added). Although the bison did not go extinct on Earth, their numbers also never recovered, the result of which has direct ramifications for the remaining Bison people living in the Reflecting World. In highlighting this atrocity, the book emphasizes the interconnectedness of human and nonhuman animal life and connects acts of environmental destruction to human conquest and greed.

One character who epitomizes the selfishness of profit-driven neoliberals is Paul, a middle-aged white man who takes up residence on the property adjacent to Nina's grandmother and her ancestral lands. When Nina first encounters him hiking on her grandmother's intentionally unkempt property, she is immediately suspicious of him. For his part, Paul is surprised to learn that the land—which he refers to pejoratively as "this wild-ness"—"actually belongs to somebody" (92). He professes to be tracking a coyote, but Nina suspects that he is searching for iron or gold deposits. Later, after she learns that Paul has been quietly buying up property in the surrounding area, she assumes that he may be motivated to secure rights to the water beneath her grandmother's land so that he can turn around and sell the water to "beverage companies [that] were always vying for new sources of freshwater" (149). Her suspicions are borne out when Paul weaponizes local property ordinances and uses them to try to bully Nina's grandmother into moving. "With a fortune at stake, Nina doubted that he'd stop pestering them any time soon" (149). Only after this man shoots Oli in a final confrontation does Nina realize that Paul is a servant of the wicked Nightmare King, a human spirit who brought an end to the joined era when, in a series of wars, he killed his rivals and drove the remaining survivors, along with the animal peoples, into the Reflecting World. According to Oli, "the spoils of his war were simple. He wanted to be the only immortal on Earth" (347). As for Paul, his anthropocentric motivation for killing animal people extends beyond his desire to curry favor with the King: he also regards them as trespassers on land that rightfully belongs to humans. As the coyote Risk explains, the people who serve the Nightmare King "got an overactive, violent territorial drive. In their heads, the whole Earth is theirs, and we don't belong" (252).

A second character the novel positions as embodying neoliberal competitiveness, self-enclosed individualism, and greed is a social media influencer known to his followers as Thou Own Dave. "A top creator on Storyte11er," a digital app that Nina regularly uses, Thou Own Dave has "30 million subscribers" (272), the result of which makes him "universe tier" in the social media hierarchy (268). In addition to sharing his own content, each day Thou Own Dave's management team wades through a pool of submissions from other creators with the promise that if a person's video is chosen, that individual will receive 50 percent of the profits the video generates in the first twenty-four hours of its publication online, which Nina attempts to do. Thou Own Dave and his team are corrupt, however, not only because they use legalese to bury contractual details that prevent individual video storytellers like Nina from earning a significant profit, but also because they have turned one of the oldest human processes—storytelling—into a commodity to be exploited for profit.

Reflecting neoliberalism's valorization of individual exceptionalism, the official narrative surrounding Thou Own Dave's success depicts him as a superspecial individual whose creative acumen and business savvy have allegedly led him to rise above the mass of content creators on Storyte11er to realize unparalleled financial success. In truth, however, Thou Own Dave is prosperous because he exploits other people. In one video he posts online, he is seen throwing small pieces of paper from the balcony of his Hollywood mansion to a group of people below. The "story" told in the video hinges on the fact that one of the papers bears his signature, and the lucky person who finds it will receive a monetary reward. As Thou Own Dave "look[s] down his nose, down the mountain, down at unseen participants in a game of chance" below him, a fight ensues between two women who lay claim to the paper at the same time (283). In the subsequent scene, a camera follows Thou Own Dave, who is clearly amused by this unexpected turn of events and its potential to generate even more views, and hence profits, as he races down to them through a house so large it "never seemed to end, as if it filled the hills with rooms" (283). Upon reaching the street below, he encounters the two women grasping the signed paper, each unwilling to let go of it. In a voice-over that was inserted in postproduction, Thou Own Dave is heard informing viewers that he told the women that if they tore the ticket there would be no prize because he hoped "*to prevent them from hurting each other*"; however, he callously adds, "*If they wanted to stand in the sun all day and see who could last longer, I couldn't stop them*" (285, emphasis in the original). In this world where stories are told not to heal or instruct but rather to titillate and shock in the name of earning wealth, Thou Own Dave is a symbol of neoliberal corruption and greed.

Along with critiquing the commodification of storytelling, *A Snake Falls to Earth* also interrogates a binary that privileges science and technology at the expense of traditional ways of knowing, such as stories.[4] Although Nina and her family are connected to the old ways, she relies on digital technology to equip herself with information she assumes will empower her. Faced with a problem or a question, she trusts the artificial intelligence on her smartphone to provide her with the answers she seeks. She uses a highpowered video camera her parents bought her to document her experiences and share them on social media, and she maintains a private video diary in which she ponders questions and problems that interest her. Yet if Nina is captivated by the promise of a "wondrous future" replete with technological advancements such as "androids, cloned dinosaurs, and VR glasses," she also recognizes its potential to "be a place of nightmares," especially when "the evening news slipped into her bedroom, carrying prophecies of disease and pain" (22). Resisting a positivist narrative that assumes that the application of science and technology are destined to improve the quality of life for people, *A Snake Falls to Earth* instead invites readers to ask, "Who benefits from science and technology?" And conversely, "Who is negatively impacted by them, and how?" In so doing, the novel exposes how these institutions are rooted in systems of oppression.

Little Badger's novel also laments how suburban sprawl—enabled by technology and industrialization—has desiccated the land in South Texas. Nina's great-great-grandmother purchased her fifteen acres in the first years of the twentieth century, but "as the nearby suburbs spread in the century that followed, covering the land with identical yellow houses, pink condominiums, and gated neighborhoods named Paradise and Sunny Vale, the fifteen acres [Rosita owned] became an island" (46). The greedy land developers who built these gated communities, however, did not properly attend to the potential for the clay-filled soil of the area to retain water in ways that inevitably led to cracking and the uneven sinking of buildings' foundations, so "Paradise and Sunny Vale had closed after a terrible case of foundation subsidence, flooding, and a class-action lawsuit" (47). These substandard construction practices, coupled with extreme hurricanes and flooding exacerbated by ill-conceived land management policies, leave Rosita's property in what Nina's grandmother considers to be pleasant isolation. Rosita and Nina's grandmother, however, know that they are custodians of the land. "When Federal Indian Removal became the law of the land, and bounties were put on Apache heads, her people resisted. In many ways, they still did" (46). Caring for the land of her ancestors becomes a way for both Nina and her grandmother to resist white colonization. The novel thus depicts caring as an act of resistance—one that is founded on an ethics of care and that demonstrates the importance of caring for the Earth, caring for animals, caring for plant life, and also caring for other peoples.[5] The novel positions directing one's care selflessly outward in direct opposition to neoliberalism's privileging of individualism and its take-no-prisoners profit-making.

Science and technology, on the other hand, are seldom depicted as an asset to communalism and caring in this novel. Instead, they are linked to systems of oppression. For example, toward the end of her life, great-great-grandmother Rosita tells Nina a story that is important to their family history. Shortly after, the girl discovers that the translator on her cell phone is unable to recognize the Lipan language Rosita uses. Later, she learns that while software engineers program computers to recognize some languages—for example, English—they exclude others, such as Indigenous languages. As a consequence, knowledge associated with those languages is irretrievable to those who don't know them firsthand. Similarly, when medical doctors are unable to account for the heart palpitations and related health issues that Nina's grandmother experiences when she travels, they dismiss her complaints as fanciful. As she tells Nina, "Tests identified zero issues, so the doctors sent me home with the same old diagnosis: it's all in my mind" (181). Foregrounding the limitations of western medicine, Nina asks, "Do you ever wonder . . . if the doctors can't help 'cause they don't understand who you really are?" When her grandmother replies, "Hm. They're only human," Nina wonders, "Are we?"; "'Of course,' Grandma answered, 'but that doesn't mean we can't be mysterious, too'" (182). On this point, the book is clear: powerful though they are, science and technology are not the only resources available to people trying to make sense of the world.

Instead, the novel validates knowledge that is associated with the traditional stories that Nina's great-great-grandmother and grandmother share with her, and that Oli and his human animal friends tell each other as an alternative, though no less valid, way of understanding the world. When great-great-grandmother Rosita asks Nina, "Quieres escuchar una historia?" the translator on Nina's cell phone presents the question as follows: "Do you want to hear a story?" (2). Then, almost immediately, when Rosita uses the plural possessive "nuestra" with "historia," rather than the indefinite "una," the app on Nina's phone translates the word as "history" (3).[6] Throughout *A*

Snake Falls to Earth, stories and histories are depicted as not only interchangeable but as necessarily interdependent on one another. As Nina thinks at one point: "This was how old *stories* went: first came a problem, then a plan. A tornado was approaching. The plan? Lasso the wind. How would the story end? Nina had no point of reference, but she'd heard a hundred other *stories*, the *histories* of a more magical era" (336, emphasis added).

Stories happen within community. Most any story requires someone to tell it and someone to receive it. In that spirit, *A Snake Falls to Earth* disavows selfish individualism, advocating instead for an ethics of care. For example, Oli and his friends take responsibility for the consequences of the Earth's environmental decay once they perceive the devastation on an individual level through Ami's desperate illness. Although the animal people are not wholly ignorant of the problems that climate change poses for life on Earth, they nonetheless assume that they won't be affected by them, until they are. As Oli explains, "Earth's recent transformation was common knowledge. Sea level fluctuations. Increases in the average temperature. Ecological devastation. Explosions in some species. . . . The decimation of other species. But until Ami got sick, it was never personal. It didn't affect me" (325).

Likewise, as Nina's character matures, her appreciation for the importance of ethical decision-making does as well. Faced with the choice of uploading a video that she and her animal people friends staged in hopes of earning money to save the Dallas toads' habitat by making it on to Thou Own Dave's channel and reaping the profits, Nina pauses and contemplates the potential ramifications of her decision:

> The video [depicting a grizzly bear pretending to attack a group of teenagers] is published on a Storyte11er account with 30 million subscribers. Nina makes lots of money, but at what cost? In response to public outcry, animal control scours the backwoods of South Texas, searching for an aggressive bear. There haven't been wild grizzlies in the region for generations, but this one must have escaped notice. Now, it's attacking children. Parents are terrified. . . . Animal control promises to relocate the animal, but a day passes. Then two. No grizzly. In the shadow of roiling thunderclouds, hunters load their guns and aim into the woods.
> Or—just as bad—copycats decide that antagonizing dangerous wildlife is a surefire route to fame. (272)

Later, when the coyote sisters propose lassoing a tornado to redirect its path away from Nina's grandmother's house, it occurs to Nina that doing so might lead it to "destroy the nearest grocery store, the hospital, or the pharmacy" (337). In a world where the consequences of one's actions ripple outward, *A Snake Falls to Earth* argues that people have an obligation to choose wisely. Indeed, the hawk Brightest makes an important point about human connectedness and the environment when they point out that Earth and the Reflecting World are not connected by the atmosphere; instead, "Our worlds are connected by the living" (326). Beings, whether plant or animal, including the human animal, are the sustaining link to the plane of spirituality.

Toward the end of the book, Mockingbird, posing as "Thou Own Dave," shows up on Dave's video feed to say this: "Thanks to Storyte11er, I've witnessed the devastation of the hurricanes in the Gulf region. It's like being there and suffering with you. . . . Families left homeless. Buildings in ruins. Floods and power outages. There's even a species of toad in dire straits because of this storm. Poor little guys. Toads never hurt anybody" (363). Mockingbird pretends that Thou Own Dave has had

> an epiphany. . . . I have the power to decrease *your* pain with *my* money. That's an incredible trade, don't you think? There's half a billion dollars in my bank account. I couldn't spend that if I tried. . . . Right now, in front of the world, I'm donating my savings to help rebuild the Gulf Coast. I hope my friends on Storyte11er will join me in the pledge to DECREASE PAIN by being SOMEWHAT LESS WEALTHY. We may not be able to fix everything, but we can make things easier. (363–64, emphasis in original)

In her false form as Thou Own Dave, Mockingbird then urges his fans to "hold me accountable" if he changes his mind, ensuring that Dave's obscene wealth will not be hoarded to the benefit of the narcissistic video-caster (364). With this conclusion to the novel, Darcie Little Badger offers not only a direct critique of neoliberalism, but also a response to it that is an ethical, caring antidote to greed.

CONCLUSION

As with Little Badger in *A Snake Falls to Earth*, Schrefer in his novel *Endangered* is an intentional ecocritic. Asked in an interview if, like his character Sophie, he also struggles with the question of whether human suffering and nonhuman animal suffering are comparable, Schrefer recalled a conversation he once had with an imam he met while attending an event sponsored by a Muslim women's organization in New Jersey. Having told the imam about *Endangered*, the book he was writing about bonobos, Schrefer indicated that he was concerned that it "was immoral to worry about animal suffering in the face of so much human suffering" (Connors, "Drawing" 31). Recounting their conversation, he explained:

> [The imam] asked me a few questions about the bonobos, and then he said, "It seems like the same systems of *power* that endanger humans in Congo also endanger animals. That is, the same poverty that is causing starvation and which leads people to shoot the bonobos with weapons they obtained from the war being waged in Rwanda is also causing people to die. By addressing one, you're not ignoring the other. You're using animal suffering to illuminate the human conflict as well. (Connors, "Drawing" 31, emphasis added)

The imam's response exemplifies intersectional environmentalism as one facet of critical multicultural analysis insofar as he is underscoring why it is problematic to conceptualize environmental justice and social justice as disparate topics. Environmental justice and social justice are better understood as apposite, two sides of the same coin, rather than as opposites.

When scholars examine children's and YA literature from the perspective of intersectional environmentalism, they create opportunities to recognize the role that power plays in constructing oppositional binaries. In turn, we can then ask how binary thinking gives rise to hierarchies that support sexism, racism, classism, heterosexism, anthropocentrism, and so on. Equally important, examining literature through a lens of intersectional environmentalism also positions us to understand how oppressive power systems frequently overlap.

Examining conservation and environmental topics through a lens of intersectional environmentalism can challenge us to reimagine our relationship with nature and with other people. This is especially important in the society of the US, which often values independence over interdependence. In her examination of the relationship between capitalism and climate change, Naomi Klein argues that satisfactorily addressing complex problems like global warming will necessitate that people adopt "not just an alternative set of policy proposals, but an alternative worldview to rival the one at the heart of the ecological crisis—embedded in interdependence rather than hyper-individualism, reciprocity rather than dominance, and cooperation rather than hierarchy" (452). In much the same way, adopting a paradigm that acknowledges the interconnectedness of people can help us learn how to address social problems such as future pandemics.

Finally, by emphasizing interconnectedness over individualism, a lens of intersectional environmentalism clarifies for critics and readers the need for collective action in addressing complex environmental problems, such as global warming and climate change, and complex social justice problems embedded in power disproportionalities, such as racism, sexism, and classism. Individual actions of the sort that neoliberal environmentalism advances—practicing recycling, driving less, using LED lighting, turning off the water while tooth-brushing, and buying locally—are undoubtedly important. However, to address climate change and create a future that is truly sustainable, people need to leverage their collective power and demand that governments around the world reduce their dependence on fossil fuels and develop alternatives to the carbon economy. Similarly, as the Black Lives Matter movement has demonstrated, our ability to live together on this planet is sustainable only to the extent that people of all races and backgrounds work together to dismantle systems and social structures that support inequality and oppression, and that deem some lives more valuable than others.

Chapter 3

US NEOLIBERALISM AND ITS RACIST ORIGINS

> That's the hate they're giving us, baby, a system designed against us.
>
> —Angie Thomas, *The Hate U Give* (170)

In *Democracy in Chains*, Nancy MacLean traces how right-wing neoliberals manipulated significant portions of the American public into voting against their own economic interests. She narrates the history of James McGill Buchanan, an economist at the University of Virginia, who reflected the outrage many southerners felt when the Supreme Court passed what is sometimes referred to as *Brown v. Board of Education II* in 1955, a later corollary to *Brown v. Board of Education* stipulating that schools should desegregate "with all deliberate speed" (MacLean xv). According to MacLean, Buchanan studied at the University of Chicago alongside scholars such as Milton Friedman, himself an early architect of neoliberalism. Buchanan resented

> the seemingly unfettered ability of an increasingly more powerful federal government to force individuals with wealth to pay for a growing number of public goods and social programs they had no personal say in approving. Better schools, newer textbooks, and more courses for black students might help the children, for example, but whose responsibility was it to pay for these improvements? The parents of these students? ... Or people like himself, compelled through increasing taxation to contribute to projects they did not wish to support? (MacLean xxiii–iv)

He conceived the blueprint to undermine *Brown II* with Machiavellian strategies, such as packing the courts and targeting public education, in what would prove to be a long-term campaign to privatize public goods and services. MacLean investigates the powerful cabal of men inspired by Buchanan's ideas who worked together starting in the 1970s to create a stealth network of radical right think tanks, academic centers, policy groups, and political action committees in order to hamstring democratic processes. Their goal was to fetter "public officials [with] shackles so powerful that no matter how sympathetic these officials might be to the will of majorities . . . they would no longer have the ability to respond to those who used their numbers to get government to do their bidding," even on such topics as K-12 education (xxvii). This cabal was lavishly funded by the billionaire Koch brothers, especially Charles Koch.

Relying on the papers in Buchanan's archives, along with many other primary sources, MacLean demonstrates how this stealth-campaign taught self-styled libertarian politicians and their funders to put political pressure on those Republicans who did not share their same neoliberal vision by funding ever more right-wing and compliant opponents in primaries. MacLean attributes to this group a variety of changes that readers of this book might also have observed over the previous two decades, including slashed funding for public education (which also includes state-funded colleges and universities), constricted voter rights laws, and gutted collective bargaining rights (xvii–xviii). MacLean writes: "Their cause, they say, is liberty. But by that they mean the insulation of private property rights from the reach of government—and the takeover of what was long public (schools, prisons, western lands, and much more) by corporations, a system that would radically reduce the freedom of the many. In a nutshell, they aim to hollow out democratic resistance" (xxx). The immediate as well as the long-term effects of these actions was to worsen race relations in the US. As we discuss in the following section, neoliberalism serves to undermine the progressiveness of social safety-net programs, school desegregation, and the advances enacted because of the civil rights movement, effectively extending the project established by the framers of the US Constitution to perpetually empower wealthy white men. While it is a truism that Ronald Reagan and Margaret Thatcher deployed neoliberalism to roll back the social safety networks that governments in both the US and UK established between the 1930s and 1960s, neoliberalism in the US was also politically motivated in large part by the desire of white elites to also roll back the social gains Black Americans experienced because of the civil rights movement. It is for this specific reason that we have chosen to narrow our focus in this volume to manifestations of neoliberalism in YA literature in the US, as opposed to casting our net more globally. Even so, we acknowledge that there are diverse communities of people that are not represented in the literature we examine, as space constraints have unfortunately limited our ability to include all that we would like.

US HISTORY OF RACIAL CAPITALISM

As the authors of this book, we recognize that the opening to this chapter is stark, but we have summarized MacLean's account of Buchanan and his fellow radical right-wing economists and politicians precisely because we wish for our readers to understand how historically entrenched the ideas of neoliberalism are in minority rule, in exploitation, and in racism.[1] The next several sections of this chapter are thus dedicated to our less than sanguine perspective on historical US race relations. Cedric J. Robinson refers to the thinly hidden racism that has shaped world history, especially US history, in terms of what he calls "racial capitalism" (2). As Robinson uses the term, *racial capitalism* is the idea that "the historical development of world capitalism was influenced in a most fundamental way by the particularistic forces of racism and nationalism" (9). Robinson argues that as the "development, organization, and expansion of capitalist society pursued essentially racial directions, so too did social ideology. As a material force, then, it could be expected that racialism would inevitably permeate the social structures emergent from capitalism" (2). *Racialism* "refer[s] to this development and to the subsequent structure [of racial capitalism] as a historical agency" (2). The effects on young people have been manifold.

One of Robinson's intellectual proponents, Siddhant Issar, argues that "racial domination is constitutive moreover of, rather than epiphenomenal to ... [the US] economy" (57). Furthermore, he asserts that: "The framework of racial capitalism highlights how capitalism works through a logic of wage-labor exploitation, while simultaneously relying on racialized and gendered logics of expropriation, ranging from the seizure of Indigenous lands to the extraction of surplus value via regimes of 'unfree' labor (slavery, debt peonage, convict leasing, gendered reproductive labor, etc.)" (60–61). Wendy Brown notes that in a neoliberal economy, "democratic state commitments to equality, liberty, inclusion, and constitutionalism are now subordinate to the project of economic growth, competitive positioning, and capital enhancement" (26). The emphasis that neoliberalism places on competitiveness and entrepreneurialism as key arbiters of individual success in the marketplace, undergirded by the persistence of structural racism in American society, means that adult Black, Indigenous, and People of Color (BIPOC)—as well as their children—seldom, if ever, compete on a level playing field.

In this chapter, we employ Robinson's concept of racial capitalism along with critical race theory (CRT) to examine how racism is endemic to neoliberalism in that it "silences claims of systemic racism through reliance on the racially-coded narrative of individual choice and intent" (Benz 58).[2] Given the many current reactionary responses to teaching US race relations in K-12 schools, and even in postsecondary curricula, we contextualize racism extensively in this chapter. After all, YA literature is clearly connected to historical racism.[3] We thus wish to examine how the genre in turn connects racism to economic exploitation, much as we examined the relationship between neoliberalism and environmental exploitation in the previous chapter. The goal of this chapter, then, is to demonstrate how neoliberalism historically deploys structural racism and racial capitalism at the expense of teenagers of color and their families. After discussing the interconnections of racism, neoliberalism, and property ownership, we investigate two older YA novels, Mildred Taylor's *The Land* (2001) and Christopher Paul Curtis's *Bucking the Sarge* (2004), and a more contemporary novel, Angeline Boulley's *Firekeeper's Daughter* (2021), as all three expose how racial capitalism works.

Cedric Robinson traces racism as it has existed for thousands of years, citing evidence from Aristotle's *Poetics* to bolster his argument (96–97). Writing fifteen years before Robinson published *Black Marxism*, Winthrop Jordan also drew a line between racism and capitalism when he argued that racism emerged, in large part, due to seventeenth-century British attempts to justify the practice of slavery by equating "Blackness" with Christian notions of sin and dirtiness (40–42). Ibram X. Kendi shows how the first enslavers in colonial America drew on a tradition of British travel literature and intellectualism to protect their economic interests by "rationaliz[ing] their enslavement of African people . . . by considering these African people to be stamped from the beginning as a racially distinct people, as lower than themselves, and as lower in the scale of being than the more populous White indentured servants" (38).

Even more emphatically, Matthew Desmond argues that the origins of racism in the US are entirely economic in nature:

> Slavery was undeniably a font of phenomenal wealth. By the eve of the Civil War, the Mississippi Valley was home to more millionaires per capita than anywhere else in the United States. Cotton grown and picked by enslaved workers was the nation's most valuable export. The combined value of enslaved people exceeded that of all the railroads and factories in the nation. New Orleans boasted a denser concentration of banking capital than New York City. What made the cotton economy boom in the United States, and not in all the other far-flung parts of the world with climates and soil suitable to the crop, was our nation's unflinching willingness to use violence on nonwhite people and to exert its will on seemingly endless supplies of land and

labor. Given the choice between modernity and barbarism, prosperity and poverty, lawfulness and cruelty, democracy and totalitarianism, America chose all of the above. (32)

Michael Vavrus espouses a similar viewpoint when he cites the historian Gerald Horne as arguing that "slave owners in the British colonies in the 1770s expressed alarm when England declared the slave trade illegal. Conservative colonial elites [subsequently] pressed for a break from England and for the creation of a new nation state that would allow legalized slavery [in part] because they feared . . . losing the labor and monetary value of their enslaved property" (Vavrus 97). Simply put, capitalism, slavery, racism, and plantation crops—most notably cotton—were the foundation on which the structural racism that persists in the US today was built.[4]

To believe that slavery benefited only elite white landowners in the Southern states is, of course, a false assumption, one that ignores the considerable wealth that white industrialists and bankers in northern states amassed as a result of slavery. First referred to as the "Triangular Trade" by British economic historian T. S. Ashton (Merritt 1), and now more commonly referred to as the "Triangle Trade," New England factory owners, merchants, shipowners, and bankers benefited as much from the heartless commerce of the Middle Passage and the depredation of slavery as did southern plantation owners. In the mid-nineteenth century, cotton was the US's largest export (Farrow et al. 4). By 1860, 472 cotton mills were operating in New England (Farrow et al. 6), and a host of New York banks were founded by cotton brokers, including one by the three Lehman brothers, who were among the men that established the New York Cotton Exchange. Moreover, J. P. [Pierpont] Morgan had a father who ensured that his son was trained to know commodity trading via cotton; John Jacob Astor's ships transported tons of cotton as an export; and Archibald Gracie was a New Yorker and international shipping magnate of cotton. (Gracie Mansion, the official residence of the mayor of New York City, is still named for him.) Even the jeweler and artisan Charles Tiffany had a father who launched his son's career with proceeds from the cotton mill he owned in New England (5). The widespread regional foundation of structural racism is further evidenced by statements the mayor of New York City, Fernando Wood, made in January of 1861 after Southern states began talking about secession: he suggested that the city secede from the Union because of its "friendly relations and a common sympathy" shared with "our aggrieved brethren of the Slave States" (Farrow et al. 3).

Like Cedric Robinson, Ibram X. Kendi, Matthew Desmond, and Anne Farrow, the critical race theorist Derek Bell also traces the long arm of economically justified racism when he delineates how white people have historically been willing to expand civil liberties in the US only when doing so has increased the economic privilege of their whiteness (9). Bell argues, for example, that the political impulse behind both the Emancipation Proclamation (1863) and the Supreme Court's *Brown v. Board of Education* (1954) decision was a concern with "foreign policy interests" (10). By attempting to free enslaved people in Southern slaveholding states, Abraham Lincoln hoped to deter England from offering economic and material support to the Confederacy at a critical juncture in the American Civil War (Burlingame). Almost a century later, in the case of *Brown v. Board of Education*, the US Department of Justice cautioned the 1952 Supreme Court that "racial discrimination furnishes grist for the Communist propaganda mills, and it raises doubts even among friendly nations as to the intensity of our devotion to the democratic faith" (Wyne). In other words, neither Lincoln and his all-white (male) cabinet in the 1860s nor the all-white (male) justices of the 1950s Earl Warren Court acted solely in the name of racial equality or the universal right to human dignity. Instead, they voiced concerns about the economic impact that slavery, and later, Jim Crow segregation, would have on the US economy when the international community judged this racism negatively. In short, economic interests, rather than genuine concern for the violence that racism inflicted on the bodies and minds of BIPOC, drove both of these landmark political decisions.

STRUCTURAL RACISM AND NEOLIBERALISM

While the relationship between capitalism and racism—i.e., racial capitalism—predates neoliberalism, sociologist Randolph Hohle connects the advent of the latter economic theory to a specific type of racism that was promulgated in the 1960s and 1970s by its forebears, whom he refers to as the white "liberal business class" (*Race*, 2). In *Racism in the Neoliberal Era* (2018), Hohle justifies using the word "liberal" so that he can call attention to this group's "moderate racial views and emphasis on hyper-individuality, or simply, crediting and blaming the self for all economic successes and failures" (45). In *Race and the Origins of American Neoliberalism* (2015), Hohle observes:

> The white response to the civil rights movement inadvertently empowered the liberal business class and set the stage for the national neoliberal turn. The [southern] liberal business class led the white

response to the civil rights movement. The liberal business class was comprised of bankers, insurance executives, and real estate elites.... The liberal business class did not support racial integration; they... led the efforts to minimally incorporate blacks into the local political economy. They used race to deregulate populist state constitutions and networked with the segregationists. (2)

Furthermore, Hohle argues that although "class plays an ancillary role to race" (4), the latter "plays a causal role in the American political system by coding and recoding political and economic preferences into categories of black and white. The most significant recoding of state policy was embedding *black* into *public*"; therefore, "the language of neoliberalism is organized around the white-private/black-public binary" (*Race* 4, emphasis added).[5] With this, Hohle demonstrates how neoliberals came to rhetorically link federal funding of the public good to poverty and African American populations, especially in the US South. In doing so, this "business class" successfully rebranded racism as "the property of poor whites that are in dire need of more education," thus deflecting attention from how racism is embedded in social systems (Hohle, *Racism* 15).

Hohle maintains that neoliberalism's emphasis on turning over management of public goods and resources to private interests (*privatization*) and reducing Keynesian federal deficit spending (*austerity*) "was never about markets or reducing spending. Austerity was about denying public services to blacks and by extension all people on the margins of society" (*Race* 37). The lack of available public services impacted people's life opportunities, and eventually included state-level antiunionization laws that created so-called "right to work" states and inspired various southern states to reject federal funding meant to enact public school integration, voting rights, and fair-housing legislation (*Race* 42–45). Southerners' calls to reduce taxation were ostensibly a logical extension of this neoliberal project because, theoretically, those who were taxed less would have more resources to become self-made, self-reliant entrepreneurs (*Race* 48–49). Ultimately, much of the tension surrounding privatization and austerity resulted in the perceptions of (white) individuals who were aligned with states' rights voters and who believed that entire groups of people, such as African Americans, were dependent on wholesale support from the federal government (*Race* 45). In the 1980s and 1990s, this racist ideology was at the heart of both the Reagan administration's and the Clinton administration's demonization of Black women as "welfare queens" (Hohle, *Racism* 123–24). In that regard, and as evidenced by the efforts of early neoliberal strategists like the economist James McGill

Buchanan, neoliberalism's origins in the US depended largely on racism, as has its ability to propagate and maintain itself.

Critical race theorists, sociologists, and a number of social psychologists have also traced strong connections between racism and neoliberalism. In an article exploring the psychology of neoliberalism, Glenn Adams and his coauthors describe the connections stemming from neoliberalism's emphasis on individualism: "Neoliberal systems build on and reinforce characteristic psychological tendencies of liberal individualism—including radical abstraction of self from context, an entrepreneurial understanding of self as an ongoing development project, an imperative for personal growth and fulfillment, and an emphasis on affect management for self-regulation—that increasingly inform dominant conceptions of mind-in-general" (190). Lisa Cosgrove and Justin M. Karter attribute the psychological disconnect embedded within neoliberalism to its positioning of people as "self-concerned agents, not members of a polis connected to a larger community" (670). According to Karim Bettache, Chi-yue Chiu, and Peter Beattie, "neoliberalism promotes indifference to structural social inequalities by reducing them to personal failures.... The neoliberal emphasis on competition and survival of the fittest also justifies inequality between different groups and discrimination against low status groups" (217–18). In addition, Bettache and Chiu argue that "the social moral axiom in neoliberalism confers universal moral inviolability to the values of free choices and self-governance" (13).

These same social psychologists suggest that, "as a mainstream ideology in advanced capitalist economies, neoliberalism prioritizes economic growth and prescribes free market solutions to almost every social, political, or economic problem or crisis" (13). Moreover, Bettache and Chiu describe the utopian thinking behind neoliberalism as ostensibly impervious to race since "the fully privatized, free market is presumably color blind. The market is like a level playing field that rewards individuals based primarily on their merits or market values. Failing is the result of not trying hard enough, not because of one's race or structural inequality in the system" (Bettache and Chiu 17). They convincingly argue that "neoliberalism should not be seen as separate from those who profit from it: [a]n Euro-White elite that, in a postcolonialist world, had a head start where it comes to its privileged position. Hence, their economic power through neoliberalism may function as a tool to strengthen White supremacy on the global stage" (Bettache and Chiu 17). Indeed, while Bettache and Chiu depict the structurally racist consequences of entrepreneurially competitive individualism, Azevedo et al. assert that "corporate hegemony perpetuates and perhaps even aggravates actual social divisions based on race, sex, and economic standing" (56). To better demonstrate the ways in which books for teenagers can reproduce or resist neoliberal and racist ideologies, we investigate them through the lens of the social science theories addressed in this section, including CRT.

Critical race theorists Richard Delgado and Jean Stefancic identify the "prime critical themes" of CRT as "the insistence that racism is ordinary and not exceptional, the notion that traditional civil rights law has been more valuable to whites than to blacks, the critique of liberalism, and the call to context" (4). By "critique of liberalism," the authors are referring to mid-twentieth-century "liberalism," which advocated for the sociopolitical advancement of civil rights (as opposed to the nineteenth-century laissez-faire "liberalism" that opposed any regulation of industry, and the late twentieth-century "neoliberalism," which effectively renewed calls for government laissez-faire of the economy). As Delgado cautions, "Placing excessive reliance on the liberal establishment can sometimes be a serious error," especially because, like other institutions, it "primarily looks after its own interests" ("Liberal McCarthyism" 40). Within economic history, *liberalism* thus refers to government leniency toward land and business regulations.

RACISM, POVERTY, AND PROPERTY OWNERSHIP

Any interrogation into liberalism, neoliberalism, capitalism, racial capitalism, and the way that government policies cleared the legal path for exploiting land usage to create housing disparities, which in turn led to education gaps, must begin with an acknowledgment that most Americans who claim to "own" land in the US have acquired stolen property, one way or the other. Indeed, one of us, Roberta, is writing this book on lands previously inhabited in Illinois by the Illini, Peoria, and the Myaamia, and later due to colonial encroachment and displacement by the Fox, Potawatomi, Sauk, Shawnee, Winnebago, Ioway, Mascouten, Piankashaw, Wea, and Kickapoo Nations. In Arkansas, where Sean works, the Osage, Caddo, and Quapaw Nations all had ties to the northwest corner of the state. The University of Arkansas further recognizes that a portion of the Trail of Tears runs through campus, and that the Cherokee, Choctaw, Muscogee (Creek), Chickasaw, and Seminole Nations passed through what is now Arkansas during this period of forced removal. The area near Jackson, Mississippi—the city in which this book was published—was inhabited by the Choctaw, Ofo, Chackchiuma, Natchez, Tunica, Yazoo, and Tioux. As the authors of this book, we also honor those Indigenous peoples whom we may have excluded in this acknowledgment due to erasure and historical inaccuracy.[6]

Land ownership, economics, and racial identity intertwine shamefully throughout US history. Political economist and teacher educator Michael Vavrus provides an example from early in the nation's founding when he contrasts the emphasis that the Declaration of Independence places on "life, liberty, and . . . happiness" with the Fifth Amendment to the US Constitution, which "states that no one should be deprived of life, liberty, or *property*" (113, emphasis in the original). Vavrus subsequently locates the emphasis the founding fathers placed on property ownership in the work of the English political philosopher John Locke, "for whom liberty was synonymous with property rights as a biblical natural right based in heritable private property" (114). As exemplified by the theft of lands inhabited by Indigenous peoples and the enslavement of Black people to work that land, however, Vavrus shows how "skin color, cultural practices, and geographic origins became a way to determine status rankings and the eventual right to own property" (118, emphasis in the original). As an example, he notes that in the aftermath of the Civil War, emancipated Blacks were promised land federal troops confiscated from wealthy plantation owners only to see that promise broken following Lincoln's assassination by a southern white supremacist.

In his book *Stamped from the Beginning*, Kendi also calls out the racism that underpinned this reversal when he observes that, in the years following 1863, when the federal government "started selling confiscated and abandoned southern land to private owners . . . more than 90 percent had gone to northern Whites over the widespread protests of local Blacks" (231). Echoing the connection that Hohle draws between black-public, Kendi argues that whereas "White settlers on government-provided land were deemed receivers of American freedom; Black people [were] receivers of American handouts" (231).

The twentieth-century French philosopher Henri Lefebvre argues in *The Production of Space* (1974/1991) that "(Social) space is a (social) product" (26, parentheses in the original). He insists, too, that the concept of space and physical space itself is defined by, among other factors, "a network of buying- and selling-points in the case of the exchange of commodities, of banks and stock exchanges in the case of the circulation of capital, of labour exchanges in the case of the labour market, and so on" (86). Thus, "*social spaces interpenetrate one another and/or superimpose themselves upon one another*" (86, emphasis in the original). Similarly, Mark Gottdiener emphasizes the capitalist impulses that influence the urban planning of social space when he argues: "The sociospatial changes within the city are ruled by the logic of capital accumulation, and the end result of this process in a capitalist society is uneven development and social inequities which are deployed spatially as well as demographically. Inequalities of class and race along with differentials in the supply of social services are most characteristic of the metropolitan sociospatial milieu" (19–20). In other words, racism and classism have inordinately driven the existence of ghettoized urban spaces. One particular example from US history explains the connection between racism and the economically motivated generation of social space: the practice of redlining among bankers in the US.

According to human geographer and sociologist Manual B. Aalbers, under the Roosevelt administration during the Great Depression, the Home Owners' Loan Corporation developed a "neighborhood rating system" eventually utilized, too, by the Federal Housing Authority (FHA) to guide banking underwriters as they made decisions about how much and even whether to loan mortgage funds to prospective buyers. The Green, or "A," level was the "best" level and constituted "hot spots" that were highly desirable for development; the Blue, or "B," level of "stable" denoted still desirable real estate areas; the Yellow, or "C," "declining" level indicated areas at risk of foreclosure; and the Red, or "D," level referred to areas where lending was to be declined because underwriters had determined the neighborhood to be "hazardous" (Aalbers 535), or as the first author of a federally distributed manual for underwriters bluntly put it, inhabited by "inharmonious racial or nationality groups" (quoted in Aalbers 539). Redlined districts became the victim of various strategies for long-term urban development, including "planned shrinkage," "urban triage," and "benign neglect," all of which were policies intended to displace low-income peoples so that areas could be razed to create better real estate markets (Aalbers 525).

One of us, Sean, experienced the consequences of redlining in 2010 when he lived in a working-class neighborhood in Columbus, Ohio, that abutted a predominantly African American urban neighborhood characterized by economic hardship. The local grocery store at the end of Sean's street sold predominantly processed foods that were high in salt and sugar, and carried only a meager selection of fruits and vegetables. A mile-and-a-half away, however, in an affluent white community where the average home cost $400,000, the same grocery chain operated a second store in which shoppers with the financial means to do so could choose from a robust selection of produce, including organic fruits and vegetables, gourmet foods, and locally sourced food items. To be perfectly clear, northern as well as southern Democrats implemented many of these social-engineering projects: for example, the redlining described above began as a practice under the Franklin D. Roosevelt administration; Daniel Moynihan was a Democratic Senator from New York who advocated for "benign neglect"; and Donna Shalala, a

Democrat who later became the Secretary of Health and Human Services under President Bill Clinton, enacted "planned shrinkage" in New York City (Aalbers 545–46, 543). Racism in urban planning historically permeated every political group wielding power in the twentieth century in the US.

It should come as no surprise that the racism underlying US property ownership recurs as a socioeconomic issue throughout YA literature. Indeed, the setting in which teenage characters live determines much about the trajectory of their character arc. We thus turn now to two novels that expose the relationship between the location of one's home, property ownership, and socioeconomics, as we examine Mildred Taylor's historical novel *The Land* and Christopher Paul Curtis's *Bucking the Sarge*, a work of contemporary realism.

HISTORICAL REALISM: MILDRED TAYLOR'S *THE LAND*

Mildred Taylor demonstrates the intersections among land ownership, capitalism, and racial identity in her novel *The Land*, a prequel to *Roll of Thunder, Hear My Cry* (1976). *The Land* begins in the 1870s, depicting the years shortly after the Civil War, and chronicles how Cassie Logan's great-grandfather, Paul-Edward Logan, came to be a landowner in Mississippi by 1887. Paul-Edward's father, Edward Logan, is a widower who raises Paul-Edward to feel that he is the equal of Edward's other three sons by his white wife, but Paul-Edward and his sister are the progeny of their father's relationship with an enslaved woman whom he treats, as he does Paul-Edward and his sister, with love and respect. Paul-Edward's mother, however, was only freed because of the Civil War, not because of any action Edward Logan takes on her behalf.

Edward passionately loves his landholdings in Georgia, where he farms, among other things, cotton. Interestingly enough, the cotton fields are hidden from the view of Edward's house. According to the son, Paul-Edward, who narrates the novel: "Beyond the pasturelands where the horses and cattle grazed were the forests. The cotton fields could not be seen. They, along with all the sharecropping shanties and the people in them, were on the other side of the woods, hidden from view. So was my mama's house" (98). It is as if Edward wants to hide from himself the legacy of Big Cotton and the slavery from which he has profited. Likewise, Edward also makes some racially tinged comments about Paul-Edward's passion for that same land, telling his third son about his maternal grandfather, an Indigenous person belonging to a tribe the white people refer to only as "The Nation" (11).

My own daddy told me about [your mama's daddy]. His name was Kanati; means the lucky hunter. My daddy said he left with some of his people headed west into Alabama or Mississippi before the soldiers made them go. . . . Kanati knew they'd be made to go because *folks like my daddy and others wanted the Nation's land*, and *there was nothing to be done about that*. The Army was set to drive Kanati's people out, and your granddaddy didn't want any part of soldiers. (42, emphasis added)

In this excerpt, Edward openly acknowledges, but seems to shrug off as inevitable, white men's greed for land ownership, a greed so great as to justify the displacement and genocide of a race of peoples.

The need to turn an economic profit by harvesting cotton on that pilfered land required the enslavement of yet another race of peoples, people who became legally defined as property, rather than as citizens with human rights, which Logan makes emphatically clear is a moral wrong; nevertheless, the author herself seems to shrug off this theft of native lands as unavoidable, since no character ever questions the putative "inevitability" of white people owning that stolen land. Instead, it is taken for granted.

The conversation about the boy's maternal grandfather continues:

"This land," I said, "it belonged to his people first."
"That's a fact," my daddy agreed. "Maybe that's where you get part of your love for the land." (42)

Edward Logan also loves the land, yet he attributes a portion of Paul-Edward's loving that same land to his Indigenous heritage in what appears to be a simplistic romanticization of Indigenous peoples' relationship with the Earth. Since both of them love the land equally, this passage seems jarring in its racism and essentialism. Why should Paul-Edward's Indigenous genetics make him somehow love the land in the same way that his entirely white father does? Embedded in these comments is an assumption that because white people will dominate the land and use it for economic gain, they have more of a right to it than those whose reliance on the land and its resources sustains life but doesn't contribute to the dominant economic model of capitalism. Not coincidentally, this same assumption underpinned the Doctrine of Discovery, a papal legal theory that offered a rationalization for white European colonists' theft of lands in the Americas, and later, for westward expansion in the US. Under European international law, land was considered vacant if it was not being used "properly," as defined by European laws and customs. And what did "proper" land use entail? Consistent with capitalist ideology, for Europeans, it "was synonymous with *improved* land for agriculture" (Vavrus 115, emphasis in the original).

In *The Land*, Paul-Edward shares his father's lust to own property. He tells the reader:

> What I wanted was land. I wanted land like my daddy's. In a way, I suppose, I was driven by the thought of having land of my own. In my early years. . . . I had figured that I'd always live on my daddy's land, that my daddy's land would be mine and I'd always be a part of it. When I discovered that wouldn't be, I created my own land in my mind. I knew that land was what I had to have. (142)

Paul-Edward's comments invite still another question: does he crave land ownership because he has inherited his father's attitudes and ideologies, or because he understands, on a practical level, that property ownership separates him from freedmen and the white men who work as exploited laborers sharecropping for white landowners? These questions are complex, interrelated, and perhaps unanswerable, but they suggest that despite the integrity of Mildred Taylor's admirably antiracist oeuvre, she still reproduces some of the basic principles that have rationalized the commodification of land, likely a result of her having grown up in a society immersed in racial capitalism. In sum, YA novels frequently depict private ownership as being preferable to tribal, communal, or public ownership.

CONTEMPORARY REALISM: CHRISTOPHER PAUL CURTIS'S *BUCKING THE SARGE*

Christopher Paul Curtis's *Bucking the Sarge* demonstrates American capitalism gone awry in a way that implicates not only corrupt white entrepreneurs, but also corrupt Black entrepreneurs. Fifteen-year-old Luther T. Farrell lives in Flint, Michigan, and works for his mother, who runs "Friendly Neighbor Loans," rents out more than fifty homes she owns, and owns three group homes for the disabled, including one that she has had her son, Luther, operate for the previous two and a half years (11, 219). Luther was thirteen when the "Sarge," as he refers to his mother behind her back, put him in charge of caring for the eight men in the Happy Neighbor Group Home for Men.

Luther refers to his mother as "Sarge" because she manages her business on "a military model" (30). As she puts it, she has to "clothe and feed a large number of people . . . [who are] a large, diverse, often unwilling and ungrateful group who most likely are where they are as a last resort" (30).

The Sarge tells her son, "It is far better to be feared than loved"—and fear her Luther certainly does (31). For example, she has taught him a form of torture to control the men at the group home, one that leaves no mark. She calls it "the Happy Neighbor Group Home finger curl. What you do is put your fingers on top of the client's and roll your fingers into their palm. The pain it gives is so tough that you can have someone jumping around like SpongeBob SquarePants on speed, and it doesn't leave any kind of mark" (25). Sarge doesn't want state inspectors to see her clients with any "bruises, scrapes or cuts that might get infected and could be seen as a sign of neglect or abuse"; indeed, Luther has learned that "if you put a visible mark on one of her clients she puts the same mark on you times five" (25). Not only is Sarge physically abusive to her son and her clients at the group home, but her boyfriend, Darnell Dixon, serves as her enforcer when tenants need to be evicted. He also "shakes people down" when they can't repay a loan or pay their rent (93). Luther both experiences and witnesses the violence that Sarge and Darnell mete out upon the citizens of Flint in their pursuit of profit.

Of the nine metropolitan areas in the state of Michigan, Flint had the highest unemployment rate in both May of 2002 and 2003, which is about when *Bucking the Sarge* is set ("Michigan Economic Indicators").[7] According to the official census data of the year 2000, Flint was 53.3 percent African American (compared to the rest of the state of Michigan, which was 14.2 percent African American), and 26.4 percent of the population of Flint lived below the poverty line, compared to 10.5 percent in the state overall ("Flint, Michigan Census Data"). Luther's best friend, Sparky, explains when and how economics changed in Flint:

> Flint's nothing but the *Titanic*, Luther. And the last life preservers they handed out were jobs in the factories back in 1976. . . . Back in the day my uncle said even if you didn't finish high school you could still get a job on the line in the factory and make enough cash to buy a new Buick every four years or buy a house or buy some clothes from Hudson's or afford cable TV or a legal satellite. You can't do that now, you can't do nothing with *two* minimum-wage jobs now. Seems like the only way to get paid is being a stickup kid, booming weed or suing someone. (128, emphasis in the original)

Sparky's commentary is a clear critique of the unequal economic conditions that resulted from Reaganomics and neoliberalism.

The Sarge herself justifies her commodification and exploitation of other Black people when she describes her low earning potential, even after earning a college degree and taking a job as a teacher to children from wealthy families during the 1980s: "I got a job in New York City at this chichi all-girls' school right in Manhattan. The people were paying twenty-five thousand dollars a year to send their kids to this school. . . . Way more than my salary. Mostly the little brats were the kids of *Fortune* 500 execs, actors, politicians" (101). After discovering that two of her students have original art by Rembrandt or Picasso hanging at home, the Sarge dejectedly returns to her "fifth-floor cold-water walk-up," where she contemplates the integrity of an economic system that is designed to disadvantage people like her:

> I asked myself how many generations down the line it would be before a relative of mine would have anything anywhere near fine, original art hanging from the walls of their home. . . . I asked myself what these little *Fortune* 500 kids had done to deserve so much when my future kids were obviously going to be starting with so little. . . . Most of [their parents] had their money left to them or they'd lucked up and had hit it big with their own businesses where someone had greased the skids for them. . . . I knew the only way my pocket was ever going to have any real weight was to set up my own business, to make the system work for me and follow the same rules they follow. . . . They milk the system for everything it's worth, and I'm trying my best to do the same thing. (100–101)

When the Sarge talks about "them," she is referring to people with privilege. Although she does not necessarily identify this privilege as "white privilege," she implies it when she speculates that the successful children in her school were not "unusually talented or intelligent" or "blessed or preordained to be where they were" (100); rather, "they've been taught to fervently believe that that was the case. . . . Believing in yourself is half the battle. . . . The other half of the battle is money" (100–101).

Two problems specific to both housing and ownership of private property stem from the Sarge's neoliberal commitment to maximizing her profit-making. First, the homes she rents are substandard. After one eviction, Luther and Sparky are cleaning out a rental and discover "the biggest, baddest, ugliest, nastiest-looking rat that had ever walked the streets of Flint"; its "tail was as thick as my thumb and as long as my forearm. He looked like he had either been in a fight and got bit or had been chewing at a sore on his back. There was a quarter-size bright pink bare spot there that was soaking wet and oozing neon-green pus along its edges" (46). Embracing austerity, the Sarge refuses to pay for an exterminator. Second, the Sarge cuts every corner she can to get "slum housing up to close-to-livable conditions" (37). Her favorite scam involves paint. Her boyfriend has "painted over dust balls the size of small watermelons, nails as thick as an elephant's leg and picture hooks big enough to snag and hold one of those nuclear submarines.... When Darnell finishes a room the walls might be a little lumpy, but you can bet every square inch is slathered with paint, and that's all that the Sarge and the renters seem to care about" (38–39). The Sarge stores all the paint "she bought real cheap a long time ago" in the basement of one of her rental houses (41).

Unfortunately, all of the paint contains lead. After winning a prize at the science fair for his oral report about how lead affects childhood development, Luther realizes that he has made a serious lapse of judgment in choosing his topic, at least as far as his mother and Darnell Dixon, ever the neoliberal entrepreneurs, are concerned:

> Darnell had told me that right after the government made leaded paint illegal a long time ago the Sarge had printed up some cards that said she was a paint disposal expert and had gone around to all the paint stores she could find and offered to get rid of their paint for a small fee.
>
> And that's what she'd been doing ever since, getting rid of the paint one gallon at a time on her houses and apartments. (195)

Furious with her son for reporting on lead paint, the Sarge gives him four days to pack up and leave home because Luther's "science fair project was going to end up costing the Sarge a ton of cash or maybe even some time in jail" (196).

Luther's compensation for managing the group home, painting her properties, cleaning up after evictions, and participating "in the Sarge's evil empire" has ostensibly been wages Sarge has been setting aside for him in a college education fund (90). He believes he has $92,000 saved towards college but discovers his mother has cheated him out of his own money. His retribution is to restore funds, Robin Hood-style, from people she has rooked, including him, and he moves to Florida with one of the elderly men, Mr. Stockard, who lived in the group home. In other words, unlike his mother, Luther compassionately thinks of other people in his community, including his best friend, the residents of the group home, and a family the Sarge has evicted with inadequate notice. He also rights a wrong he has created with the girl he has a crush on and thanks his favorite teacher for supporting and encouraging him. The elderly man Luther has been helping tells him: "What I'm talking about here is *you*, not what you have.... you're respectful, you're kind, you're considerate, you're funny.... I understand how smart you are, how ambitious you are" (177, emphasis in the original). Mr. Stockard continues: "You've accomplished all of this in spite of the fact that you've had very little positive adult influence or guidance. You've managed to turn yourself into a very decent human being even though.... your mother has been negligent in many ways" (178). Two words create a tension in Mr. Stockard's assessment of Luther: he is both "ambitious" and "decent" (178). On the other hand, Mr. Stockard contrasts the boy with his neoliberal mother, whom he describes as "one determined young sister" and "a lost-soul vampire" (145). Luther considers that to be the "best description of the Sarge" he's ever heard (146). Luther has learned that "Hard work can get you some good things, you don't always have to scheme and cheat" (186). Ultimately, he defines himself in opposition to his mother by valuing community over self-enclosed individualism.

Of course, scheming and cheating existed millennia before neoliberalism did. That notwithstanding, the tragedy at the heart of *Bucking the Sarge* is the Sarge's sense of herself as an entrepreneur, a job classification that she thinks gives her license to exploit others, including jeopardizing the lives of children with lead-based paint in an eerie foreshadowing of the ongoing lead crisis in the water of Flint, Michigan, first detected and reported to the public in 2015 (Kennedy). Reflecting our discussion in chapter 2, that real-life, man-made environmental disaster is also a byproduct of neoliberal policies that emphasize cost-saving and profit over the health of people, particularly African Americans (Benz, Fasenfest). These types of neoliberal policies encourage nefarious social Darwinist thinking, with the result that the marketplace is yet another space in which the strong are lauded for overpowering the weak.

SPIRITUAL REALISM: ANGELINE BOULLEY'S *FIREKEEPER'S DAUGHTER*

We have analyzed the Logan family's land ownership and the Sarge's property ownership because characters in each of these novels reflect historical (and often racist) attitudes toward owning property. Attitudes about land ownership differ dramatically, however, in Angeline Boulley's award-winning *Firekeeper's Daughter* (2021). The eighteen-year-old protagonist and narrator, Daunis Fontaine, attributes this difference in attitude to her family's and

Tribe's relationship to land. Daunis is Ojibwe, a nation of the Anishinaabe peoples. Commenting on the Ojibwe reservation land known as Sugar Island, she narrates: "My father's family ... is as much a part of Sugar Island as its spring-fed streams and sugar maple trees" (6). The novel also acknowledges broken treaty rights (242) and violated land claims (59) to contextualize the sense of displacement that some characters in the book experience. In the story, the ancestral site is "owned either by the Tribe or by the Flint family" (108), the largest and most corrupt family enrolled in the Sugar Island Tribe. Indeed, the Flints are rumored to be involved in the production and distribution of meth among Ojibwe tribal members. While many members of the Tribe own their own homes on the mainland across the river from Sugar Island, none owns as much as the Flint family, and approximately "half the homes on the rez are cookie-cutter houses, part of a federal housing project funded by the Housing and Urban Development [HUD] in the 1970s" (141). Newer, better homes were built after members of the Tribe began to receive per capita payments from the profits of the Tribe's casino, which became economically viable in the 1990s. Adults receive $36,000 per capita, per annum; minors, on the other hand, receive $12,000, which leads some parents to exploit their children's income. As Daunis explains to a new male friend, Jamie Johnson, "per cap isn't good or bad. It just kinda amplifies whatever's going on with a person or family" (59).

Some families use their per cap money to build better, newer homes than those put up by HUD; others buy back tribal lands that white people have procured from the Ojibwe during difficult financial times. By the end of the novel, the Tribal Council has begun to implement a banishment process lasting up to five years for members of the Tribe who are "convicted of a felony drug crime in any court" (480). Banished members are also punished by forfeiting their per capita payments. Thus, while individual members of the Ojibwe Tribe have small holdings of individual property, the overall ethos leads people to share a sense of communal ownership of reservation lands on Sugar Island and the mainland.

Perhaps the strongest indicator of neoliberal economics in the novel comes from the jealousy that some white people in the town adjacent to the reservation express about the per cap payments their Ojibwe friends and neighbors receive. Reflecting the distinction that Randolph Hohle draws between "white-private" and "black-public" (*Race* 4), some regard the per cap payments as a form of social welfare that encourages government dependency. Toward that end, a white person refers to per cap as "easy ... money" and implies that the tribal payment has made one Ojibwe teenager so irresponsible that she subsequently dies what appears to be a reckless death (253). In other cases, white people characterize freedoms afforded the Ojibwe by treaties the Tribe signed with the federal government as offering its members unfair advantages. For example, a boy who has passed as white his entire life criticizes the Ojibwe for being able to "hunt at different times than allowed by state law, or pay a reduced price for gas that doesn't include the state taxes" (242). Underscoring the extent to which these criticisms are attributable to jealousy, the same boy reveals his Ojibwe paternity when he is on the verge of turning nineteen, at which time he becomes eligible for the full adult per capita payments. Tragically, a supersmart, exceptional teenage Ojibwe boy proves to be a meth dealer—and one who has internalized the racism that underpins neoliberal economics. He justifies his decision to sell poison to his neighbors in terms of per cap greed: "Why should big-city drug dealers end up with more per-cap dollars than any tribal member?"; a teammate of his agrees: "If people are gonna buy the stuff anyway, why not buy local?" (417). Neoliberal ideologies, and the racism that underpins them, have infected the thinking of both the Ojibwe and white people.

In direct opposition to neoliberal thinking, the Anishinaabe conception of the "good way of life" holds seven values central: "love, humility, respect, honesty, bravery, wisdom, and truth" (32). The greed that leads members of the Tribe to become drug dealers violates the values of love, humility, respect, honesty, and truth; likewise, those who become addicted to meth are unable to be honest, brave, wise, or truthful. An Ojibwe teenager—a smart student exceptionally adroit at chemistry—cooks his own meth and becomes addicted to it. This young man, Travis, has been warned about the dangers of meth by ancient, mystical inhabitants of Sugar Island known as the Little People. These trickster figures are the size of five-year-olds and they play pranks on the Ojibwe, both to protect tribal children from harm and to caution miscreants against violating the seven tenets of the Anishinaabe good way of life. For example, another young man is reprimanded by the Little People for sniffing gasoline to get high; "the last time they came 'round, they cried for him. He never saw them again"—because he died lighting a cigarette while he still had gasoline on his body (296). Just before Travis murders his girlfriend and then commits suicide with the same weapon, he "*makes a hacking motion with the gun*" (1) and "*slashes diagonally at invisible enemies as if his gun has become a machete*" (283, emphasis in the original). He tells Daunis, who has been caught unawares in the underbrush and is trapped, watching the murder-suicide unfold: "*They're so mad at me.... The Little People*" (284, emphasis in the original).

Daunis eventually connects the dots between the Little People protecting youth from drug abuse and the meth Travis cooks when she realizes that a group of meth-addled Ojibwe teenagers have also been chided by the Little People:

> The Little People found the kids in the woods and scolded them.
> The FBI assumed whatever had been added to the meth-X [that Travis cooked] was a hallucinogenic mushroom, because the Anishinaabe kids who tried that particular batch of meth saw something that didn't make sense. The team working the investigation was alarmed by the group aspect of the hallucination and thought it was an unusual side effect of an unknown variety of mushroom. Whatever was added to the batch of meth-X, it didn't cause hallucinations.
> Because the Little People are real. (322)

This novel is less magic realism than spiritual realism because the narrator knows the ancient Little People exist, literally. By relying on the knowledge of tribal lore and their shared values of love, humility, respect, honesty, bravery, wisdom, and truth, Daunis is able to help the FBI identify those who are making and distributing the meth, including Travis's meth-X. Although she is heartbroken by how many members of her own family and her Tribe are implicated in the crimes, she has helped "protect [her] community" (119), which has been her goal all along. Her greatest triumph is in achieving that goal, but she does so by rejecting the lure of individual financial gain so that she can more closely treasure the Tribe's communal spirituality.

CONCLUSION

Scores of YA novels feature characters who live in ghettoized neighborhoods replete with housing as neglected as the properties the Sarge owns. Many of these novels have been published since 2016 alone, undoubtedly in response to the important influence of #WeNeedDiverseBooks, a nonprofit organization established in the spring of 2014 ("About WNDB"). As one example, Nic Stone's *Dear Martin* (2017) portrays seventeen-year-old Justyce McAllister, who writes about growing up "in a "bad area" of Atlanta; he also calls his neighborhood a "rough area" (12). Stone is undoubtedly depicting the "black concentric zone between the central business district and the white suburbs" of Atlanta (Hohle, *Race* 126), which was created by neoliberal city planning that "deregulated housing codes" (Hohle, *Race* 125), redirected public funds to develop the central business district and tourist center of Atlanta, and constructed "urban highways [that] created boundaries between the wealthy white neighborhoods and the black neighborhoods" (Hohle, *Race* 126). Another novel, Renée Watson's *Piecing Me Together* (2017), portrays its protagonist, a sixteen-year-old African American girl named Jade, living in a "run-down" apartment in a Portland neighborhood where the housing units are "just the projects with a different name" (9–10).

A similar community, one that also emerged because of segregation and underfunding, is depicted in Angie Thomas's novels.[8] Starr, the narrator of *The Hate U Give* (2017), is defensive about her low-income neighborhood: "Garden Heights is the ghetto. . . . I can call Garden Heights the ghetto all I want. Nobody else can" (139). The narrators of Thomas's *On the Come Up* (2019) and *Concrete Rose* (2021), both of which are set in the same fictionalized community, also experience the negative impact of living in the impoverished neighborhood of Garden Heights, including watching the violent death of loved ones. Ibi Zoboi's *Pride* (2018) addresses concerns about gentrification in one of Brooklyn's "broken and forgotten neighborhoods," which was "first built out of love" (1). Meanwhile, Zoboi's *American Street* (2017) is set in a west Detroit neighborhood ruined by government neglect; in the resulting poverty, drug dealers compete to stay afloat.

Because the political concept of local control dictates that public schools are funded by local property taxes, the relationship between housing and education is a close one. That this should be the case is not surprising. As Joan Marshall Wesley et al. observe, "the most pervasive applications of raw separation [between races] have been in the areas of housing and education" (12), which undoubtedly explains why these interrelated issues are so frequently addressed together in YA novels. In this chapter, we have examined the relationship that has historically existed between racism, capitalism, and home ownership, and in doing so we have shown how neoliberalism builds on that relationship. It is important to note, however, that neoliberalism does not merely represent a continuation of problematic race relations under capitalism. Instead, this right-wing econo-political ideology transforms how racism manifests itself in the US. With that in mind, in the next chapter we examine the form that racism takes in our neoliberal era, and in literature for teenagers, with specific attention paid to how educational opportunities (or the lack thereof) and the commodification of colorism are represented in the genre.

Chapter 4

RACISM IN OUR NEOLIBERAL ERA

> While the color line has been modified and dismantled in places, race and racial hierarchies still exercise a profound influence on how most people in the United States experience their daily lives.
>
> —Henry Giroux, "Spectacles of Race" (193)

In a "between the scenes" clip that was shared on *The Daily Show*'s social media account, the show's host, Trevor Noah, was asked by an audience member what he regarded as the difference between racism in South Africa, where he was born and grew up, and racism in the US, where he now lives and works. Given our purpose in this chapter, Noah's answer is striking, both for its insight and candor. Noting that the South African government made little, if any, effort to conceal the role racism played in shaping public policy, he pointed to the 1968 election of Richard Nixon (which occurred following the passage of the 1964 Civil Rights Act) as marking the start of a period in which white elites recognized a need to move racism underground so that it remained hidden. As an example of this, Noah contrasted a government policy in South Africa that blatantly prohibited Blacks from living in certain areas with racist money lending practices in the US that accomplish the same objective, albeit quietly. Expressing his preference for the former, Noah explained, "I know it sounds strange to say, but I think there's something liberating about fighting an obvious enemy as opposed to one that you have to prove exists" (@TheDailyShow). In the absence of a visible enemy, he argued, Black people are left to be "detectives of their own racism" (@TheDailyShow). In a neoliberal era, racism persists, albeit in a different, possibly more insidious, form that is not as immediately discernible as the racism of South African apartheid—or the US during the era of Jim Crow laws.

For example, conservative political efforts to erase discussions about race and critical race theory (CRT) at any level of education, from kindergarten to college, is a direct effort to obfuscate structural racism and the negative effects of racism on populations of color in the US. In the summer of 2023, the Oklahoma legislature passed House Bill 1775, which prohibits public school teachers from addressing the issue of race in ways that might make white students feel guilty for the actions of their ancestors. Specifically, in response to a question at a public forum about how teachers could address the city of Tulsa's 1921 Race Massacre without also acknowledging the issue of race, Oklahoma Superintendent of Public Instruction Ryan Walters commented: "I would say be judgmental of the issue, of the action, of the content of the character of the individual. Absolutely. But let's not tie it to the skin color and say the skin color determines it" (Krehbiel). Walters later walked his comments back, claiming to have been misquoted, but the Oklahoma House Bill still stands, limiting how teachers can talk about race (or sexuality and sexual identity). That same summer, in Arkansas, the State Department of Education announced that students would not receive credit for an AP African American studies course—replicating a similar act of curricular censorship that occurred in Florida—due to concerns that the course would violate a new Arkansas state law prohibiting teachers from engaging in student "indoctrination" (Goldstein).

In employing CRT as a tool to analyze neoliberal ideologies about race in YA novels, we find ourselves greatly indebted to many scholars of Black children's literature, including Rudine Sims Bishop, who generated the widely used concept of considering whether children's books serve as "mirrors," "windows," or "sliding glass doors" for readers ("Mirrors" ix). Maria José Bathelo and Masha Kabakow Rudman validate Bishop's impact on literary criticism by employing her phrase "Mirrors, Windows, and Doors" as the subtitle for their book *Critical Multicultural Analysis of Children's Literature* (2009). Drawing on the language of CRT, Bathelo and Rudman call on scholars to examine the "sociopolitical function of linguistic and visual signs" in children's and YA literature (2). Because we, like Bathelo and Rudman, are also "reading against culture" (3), we share their interests in discourse (109), ideology (110), subjectivity (111), and power (112), especially as these concepts can help us to productively interrogate the relationship between neoliberalism and racism in YA literature.[1]

As various children's literature scholars have demonstrated, books for young readers, including YA literature, have a long history of serving as a conduit for racist ideologies. Philip Nel's *Was the Cat in the Hat Black?*, in particular, asks readers to question the implicit racial bias in US children's and YA literature. Like him, we each recall encountering Ezra Jack Keats's *Snowy Day* (1962) in our childhoods; more perniciously, we recall seeing books such as Bannerman's *The Story of Little Black Sambo* (1899) and *Walt Disney Presents Uncle Remus* (1976) in various formats, including as part of the Little Golden Books series. For Roberta, Claire Hutchet Bishop's racist *Five Chinese Brothers* (1938) was a library staple; for Sean, it was Lynne Reid Banks's *The Indian in the Cupboard* (1980). As Nel, Kate Capshaw, and Michelle H. Martin all document, however, racism does not depend on the presence of such overtly racist tropes as those in *Little Black Sambo* to spread. Despite advancements in the publishing industry, which can be attributed to activist initiatives such as the #WeNeedDiverseBooks campaign, Black, Indigenous, and People of Color (BIPOC) characters remain greatly underrepresented in books for children and teenagers (Nel 3; Herndon). Moreover, books for young readers published in the last fifty years also frequently reproduce racist ideologies associated with neoliberalism, even though readers may not initially recognize the ideology as overtly racist or neoliberal, which is what we aim to address in this chapter.

For example, fiction, like nonfiction, often espouses the idea that the extent to which people are economically successful depends more on their willingness to work hard than it does on their racial identity or the economic exploitation of their forebears. In the case of those books for teenagers that depict Black characters who succeed as a result of their own exceptionalism, this ideology is especially pernicious. As Michelle Alexander argues, "Black success stories lend credence to the notion that anyone, no matter how poor or how black you may be, can make it to the top if only you try hard enough" (309). Christopher Paul Curtis comments wryly on the same phenomenon in an interview found at the end of the paperback edition of *Bucking the Sarge* when he observes, "We . . . celebrate 'America's first black woman millionaire,' Madame C. J. Walker who made her fortune capitalizing on black self-hatred by selling hair straighteners and skin bleachers" (7). What both Alexander and Curtis describe can lead to internalized racism for teenagers of color, especially for those living in families that have not experienced social mobility, despite generations of the family striving to do so in the face of systematic oppression.

In this chapter, we are especially concerned with identifying those aspects of neoliberalism that contribute to ongoing racism in the US. Specifically, we examine how entire demographics of people are exploited via unstable housing conditions and the allure of school privatization, both of which result in separate and unequal educational opportunities for teenagers of color. Furthermore, in too many recently published YA novels, teenagers of color demonstrate internalized racism that leads them to seek market solutions as they attempt to adapt themselves to neoliberal culture, resulting in their buying costly commodities, such as expensive clothes or shoes, skin products, hair products, and hair-styling services. The YA novels we examine at length in this chapter frequently depict teenage characters who are not only exploited because of the living conditions that result from structural racism, but who are also exploited as consumers.

In the sections that follow, we will analyze in closer detail economics and living conditions in Tiffany D. Jackson's *Monday's Not Coming* (2018), Jerry Craft's graphic novel *New Kid* (2019), and Alicia D. Williams's *Genesis Begins Again* (2019). The latter also provides us with a text for further analysis in the next section, which examines the neoliberal commodification of internalized racism. Worth noting at this juncture is the following contextualizing statement: all of the novels we analyze at length in this chapter were published during the tumultuous Trump presidency of 2017–21, an era in which race relations in the US reached what was at the time a nadir created by the maelstrom of Trump's racist rhetoric and racist police actions, including the murder of George Floyd in the summer of 2020.

PUBLIC HOUSING AND EDUCATION: TIFFANY D. JACKSON'S *MONDAY'S NOT COMING*

In the previous chapter, we examined privately owned land, privately owned rental properties, and race as they intersect with neoliberal ideologies; on the other hand, *Firekeeper's Daughter* addresses the lands of the Ojibwe reservation in terms of collectivity. Tiffany D. Jackson's *Monday's Not Coming* (2018) takes to the level of the gothic the horrors of substandard public housing that is underfunded because of neoliberal policies that emphasize austerity. In the story, the first-person narrator, Claudia, has a best friend named Monday Charles who has gone missing for almost a year. Monday lives in a condemned housing project in southeastern Washington, DC, referred to by locals as the "Ed Borough."[2] Claudia explains that "crystallized powder turned DC into a city of zombies during the '80s and '90s, hitting the southeast section of the city the hardest. Crack led to desperation, desperation led to crime, and crime led to murders and destruction. Everybody knew somebody affected by it: Daddy's family, Monday's family" (37). Although with the passage of time, "folks rebuilt, families healed," ghosts of that era still haunt the Ed Borough (37). Resembling Kendi's discussion of the broken promise the federal government made to apportion Southern lands to formerly enslaved peoples following the Civil War, Claudia explains:

> The Capitol Housing Authority built the Edward Borough housing projects during World War II on land originally given to freed slaves during the 1800s. It was meant to be a place of community, a place to start again, a place for the American dream.
> Later on, developers realized how valuable the land was, sitting right on the river, with easy access to the city. Too valuable for black folks to have.
> How convenient that crack would ravish the area developers wanted most. (38)

A resident of Ed Borough who receives an eviction notice explains, "Now they coming around serving everybody. This city has it out bad for us. They've wanted that land for as long as I can remember. Rather throw us all out and start with a clean slate than fix a broken toilet" (188). Likewise, Monday's older sister, April, observes, "White people trying to buy up Ed Borough.... Government can do whatever they want. No one owns nothing around here" (326). That April should regard the government as acting on behalf of wealthy white developers, or what Hohle calls the "liberal business class" (*Race* 2), as opposed to looking out for the interests of all those it governs, is striking. Indeed, in the novel's chilling conclusion, a member of a DC urban housing development coalition asks a question that is central to the tension between neoliberalism and government: "I think it boils down to one question: who's really responsible for your well-being—your family, the government, or your community?" (421).

Set in Washington, DC, *Monday's Not Coming* calls attention to the extreme disparities that confront Black people in the nation's capital. Indeed, the story is in many ways "a tale of two cities." For example, Claudia describes the pleasure her father finds in "driving through Northwest DC, passing the monuments, the National Mall lined by the Smithsonian museums, the Capitol, and the White House. Lived here all his life but still mesmerized by the lights bouncing off the marble goliath buildings" (217). In contrast, when they cross the bridge over the Potomac River, Claudia explains, "Like day turning to night in a blink of an eye, our part of the city felt so dark in comparison when we're so full of light" (217).

Alongside the government's culpability in creating housing disparities, Monday's mother, Patti Charles, suffers from paranoia and is convinced that the government watches "your every move" by tracking everything on the computers people use, including the books they check out from the library (89). She calls her daughter Monday "fast ass" (39, 90, 430), and Monday clearly fears the woman. As Mrs. Charles drinks more, she becomes even more verbally and physically abusive. Monday, along with her two sisters and their brother, August, is eventually placed in child protective services, though they are returned to Mrs. Charles's care after she takes "court-ordered parenting classes" (270). Mrs. Charles has clearly been the victim of physical abuse at the hands of at least one man, very likely her ex-husband. When she is talking about the bruises a neighbor has suffered at the hands of her spouse, Mrs. Charles tells Claudia's mother: "No man should put his hands on no female. Not ever! I teach my girls that every day. I lived through that long enough to know" (88). When Monday and the boy she's been hoping to date get in a fistfight, a physical altercation that Monday has initiated, Mrs. Charles tells the principal who is planning to suspend her unruly daughter: "You busy talking about what SHE did? She's a female! He shouldn't be touching no damn female! PERIOD!" (137, emphasis in the original). She goes on, "A school full of fucking adults and you letting some boy, some MAN, touch my child!" (138, emphasis in the original).

Readers eventually learn that Mrs. Charles has killed her daughter. One newspaper report suggests that neoliberal forces may have caused Mrs. Charles to become unhinged, much as financial instability is depicted as having contributed to Luther's mother's corruption in Christopher Paul Curtis's *Bucking the Sarge*. The newspaper reporter interviews at least one neighbor and concludes:

> Multiple claims suggested Mrs. Charles feared eviction, driving her to a mental break.
> "You got these buses of white folks driving around here with cameras around their necks like they're on a safari, hunting for their new home. Of course she went crazy!" (398)

But Monday has displayed signs of abuse for years, which raises the question: why were none of the adult figures in her life cognizant of her mistreatment? Readers eventually learn that eight social workers, at a minimum, are fired because of their failure to follow up on concern after concern filed in connection with Mrs. Charles's abusive and neglectful treatment of her children. Reflecting a limitation of self-enclosed individualism, Claudia's mother and father, as well as a teacher at her school, are all initially reluctant to get involved for fear of meddling in another family's affairs. In these ways, the novel critiques neoliberalism's myopic focus on individual self-interest at the expense of caring for other people.

EDUCATION AND SCHOOL PRIVATIZATION

Racist housing policies result in a *de facto* system of school segregation that creates conditions both separate and unequal. In the case of public education, the problem is further complicated by racist neoliberal policies. As we argued in chapter 3, ever since the 1954 Supreme Court ruling in the *Brown v. Board of Education* civil rights case determined that segregated schools are inherently unequal, wealthy white conservatives have sought to resegregate America's schools. Two policies that are closely aligned with neoliberalism—privatization and austerity—are integral to their efforts to do so.

As Nancy MacLean shows in her book *Democracy in Chains*, immediately following the Supreme Court's ruling in *Brown v. Board of Education*, powerful conservatives in Virginia and other southern states contemplated defunding public education to prevent Black students from attending school with white students. In subsequent years, as private academies for white students flourished, many of these same states enacted school voucher programs that allowed parents to put public tax dollars toward their children's private education. Randolph Hohle explains that, in the process of doing so, "elite and ordinary whites assembled a language of white-private as a strategy of maintaining control over the racial composition of schools" (*Racism* 168). Today, this discourse persists in neoliberal school reform efforts that seek to expand voucher programs under the guise of school choice and that cite austerity as a justification for privatizing education and opening the market to nonprofit and for-profit charter schools. In many cases, these efforts are cast as aiming to ensure that all students, regardless of race or class, have access to quality education.

In reality, however, they have the opposite effect. For example, because "the value of school vouchers are often inadequate to pay tuition at private schools," students from economically disadvantaged families may be unable to afford them (Ambrosio 325). Conversely, for children from wealthy families, school vouchers ensure that they have even more access to elite schools than they would have had anyway. As Hohle argues, "White private schools are extremely rare in suburban school districts, popping up only when a significant proportion of black or Hispanic residents exist in the suburban district" (*Racism* 166). Charles R. Lawrence III perfectly encapsulates the racist consequences of neoliberal education reform policies that aim to privatize education: "Once more we offer separate and unequal education, and this time, with a con artist's guile and deceit, we offer it as a remedy, as a solution to itself" (711).

In the twenty-first century, neoliberal policies that address education remain tainted by racism and classism, with perhaps the most egregious example being the No Child Left Behind Act (NCLB), which Congress enacted in 2002 under the George W. Bush administration. Writing in the *Suffolk Law Review* in 2005, Lawrence describes the neoliberal justifications for NCLB as follows:

> The Act's proponents claim compassion, care, and concern for poor children. It is a conservative hard-nosed compassion to be sure, they say. They will not allow liberal do-gooders to make excuses while lazy, incompetent, uncaring teachers and administrators continue to fail these children. They will take names and kick ass. They will test, hold folks accountable, close schools, create transparency, and liberate children from failing public schools. When those public schools fail they will give the kids vouchers and bring in their buddies from the corporate world to rebuild a new privately owned system. (701)

Lawrence continues:

> The No Child Left Behind Act is not simply an ill-conceived and implemented effort in pursuit of good ends. Rather, the Act does affirmative harm by diverting our attention and our resources away from the continuing substantive and structural inequities of race and class, and by perpetuating and reinforcing social class hierarchies and racist beliefs and practices that continue to deny poor, working-class black and brown children equal educational opportunity and human dignity. (706)

Lawrence was early to recognize that the Act, as it was conceived, was unlikely to close any achievement gaps because of the many factors NCLB left unaccounted for: "birth weight, lead poisoning, hunger and nutrition, reading to young children, television watching, parent availability, parent participation, and student mobility [are] all factors beyond the walls of the school that contribute significantly to the racial achievement gap" (710).

In an oft-cited article from 2007, David Hursh is even more direct about the political agenda motivating NCLB, arguing that it is "part of a larger shift from social democratic to neoliberal policies that has been occurring over the past several decades" (493). He continues, "NCLB, like other recent education policies promoting standardized testing, accountability, competition, school choice, and privatization, reflects the rise and dominance of neoliberal and neoconservative policy discourses over social democratic policy discourses" (494). Hursh asserts that "for many neoliberals, the ultimate goal . . . is to convert the educational system into markets and, as much as possible, privatize educational services" (501).

Describing the forced replacement of New Orleans public schools by charter schools following Hurricane Katrina, Hursh quotes from *Dismantling a Community*, written by the Center for Community Change in 2006: "It is a vision of private hands spending public funds. Most disturbing, it is a vision that casts families and students as 'customers,' who shop for schools in isolation from—and even in competition with—their neighbors. It is a vision that, like the game of musical chairs, requires someone to be left without a seat" (quoted in 503). As our discussion suggests, within a neoliberal economy that student is all too often BIPOC. Indeed, a pattern emerges in several YA novels about African American teenagers published between 2014 and 2018: Starr Carter, the protagonist of Angie Thomas's *The Hate U Give*, attends a prep school, as do the protagonist and her three cousins in Ibi Zoboi's *American Street* (2018); Jade attends "the best private school in Portland" on scholarship in Renée Watson's *Piecing Me Together* (2017); and the narrator of Nic Stone's *Dear Martin* (2014), Justyce, attends a prep academy rather than the public school in the "bad" neighborhood where he lives (10). All four of the authors of these novels are African American women, and all four of them seem to have lost faith in the public schools of the post-NCLB era. At the same time, however, in reproducing discourses that naturalize school privatization, these books risk eliding, if not erasing, the problematic racist histories behind that ideology. In doing so, they inadvertently evoke a social Darwinist view of schooling as they depict young people competing for access to education, with exceptional individuals prevailing at the expense of the less talented, thus ignoring that education is a fundamental human right. Even more, by focusing on talented individuals who manage to maximize their potential by attending private school, these books obscure the mass of students "left behind" through no fault of their own. In the sections that follow, we examine two books for teenagers—Jackson's *Monday's Not Coming*, again, and Jerry Craft's *New Kid*—which, we argue, offer stark critiques of school privatization in our neoliberal era.

CHARTER SCHOOLS IN *MONDAY'S NOT COMING*

Written in the long wake of No Child Left Behind, *Monday's Not Coming* puts significant energy into describing the narrator's charter middle school and her desire to gain entrance to the best possible charter high school. Despite its otherwise thoughtful critique of systemic racism, the book does not interrogate the sociohistorical, political, and economic conditions that led to the creation of charter schools. However, it is nonetheless critical of a system that regards education as yet another commodity over which young people must compete for access.

In Jackson's novel, Claudia and Monday attend Warren Kent Charter School and plan to apply to the prestigious Benjamin Banneker High School the following year, as it is highly regarded for its excellent academic program and its status as "one of the top ten selective schools" in Washington, DC— "selective meaning tough" (71). Despite the school's competitive admission standards, which include maintaining a 3.0 GPA, earning a score of proficient on a citywide standardized test, receiving strong letters of recommendation from a principal as well as English and math teachers, and sitting for an extended interview (71), Claudia is willing to submit herself to the process not because she covets the opportunities the high school offers students, but rather, because she is unable to imagine being apart from Monday, who has her eye set on attending Banneker.

Although Warren Kent Charter School is also well-respected, the novel is critical of a privatized education system whose obsession with standards and notability puts it at risk of failing the very people it is entrusted with serving. On several occasions, the novel implies that teachers and counselors at Warren Kent Charter School are overworked. For example, when Claudia visits Ms. Valente, her seventh grade English teacher, who must teach fifth grade and serve as team leader due to a staff shortage, the student finds her former teacher hurriedly grading papers in advance of a committee meeting at which she will help to select students for admission the following school year. Claudia expresses surprise that the admissions process begins so early, so her overwhelmed teacher tells her, "Work never stops around here" (226). On another occasion, when Ms. Valente accompanies Claudia to the front office to inquire about Monday's whereabouts, the teacher is surprised to learn that neither Monday nor her brother August nor her younger sister are enrolled in school. Ms. Valente tells a secretary, "I know I've only been in this school for a couple of years, but back in New York, when a student doesn't show up in class nor register for school, the school follows up"; the woman disinterestedly promises "to pass a note along" (49).

These shortcomings are incongruent with the image that charter schools such as Warren Kent and Banneker High School present to the public through sleek marketing campaigns that portray them as superior alternatives to the city's struggling public schools. Monday's older sister, April, appears to have internalized the latter narrative, as evidenced when she asks Claudia, "Did I ever tell you that I was the one who signed [Monday] up for the school lotto?" (392). April continues, "She was so smart. Reading books, like real books, when she was four. It would've been stupid for her to go to some *regular school* and not learn anything. Got on the computer at the library and signed her up. Even filled out the paperwork" (392, emphasis added). April's confidence in Warren Kent's superiority to public schools is so strong that she is willing to prostitute her body to ensure that her younger siblings can afford the cost of purchasing school uniforms and other supplies. Eventually, however, the book reveals that the faith that April and other adults place in the school is misguided.

When Monday disappears and Claudia's grades begin slipping, readers, along with Claudia's parents, learn that Monday has been doing virtually all Claudia's coursework for her for several years because the latter is dyslexic. Although some teachers, such as Ms. Valente, are cognizant of Claudia's struggles with reading and writing, most of them nonetheless fail to take action, just as no teacher or counselor or administrator adequately follows up as to why Monday and her younger brother and sister are no longer in school. While it is certainly true that students can slip through the cracks in public schools as well, the novel draws a direct line between Warren Kent's obsession with maintaining its reputation and its desire to compete for future students and the revenue streams they represent. In so doing, it suggests that the school failed Claudia and the Charles children as fully as any underfunded public school might have. Accepting responsibility for her complicity in perpetuating Claudia's struggles, Ms. Valente tells her former student:

> I tried to bring it up before, but folks just told me to keep you moving. Everything about this school is driven by our ranking. No one has time to just take a moment and really *be* with our students. You're old enough to know this now, but sometimes, all you are to this school is a score that adds up with the overall score. And the higher the score, the better the reputation. (162–63, emphasis in the original)

As a consequence of the school's professional misconduct, Claudia's parents end up having to hire a private tutor for their daughter, placing an additional financial burden on them. Still worse, the parental abuse that Monday and her siblings are forced to endure is prolonged in part because school administrators, counselors, and teachers are too busy to follow up on these students' absence from school.

CHARTER SCHOOLS AND NEOLIBERAL RACISM IN JERRY CRAFT'S *NEW KID*

In 2020, Jerry Craft's critically acclaimed *New Kid* became the first graphic novel to receive the American Library Association's prestigious John Newbery Medal, which recognizes significant contributions to American literature for children. It is the story of Jordan Banks, a twelve-year-old African American boy who longs to attend art school to pursue his dream of becoming a professional cartoonist. Unfortunately for Jordan, his parents enroll him as a scholarship student at Riverside Academy Day School, an affluent, predominantly white private school that his mother likens to Harvard and that she characterizes as "one of the best schools in the entire state" (2). Due to the school's lack of diversity, Jordan's father is less enthusiastic about the prospect of sending their son there, although he agrees to do so to support his wife. As Jordan travels between his family's home in the racially and culturally diverse neighborhood of Washington Heights and the tonier Riverdale Academy, he experiences microaggressions from other students as well as teachers, which leads him to question who he is in these two vastly different settings.

Reflecting the faith that Americans have traditionally placed in schooling as an antidote for social problems, Jordan's mother insists that education is the key to economic and social mobility for Black people in a white supremacist society. Her reluctance to send Jordan to art school is driven in part by economic concerns; she worries that Jordan will struggle to earn a living as an artist and insists that he have a profession to fall back on. At the same time, as a Black woman who works for one of the world's largest publishing houses, Jordan's mother also understands that systemic oppression results in African Americans needing to prove they are far better than their white counterparts in order to overcome socioeconomic barriers and access the opportunities that accrue to those born with privilege. For example, she tells Jordan that only forty-eight of her company's 1,200 employees are Black people, and that "to be successful in corporate America, you have to know how to *play the game*" (96, emphasis added). Jordan's father shares his belief that it is harder for people of color to play that game because the elite whites who designed it "don't give you all the pieces or even teach you the rules" (96); his wife replies, "That's why it's important that Jordan learns the rules now. And *that's* what this school can do for us" (97, emphasis in the original). The topic of systemic racism is thus a central concern of the text.

In *Racism in the Neoliberal Era,* Hohle describes a tension that exists between schooling and neoliberalism: in a society that professes to value diversity, schools "want some diversity but not too much" (186). He continues, "Whites value diversity so long as actual relations with minorities are restricted to a minimal number of racially nonthreatening bodies" (*Racism* 186). Such is the case at the ostensibly progressive Riverdale Academy Day School, where Jordan is one of only a few students of color. On his first day of school, Andy, an obnoxious white student who regularly espouses racist sentiments toward his classmates, misnames Jordan, asking him, "So what sport do you play, *Gordon*? *And what are you anyway*?" (27, emphasis added). Although Jordan corrects him, Andy persists in calling him by the wrong name. A similar scene occurs later in the book when Ms. Rawle, Jordan's white homeroom teacher, calls Drew, another Black student in Jordan's class, Deandre, which is the name of an African American student she had previously taught and whom she describes as "a real handful" (60). Initially, Drew assumes that his teacher merely made a mistake. Like Andy, however, Ms. Rawle continues to misname Drew, and on one occasion, she even embarrasses him and Jordan by inadvertently revealing that they receive financial aid to attend the school. Angered by Ms. Rawle's refusal to learn his name, Drew attempts to embarrass her in return to the whole class. When Jordan expresses disbelief that he would take such a risk, Drew tells him, "I'm starting not to care what Ms. Rawle thinks. She's never going to like me anyway. So I might as well give her what she wants, right?" (127), suggesting that he has begun to define himself according to expectations the institution holds for him. Unlike Jordan's mother, who understands attending an elite white private school as an opportunity for her son to learn the "rules" that operate in a society that is engineered to benefit white people, Drew shares his grandmother's less urbane worldview. As he tells Jordan, "She says that in order to become successful one day, I need to get used to being a 'fly in the buttermilk'!" (88).

The erasure of people's racial and cultural identities we have described in *New Kid* is not limited to interactions between students. Teachers are victims of racial microaggressions as well. When Mr. Garner, one of the few Black teachers at Riverdale Academy, encounters Jordan in the hallway and asks how he is adapting to his new school, Jordan replies, "Okay, except they keep calling me and Drew by the *wrong* names"; shortly after Mr. Garner reassures Jordan by telling him, "I wouldn't read anything into it. I'm sure it's only because you're new" (61, emphasis in the original), a white teacher passes the pair in the hallway and mistakes Mr. Garner for Riverdale's soccer coach, who is also Black. When Jordan tells his teacher, "Oh, so then you must be new, too," a visibly upset Mr. Garner replies, "I've been here *fourteen years*," suggesting that while Riverdale Academy professes to value diversity and inclusion, its commitment to those ideals is only performative (62, emphasis in the original).

Less obvious is *New Kid*'s critique of the role that systemic inequalities play in producing discrepancies between the conditions and material resources to which Black students in underfunded urban public schools and white students in private schools like Riverdale Academy have access. When Kirk, an African American teenager from Jordan's neighborhood, visits him at home to play video games, he and Jordan compare their experiences at their new schools. Jordan is surprised to learn that only a week before, a student at Kirk's public school brought a loaded gun into the building "for protection," only to have it confiscated by school security guards (144). When Kirk downplays the dangers that Jordan and other students confront at Riverdale Academy, Jordan pokes fun at the school, saying, "Are you kidding?! Last week they found a *Snickers* bar in this kid's locker. . . . We're a nut-free school, son. That thing was *packin'*, all right . . . packed with peanuts" (144, emphasis in the original). With this cynical humor, the book critiques the inequitable conditions that confront public school students in one of America's wealthiest cities.

New Kid also calls attention to the role that socioeconomic disparities play in shaping the educational opportunities (or lack thereof) that are available to Black and white students in the US. Unlike Jordan and Drew, whose socioeconomic status necessitates their staying home in Washington Heights and the Bronx, respectively, during school breaks, their wealthier classmates accompany their families on expensive trips to exotic destinations such as Hawaii, Aspen, Jackson Hole, and Alaska. Riverside Academy organizes educational enrichment activities for students, including weekend field trips, although Jordan and Drew are unable to participate in them because of the expense. In some cases, students' ability to take part in school activities is limited by their access to the prerequisite resources. For example, despite being a talented athlete, Drew lacks experience with Riverdale's spring sports offerings, which include baseball, lacrosse, tennis, crew, and fencing. As Jordan explains, Drew's lack of experience playing sports like baseball isn't attributable to a lack of interest on his part, but rather to the fact that "where he lives, there are even fewer parks than where I live" (190). In the absence of a local field on which to play baseball, Drew is unable to participate in the sport. On the other hand, his white classmates excel at activities such as downhill skiing, tennis, lacrosse, and golf because their families are able to offer them access to resources and spaces needed to participate in them.

COLORISM, COMMODIFICATION, AND STRUCTURAL RACISM IN ALICIA D. WILLIAMS'S *GENESIS BEGINS AGAIN*

Of course, *New Kid* is not the only literary text for teenagers to critique imbalances between inner-city (predominately Black and Latinx) schools and suburban (predominately white) schools. These differences are also spelled out in Alicia D. Williams's *Genesis Begins Again*, which is set in Detroit, Michigan. When thirteen-year-old Genesis and her family are evicted for the fourth time, they move to a Detroit suburb where Genesis attends, for the first time, a well-run school with more white students than students of color. It has only one Black teacher. Reflecting the significant differential in urban and suburban public school funding, Genesis and her mother immediately notice "the newness, the foreignness of this place. So far we haven't spotted a broken window or even a single ceiling tile caving in. Shoot, a school like this probably will never have lead in their water fountains" (51). Genesis describes how in previous schools, she has been "mean-mugged by the scariest, shoved by the toughest, picked on, made friends, then dumped by the best of 'em" (70). The Detroit public schools are not even reliable about supplying toilet paper, according to Genesis (142). In that regard, the novel depicts Detroit's inner-city public schools as underfunded, decrepit, environmentally dangerous, and sometimes unsafe, all because of being so chronically underfunded in the name of budget austerity. At the same time, however, *Genesis Begins Again* interrogates the connection between economics, competition, and colorism, a topic we turn to in this section.

Social-class issues within the African American community are exacerbated by *colorism*, defined by Alice Walker as "prejudicial or preferential treatment of same race people based solely on their color" (290). Writing within the context of children's literary criticism, Rudine Sims Bishop further explains: "Racism by its very nature is so insidious that some Black people have internalized negative attitudes, left over from the days of slavery, toward themselves and their appearance. Thus, lighter skin color and straight hair have often been more highly valued even among Black people than darker skin and kinky hair" (*Free* 231). Wanda Brooks and her coauthors, also writing about children's literature, make clear that colorism crosses racial demographics. They define *colorism* as "inter- and intraracial discrimination based on skin color stratification" (660). In the case of interracial colorism, members of one racial group distinguish between members of another racial group based on the color of their skin. Intraracial colorism, on the other hand, refers to members of the same racial group distinguishing between members based on gradations in their skin color.

Sociologist Margaret L. Hunter acknowledges that colorism is not only a phenomenon that affects Black people: "Hidden within the process of racial discrimination is the often overlooked issue of colorism. Lighter-skinned African Americans and Mexican Americans enjoy substantial privileges that are still unattainable to their darker-skinned brothers and sisters"; she adds, "Colorism is a problem affecting all Americans" (1). Nikki Khanna, another sociologist, delineates the pervasiveness of colorism among Asians and Asian Americans, demonstrating how women, in particular, are targeted for skin-lightening products that "conjure images of whiteness and its explicit link to beauty, flawlessness, and femininity" (2). She describes how, "throughout Asia, Africa, Latin America, and the Middle East, advertisements for skin-whitening products are aimed at consumers, most notably women, who are routinely told that their dark skin is unattractive and a social liability" (3). As a result, "neoliberalism maintains and reinforces systemic colorism and White-supremacy within local cultures across the globe" (Bettache, Chiu, and Beattie 218).

The texture of one's hair is also a topic of discussion among those concerned with colorism. Latasha N. Eley, for example, argues that "Black women are confronted with dominant beauty ideals regarding preferential skin hue and hair texture—that light skin and long, straight hair is superior to and preferred over darker skin and any length of tightly curled, afro-textured or styled hair—to cement their position as other in society" (78). Kimberly Jade Norwood and Violeta Solonova Foreman argue that this valuing of white skin persists today despite evolving understandings of race in the US, with the result that "the closer one's skin tone is to white, the better one's chances of success" (18). They note that "this distinction has had very damning effects" on Black Americans and young Black girls, in particular (19).

Cedric Herring and Anthony Hynes draw a direct connection between colorism and economic and social opportunities when they cite research that suggests "lighter-skinned people of color enjoy greater economic and social success and substantial privileges that are often unattainable to their darker-skinned brothers and sisters"; they argue that in addition to other advantages, "light-skinned people earn more money, complete more years of schooling, live in better neighborhoods, and marry higher-status people than darker-skinned people of the same race" (5–6). As critical race theorist Robert L.

Reece asserts, "the prevailing view of colorism revolves around individual discrimination and prejudice with little attention to structural mechanisms" (20)—such as those created by neoliberalism. Social psychologist Karim Bettache observes that colorism existed prior to colonialism; he notes that in some cultures, pale skin was historically linked with not being required to labor in the sun, while more recent Western colorism links tanned skin to being able to afford leisure time, so colorism in Asia belongs in a matrix that includes classism and/or colonialized racism (1132–33). Reece describes this as a tension between "preference and prejudice" (6). The "structural mechanisms" and prejudices Reece mentions indubitably include neoliberal ideology.

Yet despite a wealth of evidence that points to the roles interracial and intraracial colorism play in creating different life opportunities for people with lighter and darker skin, proponents of neoliberalism are bent on erasing the impacts of race and racism by celebrating meritocracy and individual exceptionalism as the final arbiters of people's success. To do so, they depend on the notion of *postrace* discourse, which became prevalent during Barack Obama's presidency, and which erroneously avers that, thanks to the hard-won victories of the civil rights movement, American society has progressed to a point at which race no longer impacts a person's life chances. To undo racial stratification that is attributable to racism and colorism, neoliberals resort to "power-evasive strategies such as blaming minorities of class and color for not working hard enough" (Giroux 193). In this way, neoliberalism recasts *structural* problems such as racism as *individual* problems. The result is a system that situates people who aren't perceived as contributing to society (e.g., immigrants, people with disabilities, the elderly, people receiving social welfare, etc.) as disposable. Given our understanding of neoliberalism and the fallacy of postrace discourse, we argue that texts that erase or ignore color hierarchies are problematic because they risk separating the material consequences of race from the social systems that produce them. In the following section, we examine how *Genesis Begins Again* explicitly resists neoliberal postrace discourse by calling young readers' attention to the role that color hierarchies play in producing and maintaining social inequalities.

RESISTING POSTRACE DISCOURSE THROUGH EMPHASIZING COLOR HIERARCHIES

In the opening chapter of *Genesis Begins Again*, the eponymous protagonist experiences colorism at the hands of a group of popular Black girls in her

Detroit public school. Having only recently befriended her, when these new friends see the furniture of Genesis's family spread out on their front lawn after they have been evicted, they turn on her, mocking her and resorting to calling her names such as "Eggplant" and "Charcoal," as they often have in the past, in reference to her dark pigmentation. As a result of such treatment, Genesis, like the adolescent protagonist of Toni Morrison's *The Bluest Eye*, loathes her own looks, including her "wide nose" and "big lips" and "nappy" hair, and she asks herself, "*Who you think's gonna love you with the way you look?*" (Williams 10, emphasis in the original). She is haunted as well by comments her father, who is also dark-skinned, once made when he drunkenly berated her, comparing her to her light-skinned mother, whom other people regard as beautiful. In a drunken rage, he castigates his daughter, saying, "*You were supposed to come out lookin' like her ... look at you with yo' black—*"; he does not finish his inherently racist sentence (14, emphasis in the original, ellipsis in the original). Unable to release this painful memory (14, 112, 206, 296, 355), Genesis wishes she had her mother's lighter skin and bigger eyes even more than her father seems to.

When her father surprises the family by leasing a home from a coworker in a predominantly white neighborhood in suburban Detroit, Genesis enrolls at a new school with few African American students, one of whom refers to her as "burnt" (56). Genesis then becomes even more desperate to lighten her skin. To do so, she experiments with a variety of remedies, including bathing in milk, rubbing lemon juice all over her body, bathing in water with bleach, even scrubbing her skin with a stainless steel sponge. When she one day happens upon bleaching creams online, she is surprised to discover a host of websites that "show women all the way in Jamaica, Africa, India, and Korea, all using bleaching creams. Hundreds and hundreds of women, no, maybe thousands, all feel the same as me.... She can't stand being this black" (273). Ultimately, the cream Genesis orders doesn't lighten her skin as much as it creates light-color blotches that make her look "spotted," but she has nonetheless managed to spend money, stolen from her mother, so that she can conform to standards boosted by commercialism (331).

In addition to lightening her skin, Genesis also longs for straight hair like her mother's. She is humiliated when another Black girl at her new school tells her, "I can smell your cooked hair," referring to how her mother has straightened her hair with a hot pressing comb. Noting that her own mother spends a "ridiculous" amount of money on hair and hair products, the same girl offers to straighten Genesis's hair with a chemical relaxer, which Genesis allows her to do (255, 275). The relaxer burns like "fire" (305), but she is satisfied after the ordeal is over because her hair feels "like white people's hair....

It falls down on my shoulders, smooth as silk. I give my head the slightest of shakes, and my hair moves with it!" (306). Genesis's mother is opposed to chemical relaxers as well as lightening creams, and she eventually grounds Genesis for using these products—and for buying the skin-lightener on her credit card without permission. Yet while her mother admonishes Genesis for subscribing to an "old" and "*wrong* way of thinking" (212, emphasis in the original), Genesis suggests that her mother "believes it at least a little," as evidenced by her "complaining about doing my hair, calling it 'that head' or 'tangly mess'" (212), or "when she describes someone dark complexioned and adds: 'But he or she's still good looking.' Mama may not mean it; in fact, I know she doesn't, but it's there, under the surface" (212–13).

The book implies that Genesis has acquired her obsession with light skin and straight hair in part from her parents. The tragedy that compels her self-loathing is her perception that her father also loathes her, when in reality, he despises himself for his own dark skin. The reader, along with Genesis, eventually learns that her father's internalized racism is attributable to verbal abuse he endured from his own mother, who blamed him for the death of his older brother, whom she favored for his fairer skin. She tells Genesis's father that she wishes he had been the one to die, and she callously writes off her younger son as a "never-gon'-amount-to-nothin'-like-yo'-black-nappy-headed-triflin' daddy" (356). To escape his tortured childhood memories, Genesis's father eventually turns to drink, with the result that he is unable to hold down a job or provide for his family.

On the other hand, Genesis learns that the insidious tradition of intra-racial racism and white colorism on her maternal grandmother's side of the family is attributable to economics and competition rather than being solely a function of parental disapprobation. To this grandmother the issue involves social mobility. She tells Genesis:

> "My grandpa, he knew enough not to break his back. He sold insurance.... Then he realized something—most of [his customers] weren't just regular brown- or light-skin men, but [. . .]" Grandma stops herself....
> "My grandpa understood that the only way we were going to stay ahead, as a family, was if we marry up." (150, bracketed ellipsis in the original)

In using the phrase "marry up," Genesis's grandmother is referring to her own grandfather's insistence that all four of his granddaughters marry men lighter-skinned than they so that their offspring could, over generations, have the type of competitive economic advantages that lighter skin conferred. She tells her granddaughter: "Understand that my grandpapa was a forward thinker. Our lineage is full of doctors and professors and successful businessmen. It's not luck, Genesis" (152).

Lest her granddaughter fail to appreciate that her ancestors' ability to enter the professional class was directly attributable to their lighter skin color, her grandmother adds that the people her grandfather "sold insurance to, those folks working in the mills and doing the hard manual labor were Black men. And, the poor sharecroppers? *Black* men" (150, emphasis in the original). Her grandmother goes on to describe how, after her own father took "one look" at her sister Elizabeth's new boyfriend, he stepped up to her "beau, held the [brown paper] bag next to his face, and dropped it right there in Elizabeth's lap. Then he marched out the house without saying a word. She knew what that meant" (151). Elizabeth is eventually disowned for marrying a man with skin darker than that paper bag, and years later, Genesis's grandmother "pulled out a brown bag" for Genesis's father. She tells Genesis, "Your mother—she didn't care anything about tradition and sacrifice. . . . You must understand—it was never anything personal. It's just [. . .] look around. Who's getting arrested? Who gets the worst jobs? Don't you see, honey? My papa didn't make the rules; he just understood them" (153, bracketed ellipsis in the original). Unbeknownst to Grandma, however, Genesis's mother has also suffered because of colorism. She tells her daughter: "People called me 'stuck-up' and 'Lite-Brite,' and a whole bunch of other names. . . . I hated it 'cause at school it was, 'Oh, you think you're cute,' and 'You think you're better than everybody, I'mma beat you up.' I got all that" (210). Genesis's mother loves having "a chocolate baby" because she has hoped Genesis would not also be taunted at school (210). Ironically, Genesis ends up chastising herself for making racist assumptions about a girl with light skin in her choir class who chooses to wear her hair in dreadlocks. Realizing that she is only perpetuating her grandmother's "stupid tradition," Genesis elects not to do so further (254).

Genesis ultimately comes to recognize the danger of hating herself after her African American friend Troy rails at her for using the skin-lightening cream: "What you're doing, that's not a solution. You're still gonna be Black. You'll still be called names" (311). She wonders: "Why I hate *me*? Gosh, I feel stupid. Stupid for the cream, bleach bath, exfoliation, lemons—all of it. . . . I've been caught up in the hype and what everybody thought of me, and I'm tired of it. I just want to look in the mirror and be okay with myself. That's all" (363). Here, "hype" puts the focus specifically on the economic nature of a swindle and the predatory nature of this type of commercial product ("hype, *n.*"). Genesis's epiphany also rests on her recognition that everyone is suffering from some form of painful memories: "Everybody's in pain" (361). Her self-acceptance is framed, importantly, as transcending both her appearance and her working-class background.

CONCLUSION

Like *Genesis Begins Again*, *Firekeeper's Daughter*, which we analyzed in chapter 3, nuances color ideologies. In both novels, however, the characters only do so after acknowledging the internalized racism they must live with. For example, in *Firekeeper's Daughter*, Daunis derisively refers to the "Acceptable Anishinaabe Skin Tone Continuum" as a way of describing colorism in the US. She explains that when her friend Lily "lived with her Zhaaganaash [white] dad and his wife, they kept her out of the sun so her reddish-brown skin wouldn't get any darker. We both learned early on that there is an Acceptable Anishinaabe Skin Tone Continuum, and those who land on its outer edges have to put up with different versions of the same bullshit" (13). Because her mother is white, some members of her Ojibwe tribe call Daunis "ghost" or "washed-out" (13) or "White Sheep" (30) to emphasize that she is paler than the "medium" register on the "Acceptable Skin Tone Continuum" (102). Lily, on the other hand, is "reddish-brown," so the two look like "opposites" (13). Daunis's Aunt Dora refers to Daunis's "light skin" as a "privilege," one that her own twin daughters do not share because they are mixed-race Ojibwe and African American (79). For her part, Daunis concedes that she is the beneficiary of "advantages I've done nothing to earn, they are privileges" (79). The colorism these girls experience occurs both with Native people and other white people.

Many YA novels published in the neoliberal era depict characters who discuss skin tone in ways that either assert or imply that "white" skin is superior to "nonwhite" skin; these books will often address hair texture as problematic, too. In *Piecing Me Together*, Jade derides her own "coal skin" (Watson 7) and is irritated when a white friend does not believe that she has been discriminated against in a store in Portland because she is Black; Jade thinks that her "hips and lips, hair and nose" all need to be "fixed" (85). Similarly, in Erika L. Sánchez's *I Am Not Your Perfect Mexican Daughter* (2017), set in Chicago, the narrator, Julia, contrasts herself with her mother and sister, who are "pale and thin" with long straight hair: "I'm chubby, short, and dark[-skinned]" (22). Her best friend dyes her hair multiple different colors, but as the two girls grow in self-acceptance, they both stop trying to use the marketplace to change their embodiment, as is evidenced when Julia's friend returns her hair to its natural brown color—admittedly, by dying it back to its original color at first (334). In the novel's final sentence, Julia says: "I learned to find pieces of myself—both beautiful and ugly" (340). Significantly, her least favorite teacher is a white man who has "a dumb Ronald Reagan quote" posted in his classroom (35).

Dimple, the Indian American narrator of Tanuja Desai Hidier's *Born Confused* (2002) feels that she was "born different—it started from the skin and seeped all the way in" (82). Dimple lives in New Jersey. Her aunt thinks she should be "exfoliating on a regular basis to lighten [her] skin" (11), and that aunt's daughter is deemed to be too "dark" to be eminently marriageable (101). The most beautiful Indian woman that Dimple has ever seen has long, straight hair and light-colored skin, "like sunrise on sand dune" (201). Dimple longs for straight hair, and she compares herself continuously to her blonde, blue-eyed friend Gwyn. Gwyn's attempt to co-opt the culture of India so that she can date an Indian American boy is cringeworthy. Gwyn even says, "I can't change my skin color, but I can change everything else" (278). Hidier's novel exemplifies the self-hatred of colorism too prevalent—as the scholar Sriya Shrestha has observed about Asian and Asian American women—in a complicated admixture of ancient sociohistorical forces, colonialism, neoliberalism, gender, and race (104–19).

An Na's *The Fold* (2008) traces the ethics of an expensive surgical procedure, blepharoplasty, which is a form of plastic surgery that Asian American women increasingly underwent starting in the neoliberal era (Kaw 74–89), even though the surgery has been available since 1896 (Lim). Joyce, a Korean American teenager, is offered the surgery to make her eyes look more Euro-American after her aunt wins the lottery. The novel is careful to trace the ethics, including the economic ethics, of having such a surgery, which Joyce ultimately decides against. Nonetheless, it also demonstrates neoliberal socioeconomic pressures to change one's body to adhere to white beauty standards. Joyce even asks herself, "Would she want to change her knees or her skin next?" (216).

Lilliam Rivera's *The Education of Margot Sanchez*—another 2017 YA novel with a protagonist who attends a private prep school—also addresses colorism in the Latinx community; her family takes great pride in their light-colored skin, as opposed to Gabi, the eponymous narrator of Isabel Quintero's *Gabi: A Girl in Pieces* (2014), who has this to say about herself: "My skin is there for all to see and point at and judge. Guerra. Casper. Ghost. Freckle Face. Ugly. Whitey. White Girl. Gringa. I've been called all of those names. Skin that doesn't make me Mexican enough. Skin that always makes people say, 'You're not what a Mexican's supposed to look like'" (35–36). Gabi hates having to explain her heritage to people, and she hates even worse when people say racist things in front of her, assuming that she is Euro-American. Her family is caught in a cycle of poverty made worse by her father's meth addiction, so the story contains within it a critique of the severe class disparities that especially affect communities of color.

In chapter 2, we discussed the falsely positioned oppositional binaries that lead to the exploitation of the Earth and its peoples; in this chapter, we have discussed deeply problematic effects of racism as depicted in a variety of YA novels. In the next chapter, we analyze another false oppositional binary that is interlinked with those we have discussed in the preceding chapters: constructions of gender as a neoliberally exploited oppositional binary.

Chapter 5

RESISTING POSTFEMINIST THINKING

I'll be a postfeminist in a postpatriarchy.

—Misha Kavka (29)

On August 15, 2008, a YA novel published five months earlier received a glowing write-up in the *New York Times Book Review*. The review celebrated the book for giving "hope that a girl like [the eponymous protagonist]—who has above all an unwillingness to settle—could grow up to change the world" (Freitas). The book went on to win the American Library Association's Printz Award for YA literature in January 2009, but never made the *New York Times* Best Sellers list.

A month later, in September of the same year, a second YA novel that initially received only a few positive critical reviews *did* make it onto the *Times* Best Sellers list for children's chapter books, two weeks after it was published, no less ("Best Sellers List," September 9, 2008). The YA author John Green reviewed this novel positively two months later. This leads us to ask: "Why was one book so well-received by literary critics but not the market, and the other so well-received by both?"

We argue that a distinguishing factor in the reception of these two books was the Great Recession that began in September of 2008. The most significant economic crisis since the Great Depression, it placed considerable stress on families in the US and abroad, and by extension, impacted countless children and teenagers. Furthermore, it eroded public confidence, even if only temporarily, in neoliberalism and trickle-down economics. For example, the short-lived Occupy Movement, which originated in New York City on September 17, 2011, was in part a response to the failures of the "1 percent," who, according to the Brookings Institute, controlled one-third of the nation's total wealth at the time (Sawhill).

So what about those two YA novels published in 2008? The first, which was critically but not commercially successful, was *The Disreputable History of Frankie Landau-Banks*, by E. Lockhart. Set in a posh New England boarding school, the novel depicts the privileged sons and daughters of the wealthy, who largely subscribe to Reaganism and its false promise of the "trickle-down" effects of their wealth onto others in the economy, and who are often blind to the privilege their social status confers on them. The second, which was both commercially and critically successful, is characterized by its own flaws, but we speculate that it succeeded with a mainstream audience in part because it venerated not the power of the one percent, but rather those who suffer in a society characterized by extreme wealth inequality. In the latter book, the protagonist, in particular, emerges from an impoverished working-class family to lead a revolution against an oppressive ruling class. That novel was *The Hunger Games*, by Suzanne Collins, and it went on to inspire a lucrative book series, movie franchise, and adult theme parks in Saudi Arabia and China.

Despite the differences in their commercial success, both of these books—the first a work of realism, the second a dystopia—feature strong female characters who resist conforming to their societies' traditional gender norms. Instead, they rely on the female protagonists' superior intellect, innate sense of competition, and sexual desirability as they compete against males, often besting them. In doing so, these girls appear to be the beneficiaries of the social gains the feminist movement secured for girls and women in the twentieth- and twenty-first-centuries. Discussing this phenomenon in YA dystopian fiction specifically, Sonya Sawyer Fritz celebrates the arrival of "girls who resist the forces of their broken and corrupt societies to create their own identities, shape their own destinies, and transform the worlds in which they live" (17). For Sawyer Fritz and other critics, these new girls—alternately referred to as "girls on fire" (Hentges)—appear to offer twenty-first-century readers a more progressive and empowered model of girlhood.

Smart, strong, girls-on-fire proliferate in contemporary popular culture. Well-known examples include Rey in the Star Wars sequel trilogy (2015, 2017, 2019), Clarke Griffin and Octavia Blake in the television series *The 100* (2014–20), Mirabel and her sister Luisa in Disney's *Encanto* (2021), Shuri in Marvel's Black Panther film franchise (2018, 2022), and the adult doll depicted in Greta Gerwig's *Barbie* (2023). Indeed, our students have come of age in a media environment that is saturated with images of smart, strong girls who do it all and have it all, which may explain why so many of them continue to say some of the same things about feminism in the 2020s that their counterparts said in the late 1990s and the first decade of this century, when characters such as Hermione, Frankie Landau-Banks, and Katniss first appeared in books for teenagers.

Despite these putative strides, when we ask our undergraduate students to define feminism, they often invoke injunctions about femininity placed solely on the female body. Many students identifying as female don't want to be feminists, they argue, because then they wouldn't be able to wear bras or makeup; they couldn't shave their legs or armpits; they couldn't oppose abortion; and they couldn't marry (let alone like!) men. When Roberta points out that she considers herself a feminist, even though she wears makeup and lipstick, pantyhose, a dress, nice shoes, and yes—even a brassiere!—when she teaches, students seem confused (and slightly mortified at the mention of her bra). The news of her happily married husband of more than thirty years, two sons, and a beloved twin brother, all of whom consider themselves to be feminists, as does Sean, also surprises students because sometimes even those who call themselves feminists tend to assume that only people who identify as female can qualify to be feminists. Most disturbing, the majority of both our students assume that feminists are not interested in working toward gender equality; rather, many of them falsely believe that feminists advocate solely for the superiority of women over men. They are not alone in that assumption, as evidenced by a 2014 social media movement in which girls and young women used the hashtag #WomenAgainstFeminism to explain why they neither wanted nor needed feminism. While the #MeToo movement that gained solid momentum in 2017 counterbalanced much of that type of anti-feminist sentiment, many of our students, males as well as females, nevertheless claim that feminism has outlived its usefulness. In a similar vein, some pundits rely on the same rationale to erroneously situate US gender politics using a misnomer, as if this truly were a "*post*feminist" society.[1]

In this chapter, we argue that neoliberalism, which emphasizes meritocratic competition as the engine that drives all social progress, depends in part on the notion of *postfeminism* for support, much as we suggested it does a myth of postracialism in the previous chapter.[2] After all, to accept the argument that people should have to compete in the marketplace for goods, services, and access to life opportunities such as education and a living wage, one presumably has to believe that everyone competes on equal footing. With that in mind, in the next section of this chapter, we draw on the work of feminist scholars to examine the relationship between postfeminist thinking and neoliberalism. We then identify a series of questions that we argue readers can ask of books for teenagers to assess the extent to which they reproduce or resist postfeminism, and hence, more broadly, neoliberalist ideologies.

Having established these questions, we offer a close reading of E. Lockhart's *The Disreputable History of Frankie Landau-Banks* to demonstrate how, in spite of its progressive and feminist intentions, the book reproduces a postfeminist worldview that is actually oppressive to those who identify as girls and women. In the sections that follow, we examine Nigerian American author Nnedi Okorafor's Nsibidi Script trilogy as a counterexample of postfeminist logic. We demonstrate how that series resists postfeminist ideology by calling attention to the role that patriarchal structures play in advantaging men over women and setting humans above the natural world. To conclude this chapter, we connect Okorafor's depiction of environmental and conservation topics to issues that we have examined in previous chapters, most notably, neoliberalism's exploitation of the Earth, of racialized peoples, and of women. We pay particularly close attention to what ecofeminist theory offers to literary interpretations that reject neoliberalism and postfeminist politics.

EXAMINING POSTFEMINISM AS A FUNCTION OF NEOLIBERALISM

Although some scholars argue over the definition of the term *postfeminism*, we use it in this chapter to refer to a set of assumptions that suggest society has progressed to a point when gender ostensibly raises no obstacle for educational, professional, and social advancement.[3] We argue—as have others before us, such as Rosalind Gill and Christina Scharff (1–20), Maria Adamson (314–27), Shauna Pomerantz and Rebecca Raby (287–311), and Melissa Yoong (27–41)—that postfeminism and neoliberalism are closely associated. Indeed, one could argue that because of its meritocratic worldview, neoliberalism is reliant on postfeminism for support.

To some extent, our students cannot be blamed for their acceptance of postfeminist logic. In her book *Future Girl: Young Women in the Twenty-First Century*, Anita Harris demonstrates how Western corporations co-opted the concept of "Girl Power," which originated with the Riot Grrl feminist punk movement in the early 1990s and refashioned it to reflect neoliberalism's ideal girl subject: one who is consumer-driven, independent, flexible, multitalented, competitive, and resilient. Through their exposure to popular culture and corporate messaging, our students are awash in representations of neoliberal Girl Power and the butt-kicking girls who embody it, from Buffy to Hermione, from Zelda to Katniss, from Britney to Miley Ray (and let us not forget the Powerpuff Girls!). Katy Perry encourages girls to "Roar," and Beyoncé tells them that they "Run the World." In a direct reference to YA literature, Alicia Keys sings about the "Girl on Fire," who's "on top of the world," and who's "got her head in the clouds / And she's not backing down." Against this backdrop, many of our students have come to see themselves as the beneficiaries of "feminist achievement and ideology, as well as . . . new conditions that favor their success by allowing them to put these into practice" (Harris 8). In the process, they've learned to identify successful women by "their commitment to exceptional careers and career planning, their belief in their capacity to invent themselves and succeed, and their display of a consumer lifestyle" (Harris 14).

In many YA novels, the ideal girl subject is depicted as having it all: intelligence, independence, ferocity, beauty, good grades, popularity, sex appeal, and (heterosexual) romance. With the bar for success set so high, it's no wonder so many girls and young women report feeling exhausted from their quest for perfection, as Girlhood Studies scholars Shauna Pomerantz and Rebecca Raby demonstrate in their book *Smart Girls: Success, School, and the Myth of Post-Feminism*. The exhaustion felt by girls like those in Pomerantz and Raby's research study is a direct result of the way that postfeminism—sometimes also called "lipstick feminism"—contributes to the oppression of girls and women. Arianna Marchetti defines "lipstick feminism" as "a third wave feminist movement that supports the idea of accepting and embracing femininity to help women's empowerment," but she critiques the damaging ideology behind this concept:

> Lipstick feminism is clearly in line with a new mode of neoliberal female's citizenship, in which the achievement of a "glamourous individuality" is seen as the key to women's empowerment and success. . . .
>
> This strong individualism gets in the way of feminism as a social movement and subtly leads women into believing that their attitude, and their efforts in becoming a better version of themselves will eventually determine their success or failure. . . . In other words, women are offered sexual and social recognition in spheres of employment, education, and civil society, as long as young women successfully "choose" to embody acceptable hetero-femininities. (Marchetti)

McRobbie, in her influential article "Postfeminism and Popular Culture" (2007), characterizes postfeminism as a backlash against feminism that is specifically designed to undermine the latter movement's goals and accomplishments. She also describes the "double entanglement" (255) that is implicated in postfeminism: "the co-existence of neo-conservative values in relation to gender, sexuality and family life" being coincident with "processes of liberalisation in regard to choice and diversity in domestic, sexual and kinship relations" (255–56).

Building on McRobbie's work, Julie Wilson argues that "in the postfeminist, neoliberal milieu women must perform as self-entrepreneurial, self-promotional workers on equal footing with their male colleagues yet still be invested in and appear willing to perform traditional gender roles" (34). In other words, neoliberalism has appropriated progressive attitudes, such as the assumption that both husbands and wives will work outside of the home, while at the same time perpetuating traditional assumptions about gender roles: for example, that the majority of childrearing and domestic chores falls to women, or that the latter should spend small fortunes on their physical appearance. As a consequence, women are not only expected to juggle all of these roles, but to thrive in them effortlessly while also looking glamorously beautiful.

Connecting postfeminism to popular culture, McRobbie critiques films and television series—including many that appealed to teenage girls at the time they were released, such as *Bridget Jones's Diary* (2001) and *Sex in the City* (1998–2004)—to demonstrate how putatively self-empowered women who are financially independent and sexually liberated nevertheless still seek (heterosexual) romance and a "normal" life, all the while laughing ironically and self-consciously at their own failed feminist ideals. According to McRobbie, feminist "objection is preempted with irony" ("Postfeminism" 259). She continues:

> These popular texts normalise post-feminist gender anxieties so as to re-regulate young women by means of the language of personal choice. But even "well regulated liberty" can backfire (the source of comic effect), and this in turn gives rise to demarcated pathologies (leaving it too late to have a baby, failing to find a good catch, etc.) which carefully define the parameters of what constitutes liveable lives for young women without the occasion of re-invented feminism. (262)

McRobbie notes that while teenage girls and young women are depicted as having freedom in the postfeminist regime, they are also silenced in not being able to offer any criticism of sexism, the patriarchy, or the objectification of their own bodies (262).

How postfeminism intersects with neoliberalism, which also traffics in the language of choice, competition, and individual exceptionalism, is of central concern to our project. As we demonstrated in chapter 1, neoliberalism imagines a world in which all people and entities—individual citizens, small businesses, schools and corporations—are meant to exercise their unique talents in the service of competing against others free of external (i.e., government) regulation or interference. From this perspective, success is both merit-based and predicated on a person's ability to bootstrap: those who work hard and leverage their talents most effectively are rewarded for their efforts, while those who are less talented or successful are given cause to work harder. In the process, society is divided into two groups of people: winners and losers. But a wealth of evidence suggests that people do not compete on a level playing field. For example, children who grow up in poverty are statistically likely to stay poor, and wealthy parents are better able to provide their children with opportunities that further advantage them in life.[4] As a result, neoliberalism is faced with the challenge of explaining away (or even erasing) forms of systemic oppression that disadvantage some people and privilege others. In the face of systemic sexism, this is precisely why neoliberalism relies on postfeminist discourse to absolve itself of sin.

In their essay "Reading Smart Girls: Post-Nerds in Post-Feminist Popular Culture," Pomerantz and Raby demonstrate how popular television shows that center on teenage girl protagonists often emphasize individual choice and agency at the expense of acknowledging how sexism, racism, and other forms of systemic oppression impact women. They argue that "modern-day girlhood is now defined by individualism, consumerism, hypersexuality, and the belief that girls can do, be, and have anything they want without fear of structural inequalities such as sexism, racism, or homophobia interfering with their individual efforts to achieve success. As a consequence, *such structural inequities have now come to be seen as individual rather than social problems*" (288, emphasis added).

This is precisely why postfeminism is oppressive to girls and women: it not only papers over sexism and gender discrimination, but it also perpetuates the illusion that success is a purely individual accomplishment. If teenage girls and women, as neoliberal subjects, are understood to succeed as a result of their own hard work and talents, then by the same logic, they are also responsible for their own shortcomings and failures. To return to the anecdote we shared earlier, when students in our college classes subscribe to the assumption that in a postfeminist society, feminism has outlived its usefulness, they not only ignore the very real obstacles that gender discrimination and sexism continue to pose for girls and women in a patriarchal society, but they also reject the very social movement that is best positioned to help those who identify as girls and women remedy the systemic discrimination and oppression they experience.

At a time when a growing number of YA novels and television shows marketed to young people celebrate strong-willed, iconoclastic girls who, unencumbered by their society's gender norms, successfully compete against boys in virtually all domains of life, our experience as educators leads us to wonder whether college students, let alone teen readers, are fully prepared to interrogate the questions this raises. We are not alone in our concern. Meredith Heller, for example, asks several interrelated questions that are intended to help readers of YA literature identify suspect postfeminist characters.

Sona Snircova adds even more nuance to investigating postfeminism when she observes that second wave feminism aligns with "victimary thinking" and third wave feminism with "neoliberal feminism" in terms of power and agency, especially in the ways that the third wave questions the traditional binary of the woman as victim, allowing her to become instead a perpetrator in her own right (91). For example, Snircova analyzes Helen Cross's *My Summer of Love* (2001) in terms of postfeminism. In that novel, two older adolescent girls "support the power feminists' point that impulses towards aggressive, selfish and violent behaviour are integral to female identity and more traditional feminist images of a girl as an innocent victim of patriarchal evils" (Snircova 99). This tendency to depict girls as predatory might well arise from what Jessica Ringrose refers to as cultural "panic" over successful girls, sexy girls, and aggressive girls that "shape oppositional representations of girls as *either* empowered consumers/winners *or* vulnerable victims of sexualised society" (4, emphasis in the original). Ringrose's dialectic also parallels the tension that McRobbie traces between the entrepreneurial, aggressive girl and the more traditional, albeit ironically self-reflective, girl who seeks traditionally feminine roles.

In light of the issues the aforementioned scholars raise, we encourage readers to consider the following questions as they evaluate neoliberal representations of postfeminism in YA literature.

1. Is the female protagonist an exceptional individual, especially in terms of her being more entrepreneurial and/or competitive than other characters?
2. Does the female protagonist address conflicts or social problems she faces individually, or does she instead collaborate with others to do so?
3. Does the female protagonist gain power over people by manipulating and victimizing them, or does she instead share power with others?
4. Is the female protagonist's physical appearance emphasized, and if so, toward what end? (see also Heller)

5. Are bodies turned into commodities without critique? Are they objectified for the viewing or sensual pleasure of others, as if this objectification is empowering to females?
6. Do postfeminist visions of the autonomous feminist protagonist commingle with traditional values, especially those revolving around gender norms, such as childcare, housework, and sexuality? (see also Heller)
7. Does the female protagonist appear to value independence and nevertheless yearn, either in self-parodic or earnest terms, to be partnered romantically with a man?
8. Does the female protagonist have only one mentor? Or does she have a group of mentors, including more than one woman?
9. Does the female protagonist have more than one girlfriend? If she has only one friend, does that friend survive by the end of the novel or series (Childs 188)?
10. Does the novel erase sexism (and racism, classism, etc.), as though equality for all has already been achieved? (see also Heller)

Over the remainder of this chapter, we use these questions to situate works of YA literature with seemingly strong female protagonists along a spectrum that ranges from overtly neoliberal postfeminist novels to a trilogy that appears to be less so. As we argue in other chapters of this book, we find it useful to think of YA novels as existing along a continuum, as opposed to designating them as either entirely neoliberal and postfeminist or entirely free of these problematic ideologies, since so few novels have yet been able to completely transcend the oppressive gender norms to which feminism still objects.

A NEOLIBERAL NOVEL ABOUT GENDER:
THE DISREPUTABLE HISTORY OF FRANKIE LANDAU-BANKS

The Disreputable History of Frankie Landau-Banks, by E. Lockhart, exemplifies how a novel that overtly strives to be feminist can still fall prey to the trap of postfeminism and its neoliberal machinations. In this novel, Frankie is a sophomore at an exclusive prep school in northern Massachusetts, Alabaster Preparatory Academy. Alabaster's most notorious secret society calls itself the Loyal Order of the Basset Hounds. Because it is an entirely male fraternal group, Frankie objects to the Basset Hounds on feminist principles—or at least, that is one of the rationalizations that she uses to justify her actions in the story. She is also irritated that Matthew Livingston, the group's president and her romantic interest, is unable (if not unwilling) to appreciate her intellect, cleverness, and wit. To prove her merit to Matthew, Frankie elects to disrupt a lackluster prank the Basset Hounds have planned for Halloween. Buoyed by the school-wide attention her more outrageous prank ends up drawing, Frankie clandestinely leads the Basset Hounds in conducting ever more elaborate stunts, several of which engage in social critique. Hesitant to tell the other boys that he is not, in fact, responsible for conceiving the pranks, Alpha—Matthew's best friend and the unofficial leader of the secret society—instead chooses to remain quiet while trying to unmask his imposter. When campus security discovers him in a tunnel beneath the school, they mistakenly identify Alpha as the mastermind behind the pranks, resulting in his expulsion. Wracked by guilt, Frankie confesses her "disreputable" behavior, which gives school authorities a fig leaf to hide behind as they reinstate her and Alpha at Alabaster.

Certainly, Lockhart's novel deserves credit for centering issues that are of concern to feminists, the foremost of which is the persistence of systemic gender discrimination. Despite Frankie's obvious ability and confidence, other members of her family insist on calling her "Bunny Rabbit," a nickname held over from childhood that grates on her because it casts her as "innocent. In need of protection. Inconsequential" (13). Furthermore, not only do male students at Alabaster objectify Frankie's body, they also patronize her, to her infinite annoyance. A former boyfriend who cheated on her, for example, dismisses her as "oversensitive" and "crazy" when she objects to his suggestion that she proceed slowly in her relationship with the older Matthew (143). Likewise, after Matthew angers Frankie by correcting her grammar, he attempts to placate her by calling her "adorable," leading her to think to herself, "I'm as smart as any of you, or smarter even, when all you ever think is that I'm adorable" (315). Most obviously, Frankie is left to deal with the hurt and frustration that accompany her realization that "because of her sex . . . because of her feminism . . . she would never, never, ever get in" as a member of the Loyal Order of the Bassets (195). At least on its surface, then, *The Disreputable History of Frankie Landau-Banks* appears to be a feminist novel.

While the novel appears feminist in its outlook, it is nevertheless tinged by the lipstick of postfeminism in that it mocks the feminist movement. For instance, Frankie complains about having had to hear her sister, Zada, "going on and on about feminism all summer" (129), but Zada, now a Berkeley student with "a reputation for speaking her mind" (5), espouses a suspect understanding of feminism when she asks Frankie:

> Are you seriously going to tell me you buy into the patriarchal notion that power is localized in institutions created years and years ago by people who were overly proud of themselves for having the male set of genitalia, and most of whom are either dead or drooling over themselves in nursing homes by this point? . . . *The institutions of male supremacy only have real power over you if you buy into that notion.* (202, emphasis added)

Zada's use of the idiom "buy into" is an unironically capitalistic phrase in this context, but her comments are all the more disturbing to the extent that they reproduce the emphasis that neoliberalism and postfeminism place on choice, individual exceptionalism within a meritocracy, and personal agency. Zada's comments suggest that while girls and women may have experienced the effects of the patriarchy in the past, the threat is no longer real. Instead, the concept of the patriarchy is powerful only over those who choose to believe in it. Presumably, talented girls and women who do otherwise should be able to compete against (and best) their male counterparts.

EXCEPTIONAL INDIVIDUALISM AND THE LIMITS OF CHOICE

In a review for the *New York Times*, Donna Freitas describes *The Disreputable History* as a "homage to girl-power." Frankie is nothing if not the embodiment of the "can do" girl of the Grrl Power slogan popularized by the Spice Girls in the mid-1990s. Indeed, the novel is striking for the degree to which it reproduces neoliberalism's emphasis on individual exceptionalism within a meritocracy. Frankie is "highly intelligent" (7); "attractive" (11); "curvaceous" (5); "lithe" (6); "unusually smart in certain subjects" (70); able to "regularly make her friends laugh" (70); and above all else, "a surprisingly sharp competitor" (6). Indeed, the book's third-person narrator describes her as the kind of person who might, as an adult, "head the CIA, direct action movies, design rocket ships, or possibly (if she goes astray), preside over a unit of organized criminals" (6).

One way the book emphasizes Frankie's exceptionalism is by juxtaposing her with other, more ordinary girls. Her roommate, Trish, having dated the same boy for several years, is decidedly less ambitious than Frankie, preferring to stay at home and bake crumbles rather than accompany her brothers on their "macho" and drunken adventures (68). Gidget is a "good-looking girl who had thus far managed not to date anyone at Alabaster" (59), leaving the Basset Hounds to wonder why one of their own can't "get anywhere" with her sexually (194). Whereas "lots of girls" are "so focused on their boyfriends that they don't remember they had a life at all before their romances" (103), Frankie does remember, and she proudly distinguishes herself from other girls by daring "to imagine herself in control" (86). Hence, rather than allow herself to be placed in "a box for young and pretty girls who were not as bright or powerful as their boyfriends. A box for people who were not forces to be reckoned with," Frankie instead chooses (again, characteristic of neoliberalism's emphasis on personal choice and accountability) "to be a force" (214). By depicting gender oppression as an individual, rather than a systemic, problem, and by celebrating exceptional individuals who leverage their talents to rise above others in the meritocracy, the novel undercuts its own feminist critique of sexism.

This is not to say that Lockhart's novel entirely fails to acknowledge the role that unjust systems play in privileging some groups of people at the expense of others. Frankie notes, for example, "that girls make up fifty-two percent of the student body [at Alabaster], but only about twenty percent of the upper-administration" (242). Her father expounds on the value of leveraging connections of the sort one can make at exclusive prep schools to gain access to better educational and career opportunities, but her sister Zada implies that such opportunities are limited to a particular class of people when she describes Alabaster as "an institution where the WASPs outnumbered the other Protestants ten to one, the Catholics were pretty much in the closet, and the members of 'the tribe' had largely changed their names from things like Bernstein to things like Burns" (5). And, when, by the end of the novel, Frankie wonders why school authorities expel Alpha rather than give him a second chance, the third-person narrator attributes it to Alpha's socioeconomic background, noting that, as a scholarship student, "He's got no money" (311). Frankie herself is a beneficiary of both social class and sexism, as she manages to avoid being expelled from Alabaster simply because "a sweet-looking girl with no prior record of misbehavior gets a more lenient sentence (even with a full, written confession) than would a senior boy with a history of visits to the headmaster's office" (330–31). In short, the problem is not that the novel ignores the reality of systemic oppression; rather, it presents systemic oppression—such as classism, anti-Semitism, and sexism—as problems that can be overcome by talented, goal-oriented individuals.

As an example, one of the pranks that the Loyal Order of Basset Hounds carries out under Frankie's direction involves their stealing the statue of a guppy that had been erected on school grounds three years after Alabaster was founded and that alumni embrace as an icon. In the wake of the statue's disappearance, Dr. Richmond, the school's headmaster, receives a letter written by Frankie under the auspices of "The Fish Liberation Society" informing him that the statue will be returned when the school agrees to move its weekly student body meetings from the chapel, which is laden with Christian iconography, to another secular building on campus. This is not the first time such a request has been made in the school's history. In the past, a "small number of non-Christian or atheist students" had made similar requests, only to be "cowed by Richmond's assertion that the stained-glass crucifixions and Virgins were part of the Alabaster tradition students had enjoyed for nearly 120 years" (287). As an exceptional individual, however, Frankie single-handedly manages to do what others before her could not: in the end, the administration consents to move future student body meetings elsewhere in exchange for the guppy's safe return.

EMBODIMENT AND DIVISIONS OF LABOR

The historical justification for the division of labor between males and females has ridden for eons on the concept of embodiment. Two facts are true: first, some jobs are more physically and emotionally demanding than others; second, some women are physically and emotionally stronger than some men. Embodiment certainly affects how all people live their lives, but it does not serve as a justification for devaluing the work that those who identify as women perform.

In *The Disreputable History of Frankie Landau-Banks* female embodiment is compounded by notions of male privilege. Alpha, for example, callously refers to his mother as "the menstrual unit, the maternal unit" (16), displaying male privilege while he simultaneously denigrates his mother's embodiment. All of the students at Alabaster live in a world divided by this combination of gendered embodiment and male entitlement. The all-male Basset Hounds are "deeply confident of their merit and their future" (46); "their money and popularity made life extremely easy for [them].... They were secure" (104), so they set the agendas and have their girlfriends send out the invitations, as Elizabeth does when Alpha asks her to invite girls to the first beer party of the fall semester. These boys also patronize girls, as Matthew does Frankie when he "chucked her under the chin, like you do to a dog" (114). He refers to her as "harmless" (211), which unsettles her greatly (214). Additionally, a group of boys dressing up as girls for Halloween faux-lament, "There are so many girl-things we don't know"—like, for example, shaving armpits or what it means to wear a "shrug" (230). In other words, these boys consider feminine embodiment entirely in trivial terms.

Goaded by her boyfriend calling her "harmless" behind her back, Frankie disrupts the Basset Hounds' plans by posing as Alpha on email and changing a prank the group had planned for Halloween. Before landing on her ingenious idea, however, she first laughs at her own embodiment (and the embodiment of all who identify as women), thinking:

> It just seems so funny to dress up your boobs. Like when no one is going to see them. Or even if someone is. It seems so undignified to deck out your private bits in flashy bits of lace you'd never wear on the outside of your clothes for a million years. . . .
> Boobs are just inherently undignified.
> These are what I've got that keeps me out of the Loyal Order. Yes, it's my chromosomes, and maybe other things, too, but for a symbol of the difference between me and the boys—I could do worse than boobs. Or a bra. (225–26)

Frankie proceeds to order a parachute, and she convinces the Basset Hounds to buy a number of pretty and amusing brassieres. On Halloween morning, Alabaster students awaken to find the bras pinned to portraits of headmasters and board members, all of whom are men. Moreover, a "small nymph statue near the pond wore a practical underwire in beige. The guppy wore a hot purple A-cup. Even the large tree in front of the library sported a bright red double-D" (239). The crowning glory, however, is the "large, pale brown parachute" atop the dome over the library; "in the center of the parachute, the dome's nub had been painted a rosy pink, and in case anyone missed the idea, from the front of the library hung a large, painted sign reading: IN THE LADIES WE TRUST" (239–40, emphasis in the original).

Girls themselves dispute the intended meaning of the prank. Trish thinks "it's like making fun of women. . . . Like saying, look how stupid these old guys look wearing clothes that women wear every single day" (241). Another girl calls it "objectification. . . . All these guys were making boob jokes in math this morning" (241). These two girls challenge each other as to whether this is "objectification" or "denigration," but Trish ultimately acknowledges that those two words amount to the same thing. Yet another girl celebrates that "it's funny! . . . Maybe it's just saying, boobs are great! Because they are. I bet guys secretly wish they had them" (242).

Earlier in the novel, Frankie has argued with her roommate, Trish, insisting that guys "have got to look at girls' faces every once in a while. Otherwise how are they going to recognize anyone?" (48). At the time, Trish answers, with amusement, "I'm betting that if all of us started padding or wearing minimizers, the boys of this school would be completely confused and unable to identify at least half of the female population. Haven't you seen the way they always talk to your chest? . . . But that's what they do. They talk to the Ladies. If you know what I mean" (48). Thus, in September, Trish appears complacent about the male gaze's objectification of the female body, so her willingness to refer to the denigrating objectification of breasts by October 31 indicates either some rapid level of character growth or a character inconsistency. In any event, on October 31, Frankie guilelessly wonders to the group of girls who are speculating about the meaning of the "In the Ladies We Trust" prank: "Couldn't it be pointing out how there are like, no women in any of the paintings on campus? . . . Couldn't it be saying, 'Where are the women to fill out these bras?'" (242). She further speculates: "What if we consider that maybe all those bra-wearing founders and headmasters are trying to get in touch with their feminine side? They're dressing in drag, the way so many guys do on Halloween, because it's their only chance to experience any of the *power* of femininity" (243, emphasis added). With Frankie, everything always comes down to power and how she wants to use it for transactional purposes.

Political theorist Wendy Brown identifies how future-oriented and transactional neoliberalism is when she writes:

> Today, *homo oeconomicus* . . . has been significantly reshaped as financialized human capital: its project is to self-invest in ways that enhance its value or to attract investors through constant attention to its actual or figurative credit rating, and to do this across every sphere of its existence. . . . Neoliberal *homo oeconomicus* takes its shape as human capital seeking to strengthen its competitive positioning and appreciate its value, rather than as a figure of exchange or interest. (32–33)

Catherine Rottenberg perceives this sense of competition and appreciation of one's self as an asset in terms of the "futurity" (94) of neoliberalism and what she condemns as "neoliberal feminism" (21). She also argues: "there is a striking gendered aspect to the avowed emphasis on futurity. Futurity as a technology of the self is arguably *most evident* in neoliberalism's hailing of young upwardly mobile women who are still constantly told that they must worry about their 'biological clock' if they want to 'have it all'" (94, emphasis in the original).[5] Frankie is very focused on her future, especially her career, but because she is so fixated on her own futurity, she does not yet understand what Rottenberg critiques as the expectation that neoliberal feminists can find ways to outsource childbearing, childrearing, and lactation—which is what allows Frankie to define breasts as "inherently undignified" (226). Not unlike her fellow students, she sees breasts in terms of commodification: both in the ways that the boys at her school use them to identify girls and in encouraging others to spend so much money on brassieres for her prank.

FEMALE FRIENDSHIP AND THE ERASURE OF INEQUALITY

Two additional metrics can help readers recognize problematic postfeminist tendencies within a literary work. When girls have only one or no female mentors, and when they have one or no female friends (or when that one friend dies), those girls become isolated and unable to create a female community. As Ann M. M. Childs notes, this is a problematic tendency in YA literature, especially when female characters privilege their hetero-romantic partners over their female friendships, which "privileges females' heterosexual relationships as the only important ones and, therefore, males as the most important social connections" (188).

Similarly, Amy Montz criticizes the perpetuation of the type of woman vs. woman competition at work in, for example, stories such as the fairy-tale "Cinderella"; Tharini Viswanath refers to this as "competitive femininity," which she argues prevents girls from creating successful communities that can effect change (111). When rejecting the help of other girls appears to be a conscious choice on the character's part, any novel becomes that much more postfeminist, especially when individualism seems to be more important to the girl character than functioning within a social group. Frankie has only one girlfriend—her roommate, Trish—and considers herself to be superior even to that friend. And she has only one mentor, her sister, who is a mere three years older than she and studying across the country in California. Despite Frankie's potential to have created a campus-wide protest about the objectification of the female body that might have been led by a group of girls, she is instead satisfied with having gotten so many people talking about the bra prank she designed. Before the prank, she had hoped that Alpha "would suspect someone outside the pack and finally accuse her, angry but admiring her genius, acknowledging her as the superior mind" (245). In other words, she ultimately cares more about earning Alpha's admiration than she does about using her power to foment impactful gender protest; she seems more interested in "becoming one of the boys" than in changing the patriarchy that privileges them.

Frankie's exceptionalism and competitive spirit also complicate her relationships with the other girls at Alabaster because she is cognizant of how she differs from them. She regards herself as more intelligent than Star, a fellow sophomore whom Frankie (unironically) dismisses as "insecure and suspicious of women and girls who weren't similar to her" (81). She feels affection for Trish, but questions her ambition and holds her at arm's length in part because Frankie worries that "were Trish to ever fully comprehend the way Frankie thinks, the subjects she ponders all the time when she appears to be quietly doing her homework—Frankie's anger and hunger—she would pull away" (338). Ironically, Trish proves to be the only student at Alabaster who correctly infers the symbolic meaning of Frankie's "Fish Liberation Society" prank, suggesting that she would make a formidable ally and that Frankie has been underestimating her roommate all along (302). Toward the end of the novel, when Frankie's efforts to infiltrate the Basset Hounds are made public, she "wishes she were a different kind of girl. Someone simple, sweet, and unambitious" (340). Because she has such a low opinion of other girls, Frankie sacrifices the collective power she could otherwise leverage by working with her female classmates to combat gender oppression, instead going it alone in the neoliberal tradition and thus ultimately failing in her goal. In other words, if Frankie were as intelligent as she thinks she is, she would have recognized that a group of women has more power to fight the patriarchy than one girl acting on her own.

Postfeminist thinking values the individual actions of an exceptional girl or woman over the collective power of a group. In this very specific way, the values of neoliberalism undercut the whole purpose of the feminist movement, which is to empower women not only individually but as a group. Even the one adult woman in the novel whom Frankie admires abandons collective action, choosing instead to turn Frankie into the administration for her miscreant behavior. Ms. Jensson, who teaches Frankie's favorite class, "Cities, Art, and Protest" (53), is in her first year of teaching at Alabaster. In completing one of Ms. Jensson's assignments, Frankie writes a paper that examines community clubs that historically organized in the name of protest and disruption in cities such as San Francisco and Portland. The paper inspires many of the pranks that Frankie later manipulates the Basset Hounds into performing, and the due date for the assignment coincides with Frankie's most elaborate prank. Ms. Jensson ultimately turns the paper over to the school's administrators as "evidence" in the case against Frankie because she is "eager to disassociate herself from the perpetrator in order to keep her new job" (320). Without prompting, she even "helpfully made notes'" on the paper "for the headmaster to ensure he wouldn't miss any of the connections" between Frankie's paper and the pranks (320). As much of a feminist as Ms. Jensson appears to be, she, too, rejects the opportunity to form a bond with another female and defends only her own self-interest.

Frankie's feminist sister and their mother also criticize Frankie's actions, pushing her into therapy to deal with her "aggression" (336). The therapist suggests field hockey as a form of cooperative teamwork, but the sport is only played by girls, and "Frankie [is] not interested in playing a sport that was rated as nothing by the more powerful half of the population" (336). The novel concludes with her thinking: "It is better to be alone . . . than to be with someone who can't see who you are. It is better to lead than to follow. It is better to speak up than stay silent. It is better to open doors than to shut them on people," but without her being able to consider how difficult it is for most women to be the type of privileged leaders with voices that open doors for others, the novel ultimately fails Frankie's self-proclaimed feminist values (342).

Erasure of social disparities created by structural inequalities is an essential aspect of neoliberal ideology. If any individual can succeed by being excellent, then any systemic failures of social structures or stratification are, ostensibly, meaningless. As postracialism does with racism, so too postfeminism erases the structural flaws in an inherently gendered society by implying that talented girls who try hard enough can overcome gender-based inequalities. This erasure of inequality often happens at the level of the individual relationship within neoliberal/postfeminist thinking. Girls who think they do not need community because they are superspecial are girls who will never advocate for women to unite in collective action to address gender inequality. Girls who are convinced that they can manipulate the patriarchy with their own special talents are also unlikely to build strong relationships with other girls—and in turn, they prove to be among the pillars that uphold the patriarchy. Girls who feel empowered because they measure up against an imaginary checklist of male qualities, as Frankie does, are not truly empowered. Just as race is not a factor among the lily-white student body of a school named for whiteness itself, Alabaster, Frankie's initial feminist posturing is eventually erased from the novel, too. Erasure is an effective tool in the way that it obviates social justice for historically marginalized groups.

Approximately a third of the way through *The Disreputable History of Frankie Landau-Banks*, the narrator wryly asks a series of rhetorical questions: "How does a person become the person she is? What are the factors in her culture, her childhood, her education, her religion, her economic stature, her sexual orientation, her race, her everyday interactions—what stimuli lead her to make choices other people will despise her for?" (107). Frankie values her own exceptionalism, particularly her intellect, and she is willing to serve as her own self-advocate. Tellingly, her willingness to act on these attributes ultimately lands her in therapy. Nevertheless, toward the book's conclusion, the narrator unironically expresses hope that, in the spirit of meritocratic exceptionalism the novel advances, Frankie will grow up to change the world, presumably by opening doors that have traditionally been closed to women.

Therein lies the issue: in spite of its feminist ambitions, in the end, *The Disreputable History of Frankie Landau-Banks* ultimately leaves readers with the impression that, so long as Frankie is flexible, resilient, and continues to work hard, she will one day overcome gender oppression and realize her dreams. In doing so, the book reframes a complex, systemic problem as an individual matter. Ending gender oppression requires more than one person having a strong work ethic and an entrepreneurial spirit. It necessitates addressing the myriad ways in which gender discrimination (like racism) is inscribed in our legal system; in health, educational, and religious institutions; in the economy, at all levels; in the political system; and in virtually every aspect of American life. To create meaningful change, people need to work together to leverage their collective power. With that in mind, we now turn to a set of YA novels that demonstrates how the genre can resist the emphasis that postfeminism—and through it, neoliberalism—places on exceptionalism, choice, and individual agency.

FEMINIST REJECTIONS OF NEOLIBERALISM: THE NSIBIDI SCRIPT SERIES

Nigerian American author Nnedi Okorafor's Nsibidi Script series—which, at the time of this writing, consists of *Akata Witch* (2011), *Akata Warrior* (2017), and *Akata Woman* (2022)—is premised on a resistance to exploitation: of the Earth and its resources, and of all peoples, especially Black women. As such, we interpret the Akata books as Orkorafor's intellectually honest critique of neoliberalism—and relatedly, postfeminism. Set in Aba, a city in southeastern Nigeria, the novels are focalized through the perspective of the protagonist, Sunny Nwazue, a twelve-year-old girl who was born in New York of Nigerian parents but who later returned with her family to live in Nigeria. Sunny has albinism. Other than having "light yellow hair," hazel eyes, and skin that looks like "sour milk," she has "West African features, like [her] mother" (3).

In the first book of the series, Sunny learns that she is a "free agent" of the "Leopard People," as the magical folks of West Africa refer to themselves (*Akata Witch* 52). Most Leopard People are born into magical families, but a "free agent" is a person whose magic is inherited indirectly, rather than from a parent. In Sunny's case, she inherited her magical powers from her maternal grandmother. Each Leopard Person has a unique spirit identity and special talents, but because Sunny is a free agent, she has not yet learned that her albinism gives her the special talent of gliding in and out of physical spaces unseen, and she eventually discovers that her spirit identity is Anyanwu, the Igbo solar deity. Unlike Lambs (as nonmagical people are called), Leopards can perform juju, which is "like anything else: some good, some bad, some just is" (35).

Because Sunny's magical powers skipped a generation, she has been unaware of them for the first twelve years of her life. After she is made aware of her identity, however, she joins with three other Leopard teenagers—Chichi, Orlu, and Sasha—to become an *Oha*: a balanced group of Leopard People—usually four adults—that come together as a coven and fight the evil inherent in bad magic. Like other groups of characters in children's literature, Sunny's coven in the Nsibidi Script series resembles what Maria Nikolajeva calls a "collective character": each individual has a specific set of talents, and together, the group functions as the equivalent of a highly rounded character (Nikolajeva, *Rhetoric* 67–87). Chichi, who is among the first people to recognize Sunny as a fellow Leopard Person, is known for her fierce intelligence, her eidetic memory, and her royal bloodline from Nimm warrior-queens. Orlu, a classmate of Sunny's and the group's most level-headed, compassionate, and kind member, can "undo bad things," such as bad magic, using his hands to unweave juju spells (23). Sasha is a fiercely competitive, athletic, and impetuous African American boy who, like Chichi, also has a photographic memory and a passion for knowledge about magic. He was sent from Chicago to Nigeria by his parents, who worry that his lack of respect for authority figures, especially the police, puts him in danger in the US. As for Sunny, her greatest power is borne of her albinism: she not only possesses the ability to become invisible and pass through solid objects, but she can also manipulate time and pass between the spirit world and the nonmagical world more easily than most Leopard People.

In *Akata Witch*, evil is channeled through the personage of Black Hat Otokoto, a nefarious oilman who has ties with the US and who strives to profit from Nigeria's many natural resources, including its oil reserves. To do so, Black Hat plans to summon Ekwensu, a masquerade (or spirit) "of such deep evil that her name was rarely spoken, even in the Lamb world" (324). To bring her back from the underworld, where she was banished millennia before, Black Hat must perform juju that includes killing young children so that he can add their spirit powers to his own. He commodifies their bodies and (literally) consumes their lives. Although parents in the region are aware that children are being kidnapped and murdered, they do not know they are being exploited as sacrifices in the name of dark magic. Toward the end of the first book, Black Hat manages to invoke the evil Ekwensu, and she emerges from underground, emitting "an oily, greasy smell, like car exhaust," thus linking her to the oil that Black Hat seeks to exploit for profit (324). Black Hat ultimately kills himself, however. Sunny and her coven manage to vanquish Ekwensu temporarily, but they fail to eliminate the threat she poses to the people and environment of Nigeria, setting up the sequels in the series. They have succeeded in this first step of their quest, but only because they have functioned as a collective unit.

LOVING THE WORLD:
AKATA WARRIOR AND *AKATA WOMAN*

In the second book, *Akata Warrior*, the coven again confronts Ekwensu. The first time they do so, Sunny banishes the masquerade with words she has learned from her spirit-self, Anyanwu. In a subsequent encounter, Sunny relies on combat, scaling Ekwensu's physical manifestation as a growing tree and pulling off one of the masquerade's spirit masks, exposing the monster for what it truly is: a demon intent on making "the world into the apocalyptic place" that Sunny has previously witnessed in a vision (432). In a separate subplot, Sunny uses her magical powers to avenge her older brother, Chuckwu, after he is tortured and nearly killed as part of his initiation into a dangerous fraternity at the university he attends. In the absence of another adult, Chukwu later travels with Sunny and her friends on their journey to confront Ekwensu, and toward the end of the second book, he inadvertently learns of his sister's magical powers.

By the time of the third novel's setting in *Akata Woman*, all of the four teenage Leopard characters have learned more about their powers, and all but Sunny have turned sixteen. They witness historical aftereffects of the Biafran Civil War, fought in 1967, when the Igbo peoples of the southeast attempted to secede from Nigeria.[6] Thirty months of brutal fighting ensued, and at least a million Igbo peoples were killed by the Hausa and Fulani ethnic groups of northern Nigeria (Nwaubani; Achebe 74–77, 95–98). Fighting for the Nigerian military in opposition to the secessionists of Biafra was a military officer who became a historical figure, Sani Abacha. He later staged a military coup to become the dictator of Nigeria from 1993 to 1998; he was notorious for supporting Shell Oil's exploitative extraction practices in Nigeria and for having assassinated various environmentalist leaders who opposed the expansion of oil production in the country ("Abacha" 1–3). Okorafor presents Abacha's corruption as having leached into the Leopard People: corrupt leaders among the female Nimm warriors have promised Abacha juju to make him immortal and victorious. In the process, they have stolen a treasure from the powerful spider spirit, Udide, which Sunny and the rest of her coven work to recover. Ultimately, upon finding Udide's artifact, Sunny is able to read the mystical Nsibidi script on it well enough to understand that it is "a memoir fueled by, recipes inspired by, a weapon created from, a testament to, a mystical command book centered on love. The journey of it, the power of it, the healing of it, the price of it, the weight of it, the juju of it" (387). Sunny in turn works powerful juju that she has learned from this script, weaving a spell called "love rules all" (388). Okorafor is thus consistent throughout the series in delivering the message that loving people, loving the Earth and its resources, and loving and venerating mystical and ancient traditions are among the most effective ways to heal the environment and the broken humanity of the twenty-first century.

COUNTERING POSTFEMINIST INDIVIDUALISM

Equipped with powers and abilities that mark her as exceptional, Sunny initially appears in *Akata Witch* to resemble the postfeminist supergirl. As a free agent, she is an outsider in Leopard society, and she is also marginalized socially in Lamb society as a result of her albinism. Despite this, Sunny proves to be a powerful witch, even among Leopard People, due in part to the fact that her spirit-self, Anyanwu, is ancient, revered, and highly skilled at juju. In *Akata Warrior*, a witch who is further along in her learning refers to Sunny as "some sort of *chosen one*" (153, emphasis added); that assessment is seemingly reinforced toward the end of the book when Sunny, having vanquished Ekwensu, joins Anyanwu in breaking kola—a ritual of honoring another—with the Supreme Being, Chukwu. Nevertheless, the series is less interested in celebrating exceptional individualism than it is in emphasizing collectivism. Despite her exceptionality, Sunny is able to defeat evil only when she works with the combined powers of her coven, suggesting that shared knowledge, unity, and teamwork are preferable to individualism and self-advancement.

The series also critiques postfeminism's emphasis on consumerism. In Leopard society, people are socialized to value knowledge over material wealth. Lambs, on the other hand, "think money and material things are the most important thing in the world" (*Akata Witch* 81). As Orlu tells Sunny, "You can cheat, lie, steal, kill, be dumb as a rock, but if you can brag about money and having lots of things and your bragging is true, that bypasses everything. Money and material things make you king or queen of the Lamb world. You can do no wrong, you can do anything" (*Akata Witch* 81–82). Black Hat's capitalist thirst for Lamb wealth—and, more important, for power over both Lambs and Leopard People—is at odds with the cultural values of the Leopard People, whose economy is centered around knowledge. Any time a Leopard Person gains "knowledge and wisdom," they earn "*chittim*," a form of currency that consists of curved rods of gold, silver, bronze, and copper (*Akata Witch* 38). In a reversal of Euro-American values, however, the least valuable of these rods is gold and the most valuable is copper. Furthermore, Sunny is encouraged to earn chittim not just as currency, but because "you owe it to yourself" to learn, as another character puts it (229). In the series, financial greed is thus identified as morally wrong and associated with Euro-American values. In contrast, knowledge is, quite literally, the coin of the realm among Leopard People and the greatest possession a person can own.

The Nsibidi Script series also criticizes postfeminism's emphasis on consumerism and self-enclosed individualism. As one elder explains, Americans "don't teach [children] to understand others, they teach them to expect *others* to understand them" (*Akata Witch* 303, emphasis in the original). Okorafor connects extreme wealth disparity in Nigeria to a failure of empathy as well. When the teenagers attend a festival in the city of Abuja, they stay in a suite at a Hilton where a former US president is said to have stayed (209). Although it is "the biggest and most lavish hotel in the city" (*Akata Witch* 209), Orlu tells his friends: "I hate this hotel and everything it stands for. . . . The over-extravagance when people are living so badly just outside the hotel, it's obnoxious" (*Akata Witch* 211).

Unlike Harry Potter, who, as a neoliberal hero, is usually celebrated as the one wizard capable of defeating Voldemort, Sunny's mentors continually remind her that her powers notwithstanding, she is ultimately replaceable: "The world is bigger and more important than you" (*Akata Witch* 54), they instruct her, and they encourage her to remember that "it will go on, regardless" (*Akata Witch* 119). In a similar manner, they also encourage her to place societal problems ahead of her own self-interest, arguing that the former are "bigger than you" (*Akata Witch* 170) and cautioning Sunny, "There are more valuable things in life than safety and comfort" (*Akata Witch* 228–29). When she and her friends ask Leopard leaders whether they have previously deployed other witches to stop Black Hat, an elder replies, "We have and will continue to until Black Hat is taken down. . . . More is at stake than your lives" (*Akata Witch* 310). In contrast to the Harry Potter books, then, the Nsibidi Script series does not present Sunny and her friends as exceptional individuals who are predestined to save the world; rather, when the four members of the *Oha* coven succeed in stopping Black Hat and Ekwensu, they are able to do so only because of their teamwork.

Teamwork is also on display in *Akata Witch* at a festival when two teams of Leopard teenagers play what Sunny and Sasha call "soccer" and what Chichi and Orlu call "football." Sunny is a talented footballer, but initially, some players dismiss her because she is a girl. In the end, however, her friend Sasha intervenes, telling them, "It's stupid to judge without knowing what you're judging" (251). Given the opportunity, Sunny's talents shine during her try-out, and she eventually makes the team, becoming one of its more valuable members despite sexist verbal abuse she experiences from members of the opposing team. Early in the game the captain of the other team ridicules her because of her gender. Initially, this hurts Sunny "more than usual. This wasn't just about her being albino, this was about her being a girl—an ugly girl" (256). When the game begins, however, she quickly takes advantage of the opposition's scorn, passing the ball to another player who scores the first goal. In other words, she assists in making the first point; she does not make it herself. As the novel, emphasizing the importance of teamwork, explains, Sunny knows that "she wasn't just good at kicking a ball around, she was good at playing *with a team*" (258, emphasis added). Near the end of the game, the opposing team's captain taunts her again, telling her, "Girls belong on the damn sidelines," to which Sunny, refusing to accept his sexism, retorts, "Do you know what century it is?" (260). Sunny's team loses the game by one point, but they win considerably more chittim than the winning team because they have played as a team and without sexism.

EMBODIMENT, INTERRELATIONSHIPS, AND FOREGROUNDING SOCIAL DIFFERENCE

In critiquing neoliberal postfeminism, the Nsibidi Script series also emphasizes the importance of "balance" in terms of gender, knowledge and power, tribes and/or races, and even income level (*Akata Witch* 84). In that regard, the series is profound and deft in its ability to confront and critique neoliberal values of power, wealth, and exploitation. Okorafor is unstinting in her criticism of both US and Nigerian corruption, including critiques of Nigerian sexism, colorism, ableism, homelessness, and the failure to address widespread problems of living standards, sanitation, and the exploitation of oil. US citizens are consistently identified by their greediness and intolerance.

Of all the characters, Sunny most clearly conveys ideologies about differently abled women whose skin tone is unlike that of the dominant culture. Toward that end, she has many strong female role models among the Leopard People. Chichi's mother, who is of royal blood, is the first to identify Sunny as a free agent. Sunny's mentor, one of the elders, is an independent woman named Sugar Cream; she teaches Sunny that her grandmother was the Leopard Person who mentored Black Hat, until he proceeded to kill her and eat "some of her flesh"—consumption, again—so as to gain her powers (*Akata Witch* 193). In contrast to Sunny's grandmother, Sunny's mother, Dr. Kwazou, fulfills the docile role that Nigerian wives are expected to play (seeming to belie the fact that she is a physician). Sunny's father is a lawyer who loathes his daughter and says vile, sexist things to her, calling her, for example, "Stupid, stupid girl," threatening to "flog" her "tirelessly," and disrespecting her for being albino (*Akata Witch* 5, 88). She professes to hate him and believes firmly that he hates her. Eventually, after he tries to pummel her, Sunny's mother reveals that her father never wanted a daughter. "A beating won't save you," he screams as he storms out of the house; for her part, Sunny cries at the sadness of their relationship (*Akata Witch* 338). Only then does her mother tell her about the talents Sunny has inherited from her maternal grandmother.

The series balances the abuses of Sunny's patriarchal family, however, with a series of trustworthy female and male mentors, including her teacher Anatov, a wise man who has counseled her to learn for her own benefit, and another elder, Ali, who gains empathy for Sunny when he realizes she has had apocalyptic visions of the end of the world. As the members of her *Oha* coven learn, each such group must contain two males and two females for balance—and leadership throughout the Leopard world similarly balances the power of males and of females. At the end of *Akata Witch*, the nurturer who restores a dead young boy and a dead young girl to life is a male (Orlu), and it is a female (Sunny) who defeats the evil spirit Ekwensu after Black Hat evokes her. In terms of gender, then, the Nsibidi Script series provides valuable insights into the importance of power being balanced between those who identify as male or as female.

In contrast to postfeminist depictions of girls who do and have it all, female-identifying characters in the Nsibidi Script series are not idealized. To the contrary, most of the Leopard Women have some sort of physical difference. Sunny's mentor, Sugar Cream, for example, has scoliosis of the spine, so her backbone is twisted as much as a serpent's can twist. The reader eventually learns that her spirit animal is a snake, and she can transform herself into that creature when she needs to. Additionally, diminutive Chichi is "fine-boned, dark brown, and elfin, but her voice was loud and strong and arrogant. So was her smile" (*Akata Witch* 15). Sunny, too, is discriminated against in the Lamb world because of her albinism, even though it is the source of her strength in the Leopard world. The Leopard women, in particular, are strong, complex, and self-sufficient, but also flawed in ways that help them to grow stronger. In short, no woman in this series serves as a sex symbol or fills the role of "lipstick feminist."

Despite these depictions of females as complex, traditional gender roles are occasionally assumed to be the norm in these books. In *Akata Warrior*, Sunny and Chichi always cook for the boys in their coven; Sunny's mentor, Sugar Cream, also scolds Sunny for not being able to cook tainted pepper soup adequately. The series occasionally evinces "double entanglement" of the sort that McRobbie associates with postfeminism (McRobbie, "Postfeminism" 255). Although Sunny is powerful, she also adheres to traditional Nigerian values that work to keep young girls virginal, thus reproducing conservative attitudes toward sexuality. Chichi, on the other hand, is the exact opposite, more sexually and romantically adventurous than Sunny, which turns the two of them into a tamed-down version of the virgin/whore dichotomy that permeates folklore and cultural mores in many countries around the world. Finally, the women in the Leopard world regulate and punish girls who fall out of line. Sugar Cream locks Sunny in the magical library's basement with a soul-sucking djinn as punishment for revealing her spirit face and juju to a Lamb. Sunny's punishment lasts for three days, but the punishing face of authoritarian women is balanced by the face of a powerful female spider who helps Sunny's spirit-self, Anyanwu, defeat the evil djinn. Women, indeed, have power in this series; sometimes they use it for good, but sometimes they use it to discipline others; on still other occasions, they use it for evil purposes, as Ekwensu does.

Balancing these gender-normed traditional roles are what the series has to offer in terms of rejecting heteronormative marriage and motherhood. For example, Chichi and her mother represent a special class of women known as Nimm warrior women. They are perfectly happy living in a relatively squalid hut filled with more books than furniture. As Orlu tells Sunny,

"Nimm women all have 'Nimm' as a last name, and they're never allowed to marry. And they reject wealth" (*Akata Witch* 214). Just as the women in Chichi's matrilineal family reject ownership of property, they also reject the ownership that is engendered by patriarchal marriages, offering a critique of the sexism that oppresses women, especially those like Sunny's mother, who are married to domineering and abusive men. Sunny's mother displays loving maternal care for her daughter in traditional ways, just as Chichi's mother does in less traditional ways. As Chichi says, "My mother is more than a mother to me. . . . My mother tells me everything. She's not your typical mother" (145); she's "a badass" (165). In that regard, Chichi's mother is presented as ideal.

In the final chapters of the third book, *Akata Woman*, Sunny learns something important about both her spirit-self, Anyanwu, and motherhood. Sunny and Anyanwu are seated on the ground opposite one another, rolling a ball back and forth between them, when this conversation transpires:

> Anyanwu rolled the ball to her harder than normal and Sunny caught it. She placed it in her lap. "We've all been treating you like . . . like a type of mother, a mother who is genius-level amazing and births a child . . . and then everyone expects her to step away from her genius . . . to come down and nurture her baby, to make herself less, so her baby can understand. But that's not right; amazing mothers should continue being amazing . . . and you're not my mother, you are me." She pressed her hand to her chest. "And I am you." She paused, looking hard at Anyanwu. "I would have been angry, and I would have kept walking away, too. But you also kept coming back. Thank you for that."
>
> Anyanwu responded aloud and Sunny smiled at this acknowledgment. "Because I am you, Sunny," she said. "And you are right. You all—you, Sugar Cream, Sasha, Chichi, Orlu, Anatov, even the Mami Wata oracle Bola—you've all viewed me as the one who must come down to you. But it is YOU who must come UP to meet ME." (396, emphasis in the original)

Here, Okorafor reverses the script of mothering, positioning mothers not as women who stoop down to nurture, but instead as people who are strong, smart, and perhaps most important, role models of integrity. She is demonstrating the ethics of care in terms of mothering. As Mary Jeanette Moran describes that process being depicted in children's literature, this type of mothering tends to "emphasize the importance of a nurturing, reciprocal web of relationships" as being necessary for mothers to retain their "[individual] relationally autonomous identity" ("Balance" 273).[7] Both Chichi's mother and Anyanwu, as ethical mothers, are the polar opposites of the neoliberal mother in YA fiction, who raises her strong, postfeminist daughter only for the latter to be captured by a man who will elevate her social status. Equally important, Anyanwu's conversation with Sunny implies that a spark of the divine—or a capacity for greatness—exists in all people, not merely an exceptional few. The question is thus not whether one will choose to exercise one's talents to rise above systemic oppression, but rather, whether one uses them to work alongside others to undo it.

A FEMINIST CRITIQUE OF POSTRACIALISM

Issues of race might seem initially to be inconsequential in a series that is set in a country free of the racism born of slavery, one of the original sins in the United States. But in at least two ways, racism is problematized by this Nigerian American author. First, and most obviously, Sunny's albinism provides a reason for other people, especially her peers—but also her father—to discriminate against her based on skin color alone. She explains, "I knew I looked like a ghost. All pale-skinned" (*Akata Witch* 4), and indeed, her peers call her "ghost" to mock her throughout the story. In the first full chapter of *Akata Witch*, Sunny's (white) teacher in Nigeria grows furious with every student in the class except Sunny because of their lazy writing. She ferrules the other students, hoping to "beat some ... sense" into them (10). After school, a bully shouts at Sunny, "Did you *like* seeing that white woman beat us like that? Does it make you happy because you're white, too?" (12, emphasis in the original). The girl who has been bullying Sunny calls her a "stupid pale-faced *akata* witch" (11), an Igbo term for "bush animal," but one that is also slang for "black Americans or foreign born blacks" (11). In Sunny's mind, it is a "very, very rude word" (11), which is not surprising considering that, throughout her lifetime, she has been discriminated against, both for the color of her skin and for being born in the US.

Another subtler exploration of racism emerges from the difference between the Leopard People and the Lambs—an exploration not unlike Rowling's distinction between wizards and Muggles. Sunny discovers that some Leopard People consider themselves superior to both Lambs and free agents when she reads a book, *Fast Facts for Free Agents*, which is written by a classist and racist woman, Isong Abong Effiong Isong, who considers Leopards to be "high society" (*Akata Witch* 98), Lambs to be "idiots" (18), and free agents to be "the scourge of the Earth" (113). In her book, Isong discusses how Leopards "embrace those things that make us unique or odd.... One's abilities mark him or her.... Often they are things that Lambs make fun of, imperfections. They can be physical, psychological, behavioral" (99). Isong concludes this passage: any free agent will need "a patient pure spirit who is willing to help someone as needy and ignorant as you" (99). Sunny objects to this author's frequent descriptions of free agents as incompetent, throwing the book across her bedroom at one point and thinking, "How am I supposed to read this? ... What a pompous, discriminating idiot of an author. If they have racism in the Leopard world, this book is so 'racist' against free agents!" (*Akata Witch* 97). When Sunny confronts her teacher Anatov about the book's "condescending tone" (99), he tells her that, as an African woman, Isong also discriminated against African Americans. "Prejudice begets prejudice," he tells Sunny; "Knowledge does not always evolve into wisdom" (113). The lesson is a powerful one, given the Leopard valuation of wisdom. Anatov tells Sunny and the others in her coven: "Learn how to *learn*. Read between the lines. Know what to take and what to discard.... We don't teach as the Lambs do. Books will be part of your learning but experience is important, too" (*Akata Witch* 112, emphasis in the original).

Rejecting postfeminism and postracism, Anatov eventually moves the lesson to an explicit discussion of the intersectionality of race and disability. "The book spoke of Leopards as if we are the most confident beings on Earth and beyond. Don't get her wrong, we are a confident people. And we do embrace those things that make us unique. However, we have insecurities and problems like any other humans" (*Akata Witch* 113). Anatov wants his students to know that although Leopard People value what Lambs perceive as "disability," they are still vulnerable to being themselves racist and classist. For example, Orlu objects when Chichi tries to teach Sunny that one Leopard tribe is better than another:

"The Efik people have the strongest juju in the world."
 "In whose opinion? Not the Igbos,'" Orlu said irritably. "Sunny, there are Leopard People all over the world from every tribe, race, whatever. None is better than the other." (*Akata Witch* 45)

Sasha also complains about snobbery, tribalism, colorism, and racism within the Leopard world. In the US, he explains, "everything's biased toward European juju. The *African American* headquarters is on the Gullah Islands in South Carolina" and is not really part of the US Leopard headquarters in New York (*Akata Witch* 79, emphasis in the original). Via the mechanisms of tribalism and Sunny's albinism, the series critiques racism, much as it does sexism, openly acknowledging its existence within Nigeria. As a mystical figure says to Chicago-born Sasha in *Akata Woman*: "Seeing is not the same as caring.... You're American; you should understand that more than anyone" (243). The books in the Nsibidi Scripts series thus address the subtle and not-so-subtle evils of racism, sexism, ableism, classism, and disregard for the environment. The novel's antagonists—Black Hat, Ekwensu, Abacha, and Chichi's corrupt Nimm cousins—could not become the power-seeking, greedy killers they are had they not internalized the Euro-American thirst for economic power along with a willingness to devalue the lives of other human beings, including children and teenagers.

INTERSECTIONAL ENVIRONMENTALISM AND ECOFEMINISM

In chapter 2, we explained how intersectional environmentalism builds on the work of ecofeminist scholars in arguing that environmental justice and social justice are not unrelated topics. Reflecting that understanding, in the Nsibidi Script books, oil and corporate exploitation of the environment wreak havoc for humans as well as nonhuman animals, much as they do in real-world Nigeria. When Ekwensu reappears in *Akata Warrior*, she feasts upon oil spills across the Niger Delta. A member of an environmental watchdog group says, "This place is already mutilated by oil pipelines; now the forest and waters are poisoned" (212). He continues, "These oil companies are so sloppy in their mining of crude oil. They don't care. It's not *their* home" (213, emphasis in the original). Another character calls the oil companies "stupid" (212), and Sunny's father refers to them as "idiots" (211). It is perhaps not surprising, then, that when Sunny finally confronts Ekwensu toward the end of that novel, the girl witnesses the spirit from the vantage point of an ecofeminist:

> *Forest, silt, craggy waters, all drenched with greasy black ooze.* Sunny knew this place. She'd seen it on the news. *The bitter smell of dead rotted trees, sulfurous like a thousand farts. The place is silent because everything is dead. Then I saw Ekwensu bubble up from a great pool of black-brown mud surrounded by a ring of dying trees. Mud bubbling and blurping as she rose. Then she began to spin and one of her faces spat out an orange-yellow spark. It arced into the pool of blackened mud and the whole place went up in flames. I pulled back far enough to see the first burn, then the nearby town, and another town, all as*

> *Ekwensu danced in the burning forest.* (*Akata Warrior* 432, emphasis in the original)

If oil production and consumption are the root of all evil in this ecofeminist series, plants and vegetation provide the antidote to the extraction of carbon-based fuels from the Earth. For example, in the third book, *Akata Woman*, Sunny and the rest of her coven travel through many worlds, including an Afro-futuristic version of Earth that is entirely plant-based and where plants have evolved to provide fuel, air conditioning, lighting, and all other necessary forms of technology.[8] Most people who live in this place are happy because their needs are sufficiently met; sentient trees even build houses inside of themselves for the people to live in.

Ecocritical theorist Ynestra King defines ecofeminism in terms of industrialization's "opposition to nature," which "reinforces the subjugation of women"; she maintains that "life is an interconnected web, not a hierarchy" and that ecosystems "must maintain diversity," because humans, after all, can only survive within the environment, not in opposition to it (19–20). In chapter 2, we also examined the relationship between intersectional environmentalism and neoliberalism, but as we conclude this chapter about the relationship between neoliberalism, postfeminism, and gender, we must clearly acknowledge that exploitation of the environment is linked to gender exploitation. As Alice Curry argues in her ecofeminist theorization of YA literature, "Acknowledgement of the earth as a material entity ties the earth to other 'bodies' and particularly the female body" (194). Similarly, Karen J. Warren observes that "there are important connections between how one treats women, people of color and the underclass on one hand and how one treats the nonhuman natural environment on the other" (xi). With that in mind, we maintain that the expressions of postfeminism, postracialism, anthropocentrism, and other neoliberal ideologies in books for teenagers create conditions that require readers to pay close attention to how people who are not cis-het white men, along with nonhuman animals, plants, and the very Earth itself, have historically been, and continue to be, exploited in the name of mercenary capitalist profits.

CONCLUSION

As authors, we both once hoped that the myth of postfeminism would be thoroughly discredited by the #MeToo movement. Likewise, we once assumed that the US Supreme Court's 2022 *Dobbs v. Jackson Women's Health*

Organization ruling, which held that abortion is not a constitutional right, would further undermine postfeminist discourse. However, as evidenced by the many examples we shared at the beginning of this chapter, the trope of the beautiful, brainy teenage girl who competes against boys and who succeeds in virtually all her endeavors remains a fixture in many YA novels, not to mention films, television shows, music videos, computer games, and other forms of popular media that are directed at teenage audiences. Indeed, the frequency with which this trope appears in popular culture may explain why so many of our students—females as well as males—believe that feminism has outlived its usefulness.

Angela McRobbie observes a pattern that reflects the ebbing and flowing tides of various waves of feminism, asking: "What then is the cost of feminism's seeming rehabilitation or at least acknowledgement of its existence once again? Could an answer to this lie in the attempt to attach something of feminism to an ethos of competitive individualism? . . . This is offset by the renewed emphasis on individualisation and on the equating of female success with the illusion of control" ("Notes" 4). An ironic tension exists between the notion that strong, supersmart girls are somehow autonomous from others, when they are actually victims of a highly controlling econopolitical ideology that has taught them to immerse themselves in a culturally induced form of autonomous self-regulation. This is one of the many costs of living in a neoliberal society.

As we have argued in this chapter, neoliberalism seduces those who identify as girls and women by reassuring them that in a postfeminist society, anyone can be successful—professionally, educationally, economically—provided they are willing to work hard, leverage their talents, self-regulate to social norms, and compete for opportunities that come their way. But this raises the following question: are all opportunities really open to all who identify as female, even when they accept postfeminist (il)logic? In the society that postfeminists and neoliberals envision, gender and age have little or no bearing on a person's life outcomes. Instead, what matters is people's work ethic, their attitude, and their tenacity. And yet, reality intrudes on the illusion that postfeminism aims to create in a number of ways. From the gender pay gap to discriminatory hiring practices to the trafficking of female bodies to the US Supreme Court ruling that overturned *Roe v. Wade* to women's ongoing fight for bodily autonomy to Donald Trump's campaign invectives hurled at Kamala Harris, a host of well-documented measures attests to the fact that gender discrimination is anything but a relic of the past.

The messaging of postfeminism is even more insidious when one acknowledges that in emphasizing individualism and competition at the expense of collectivism and collaboration, this ideology dissuades girls and women from supporting, let alone contributing to, the very social movement that is best positioned to address sexism and gender discrimination. Postfeminism invites girls to prioritize heterosexual romance over friendship with other girls (Childs 188) and promotes "competitive femininity" (Viswanath 111), pitting girls and women against each other, fracturing their relationships, and isolating them still further. As a consequence, their access to the social, economic, and political empowerment they might otherwise exercise if they were to work together as a collective is further diminished.

In the next chapter, we build on our previous arguments about collectivity, intersectional environmentalism, critical race theory, and ecofeminism to address one of the great paradoxes of neoliberalism: namely, that in advancing discourses such as postfeminism and postracialism, neoliberalism attempts to erase the effects of sexism, racism, ableism, heterosexism, and other -*isms* at the same time that it reproduces social hierarchies on which these and other forms of systemic oppression depend. To demonstrate this point, we examine biopolitics—that is, the relationship between the political and the biological—to demonstrate how novels sometimes embrace the biopolitical and sometimes reject it in relation to neoliberalism.

Chapter 6

BIOPOLITICS AND NEOLIBERAL ERASURE

> They knew that the Indigenous ones relied on bison.
> So the bison had to go.
>
> —Darcie Little Badger, *A Snake Falls to Earth* (72)

In January 2020, two twenty-nine-year-old women worked in health care in a city of more than eight million people: Wuhan, China. Ms. Deng Danjing, a registered nurse who worked at Wuhan No. 7 Hospital, was the mother of a five-year-old girl. Eighteen miles away, Dr. Xia Sisi worked as a gastroenterologist at Union Jiangbei Hospital. She was the mother of a two-year-old son. Both of these mothers of young children contracted COVID-19 while working, and by February, both were infected with the disease and lying sick in their own hospitals. On March 13, 2020, the *New York Times* ran a poignant story about the two women. Ms. Deng Danjing survived; Dr. Xia did not. No one knows why (Wee and Wang).

As readers of this book already know, the coronavirus pandemic that started in 2019 (COVID-19) was a global emergency. On December 31, 2019, officials in Wuhan City, reported to the World Health Organization's (WHO) China office that forty-four people were ill—eleven of them seriously—with a novel virus of unknown origin. Fearing that transmission of the virus might have moved from animals to humans, officials in Wuhan quickly closed the public market where fresh food (including seafood) and live animals were sold. By January 13, 2020, a case of the novel coronavirus occurred in Thailand. By January 30, the virus was identified in eighteen countries ("WHO Timeline"). According to the US Center for Disease Control and Prevention (CDC), on February 23, the Italian government shut down its country, and on March 11, 2020, the WHO declared the virus a pandemic ("CDC Museum").

Ms. Deng and Dr. Xia are young women who put faces on this international tragedy. Stories like theirs led many people in the world to ask questions that reflected distrust of governmental entities. Why would one mother die and the other survive, when they were getting the same basic treatment? Even more insidiously, some people—including prominent politicians and media pundits—speculated that China developed this virus in a lab intentionally. Or did it really migrate from animals to humans in the Wuhan public market? In the US, why did the CDC approve the use of hydroxychloroquine on March 20, 2020, when it eventually proved to be ineffective at best and lethal at worst ("CDC Museum")? Was it wise to shut down the economy with stay-at-home orders? Did children really need to wear masks at school? Could the so-called "learning-loss" of students who attended school virtually ever be regained?

When President Donald Trump took to social media on March 16, 2020, to label the pandemic the "Chinese Virus," he stoked even more distrust, sparking a virulent uptick in anti-Asian expressions on social media platforms (Hswen et al.). As science-deniers refused to wear masks, the use of that simple preventative measure became a political statement for people who sought to exercise their individual freedom as Americans, seemingly without concern for the welfare of others. Some of the same citizens also refused to get vaccines once they were available.

Perhaps more than any other event of our lifetime, the COVID-19 pandemic illustrates the concept of *biopolitics*. According to Foucault, biopolitics involves the interface between living beings and the law (*Birth* 317), such as statutes regulating food, water, and sanitation, or conversely, failures of such regulations, such as the infamous Tuskegee Syphilis Experiment, wherein researchers knowingly left African American men infected with the disease in rural Alabama to die so they could study its natural progression. Another example of biopolitics involves the lead contamination that poisoned the water in Flint, Michigan, affecting children especially, as we have discussed in chapter 3. In a neoliberal economy, the market comes to regulate biological phenomena— people, animals, natural resources, the environment—but the term *biopolitics* indicates that a relationship exists between biological forces and government control, which is why we think of examples such as state governments in the US issuing "stay-at-home" mandates in March 2020, as *biopolitical*.

Neoliberalism relies on biopolitical power: the individual on whom the free-market economy depends is both empowered by and repressed by government regulatory power over the environment, over the cultivation and processing of food, and over medical issues (including regulations at every stage of human life, from the legality of birth control to assisted suicide, and from regulations of pharmaceuticals to regulations of funerary arrangements). One of the inherent contradictions in neoliberalism is the paradox by which the free market is sustained by infinitely complex biopolitical regulations: many farmers in the US, for example, oppose any form of government regulation—except those programs that free the farmer from fear of economic loss, such as crop insurance and farm subsidies. Additionally, Foucault notes the role of biopolitics in reinforcing segregation and stereotypes when he observes that biopolitics "also acted as factors of segregation and social hierarchization . . . guaranteeing relations of domination and effects of hegemony" (*History* 141). Enforced segregation in the southern states of the US, for example, could not have existed without the biopolitical dynamics between (false and essentialized) pseudo-biological concepts of race and legal statutes, such as Jim Crow laws.

In an era in which fifty years of settled abortion rights have been overturned by the US Supreme Court, when young Black men are murdered at the hands of the state, people of color are incarcerated in mass numbers, Muslim Americans are surveilled and harassed, anti-Semitism is boiling over in popular culture and politics, and immigrant families are separated on the southern US border and immigrant children are detained in cages, one might expect that sexism and racial hierarchies would be roundly critiqued in dystopian and postapocalyptic fiction for young adults. More often than not, however, popular books in these genres are set in futuristic societies that are as gendered as our current culture but that are purportedly blind to race. In these books, many characters' success is linked to ability and initiative instead of identity politics or discrimination. Nevertheless, there are exceptions to this pattern, as futurist fiction for adolescents can also examine and critique neoliberalism's reliance on biopolitics to support and reproduce systemic oppression. After providing theoretical information about biopolitics, we turn in this chapter to close readings of such futurist novels as Sherri L. Smith's *Orleans* (2013), Marissa Meyer's *Cinder* (2012), and Paula Mendoza and Abby Sher's *Sanctuary* (2020). We next analyze oil production as a biopolitical issue, demonstrating it as a factor that propels the narrative arc in a handful of novels written for a general audience, but which feature adolescent protagonists. To conclude, we interrogate how biopolitics play out in several of the YA novels we have already analyzed in this volume to demonstrate that this pervasive issue appears in a broad range of genres, including realism and speculative fiction alike.

HUMAN CAPITAL AND THE BIOPOLITICAL

Foucault observes that the study of political economy has traditionally "declared that the production of goods depends on three factors—land, capital, and labor—while leaving the third unexplored" (*Birth of Biopolitics* 215). He argues that the human worker should instead be studied "as an active economic subject" because "the ability-machine of which it is the income cannot be separated from the human individual who is its bearer" (*Birth of Biopolitics* 223, 226). In other words, in a neoliberal economy, workers cannot be fully separated from either their productivity or their worth as workers. Foucault understands this transformation of thinking about people in terms of their being *human capital.*

Foucauldian scholar Christopher Breu extends this economic theorization into biopolitics, arguing that the latter concept "suggests that a relationship between biopolitics and neoliberalism can be adduced in relationship to the neoliberal concept of 'human capital' as the means by which human life and biology are regulated under neoliberalism" (15). In a neoliberal economy, "immaterial production" begins to replace material production as the core of the economy, so that cities that once depended on "a largely industrial, shipping, and manufacturing base" now become "organized around the [globalized] electronic, service, and financial sectors of the economy" (Breu 21, 134). In other words, neoliberalism prioritizes the production of any individual (including their immaterial production) as a cog in the economy, such that even the individual's biologically situated body is regulated through economic forces. In this context, people are viewed as biopolitical human capital fit for exploitation by governments and corporations.

Examining neoliberal biotechnologies in literature for young people, Naarah Sawers argues that their advent "makes problematic any definitive understanding of the self or subjectivity," explaining that "agency is crucial to understanding how humanity is enacted as performativity in posthuman narratives for children and young adults" (171, 173). Likewise, Stephanie Guerra suggests that "the possibility of creating or altering subjects to accommodate corporate interests . . . echo[es] through fiction [with] questions at the very heart of bioethics about what it means to create, design, and alter human life, and the potential of such staggering capabilities in the hands of profit-seeking corporations" (290). Thus, Sawers (170) and Guerra (288), like Clare Bradford et al. (16) understand that children's and YA literature focuses on agency and subjectivity, whether the novel at hand is a celebratory tale about the potentiality of technoscience or a cautionary tale about dystopic forces of globalization at work in a dark authoritarian future.

In the sections that follow, we examine how dystopian and postapocalyptic fiction for teenagers can employ biopolitics in ways that either reproduce or resist social stratification. To do so, we examine two YA novels—Sherri L. Smith's *Orleans*, a work of postapocalyptic fiction, and Paula Mendoza and

Abby Sher's *Sanctuary*, a dystopia—as works that depict neoliberal reliance on biopolitics specifically to critique the erasure of race. In addition to showing how biopolitics can be used to replicate social stratification, *Orleans* and *Sanctuary* also acknowledge the erasure of race and the elision of the local and the global as problematic. Marissa Meyer's *Cinder*, on the other hand, also employs a posthuman use of biopolitics, but it elides race almost entirely, and as a consequence, reproduces the myth of postracialism on which we have suggested neoliberalism depends. Because *Orleans* and *Sanctuary* rely on biopolitics in their direct rejection of racist neoliberal thinking, we argue that these two novels warrant attention from literary critics as well as teachers, librarians, and other adults who work with literature for adolescents.

BIOPOLITICS AND RACE ERASURE IN *ORLEANS* AND *CINDER*

Smith's *Orleans* features an African American protagonist and portrays a new world order in which the ideologies of neoliberalism have been followed to their logical and most destructive extreme. In the world of Orleans, blood, rather than race, provides a logic for social hierarchization. In the novel, a series of hurricanes, each more powerful than the last, has ravaged the city formerly known as New Orleans, unleashing a plague-like epidemic—Delta Fever—that has decimated the population. Unable to discover a cure for the blood-borne contagion and unwilling to shoulder the financial burden of continually rebuilding the hurricane-ravaged city, the US government, to protect its economic interests and workforce, abandons the people of the Gulf Coast, literally segregating the southern states of this region from the rest of the population by constructing a vast concrete wall patrolled by armed soldiers and blood-sniffing drones. The people trapped south of the wall have learned how to survive in tribes based on their blood type, and the book repeatedly maintains that no one can survive without a tribe. In *Orleans*, individualism matters far less than group identity. Nevertheless, because some blood types are less susceptible to Delta Fever than others, individuals with those blood types assume greater economic value, and so people live aware of their biocapital worth and serve as their own blood entrepreneurs. The result is a terrifying free-market system that, in the absence of government regulation, reduces every physical body to the status of a biocommodity.

The subsequent blood warfare that results from an unfettered economy structured solely around survival is also brutal. The novel communicates an ideological critique of economies predicated on maintaining a rigid system of haves and have-nots, as when the protagonist, a teenage girl named Fen, wonders, "Ain't it be like that everywhere? Either you got it or somebody else do?" (167). In contrast, the small-scale economies that succeed in Orleans involve some type of regulation. For example, each blood tribe provides security at the Market, which "be right at the edge of the Mississippi, with her back up against the Old French Quarter" (18). In this way the blood tribes, having filled a vacuum created in the absence of government intervention, serve as the collective force regulating the Market, so that each group can trade safely.

Orleans imagines a postapocalyptic world in which the logic of neoliberalism has prevailed: social and political institutions that once safeguarded citizens' interests are broken, with the result that people compete against one another to survive. Fen's tribe has been dispersed because of a massacre led by another tribe; the leader of Fen's tribe, Lydia, dies immediately after the massacre while giving birth to a child, Baby Girl. Fen vows to deliver Baby Girl safely over the wall before the infant can contract Delta Fever, which typically occurs within a week of birth. Despite the fact that churches have long been considered safe zones in the Delta, Fen learns that even they have become corrupting centers of commerce. She seeks sanctuary in a Christian church they happen upon. Fen thinks to herself it "ain't seen God in a long time," an observation that proves prophetic later when she learns that a voodoo priestess named Mama Gentille has co-opted the structure to lure the unsuspecting children of freesteaders—people who try to live independent of a tribe—with the goal of selling them into bondage in the blood trade (76). Fen confronts Mama Gentille about this, but the latter dismisses the criticism, stating, "God a business, just like any other" (102). Thus, Fen, as narrator, critiques neoliberalism: Mama Gentille is corrupt because she places her own individual economic interests ahead of others, exemplifying how neoliberalism conceptualizes people as a biological resource (or in neoliberal terms, human capital) to be used and discarded.[1]

Throughout *Orleans*, Fen demonstrates an understanding that her survival is threatened if she cannot function within a group; indeed, in her world, unchecked individualism, rather than conformity to a group, is a liability. In contrast, Cinder, the eponymous protagonist of the first book in Meyer's Lunar Chronicles series, values her individualism and her entrepreneurship above all other skills. At no point in *Cinder*, or in any of its sequels or prequels, is capitalism depicted as anything other than the most logical and efficient way to maintain social order. Viewed through the lens of individualism and its role within free-market economies, Meyer's novel exemplifies the type of YA dystopia that erases the impact of race as a social factor.

In *Cinder*, the titular character has a booth in the city's bustling marketplace where she is regarded as "the best mechanic in New Beijing" (10). Although merchants in the marketplace sell local material goods, such as baked goods and silk, Cinder sells her specialized knowledge and services—immaterial goods—as a mechanic. Meanwhile, Queen Levana, Cinder's nemesis who rules the Moon, has relied on biopolitics to create two weapons of war: a mutant army and the letumosis plague. Emperor Kai describes the latter crisis in the language of neoliberalism: "My father was fighting a war against letumosis, the pestilence that has ravaged our planet for over a dozen years.... The good people of the Commonwealth, and all our Earthen siblings, have lost friends, family, loved ones, neighbors. And with these losses, *we face loss of trade and commerce, a downturn of economy, worsened living conditions*" (311, emphasis added). Biopolitics—here, taking the form of biowarfare—are problematic not only because of the loss of human life, but also—and apparently more important—because the plague is bad for business.

As in *Orleans*, biopolitics also determine social stratification in Meyer's novel. While Cinder, as a cyborg, is considered "36.28 percent not human," her best friend Iko, a robot, occupies the lowest caste of all, that of the android, which is 100 percent not human (82). Cyborgs are Earthen culture's pinnacle achievement of the free market, but government decree defines them as second-class citizens. Presumably, this second-class citizenship guarantees "fully human" citizens a competitive advantage in the marketplace, which results in social stratification and explains why Cinder tries to hide her cyborg status from others. The text positions cyborgs as "other" compared to humans, resulting in a distinct form of biopolitical social stratification.

In *Orleans*, however, social stratification depends on blood type, as well as on whether a person lives in a tribe or as a freesteader. Based on a logic of biopolitics, people band together in tribes solely according to their blood type. Life is precarious in Orleans, however, as biopolitics also provide the city's citizens with a rationale for social stratification. Because O-blood types carry the disease but are not adversely affected by it, they are considered economically more valuable than people with other blood types; as a result, they are preyed on by Blood Hunters, who traffic in the sale of their blood. Other tribes, due to their biological susceptibility to Delta Fever, must also sustain themselves through transfusions of blood harvested from members of the O-blood tribes. Due to their complete independence, freesteaders face the most risk. Fen hierarchizes the above castes when she explains, "In Orleans, you either a tribe, a religion, a hunter, or a freesteader. Better a tribe than a religion, but freesteader be as good as free-deader" (82). The vulnerability of people depends entirely on their biopolitical connection to a collective.

Yet another layer of bio-social stratification exists in *Orleans*: people who are not infected with Delta Fever (i.e., those in the Outer States) are considered more valuable to the free-market economy in Orleans than those who carry the disease. After the US government protected its workforce by segregating the people of Orleans from those in the Outer States, the federal government claimed Louisiana as a base for strategic military operations, assembling its forces on the border there en masse and summarily killing anyone caught crossing the wall. Daniel is a military scientist who has engineered a virus he hoped would destroy Delta Fever, but which in fact threatens to kill anyone living in the Delta who has the fever's pathogens in their blood. He understands the lengths to which the government would go to protect its economic interests. He worries that the government, upon learning that "the Delta could be recovered, stripped of Delta Fever and harvested for its natural resources—timber, oil, shipping lanes, and more ... might very well use it. Genocide in the name of money" (47). His suspicion is not unfounded, as the text implies that the government is arming the blood tribes with weapons to facilitate their self-annihilation so that the Outer States can capitalize on the Delta's resources. Delta Fever thus offers the federal government a rationale for "managing" the population via genocide.

RACE, EXPLOITATION, AND THE ELISION OF THE GLOBAL AND LOCAL

Bradford et al. express concern that "subjectivities in the new global order are both dispersed and integrated," and they identify a problem "associated with the widespread use of the term 'globalisation': as an all-encompassing signifier it evades charges of ethno-euro-anglocentrism" (42, 41). They also rely on Harvey's recognition that "globalization is about the socio-spatial relations between billions and individuals" to argue that "globalising processes reconfigure social space" in a "universalising process" that can lead to erasures of specificity, such as racial and ethnic identity (Bradford et al. 42). Harvey directly connects race to neoliberalism via the mechanism of social class and the exploitation of workers: "Employers have historically used differentiations within the labour pool to divide and rule. Segmented labour markets then arise and distinctions of race, ethnicity, gender, and religion are frequently used, blatantly or covertly, in ways that redound to the employers' advantage" (*Brief* 168). Harvey argues that the "mobility of global capitalism" allows it to move into markets where laborers can be exploited;

race and ethnicity are often implicated in the exploitation that globalized capitalism affords (*Brief* 168–69).

Roland Robertson, however, critiques those uses of the term *globalization* that rely on a simple global/local binary and that ignore how much of "what is called local is in large degree constructed on a trans- or super-local basis" (26). He believes the term *glocalization* better "describes the interactions of the global and the local" (26) since it more precisely captures the interplay between local forces and the global economy (26). Additionally, Robertson argues that the concept of glocalization helps us to avoid what he recognizes as a tendency to confuse "globalization" with "homogenization" (31). He acknowledges that people are capable of evading or resisting homogenizing forces, noting that corporations "increasingly tailor their products to a differentiated global market" (46). Thus, to cater to international markets, McDonald's sells products such as rice McWraps in China, the McLobster Roll in New England, and India's McPaneer Royale. In every case, McDonald's profits off of local flavors that are often sold to exploited laborers confined to work in the country of their birth because of immigration policy and/or their lack of personal capital.

An inherent contradiction in neoliberalism is the paradox by which ostensibly laissez-faire markets are sustained by infinitely complex biopolitical government regulations. For example, neither slavery nor later enforced segregation in the southern US could have existed without the biopolitical dynamics between insidiously hierarchized racialization and legal statutes. This phenomenon occurs in *Orleans* when the US government chooses to protect its workforce by cordoning off the Gulf Coast region, leaving an entire population of people to die from Delta Fever. Similarly, Cinder's status as a cyborg advantages her in the marketplace, while simultaneously offering her society a rationale for treating her like a second-class citizen.

Sarah Trimble connects stories about contagion and disease—such as letumosis in *Cinder* or Delta Fever in *Orleans*—to anxieties about how "transformations of the state under neoliberalism (re)shape the national response to disease" (298). Specifically, Trimble links "the dis/ease generated by neoliberalism and the new proximities wrought by globalization" to "a patriarchal survivalist fantasy that articulates among whiteness, rage, and (corporeal) fortification" (298). Although *Orleans* is predicated on a narrative of "dis/ease," it rejects many narratives of neoliberalism and problematizes what Trimble calls "white rage" (303). In *Orleans*, contagion is not a metaphor for white middle-class fears that the world is becoming corrupt; rather, the social construction of race itself is problematized as the original source of this culture's contagion.

BIOPOLITICS AS A FRAME FOR *ORLEANS*'S SOCIAL CRITIQUE

According to the official narrative surrounding the creation of the Institute for Post-Separation Studies in *Orleans*, a team of doctors, psychologists, researchers, and graduate students who were "willing to dedicate their lives to the cause" stayed behind in the city after the government abdicated its responsibilities there to study whether constructs such as race and gender would matter once people stratified along bloodlines (74). Racial divide, then, proves to be the most powerful metaphor for corruption in the novel. Had scientists not wished to have a project in which they could study a postracial cultural system, the text implies that a cure for Delta Fever might have been more strenuously sought.

When Fen leads the military scientist Daniel to the Institute in a trade by which he promises to help her get Baby Girl over the wall, he is horrified to learn how callous its leaders have been in the name of science. Instead of developing a cure for Delta Fever, these scientists selfishly allowed people to perish so they could pursue their research agenda, prompting Daniel to compare this abuse of institutional power to the real-life Tuskegee Syphilis Experiment. Fen tells him that "studying tribes" has been the Institute's "pet project" because the lead scientist "ain't interested in the Fever" (207). Daniel replies, "Ending racism. . . . For the most part the rules of blood make race irrelevant. Blood types cross all ethnicities" (207). Fen agrees, stating, "If folks stop hating each other 'cause of skin color, the only difference be blood type," which leads Daniel to conclude, "A new form of racism. . . . It's like Tuskegee all over again. They never wanted a cure" (207). Revealing her distrust of social and political institutions that have consistently failed her, Fen thinks to herself, "I don't know nothing about Tuskegee, but if it mean folks with power always gonna abuse it, then I got to agree" (207).

Biopolitical rules of blood appear to have shifted rules of class and race, but Smith does not entirely erase the latter as a concept from *Orleans*. Fen refers to one character's "ruddy brown" skin (35) and another's "mahogany face" (249). One woman has skin "too dark for blond hair" (123); a smuggler is described as "white, whiter than you see in Orleans anymore, with yellow-blond hair stuck to his forehead with sweat" (77–78). Fen also refers to the way the people of the region have become "mixed up" racially (78). Indeed, one of the few people in the novel described as "pink" is a corrupt priest wearing make-up to disguise his illness because he wants to commodify Baby Girl and give himself a blood transfusion, which will in turn kill her (297).

Another exception to the creolization of races is Asian Americans, who are largely immune to Delta Fever and who have developed their own shanty town along the river, although it is a culture among which mixes "Koreans and Japanese, Chinese and Vietnamese and Filipino. But nothing else. Folks in Orleans all be mutts except for the Asians" (144). As Fen tells Daniel, "The Fever ain't take to Asians the way it did the rest of us, so they like a tribe that way" (144). These people are thrifty, economical, tight-knit, and "they used to trading" (145), so even in this otherwise carefully antiracist novel, Smith depicts this group in terms of the "model minority myth" that "has been used to explain the assumed success of Asian Americans by essentialising this heterogeneous group of people as hardworking, docile, self-sufficient, and family oriented" (Chen and Lau 292).[2] Smith's reliance on this stereotype reinforces how inescapable racial stratification still is in US constructions of social groups, even when an author such as Smith is committed to exposing racism as a function of neoliberalism.

Dystopias such as *Cinder*, on the other hand, reproduce neoliberal values insofar as they celebrate free markets and individualism while also eliding race and ethnicity to minimize the destructive impact of racial discrimination and the importance of local culture. In contrast, we interpret *Orleans* as offering a counter-narrative to neoliberalism and the value that it purportedly places on liberating both markets and people from regulatory constraints. Rather than celebrating the exceptional, self-enclosed individual who trades on her unique abilities to overcome adversity, Smith's novel acknowledges that race and class serve gatekeeping functions in white supremacist societies. In Fen's world, hope for the survival of humankind depends not on unchecked individualism but on its opposite: people's willingness to set aside their self-interest and work for the betterment of the social group. The novel argues that our future as individuals is implicated in our relationships with the environment, in our valuing cultures from varying racial and ethnic groups, and, ultimately, in the well-being of the social collective. As Fen says, "we in this together" (207).

BIOPOLITICS AND GENOCIDAL LOGIC IN *SANCTUARY*

As with Smith's *Orleans*, Mendoza and Sher's *Sanctuary* examines the role that biopolitics plays in producing racial hierarchies—in this case, when recent immigrants of color cannot access resources that are readily available to US citizens. This deprivation of resources reaches such extreme measures that the dominant group, mostly depicted as descendants of white colonizers, ultimately pursues the nefarious (il)logic of genocidal biopolitics. Set in the near future, this dystopia examines what happens when the US government watches the economy implode due to natural catastrophes caused by damage from climate change. These problems are exacerbated by the government's own failed responses to the obvious peril and results in an authoritarian leader implementing draconian anti-immigration laws that are designed to scapegoat immigrants.

The book's teenage protagonist, Valentina González Ramirez, or Vali as she is known to her family and friends, immigrated to the US with her mother, father, and Tía Luna when she was four years old to escape the violence that engulfed their native Colombia. For a time, they live peacefully in California, but after Immigration and Customs Enforcement (ICE) officers arrest and deport her father, Vali, along with Mami and younger brother, Ernesto (Ernie), flee to Vermont, where they live and the brother and sister attend school for several years. This small family's situation becomes more perilous, however, after the US president, a thinly veiled caricature of Donald J. Trump, is reelected for a third term and creates the Deportation Force (DF), a shadowy government agency authorized to detain suspected immigrants without a warrant. The DF is permitted to operate outside of longstanding federal laws originally designed to constrain law enforcement agents from abusing their powers.

When Vali is sixteen and still living in Vermont, a fifteen-year-old Latina immigrant wearing a Mickey Mouse T-shirt inadvertently steps on a landmine while attempting to cross a swath of land adjacent to the "Great American Wall" separating Tijuana from San Diego (2). Vali watches on her cell phone as a group of protestors and human rights activists rebel, pushing against the wall from both its California and Mexican sides. This quickly leads the US president to order another wall to be built separating California from all contiguous states. In response, California secedes and declares itself to be a sanctuary nation, separate from what Californians now begin to call the "Other 49" (286). The existence of this sanctuary nation-state motivates Vali, Mami, and Ernie to embark on a dangerous cross-country trip to reunite in San Diego with Mami's sister, Tia Luna. When the DF arrests Mami early in their journey, however, Vali and Ernie must complete the difficult trek themselves. They eventually accompany a small group of fellow immigrants and a dangerous so-called "coyote" they have all hired to smuggle them across the country in the back of a truck, where they huddle beneath frozen cow carcasses that are thawing as they hang from hooks in the ceiling (151). The hierarchical neoliberal society that *Sanctuary* envisions is thus premised on a logic of exploitation and expendability: people who are perceived as contributing to the economy are provided for by the government, while those who are perceived as a drain on it—in this case, because they are legally prohibited from contributing to the economy—are cast aside and stripped of even their basic humanity. As Vali thinks to herself in the back of the truck, "We were all just pieces of meat, really. Some of us with loss and shame weighing us down. The rest dismembered and frozen. All of us, beasts of prey" (163).

Vali connects the commodification and corporatization of neoliberal capitalism to the violence that engulfed her family in Colombia long ago. She explains that at the time, she was too young to understand that "there were big corporations trying to take over our town when I was little. That people were getting death threats and being murdered as they tried to stop the corporations from taking the gold under our mountains" (17). Consistent with neoliberalism's conceptualization of government as existing to protect and advance the interests of business, Vali likens the violence bred by corporate greed to a "quieter war," though she acknowledges that it is "almost deadlier, because it was so stealthy and cruel. A war camouflaged inside the shadows of peace" (17). Vali left Colombia with her parents when she was four, but after they survive a harrowing emigration to California, they discover that an equivalent racial hierarchy rationalizes the economic exploitation of immigrants in the US. For example, she describes a series of proclamations the president issues "about how 'illegals' were trying to ransack and ravage the country. The economy was in danger. The land was in danger. Everybody's taxes had to triple because there were evil foreigners lurking everywhere, ready to pounce on innocent Americans and take everything they'd worked so hard to achieve" (33). Vali's descriptions make clear that the majority of those labeled "illegals" are from countries identified as Spanish-speaking, African, or Middle Eastern. In another example of the abasement immigrants from these countries experience, Vali explains how the president "banned all public restrooms from dispensing tap water" as "part of his campaign to crack down on 'illegals taking all of our natural resources'" (112–13). White American citizens, on the other hand, prove to be the primary beneficiaries of this imbalanced economy. Whereas the section of the small Vermont town where Vali, Mami, and Ernie have lived quietly for years has "been on water rations and electricity curfews for close to a year now," those houses that are nearer to the magnet high school she attends across town have "drone irrigation, freshly painted storefronts, and real meats and vegetables in the grocery windows" (39–40). Likewise, she describes people she encounters on the streets by her school as "clearly wealthy and white," and she notes that "their homes looked sturdier; their grass looked thicker. They *belonged* here" (40, emphasis in original). Vali intuitively understands that when the economy in which one's access to resources—such as water, food, shelter, and even freshly grown grass—is regulated by nationalistic biopolitics, she and any others who share her perceived caste automatically occupy the status of *other*.

To maintain this oppressive economic system, the government requires that citizens bring a birth certificate or some other proof of citizenship to a local clinic so they can have small identification chips implanted in their wrists. As Vali explains, "The chips would have all of our information on them—ID number, birthplace, blood type, medical history, even allergies" (21). By scanning a person's wrist with a handheld electronic device, such Althusserian Repressive State Apparatuses as ICE and the Deportation Force are able to determine "who belonged here once and for all" (21). This federal stricture leads to the creation of a black market that enables those with enough money to have a chip implanted illegally. Although Vali and her mother purchase implants for five thousand dollars each, the family does not have enough money for Papi to also do so; as a result, he is eventually detained by the government and deported. He is later found dead on the trail to the mountain village in Colombia from whence he once fled with his sister-in-law, his wife, and their young daughter. But since his son was born in the US, Ernie is granted full access to all rights as a citizen. Because Ernie's wrist chip was legally implanted, it will never malfunction, a risk that both his mother and sister confront more than once in the book. Between these trackers and the government's racist rhetoric contorted into patriotism, the novel paints a vivid portrait of the neoliberal genocidal logic through which *Sanctuary* acknowledges the deterministic role that biopolitics play in the creation of hierarchies that define some people's lives as more expendable than others.

This point becomes particularly evident when Vali, Mami, and Ernie frequent a public transportation station in the initial phase of their flight from Vermont because they want to purchase tickets for a bus to Queens, New York, where a friend of Mami's will help them escape to California. As the small family stands in line waiting to pass through the security checkpoint and have their wrist implants scanned, Vali notices that the Deportation Force "officer manning the machine looked pissed off and tired" (88). He permits a group of "blond-haired, blue-eyed [college] students" to "just stick out their wrists and walk through without a second glance," but when Vali, Mami, and Ernie reach the front of the line, the guard "stood in front of [them] like a human blockade and let a creepy grin ooze across his lips" (88). The white college students flippantly dismiss the procedure as a trifling "pain in the ass," but for Vali and her family, the man's racism, emboldened by the power of institutional authority, signifies the difference between remaining in the US and being detained and returned to a war-torn country (87). Blond-haired, blue-eyed college students need not fear the genocidal logic of this novel's neoliberal government; that fear is reserved for immigrants of color, such as Vali and the members of her family.

BIOPOLITICS AS A FRAME FOR *SANCTUARY*'S CRITIQUE OF HUMAN CAPITAL AND MERITOCRACY

As a genre, YA dystopia is didactic insofar as it aspires to "teach serious lessons about the issues faced by humanity" (Basu et al. 5). In *Sanctuary*, Mendoza and Sher take neoliberalism's commodification of human life to its most destructive and horrifying extreme, describing a system in which people are kept alive only for as long as they are valued for their utilitarian abilities. When Vali and Ernie finally reach the transfer point in Oklahoma where the coyote driving the meat truck was meant to deliver their group, they are horrified to learn that the second set of coyotes they encounter, Ronny and BJ, have no intention of aiding them further, much less helping them reach California. Instead, these white men, self-styled as entrepreneurs, have devised a business plan by which they profit from sex-trafficking the bodies of female immigrants to members of the local Deportation Force. Vali and Rosa—a fellow immigrant who has ridden with her two young children in the back of the meat truck alongside Vali and her brother—quickly attract these men's lecherous eyes. When Rosa's infant daughter, Guadalupe, begins to cry, Ronny grows angry, prompting his partner, BJ, to reassure him, "We're gonna get paid, I promise.... And we got some nice fresh meat" (194). When he lifts a lantern up to Vali and Rosa "to get a better glimpse of [their] bodies," Vali is reminded of how her mother performed a similar gesture while she examined cattle when she worked on a dairy farm "in Vermont, sizing up the cows' flanks" (193).

As BJ shepherds this latest group of captive immigrants through the rancid house, the newcomers are sickened when they encounter two heavily sedated, "glassy-eyed" women, both of whom wear only "oversize T-shirts" and who are "tied to an empty bed frame with a rope" (197). Vali and her brother have met a young Filipino man named Malakas in the back of the truck. When he attempts to intervene on Vali's behalf, BJ puts a gun to his head and informs him that a recent update to the national database means that the government is now able to track immigrants who have had a black market chip implanted in their wrist. He continues, "The only reason why you haven't been caught yet is 'cuz the officers around here know me. They like me. Or, at least, they like what I have to offer" (198). When Ronny returns later with a Deportation Force officer clearly there on the assumption that Rosa is his to rape, a skirmish ensues, and another passenger who has been in the meat truck, Volcanoman, shoots one of their assailants, enabling the group from the truck to flee.

A second example of how *Sanctuary* critiques the commodification of people as human capital occurs some time later in the story when Vali, Ernie, Malakas, and Volcanoman, now the only remaining survivors of the original group from the meat truck, ride atop the roof of a self-automated freight train bound southwest to California. From her perch atop the train, Vali borrows Malakas's high-powered binoculars to survey the surrounding landscape. In the distance, she observes a series of "huge tents pitched in the middle of the desert" (237). Upon closer examination, however, she realizes that the tents contain metal cages in which people of all ages are held. As she pans the scene still further, she spies "a line of hunched silhouettes emerging from another one of the tents. All of them stooped over, walking with the pained stagger of someone half dead. They were attached to each other with what looked like neck collars and leashes. Surrounded by armed DF officers" (238). When she finally reaches California and tells her Tía Luna what she has seen, her aunt, an activist for immigrant rights, informs her that the camps are in fact "labor camps" the president has created for the purpose of forcing "illegals [to] pay off their debt to America" (285). In a scene evocative of recent presidential administrations' brutal treatment of immigrants along the southern US border, Vali's aunt tells her that, having ceased its program of deporting people, the government "puts undocumented immigrants in cages and forces them [to] work without pay and with no end in sight" (285). In this way, the book shows how, when taken to its extreme end, neoliberalism's reliance on biopolitics and its embrace of ideologies that rationalize commodifying people as human capital result in a system inescapably akin to slavery.

As a work of dystopian fiction, *Sanctuary* also critiques neoliberalism's emphasis on self-enclosed individualism and its underlying assumption that in the US, people compete on a level playing field, regardless of identity politics. Unlike the protagonist of *Cinder*, who rises above discrimination and adversity because of her exceptionalism, the characters in *Sanctuary* are not disillusioned by the myth of meritocracy. Instead, they are well aware of the obstacles they encounter as immigrants in a white supremacist society. For instance, at a second clearing point before Vali and her mother and brother can even arrive via bus to New York, Mami, fearing the black market chip implanted in her wrist will malfunction, hands her backpack—with its precious contents of food, water, cash, and a knife that proves pivotal later in the novel—to her daughter. Moments later, Mami is detained by members of the Deportation Force, and whether she is deported or imprisoned in a government labor camp is left uncertain. What is not ambiguous is Vali's mother's emphatic last word to her daughter: "*GO!*" (93, emphasis in the original). Vali subsequently leads her brother to a safe harbor church in Queens, where the nun who welcomes them later pays $10,000 to the coyote truck driver to transport them to California. In the back of this truck with its melting meat, Vali and Ernie meet the explosively tempered Brazilian they nickname "Volcanoman" due to his impatience with Rosa's four-year-old son, Tomas, and the teenage Filipino boy, Malakas, who eventually accompanies Vali and her brother all the way to California.

The group's emphasis on collective action as an antidote to the government's genocidal logic is evident when the aforementioned coyote's maniacal partners try to rape Tomas's mother, leading Volcanoman to shoot one of them. Four-year-old Tomas flees alone in terror from the gunshots. The rest of the group also escapes their captors in the chaos, only to discover that the frantic Tomas has drowned while running from the violence. Rosa refuses to leave her son's body, despite incoming drones that have tracked her and her son through their malfunctioning identification chips. Vali, Volcanoman, and Malakas urge her to flee with them and Ernie so that she can save her remaining child, but Rosa stands her ground, holding her dead and her living child close to her chest, urging the others to "GO!," just as Vali's mother has also once commanded (216):

> There was not a scrap of self-pity in her voice. She was grounded and sure of what she wanted. As if speaking not only for herself, but for every mother who'd ever lost a child before her. She rocked back and forth with both her children in her lap. The baby still drinking from her breast....
> She was not a martyr. She was a mother. (215–16)

Moments later, the drones drop nets that ensnare Rosa and her children, lifting them into the sky and away from the now camouflaged group that has tried to save them.

Tomas's death and his mother's subsequent refusal to abandon his dead body transform the remaining refugees into an emotionally connected collective. Volcanoman can admit that his volatility stems from having witnessed his mother shot while two gang members in Rio de Janeiro tried to rape his sister. Both his mother and his sister manage to survive, but because his mother knows Volcanoman is gay, she does everything she can to send him to the US to keep him safe from homophobic murderers, once again demonstrating how biopolitics can provide a logic for genocide. Like Rosa, Volcanoman's mother is not a martyr; rather, she is terrified that people in the community where they live will kill her beloved son because of his sexual orientation. Malakas's mother, too, has sacrificed greatly to pay for her son to emigrate to the US so that he can escape the environmental degradation of the Philippines. Just before he leaves their island home, his mother tells him "to look at the moon" every night, promising that she will, too, so that they "would be, kind of, together" (187). This is what has kindled Malakas's original interest in astronomy—and it is that sense of being unconditionally loved that gives him strength to persevere after he learns that his mother died when his hometown was "washed away" because global warming has created such ferocious storms, cyclones, and mudslides in the region (188). His knowledge of science, along with his ability to give and receive love, add to the group's collective strength. By acknowledging the shared economic and social obstacles that Vali and other characters in the novel confront because of the genocidal logic of a government that rages against them and denies their potential contributions to the society, *Sanctuary* exposes hierarchical notions of American meritocracy as one of the lies on which neoliberalism is built. In doing so, however, the book also positions readers to understand other people as potential allies, rather than competitors, and to recognize and honor their shared humanity, even in death.

At the novel's climatic moment, when Vali, Malakas, and Ernie plunge into the raging waters of the Colorado River in their last, desperate attempt to reach California by swimming, she is made aware of the connectedness she feels towards others. As she braves the river's currents, pulling Ernie along by her side, she thinks, "Whether or not I had the skills to stay afloat, I felt like there was a greater current moving me forward. Maybe connected to the sun and moon or the magical weightlessness of everything floating, gliding, compelling us forward" (277). She continues, "Definitely connected to Mami and Papi and the girl in the Mickey Mouse T-shirt. Because we were all woven from the same thread. Braided together in an intricate pattern. *It was only on land that humans could draw all these boundaries and build these gigantic walls*" (277, emphasis added). In this way, the novel acknowledges the power that people exercise when they work together as a collective.

Compared to the fifteen-year-old in the Mickey Mouse T-shirt whose self-motivated death march serves as the activating circumstance for the US crackdown on immigrants, intelligent, strong, courageous Vali might initially appear to be a smart, strong, superspecial hero. She is, however, only relatively successful during her quest. She gets herself and her younger brother to California, but at a great cost, as they are both clearly traumatized by the experience. On a personal level, she has lost her mother, her best friend in Vermont, and a litany of others for whom she grieves: "Rosa, Tomas, Guadalupe, Volcanoman" (303). On a larger scale, she has made no impact whatsoever on the systems that have oppressed her and millions of other people. Immigrants are still being persecuted in the Other 49; immigrants once thought to have been deported are now found to be detained in squalid conditions in forced labor camps that evoke death camps, and Vali has been emotionally scarred by violence, threats of rape, and multiple traumas. Unlike the superspecial individuals who serve as exceptional, self-enclosed neoliberal heroes in such dystopias as *Legend* and *Cinder*, the protagonist's success in *Sanctuary*, as in *Orleans*, is defined by survival, a survival that is itself predicated entirely upon working within a collective in which each flawed human's individual skills nevertheless provide value to the group.

HISTORICAL INTERLUDE: BIOPOLITICS AND PETROLEUM

In this chapter, we have written about race as a biopolitical construct, and in chapter 3, we have written about how racism was initially used to justify enslaving peoples as free labor in Anglophone countries so as to expand the profitability of agriculture and commerce, particularly in cotton mills in the US and UK. Baldly stated, commerce necessitated slavery, which in turn necessitated racism. The politics of slavery were based on constructions of the physiological—as determined by skin color, other physical characteristics, and place of origin—all of which were effectively defined in biological terms for 400 years. Slavery is a heinous example of damaging, misguided, and genocidal biopolitics.

We turn now to yet another biopolitical disaster for the global economy: the commodification of petroleum products and the global thirst for oil, both of which are the direct result of biopolitical decisions made for the last 150 years by international political figures. (We touch on this topic briefly in chapter 5 with our discussion of Nnedi Okorafor's Nsibidi Scripts series.) Petroleum products have not only created air pollution, water pollution, and increased cancer rates worldwide, they have also led to a dramatic increase in carbon production, thus imperiling the planet's ability to sustain human life in the future. Despite this, much international legislation and many alliances have historically protected the ongoing use of these fossil fuels. For example, following World War I, the UK supported an Iranian shah who allied himself with the UK's oil interests, but during World War II, fearing that Iran would make an alliance with Russia or Germany, the UK ousted that shah. When the Iranian Parliament voted in 1951 to nationalize their oil industry, the UK turned to the US for help in overthrowing the sitting government so that the Shah's son, Mohammad Reza, could serve as a ruler friendly to the Allies. At the heart of the shifting tensions in Iran was a precious biopolitical commodity, petroleum.

Later, in the autumn of 1973, the Organization of Arab Petroleum Exporting Countries (OAPEC), with the addition of Iran, placed an embargo on the nations that were most supportive of Israel during the 1973 Arab-Israeli War. The embargo initially affected Canada, Japan, the Netherlands, the UK, and the US. This embargo led to a quadrupling of oil prices for the affected countries ("Oil Shock"). Effects of the OAPEC-created oil shortage were felt globally, and many nations experienced turbulent protests, including nations such as India that were neither oil exporters nor involved in the 1973 Arab-Israeli War. Nevertheless, by 1975, high petroleum costs in India were among the factors that led Prime Minister Indira Gandhi to declare a state of emergency (known as "The Emergency"), which led to further political crisis in the country (Dahr 218–19).[3] Readers of *The Life of Pi* (2001) will recall that Pi Patel's family decides to leave India in June 1977, shortly after elections put an end to The Emergency (90); readers may also remember that an oil tanker ignores Pi's lifeboat, gliding carelessly by without noticing a teenage boy languishing, adrift in the ocean (234–35). Most important, when incredulous Japanese officials question Pi about the events he has narrated to them, they ask why the sinking ship he was on did not sound out a distress signal before it sank. The teenager responds, "In my experience, when a dingy, third-rate rustbucket sinks, unless it has the luck of carrying oil, lots of it, enough to kill entire ecosystems, no one cares and no one hears about it. You're on your own" (312). *The Life of Pi* is thus citing a cynical but accurate biopolitical truth about oil production and consumption in the late 1970s.

By 1979 in Iran, Shah Reza's greatest critic, a theologically conservative Muslim leader, Ayatollah Khomeini, rose to power following a revolution that had immediate effects on world history: the Ayatollah mobilized evangelically conservative Shiites in Iran to oppose the Sunni regime in Iraq, setting the stage for US wars that would start in 1990 and continue again in 2002. Similar to *The Life of Pi*, Marjane Satrapi's *Persepolis* (2003) delves into the oil-fueled events of the 1979 Iranian Revolution. As Satrapi writes in her introduction to this graphic narrative: "In the twentieth century, Iran entered a new phase. Reza Shah decided to modernize and westernize the country, but meanwhile, a fresh source of wealth was discovered: oil. And with the oil came another invasion" (n.p.). Moreover, a hostage crisis in Iran in 1979 was a major factor in Ronald Reagan's defeat of President Jimmy Carter in 1980, at which point Margaret Thatcher was prime minister of the UK. Because the Iranian Revolution further disrupted global oil prices, the US experienced a recession in 1981 and 1982, as did much of Europe. In response to this oil crisis, the US and UK leaders, Reagan and Thatcher, set about dismantling the social safety networks put in place during the Great Depression of the 1930s. Both of them argued that free markets would result in "trickle-down prosperity" for everyone.

That never happened.

Instead, recession after recession followed: in 1990 and 1991, oil prices during the first Gulf War, "Desert Storm," triggered yet another recession. In that era, Salman Rushdie wrote of a fairy-tale city in *Haroun and the Sea of Stories* (1990): "In the north of the sad city stood mighty factories in which ... sadness was actually manufactured, packaged and sent all over the world, which never seemed to get enough of it. Black smoke poured out of the chimneys of the sadness factories and hung over the city like bad news" (15). Rushdie's description of the smoke-belching factories could describe any fossil fuel-reliant manufacturing plant, but its equation with "sadness" and "bad news" underscores that the use of most industrial fuel results from intentional political decisions that exploit carbon-based products and poison the air that people must breathe and the water that they must drink. We share this brief history of petroleum to emphasize the point that YA literature is not alone in examining the intersection of neoliberalism and biopolitics. Rather, these three bestselling works—Rushdie's *Haroun and the Sea of Stories*, Martel's *The Life of Pi*, and Satrapi's *Persepolis: The Story of a Childhood*, each published in English between 1990 and 2003, and each initially marketed to adults rather than youth—allude directly to carbon-based econo-politics while also touching on the interconnected relationships that exist in the interactions among youth, politics, and neoliberal capitalism itself.

BIOPOLITICS AND CONTAGION ACROSS GENRES

Throughout this chapter, we have provided close readings of novels that link biopolitics, immaterial production, and literature across genres. Works of YA futurist fiction lend themselves in particular to examining the neoliberal relationship between ideas of biopolitics and contagion. As in Smith's postapocalyptic *Orleans* and Meyer's dystopic *Cinder*, the citizens of Lu's *Legend* are victims of a deadly plague, one that affects lower-class people even more insidiously than it does those with the resources to fight it, something we analyze in chapter 1. Indeed, the government itself spreads the disease in order to have victims on which to experiment for cures, thus further weaponizing the plague for use against governmental adversaries.

In Taylor's mythical Daughter of Smoke and Bones series, which we examine in chapter 2, biopolitics also involve corrupt governments that employ biological antidotes to address their leaders' genocidal logic. For example, both angels and demons wage war as a form of genocide, hoping to annihilate the other population. The biologically caste-aware angels breed infinitely to create subalterns as biopolitical cannon-fodder for their war against the demons. Moreover, two resurrectionists among the demons can reincarnate people from teeth and their soul, captured in smoke, which invokes Holocaust imagery but without necessarily inviting readers to question the imagery. The basis of this genocide is certainly biopolitical: although angels and demons appear to constitute different lifeforms, their ability to breed together suggests that they are not any more genetically distinct as populations than Jewish people were from the perpetrators of Nazi Germany.

In realist fiction, too, biopolitics play a clear role. For example, the bonobo population in Eliot Schrefer's novel *Endangered* (discussed in chapter 2) is threatened in part because of human poaching and in part because of the richness of Congo's natural resources. As a UN guard tells the earnest protagonist who has upset the natural order by purchasing a poached young bonobo:

> "We're in the richest country in the world as far as minerals. Some very fancy metals that go into electronics can be found only here. What's lying unused in the Congo soil is worth more than the combined yearly GDP of Europe and America. So: How did a bunch of impoverished scraggly Rwandan mercenaries overthrow the standing government of the Democratic Republic of Congo? With lots of help from rich friends. Rwanda is the biggest exporter of coltan, diamonds, and gold. Rwanda has none of these, but it's next door to Congo. Follow?"
>
> "It's not about Tutsis. It's about access to the mines. These rebels have investors that want access to minerals."
>
> "Right. The rebels enslave the people and get free miners. In turn, they use the billions of dollars they make to buy more arms and terrorize more people." (157)

As our previous discussion of intersectional environmentalism in chapter 2 makes clear, exploiting the Earth's heavy metals leads inevitably to exploiting people.

Heavy metals also create a biopolitical nightmare in Curtis's *Bucking the Sarge*, which we attend to in chapter 3. Luther T. Mott's science fair entry "combined the traditional science fair project with some top-rate investigative journalism and detective work to expose a horrible fact of life in twenty-first century Flint, Michigan" (194–95). Luther has written about "the continued, criminal plague of leaded paint in many of our inner-city homes and apartments," a plague to which his own mother has contributed mightily as a slumlord (195). That "continued, criminal plague" put the emphasis on bio*political* when Flint residents learned in 2015—more than ten years after *Bucking the Sarge* was published—that their drinking water was contaminated with lead, endangering the health of thousands of children and teenagers. State-appointed local politicians were responsible for the 2014 decision to switch water supplies to the more dangerous, less regulated water supply that contained lead (Denchak).

Pollution and its biopolitical fallout also emerge as a significant factor in *A Snake Falls to Earth*, discussed in chapter 2, with its magic realist depiction of environmental devastation on Earth. Similarly, as we note in chapter 3, mystical creatures in *Firekeeper's Daughter* seek to save teenagers from involving themselves in the economically motivated biopolitical production of meth. Extending our discussion of the Hunger Games trilogy in chapter 1, we note that biopolitics also inform every aspect of the games in the trilogy: the gamekeepers manipulate the biopolitical with devices injected into the bodies of contestants in the arena; they develop and deploy mutations; they change the contestants' embodiment with skin care and prosthetic limbs that improve upon the original body parts. All these forms of biopolitics are condoned by the central government in the Capitol of Panem, as is the government-controlled starvation economics of both District 11 and District 12.

Gender, too, reaps undue consequences from the neoliberal manipulation of biopolitics and commercialism, even at the level of commodities made from the skin of endangered species or the proliferation of plastic enwrapping myriad beauty products. For example, in Boulley's *Firekeeper's Daughter*, Daunis's white grandmother, GrandMary, scrutinizes Daunis's clothing, expecting perfection from her granddaughter. GrandMary "believes in greeting the day with a perfect red smile" and insists on smelling her own expensive rose-scented hand cream at all times (9). Gossips in the town refer to her past "Perfect Life" before her daughter had a child out of wedlock. That child, Daunis, perceives the difference between GrandMary and her Ojibwe grandmother as follows: they "could not have been more different. One viewed the world as its surface, while the other saw connections and teachings that run deeper into our known world" (10–11). GrandMary is motivated by the biopolitics of appearance, a superficiality that Daunis's Ojibwe grandmother rejects.

Angela McRobbie gives a nuanced explanation as to how physical body size and superficial beauty are an outgrowth of neoliberal biopolitics. After tracking the limits of the feminist movement while simultaneously perceiving an increase in feminine drives for physical perfection, she asked herself, "Why had it become so commonplace for girls to say they hated their bodies?" ("Notes" 8). She finds the answer in neoliberal biopolitical visions of "'complete perfection.' By the perfect I mean a heightened form of self-regulation based on an aspiration to some idea of the 'good life.' . . . Various technologies bring the perfect into life, or vitalise it as an everyday form of self-measurement" ("Notes" 9). She continues with an exhaustive (and exhausting) list of questions that underscores the interrelated machinations of economics, technology, and human embodiment, especially for those who identity as girls and women:

> How well did I do today? Did I manage to eat fewer calories? Did I eat more healthily? Did I get to the gym? Did I achieve what I aimed to achieve at work? Did I look after the children with the right kind of attention? Did I cook well after the day's work? Did I ensure that my family returned from school and work to a well-appointed and well-regulated home? Did I maintain my good looks and my sexually attractive and well-groomed body? (9)

In a brilliant analogy that speaks to neoliberalism's fixation with self-regulation, Robbie calls these calculations "a kind of neoliberal spreadsheet, a constant benchmarking of the self, a highly standardised mode of self-assessment, a calculation of one's assets, a fear of possible losses," while she also critiques the ubiquity of cell phone photos and identifies how these self-conscious measurements align with Foucault's concepts from *The Birth of Biopolitics* regarding "human capital" ("Notes" 10). To McRobbie, the greatest irony is that those who employ neoliberal biopolitics of the perfect are self-regulating, self-judging, and self-loathing. They are not necessarily dominated by the patriarchy because they have internalized its male-centric neoliberal values; instead, "the perfect suggests that it is only viable to compete against other women. . . . The perfect does this by directing itself to girls and women only, and in so doing ensures the maintenance of boundaries against the threat of erosion through queer or transgender politics" ("Notes" 17). McRobbie implies that neoliberalism creates a self-sustaining form of disciplining the body, as Foucault might say. In our view, concepts of "perfection" also mask a problem that neoliberalism must hide: systemic gender imbalance.

CONCLUSION

Neoliberalism has the potential to remain masked in YA literature, especially in books that depict perfectionism among teens who identify as female or those that celebrate talented individuals, such as Cinder, who seemingly rise above their biopolitical social conditions purely as a result of their exceptionalism, regardless of poverty and/or gender and/or race and/or ethnicity and/or ability. On the other hand, novels that permit readers to confront and reject biopolitical neoliberal ideologies and values, such as Sherri L. Smith's *Orleans* and Paola Mendoza and Abby Sher's *Sanctuary*, can help teenage readers connect fictive worlds to social critiques of the world in which they live.

In the next chapter, we trace the relationship between neoliberalism and knowledge production. To do so, we explore how biopolitics and immaterial production affect the ways that knowledge is commodified and subsequently exploited in a neoliberal economy. We work from the premise that knowledge, whether construed as a neoliberal commodity to be traded or a collective resource to be shared, always already involves the biopolitical. Knowledge, after all, is generated by and stored in human brains—and no one's embodied mind is immune to the econo-political ideologies that surround them.

Chapter 7

KNOWLEDGE PRODUCTION AND NEOLIBERALISM

> Baby Girl, you don't know the world like I do.
>
> —Sherri L. Smith, *Orleans* (202)

In *The Order of Things* (1994), Michel Foucault asserts that every age is characterized by its epistemes, that is, by its systems of categorization (57–58). In his later work, *The Birth of Biopolitics*, Foucault defines neoliberalism as *the* American episteme in the second half of the twentieth century (222), which it arguably still is. Foucault claims that the populous constitutes the root problem of contemporary economics (*Biopolitics* 21), and he defines neoliberalism as the way that "scarce means are allocated to competing ends" (*Biopolitics* 222), which, of course, puts individuals within the population in competition with one another for those scarce resources. It follows, then, that the study of how people think and know what they know, called *epistemology*, also reflects the market forces at work in shaping the population's experiences within neoliberalism.

Epistemology is inseparable from sociopolitical and economic practices, such as how schools are structured and funded or how children are taught. Does discourse surrounding education position for-profit and private schools as enhancing students' future economic prospects and publicly funded schools as lessening them? Are teachers fairly compensated based on their academic credentialing? Are they in control of the curriculum, or is it dictated to them by external agents? Are school facilities safe, both physically and psychosocially, for all students, so that all students can maximize their learning? Readers of this book know that neither all schools nor all teachers—indeed, not all students—have the same access to sociopolitical and economic assets, which consequently affects how those students can learn. In short, sociopolitical and economic structures, especially those structured by neoliberalism, have an enormous epistemological impact on how children and teenagers know what they know.

Hans N. Weiler extends Foucault's sense of the epistemological relationship between power and knowledge to the "political economy of the *commercialization of knowledge*" (2, emphasis in the original) when he argues:

> Certain kinds of knowledge have always had their economic utility, but it is an important part of our times that *the creation of knowledge* has come to be regarded and treated so pervasively in economic and commercial terms. . . . The very nature of modern economic activity has become so massively dependent on up-to-date knowledge of constantly increasing scope and complexity that the linkage between knowledge and both productivity and profitability has become virtually inescapable. (5, emphasis added)

Weiler identifies the "power relationships" within neoliberalism as being "dictated by both the interests and the resources of the commercial users of knowledge" (5). He also asserts that knowledge production inheres to "the politics of production and profit, which are arguably the most powerful political dynamics in today's world" (5–6). In other words, knowledge production and those who control how that knowledge is "produced" become inseparable from neoliberalism's unquenchable thirst for profit-making. Moreover, as Jana Bacevic argues, the epistemology of neoliberalism privileges "individuals' behaviour online that becomes aggregated into 'Big Data'" and in turn supports "ever-more sophisticated modes of surveillance" and "privatisation" of debt, including but not limited to "student debt" (381). In other words, the epistemology of neoliberalism is defined in terms of data and dollars; as such, it is of central concern to our examination of how this econo-political theory finds its way into literature for teenagers.

The philosopher Nancy Tuana identifies how problematic it becomes when the knowledge held by dominant economic interests leads to the wholesale invisibility of entire swaths of the population—women, people of color, queer people, religious minorities, or those with disabilities, for example—whose experiences have not in the past been explained by standardized epistemologies of finance and data. Refuting the problematic construction of neoliberalism's totalizing economic epistemology, she documents how during the 1990s, "liberatory epistemologists aimed to transform the subject of knowledge in the sense of *focusing on knowledge obscured by dominant interests and values* to identify and provide tools for undermining the knowledges and practices implicated in oppression" (125, emphasis in the original). As she points out, "gender oppression does not happen in a vacuum but is complexly linked to colonialism, racism, heterosexism, as well as class biases, Eurocentrism, androcentrism, ableism, and other manifestations of power/privilege" (126). Tuana extols the virtues of liberatory epistemologies that "reveal the workings of power in the governance and disciplining of knowledge practices and institutions in order to generate paths to freedom" (126). She praises one such liberatory epistemology as that described by Charles W. Mills in *The Racial Contract* (1997): "Mills views the racial contract as resting upon an inverted epistemology in which those in privilege are ignorant of the privileges they reinforce and benefit from" (132). Indeed, Mills defines whiteness as a "contract" that is "political, moral, and epistemological" (12) and by which white people "categorize the remaining subset of humans as 'nonwhite'" (11). As with Foucault, Mills relies on epistemological concepts of classification or categorization to demonstrate how one dominant group constructs the world to its own benefit. In short, according to these philosophers of social justice, neoliberalism is of most benefit to those with economic privilege, usually the portion of the population identified as white, cis-het-male, and upper-class. Thus, the knowledge production of disadvantaged groups is further subordinated by those in power.

In this chapter, we build on our discussions earlier in this volume about individualism, ecocriticism, racism, gender, and biopolitics to examine epistemology and knowledge production as tools of neoliberalism. Using novels that we have discussed in previous chapters, we first identify neoliberal ideologies that rely on epistemologies of competition, often to the disadvantage of those characters who exist outside of (white) patriarchal structures. We then contrast these texts with epistemologically liberating YA novels—such as A. S. King's *Dig* (2019) and Kalynn Bayron's *Cinderella Is Dead* (2020)—that critique racist, sexist, queerphobic, and heterosexist neoliberal epistemologies by subverting, and even openly critiquing, the inherited systems of knowledge that privilege one or more social groups at the expense of another. In the chapter's concluding section, we contrast the ways in which Marissa Meyer's *Cinder* (2012) and Sherri L. Smith's *Orleans* (2013), which we have examined in chapter 6, both utilize narrative positioning as a form of knowledge production.

EPISTEMOLOGIES OF COMPETITION

When one conceptualizes knowledge as a commodity that one can trade on and profit from, as we argue is the case for neoliberalism, then knowledge itself becomes a contested site over which people compete for access. Suzanne Collins's Hunger Games books, for example, are premised on a shortage of commodities, especially a shortage of food in District 12. Food is not, however, the only commodity withheld from the young by the Capitol and by some of the adult characters in the series. Knowledge is also commodified and controlled. In the first book, Haymitch rewards the knowledge that Katniss gains in the arena with material gifts of food and supplies each time she discerns what he wants her to learn. In *Catching Fire*, he knows what Katniss does not: namely, that District 13 intends to blow up the arena to rescue her. Katniss's successful participation in these games is predicated on her remaining ignorant; even Peeta is in on the secret. Presidents Snow and Coin trade in secrets to their own advantage as well, and both keep their respective citizenries ignorant in order to maintain power over them. In *Mockingjay*, Finnick successfully leverages his knowledge of Snow's political misdeeds, which include poisoning his political enemies and trafficking the bodies of victors to wealthy patrons for profit, as the former Tribute works to weaken Snow's political standing. Likewise, Katniss learns that Coin intends to have her killed to preserve her grip on power, thus setting up a knowledge-based competition between these two characters that is only resolved when Katniss assassinates Coin.

The Hunger Games is not the only young adult series to demonstrate how a neoliberal economy commodifies immaterial concepts, such as knowledge itself. In Marie Lu's *Legend*, which we discuss in chapter 1, an authoritarian government regards June as a threat after she discovers that the government killed her father, a scientist, once he learned about its plan to release a plague in the city's poorest sectors to cull the population of those it considers genetically inferior. June's potential to use that knowledge against the government marks her as a threat to be eradicated. As she notes, "I'm a prodigy who knows the truth" (251). This biopolitical knowledge could prove lethal to her.

Literature for teenagers need not reproduce neoliberalism's conceptualization of knowledge as a commodity people compete over, however. To the contrary, in the next sections, we examine how two recent works of young adult fiction—*Dig* by A. S. King and *Cinderella Is Dead* by Kalynn Bayron—depict characters who are empowered as a result of participating in shared knowledge economies.

NEOLIBERAL EPISTEMOLOGIES IN TENSION WITH LIBERATORY EPISTEMOLOGIES

A. S. King's *Dig* is focalized by eight narrators who tell their stories in a nonlinear fashion so that readers learn about the present before they learn about the past, even though the key to five of the teenagers understanding their lives lies in the well-kept secrets of their grandparents. *Dig* exemplifies some of the problems that result from treating knowledge as a commodity over which people compete, but it also juxtaposes problematic neoliberal knowledge-hoarding against a backdrop of the liberatory empowerment that results when these five teenagers collectively share their knowledge with one another, while they also surface the trauma of knowing about racism in the US.

The novel's past involves Marla and Gottfried Hemmings, who are the parents of five siblings, most of whom are estranged from them and from one another, a sign that Marla interprets as evidence that she and her husband "did it right—they raised independent kids who could do the same as they did. Work hard and save money. . . . Marla had rules. *No contact with the [adult] children because we want them to thrive*" (52–53, emphasis in the original). In point of fact, none of the five is thriving, and two live in abject poverty because Marla will not allow Gottfried to help them financially, even though the couple has ten million dollars in the bank. Instead, Marla believes in boot-strapping self-reliance. Gottfried blames Marla's "meanness" for their children's absence from their lives; she blames him for being away from home so much, making money, while the children were growing up (250). He thinks, "It's got to be someone else's fault, these missing grandchildren, this collection of grown children who never come around" (307). Neither can accept responsibility for this intergenerational familial estrangement.

Gottfried's secret story to himself about his unhappiness reverberates in a poignant motif throughout the book; he is haunted by two mating robins that he accidentally drove into and killed when he was seventeen years old, a story that is rehearsed on the first two pages of the novel. Whenever he thinks about the robins, he cries, grieving that he killed them during their mating ritual. He never told Marla about the robins, but they are clearly linked in his mind to loss and grief, especially to the loss of his children and grandchildren, whom he pictures as "five robins" (308). He eventually can admit to himself, however, that he and Marla are "complicit" in the death of one of their grandchildren as a direct result of their stinginess and negligence (308).

Gottfried's father was a potato farmer in Pennsylvania. Early in his adulthood, Gottfried used his business acumen to betray his father and ruin the family's farming operations by making intentional bookkeeping errors. As the senior Mr. Hemmings puts it, "A man can't fuck up the books this bad and not mean to" (122). When federal authorities begin to investigate, the family liquidates the farm, and Gottfried uses his apportionment to become a real-estate developer. His business knowledge serves him as a tradable commodity because he calculates how to use what he knows to get what he wants: the land for a real-estate development and ultimately ten million dollars. But just as he has killed the robins, Gottfried has effectively killed his relationship with the nuclear family into which he was born. Although he "feels proud of what he did to survive" and believes himself to have been a "good father. Good husband. Good provider" who "looked out for his family" (371), he "never once thinks about how it would feel if his own son would do the same to him as he did to his father" (371–72). Like a true capitalist, Gottfried equates being "good" as a father and husband with providing material comforts for his family. Gottfried's misery stems from the empty comfort of having an excessive amount of money that he effectively earned by raising children who "hate" their parents (250). As he tells Marla, "Kids with shitty parents eventually figure it out" (250).

While Gottfried's story is one of capitalism, corruption, hoarding, and the commodification of his business knowledge, Marla's story is embedded in the horror of US racial history. In 1962, at the age of twelve, Marla was hit by a car while she was visiting Arkansas. She needed three units of blood, but the only blood available was "negroid blood," which Marla's mother instructed the nurse to use, with gratitude that the nurse is a "Yankee" (327). Later, in the 1970s, Marla's Uncle Bill calls her names like "half blood" and asks, "So does this mean you're gonna sit on your ass and collect welfare now?" (328). Marla has internalized this racism so thoroughly that she believes those units of blood have somehow tainted her children, which appears to be part of her motivation for insisting that they all be independent, even when they have been ill with cancer or are the victims of spousal abuse.

Marla's racism affects her at every level, right down to her disdain for people who eat fried chicken, which she calls "soul food" (188). She is a perfectionist, one who has the interior walls of her house painted every year: "Her religion is her kitchen. Her freezer. Her flower beds. Interior paint" (158). She also obsessively serves her family lamb chops, as if the fact that this cut of meat is from lambs makes the meat somehow innocent and her somehow a person who nurtures the young. "Marla wants everyone to know how caring she is," the narration explains in free indirect discourse (84). The character Marla then thinks, "I have to get myself together and be a grandmother to a kid who hates me because I care so much about him that I make lamb chops and he won't even eat them" (85). Much of the story is set around Easter, which puts in play symbolism of the Lamb of God as sacrificial, but as Marla's lamb chop-loathing grandson thinks to himself about white people, "We blow everything off because we're so concerned with looking good we just can't feel. . . . You can't fill that hole with a fucking lamb chop" (288). Marla's hypocrisy is deeply disturbing.

Moreover, Marla's and Gottfried's secret self-stories are knowledge-hoarded in ways that benefit no one, not even themselves as individuals. Another secret story compels this plot; that story, however, is not a shameful secret secluded in the recesses of one character's mind. Rather, it is the story of Marla and Gottfried's granddaughter who has been raped, murdered, and buried deep in a forest by two brothers, the younger of whom is one of the book's eight narrators. Gottfried knows that he and his wife are complicit in their granddaughter's death because they refused to lend her father, Matt, money when he needed it. Consequently, Matt is so penurious that he has refused to buy his daughter brassieres or tampons. Matt's wife moves with their daughter to get a job in Pennsylvania, which ultimately leaves the girl vulnerable to the predators who rape and kill her. After her death, she thinks of herself as "The Freak," and readers never learn her given name. Her spectral self "flickers" in and out of people's lives, especially those of her first cousins, Marla and Gottfried's other four grandchildren.

Tenth-grader David, sometimes referred to as "the shoveler," is the first cousin the reader witnesses meeting The Freak. He feels isolated because his mother moves so frequently and shoplifts so often. He also does not know who his father is. He finds solace in shoveling; he initially shovels snow, but he metaphorically is trying to dig himself out of the tunnels of his own depression. Once he thinks of himself as "the shoveler," Matt finds the idea of becoming a farmer appealing, especially once he learns that their family were once potato farmers.

Like David, eleventh-grader Katie's mind also digs into metaphorical tunnels—which turn out to be the manifestation of a form of depression they have both inherited from Marla. Katie's best friend is an African American male, although she eventually realizes that she has been exploiting him because befriending him is the best possible way to irritate her racist mother, who is proud of a hideous handbell shaped in the form of a "caricature" of an enslaved woman (284). Marla once brought the gift home from a trip to one of the southern states. Katie is also a drug dealer who deals from the drive-thru window of an Arby's restaurant in yet another act of rebellion against her rigid and reprehensible mother.

A fourth cousin, Malcolm, is a tenth-grader who knows that his father is dying of pancreatic cancer. Together, they travel back and forth from the town in Pennsylvania where Marla and Gottfried live to Jamaica, where Malcolm's father transforms THC into edible paper products for others who suffer from cancer. Sometimes, Malcolm resents this business his father is running, but on the other hand, his father articulates one of the novel's most central truths: "You can't buy life. You can make life and offer it to anyone who needs it" (280). Malcolm's father has also taught him that "all that mattered was *human connection*" (278, emphasis in the original). And Malcolm's father gives his business product away free, rather than selling it, reasoning, "If I sell it, I'd be as bad as the drug companies" (280). This man lives—and is dying—in defiance of neoliberalism.

The fifth cousin is Loretta, perhaps the youngest of the grandchildren and certainly the least mature. She lives with Marla and Gottfried's middle daughter and her verbally, physically, and emotionally abusive husband, who is also Loretta's father. Marla has continuously refused to help their daughter, even though her family lives in a flea-ridden trailer that lacks adequate access to food, clothing, or grooming supplies. To cope, Loretta has, in her own mind, converted their trailer into a circus wagon and herself into a circus ringmistress. Her closest friends are the well-trained fleas in the flea circus she uses to divert her attention from her squalid living conditions. Loretta serendipitously reconnects with her grandparents when the hypoglycemic Marla is hospitalized for a concussion after fainting at the sight of her husband eating fried chicken at a farmer's market. Loretta's mother is in the same hospital because her husband has beaten her nearly to death. Once they reconnect, Loretta and her grandfather, Gottfried, take delight in getting to know one another again.

Throughout the story, The Freak appears in one form or another to each of her cousins: she is a member of the audience in Loretta's imagined circus, and she finds Katie in her mental tunnels. She flickers into the path of David's snow shovel and uses a lighter that her murderers dropped by her corpse to try to light snowflakes on fire. The Freak also appears swimming in the ocean in Jamaica when Malcolm is crying, wishing he had a sister. She promises to be one for him and then leaves the GPS coordinates where her body can be found for him to discover, although he does not understand the significance of the clue at the time.

Each of these five teenagers suffers from feeling disconnected from other people, and each of them finds redemption in connecting with their Hemmings cousins. Their ability to unite as family members occurs on Easter Day, while their parents are bickering with each other, as well as with Marla and Gottfried, and while four of these first cousins share candy from their Easter egg hunt, rather than competing to be the winner who finds all of the eggs first. Gottfried marvels that they are sharing, but he also criticizes their parents for not teaching them the simple elements of competitiveness: "You could have at least taught these kids how to do an Easter egg hunt," he complains (353). Malcolm's father, on the other hand, openly criticizes Marla and Gottfried for raising him and his siblings "to be competitive" (353).

In addition to appearing to her Hemmings cousins, the Freak has also shared various forms of knowledge with each of them. She has shared her corpse's whereabouts and her reassurance with Malcolm; she has given David information about getting a job and purchasing a car; she has emotionally supported Katie in her tunnels; and she has helped Loretta to find a red sequined dress that suits well her role as Ringmistress. Far more important, however, when the four surviving cousins begin to share the knowledge each of them has about their family, they recognize the role of The Freak in their lives, and they are able to gain justice for her and finally help put her remains to rest. Sharing knowledge proves to be far more productive and liberatory in this novel than hoarding it or competing for it does.

The problem with neoliberalism's emphasis on competition is linked in this novel with the inherent evil of racism. As we have discussed in chapter 3, slavery was the original economic system that drove the American economy into global competitiveness long before the US was even a country. Drug-dealing Katie knows about and acknowledges white privilege. Indeed, she is one of the two narrators who overtly conveys the novel's antiracist ideology, sharing her knowledge directly with readers. For example, she addresses the reader:

> You probably think I'm some cliché kid who hates her parents. I don't. I have reasons I don't like to spend time with them. For one thing, they hate gay people. And Jewish people. And Black people. And Mexicans. And Muslims. My mom doesn't even know a Muslim from a Sikh. She just talks about how great it is that their god makes them wear "turbans" so she can pick them out in a crowd. She thinks this is funny. (102–3)

Katie hates that her mother uses the worst possible racial epithet she can to describe Black people and then justifies doing so with "the ridiculous excuse that rappers say it all the time so why can't she?" (237). Katie criticizes her high school for its racism, too, and despises how some people hide their racism with the term "heritage—as if it were in our blood to be assholes to other people, as if we'd inherited it" (144). Eventually, however, Katie recognizes that she herself has been using her Black best friend both to annoy her mother and to hide from her own white privilege. She finally admits to her own privilege when she criticizes the kids at her school who "never have to think about how white they are. They get to run stop signs, drink beer, and do all kinds of stupid shit and they never think about why they get away with it. I guess I do that, too" (193).

Katie's cousin Malcolm is also cognizant of and angry about his white privilege, which he becomes acutely aware of while spending time in Jamaica with his father. He understands that "white isn't just a color. . . . White is a passport. It's a ticket. The world is a white amusement park and your white skin buys you into it" (82). Later, Malcolm adds, "entitled white culture encourages those inside it to never look outside their own fucking worlds" (288). He considers his grandmother, Marla, to be "the most entitled woman on Earth" (158), but like Katie, he eventually needs to confront his white privilege when he acknowledges that his crush on a young woman in Jamaica is about "really just looking for a way out of where I am. She deserves better. She's a human, not a door" (286). Malcolm realizes that he needs to stay in Pennsylvania, rather than move back to Jamaica, because "people there already know the truth about poverty. They don't think it's a coincidence that they're descendants of slaves and also poor in a country that was ruled by Colonialists for so long. I'm needed here because this is where the ignorance is. Even my own" (382). Malcolm's ability to admit his own bias is based, interestingly enough, in the context of the knowledge sharing experiences he has had with his cousins.

While these two characters directly critique white entitlement, the racism of other characters is cleverly cloaked in ways that the Hemmings cousins must discover, so as to uncover it and learn more about the deeply embedded insidiousness of US racism. Marla's racism, for example, is hidden even from her husband, although Katie knows how deeply that racism runs beneath the surface because Marla once told her that "black people have different blood than ours. . . . It's got disease in it" (109). David recoils when an older man who befriended him and whom he has begun to think of as a father figure reveals a tattoo under his T-shirt that reads "100% WHITE POWER" (256). This man has the words etched onto his very skin, and yet they lie hidden beneath the layers of his shirt and T-shirt, so that only once David reads the words can he gain the knowledge he needs to discover how toxic this man is.

The elder of the two brothers responsible for The Freak's death is another white supremacist. Early in the novel, the Freak wants to warn her cousin David "not to talk to anyone who carries a snake" because "you can't always see right away who's carrying a snake" (35). Indeed, Bill—the older of these two brothers—carries a large yellow serpent wrapped around him under his shirt. Bill is a recruiter for a white supremacist group; his friends in the group are skinheads, and Bill directs his younger brother to "*look for other guys like us. Bring them to see the snake after school. The more, the better. We'll win this country back*" (180, emphasis in the original). The reader eventually learns that Bill raped his younger brother Jake when Jake was twelve years old in much the same way that Bill encourages Jake to rape The Freak. Bill tells Jake that he's "not responsible" for what he does when he is "pissed off" and helps Jake bury the girl's dead body, hiding this act of carnal knowledge beneath a layer of dirt (181). Jake subsequently realizes that he does not want to be like Bill or Bill's friend, Jefferson Davis Kirwin, who is a registered sex offender, so Jake decides to confess their crime despite knowing that doing so will likely land him in jail and permanently estrange him from Bill. He reasons, "Truth isn't so bad once you look at it" (336), suggesting that, like the Hemmings cousins, he has learned that it is better to share knowledge of the truth than it is to hide it.

With the name "Hemmings," this novel alludes to a truth in US history, one of racism that remained hidden for centuries in plain sight. Thomas Jefferson, the author of the Declaration of Independence and a slave owner who celebrated farmers as the backbone of the US, had six children by his wife's enslaved half-sister, Sally Hemings.[1] Sally was three-quarters white; her children, four of whom lived into adulthood, were seven-eighths white. Three of them "passed" as white people in adulthood, while one retained his identity as Jefferson's African American son. A 1998 DNA test had confirmed that a male Jefferson passed a Y chromosome on to the male members of this now large, extended family ("Sally Hemings"). Although *Dig* clarifies that the fictional Hemmings' potato farm in Pennsylvania was founded in the 1700s, it takes little to imagine that A. S. King is nevertheless evoking the famous Hemings family, whose ancestry is as intertwined with the Jefferson family as rhizomatic potato plants are. As an interesting side note that helps support this connection, Thomas Jefferson brought the recipe for fried potatoes to the US back with him when he returned from serving as the minister in France in 1789 ("Four Foods").

The central metaphor at work in *Dig* is that of the potato plant, a point to which readers are first alerted by an epigraph: "A man who prides himself on his ancestry is like the potato plant, the best part of which is underground" (n.p., repeated 360). While Marla is preparing an Easter dinner that will include three different types of potato dishes, she thinks, "When you water a potato plant, the liquid seeps into the soil. Helps the spud grow underground. The leaves may love seeing the sun, but the tubers need the dark. They seem so different—so unrelated—but when the blight hits and the whole plant goes, then you know everything was related" (326). Gottfried has similar thoughts: "A potato plant. Leaves up top, potatoes down below. All those stems and roots joining the two—like veins and arteries. His father always said that families were the same. Everything was connected, everything worked in synchronicity" (371). The potato plant serves as a shared metaphor providing the family with knowledge they can choose to accept or not: they are all interrelated because they are members of the same family, even those who are buried underground.

Gottfried thinks of his grandchildren as "accidental" volunteer potato plants that have grown despite never being tended (371). As The Freak describes it while she is standing in a field looking at "random potato plants":

> They are random because these are abandoned potatoes from last year's crop. Volunteers. They make more potatoes without meaning to if you leave them alone.
>
> Accidental fruit. Accidental fruit that makes more fruit. Accidental seeds. More marvelous than the kill rate of Roundup. . . .
>
> Fact: No one needs to do anything to help these plants thrive.
>
> Fact: Sometimes accidental seeds are stronger because no one gives a shit about them.
>
> Fact: The crop from a volunteer plant tastes just as good. (208)

Indeed, The Freak has learned about the agricultural history of the potato from flickering into two different college classes. In the first, she learns from a male professor that European dominance may well have emerged because of the potato, *Solanum tuberosum*: "any part of the plant that sees light can hurt you if you eat it. Even kill you. . . . The world we live in—this dominion of Northern Europeans—is the way it is because of *Solanum tuberosum*. If you ask me, it's ironic that our ancestors were able to avoid poisoning themselves on the plants, and yet rose to poison the whole world with themselves" (36).

A second professor, "a tall African American woman" lecturing to a room in which "every student is white," has this to say about the potato:

> *Solanum tuberosum*, our modest friend from the Andes, saved you from certain mediocrity. Grew your population while others withered—doubled it in some places. Rose you up. Rose up your children, your servants. Starched you rigid into your beliefs. The key to the kingdom was yours for the taking. . . .
>
> Your ancestors arrived in the New World, strong and ready . . . to wipe out whatever and whomever stood in their way. (111–12)

The professor then links potatoes to slavery by talking about "the last four hundred years" of the European conquest of North America, which seems to have been neither accidental nor swift to her (112).

In addition, David's mother, who prepares potatoes for their supper each night, reveals to him that her family was "famous for potatoes" during its "two-hundred-year-old-family history" (297). She tells her son, "I don't think my dad knew how bad it would mess things up" when he sold the farm (298). Later in the same conversation, she talks to David about the virulence of the racism in her hometown:

> "That's how things are. It's just normal for these people to think the way they do. Runs in the family, usually."
> "Like potatoes," [says David].
> "Like potatoes," she says. (299)

Over their shared Easter dinner, Katie wonders what is "wrong with the roots of our family" because she has not yet come to know that Marla's racism, along with both grandparents' greed, lies at the basis of what has harmed their family so toxically (354).

After the four living cousins have shared their knowledge, including knowledge of their family's racism, with each other, David asserts that the racism is "in our genes.... We have to attack it on a cellular level" (388). Katie concurs, exclaiming, "Totally. Cellular" (388). The cousins are focused on eradicating the toxicity of their own personal history. The Freak, on the other hand, links the contemporary cultural spirit of the Trump era as "hateful shit.... News shows and conspiracy theories. Rape jokes and dank memes. You're so used to the humor of the put-down that you didn't see that you slid down a hole and into a tunnel" (384). In a direct appeal to readers, she implores, "DIG YOUR WAY OUT!" (384, emphasis in the original), and then continues: "The Freak is tired of the Easter egg hunts, the race—the competition.... NOBODY WINS! CHANGE YOUR MIND!" (385, emphasis in the original). In her final lines, still addressing the reader directly and referring to herself in the third-person, The Freak calls on readers to share the knowledge they have gained about racism from this story:

> The Freak knows you can't control all of those things. Look at the power she has. She can go anywhere and do anything. The one thing she can't do is change the minds of the living.
> THAT'S YOUR FUCKING JOB! (385, emphasis in the original)

In this way, the text both empowers and implores readers to object to white supremacy, the exploitation of the female body, the classism, the competitiveness, and the consumerism that together form the neoliberal world from which this novel emerges. Perhaps most important, *Dig* rejects the neoliberal epistemology of hypercompetitive, individualist, perfectionist white privilege in favor of more emancipatory politics that include cooperation, collectivism, and community-based antiracism—all of which, the novel insists, must be predicated on knowledge sharing.

HEGEMONIC KNOWLEDGE VERSUS SHARED KNOWLEDGE: BAYRON'S *CINDERELLA IS DEAD*

Kalynn Bayron's *Cinderella Is Dead* is a racially aware feminist and LGBTQ+ critique of the "Cinderella" fairy tale set in Mersailles, a country that is dominated by a repressive tyrant, King Manford, who carefully hides from public knowledge the secret of his personal origins and the source of his power over his subjects. According to Sophia, the story's protagonist and first-person narrator, in the city of Lille, the seat of government where she grew up and lives, the wealthy "hoarded their wealth, improving their own lives while the rest of the city fell into decay"; in poorer districts, the air is "tinged with the distinct smell of excrement, human and animal alike" (31). In this patriarchal and class-based society, the rich use their wealth to buy privilege for their children; daughters, especially, are regarded as investments. King Manford's subjects complain about excessive taxation, but no one dares rebel because the military and threat of imprisonment serve as what Althusser would refer to as "Repressive State Apparatuses" (92–95). These RSAs enforce the king's will via financial mechanisms: "Failure to comply will result in imprisonment and seizure of all assets belonging to [a person's] immediate family" (Bayron 14). Manford even goes so far as to call human beings "a commodity" (368), although in the economy he has created, gender exploitation means that women are more commodified than men.[2]

The laws, politics, and economy of Mersailles are regulated by a story: namely, the state-sanctioned version of the country's origin tale, "Cinderella." Two points are salient: first, this story defines the sexist econo-political mores of Lille, and second, it shapes the epistemology of the city's citizens, thus exemplifying how one dominant group can hegemonically construct the world to its own benefit at the expense of all other groups by disciplining institutions and knowledge practices in ways that support oppression.

Each household is required by law to own a copy of the state-sanctioned "Cinderella" story, and girls are expected to commit it to memory and model their behavior after that of the famous princess. As Sophia explains, "Everything we do is measured against Cinderella's story" (57). Indeed, "the founding tenet" of the law in Mersailles "is that women, no matter their standing, are at the mercy of the fickle whims of men" (48). Reflecting one pattern of postfeminism we discussed in chapter 6, these women immerse themselves in the equivalent of neoliberal perfectionism. Like the "perfect" princess they are expected to emulate, girls between the ages of sixteen and nineteen are legally obliged to attend an annual ball at which they can be claimed for marriage by males of any age. In a gender-based economy that exploits the labor of women, "girls who aren't chosen by their third ball are considered forfeit, ending up in workhouses or in servitude. But in recent years, several girls have disappeared into the castle and were never heard from again" (33). Readers eventually learn that Manford, who is in fact Prince Charming in disguise, sacrifices them through a vampiric process during which he drains them of their lifeforce so that he can live eternally.

The state-sanctioned version of Cinderella's story also regulates the economy of Mersailles, which is predicated on consumption and which disciplines, in the Foucauldian sense of the word, girls to perform traditional femininity. For example, at Lille's outdoor market, Sophia observes vendors selling "jewelry and dresses from the city of Chione in the north, and satin gloves, makeup, and perfume from the city of Kilspire in the south" (17). In a shop window, she spies a young girl dressed in a wig "layered in pink peonies, topped with a small model of Cinderella's enchanted carriage"; in another, "Cinderella's glass slippers sit on a red velvet cushion" adjacent to a placard that reads, "Palace-Approved Replica" (15). To increase the chances that Sophia will catch the eye of a man at the ball, her parents arrange for her to wear expensive garters and stockings, as well as ribbons in her hair. The team of women they hire to dress her "rub scented oils into [her] skin" (64), sprinkle her "décolletage with a fine pearly powder that sparkles in the dancing candlelight" (67), and give her a magic elixir purchased from a local vendor that promises to bring good fortune. Even the carriage that carries Sophia and her friend Erin to the ball is "decorated with lavender curtains and matching ribbons" and is drawn by "two snow-white Clydesdales, . . . each wearing a lavender sash to match the carriage" (73).

Along with depicting a consumerist economy that disciplines girls to perform traditional femininity perfectly, the book also critiques an economic system that privileges one group of people (heterosexual men) at the expense of all others. When Sophia visits the home of the seamstress who sewed her ballgown, she overhears a violent argument between the woman and her husband, who accuses his wife of withholding earnings from him despite a law that decrees, "Every cent you make belongs to me" (47). Later, when Sophia stops at a merchant's stand to buy rice, the vendor angrily demands to know how she came by her money, noting, "Women aren't allowed to keep no money" (179). These gendered laws and economic practices were put in place two hundred years earlier by Prince Charming, who was married to Cinderella before he became increasingly tyrannical. According to Sophia, "The changes in the very beginning were subtle. A curfew was imposed for the safety of the women. Women were required to wear long dresses to protect their modesty. Men were elevated to positions of power because they knew best" (216). Exemplifying how the powerful can exploit their control of social and economic resources to discipline institutions and knowledge practices, Prince Charming predicates the country's economic and political system on everyone *knowing* that women are to be protected, that they can own neither property nor money, and that they live entirely within their husband's control. After two hundred years of living with laws framed by a dominant cultural narrative that privileges cis-heterosexual male supremacy and domination, cis-female subjugation serves to shape how the citizens of Mersailles learn and how they know what they know.

By emphasizing the role that the state-sanctioned version of the Cinderella story plays in normalizing oppressive legal and economic practices, *Cinderella Is Dead* reflects the connection that Foucault draws between power and knowledge. As Sophia explains, "Cinderella's story is the reason I'm being forced to go to the ball, the reason my parents have gone into debt to provide me a dress and shoes and all the pretty things I could ever need. Her story is the reason why none of the things I want for myself matter" (68). Sophia is a gender-nonconforming person who, when she turned twelve years old, came out to her parents by telling them that she would "much rather find a princess than a prince" (35). She thus destabilizes several binaries that structure her patriarchal, heterosexist, and classist society. Unlike other girls her age, she does not aspire "to be saved by some knight in shining armor. I'd like to be the one in the armor, and I'd like to be the one doing the saving" (25). Likewise, in a society shaped by heterosexual norms, she experiences pressure from family and friends to keep her sexual identity a secret, which causes her to feel alone. Only after she meets Constance, a queer teenage descendant of one of Cinderella's supposedly "evil" stepsisters, is Sophia introduced to another version of Cinderella's story. Sophia shares with Constance the knowledge that Cinderella actively resisted her society's materialistic and oppressive gender ideologies.

Cinderella is neither a love-struck girl nor a passive victim of her stepfamily's cruelty in the version of the story that Constance tells Sophia. Instead, with help from her stepmother and stepsisters, who love and care for her, she attends Prince Charming's ball with the intention of assassinating him for executing her parents after they spoke out against his oppressive laws and attempted to rally public support to depose him. However, the plan is foiled when Prince Charming's mother, a witch dressed in the guise of a beneficent fairy godmother, gives Cinderella a potion that causes her to fall in love with, and later marry, Charming. When Sophia asks Constance how she *knows* so much about Cinderella's history, Constance indirectly speaks to Manford's efforts to control knowledge, telling her, "I keep the stories no one else is allowed to hear, the things Manford and his predecessors don't want anyone to *know*, the true history of my family" (141, emphasis added).

The critical race theorist Richard Delgado refers to the type of story that Constance describes as a *counterstory*. According to Delgado, counterstories are told by "out-groups, groups whose marginality defines the boundaries of the mainstream, whose voice and perspective—whose consciousness—has been suppressed, devalued, and abnormalized" (71). He notes that the "dominant group" crafts stories that "remind it of its identity in relation to out-groups and provide it with a form of shared reality in which its own superior position is seen as natural" (71). Counterstories, on the other hand, "aim to subvert that reality" (71). This sharing of suppressed knowledge is evident in *Cinderella Is Dead* when Luke, a friend of Sophia's who is also gay, asks whether she has "ever heard of a man marrying another man? A woman being in love with another woman? Or people who find their hearts lie somewhere in the middle or with neither?" (60). When Sophia replies, "Only as a cautionary tale that ends with people imprisoned or dead," Luke explains, "The kings that have ruled Mersailles would like you to believe that you're alone, but it's not true" (60). Later, when Sophia tells Luke that she has never heard of anyone managing to leave Mersailles without Mansford's permission, he replies, "Neither have I, but that doesn't mean it hasn't happened. We've also rarely heard about people like us and yet here we are. Just because they deny us doesn't mean we cease to exist" (104).

Beyond depicting characters who exchange counterstories (and hence knowledge) to subvert dominant cultural narratives surrounding race, gender, class, and sexual identity, the novel also critiques the role that the Disney corporation has historically played in controlling cultural epistemology by insisting on the dominant image of Cinderella as a white, traditionally feminine cis-het woman. On one level, the novel references the song "Bibbidi-Bobbidi-Boo," made famous in the 1950 Disney animated film, when Constance wonders whether Amina, a witch and Mansford's mother, can "bibbidi-bobbidi-boo" her cottage back in order following a visit from her irate son (283). More important, in an episode of *The Storyteller's Thread* podcast, Kalynn Bayron, who is both African American and a queer author, connects her decision to write a multicultural version of the Cinderella story populated by Black, brown, and gay characters to her own experience as a child who only ever encountered fairy tales that were "very white, and straight, and cis" (Connors, "Interview"). In addition to diversifying the story, Bayron describes her interest in "deconstructing some of the very problematic themes that... run throughout that story." With that in mind, we argue that it is possible to read *Cinderella Is Dead* as contrasting two forms of knowledge: hegemonic knowledge, which is epistemologically controlling, and shared knowledge, which is depicted as epistemologically liberating.

Sophia connects the state-sanctioned Cinderella story to hegemonic knowledge when she describes it as positioning girls to believe that if "we are diligent, if we know the passages, if we honor our fathers, we might be granted the things Cinderella was" (21). When she happens upon a group of older women exchanging tales about Cinderella's tomb, Sophia dismisses them as still "more stories [meant] to trick young girls into obedience" (22). However, although she understands how the state-sanctioned version of the Cinderella story aims to control girls, she is not immune to its effects. Upon hearing the version of Cinderella's story Constance's family has passed down to her, Sophia protests, "But the story—Cinderella's story doesn't say anything about that. That's not how it goes," leading Constance to reply: "It is a lie" (144). When Sophia finds herself "questioning everything [she'd] ever thought was true about the tale" (143), Constance tells her, "You have to set the story you know aside, Sophia," which she subsequently is able to do, but only with Constance's help (146).

By juxtaposing two versions of the iconic ballgown scene in the Cinderella fairy tale, the book contrasts hegemonic knowledge, which it depicts as controlling and intrusive, with shared knowledge, which is celebrated as liberating. Toward the beginning of the story, when Sophia prepares to attend the royal ball, the language she uses to describe the transformation into perfection that she experiences is riddled with violent imagery. The women that her mother employs to dress her are said to "tug at [her] corset," prompting Sophia to "yelp"; as she struggles to breathe, "the walls and ceiling switch places... before [her] eyes" (64), leading her to fear she might vomit (65). The women "tug at [her] hair," so that "tears well up in [her] eyes" (65), and her mother instructs them to apply lipstick the color of "blood" (66). After her hooped petticoat is attached to her frock, the weight of it causes Sophia to feel caught like "an animal in a trap" (66). As she notes, the cumulative result of the transformation she is forced to undergo is a "remind[er] that this isn't about what I want or what I like. It's about what everyone else thinks is best" (67). In contrast, when Sophia is given the opportunity later in the story to ask a magical tree for something that will help her to assassinate Mansford at a second royal ball, she does not ask for a weapon. Instead, she requests "a dress" (316). That she does so, we argue, is attributable to the agency she feels upon hearing Constance's version of the Cinderella story, which disrupts the hegemonic narrative Sophia has grown up hearing.

As well as emphasizing shared knowledge as epistemologically liberating, *Cinderella Is Dead* also rejects neoliberalism's assumption that exceptional individuals are best equipped to address problems that confront their society. Instead, the text emphasizes collective action and shared decision-making, which is dependent on knowledge being shared freely, as the antidotes to complex social problems such as sexism and heterosexism. Toward that end, the book concludes with a third version of the Cinderella story, one that Sophia is said to have written down and that is presented as the "People's Approved Text" (383). In this rendition of the story, after having helped depose Mansford, Constance, as the sole-surviving heir of Cinderella, emerges as the new ruler of Mersailles. Rather than govern independently, however, she elects to preside over a "council made up of six individuals, handpicked by her" (384), who by sharing their collective knowledge, will enable her to govern more equitably and justly. This third version of the Cinderella story ends with a direct appeal to readers: "Do not be silent. / Raise your voice. / Be a light in the dark" (385). Oppression, the book implies, can only be overcome when people call others' attention to it, which is itself a form of knowledge sharing.

KNOWLEDGE PRODUCTION, EPISTEMOLOGY, AND NARRATIVE LEVELS

Living with self-awareness about race is an epistemological issue, as W. E. B. Du Bois first noted in 1903 when he referred to "this double-consciousness, this sense of always looking at one's self through the eyes of others.... One ever feels his twoness,—an American, a Negro; two souls, two thoughts" (5). White privilege, then, is its opposite: the ability to live *un*-self-aware—that is, without knowledge—as to how race provides economic, social, and political advantage. Indeed, what is privilege if not the very ability to be confident that one's ontological and epistemological position is secure and unthreatened and hence does not warrant examination?

Much of the impetus for the globalized neoliberal economy that has characterized US society in the first quarter of the twenty-first century has come from European and Anglophone corporations whose leadership has the privilege of ignoring race (not to mention gender, sexuality, ability, and class) as an ontological and epistemological experience. When knowledge is commodified, it is often depicted as deracialized, as if knowledge knows no race (or racism). Interrogating how knowledge production occurs in books for teenagers can expose racial privilege and racism. In some cases, characters immersed in social stratification created by immaterial production have the privilege of ignoring race, as do Katniss, Cinder, and June, along with Martha and Gottfried in *Dig*. Although the storyworld Bayron imagines in *Cinderella Is Dead* is populated entirely by Black and brown people, Sophia and Constance disrupt binaries associated with gender and sexuality, and hence do not have the privilege of ignoring those constructs.

Texts communicate about knowledge production in at least two ways that can guide readers to confront neoliberalism's racist privileging of knowledge (as immaterial production): first, through individual characters' epistemological insights, including how they trade on what they know, and second, through the way that texts communicate information to the reader. These two mechanisms—particularly the narrator's insights—have the potential to demonstrate the "resistant logics" by which texts can respond to the hegemonic forces of neoliberalism (Crary 134). With that in mind, we conclude this chapter by examining the narrators' relationships to knowledge structures in two novels we have already discussed in chapter 6: Marissa Meyer's *Cinder* and Sherri L. Smith's *Orleans*. In doing so, we demonstrate how textual positioning of the narrator's knowledge production can be connected to neoliberal racism.

In conceiving knowledge as content to be learned, *Cinder* depicts it as a commodity to be traded on. This commodification of knowledge occurs when characters in the story use their own knowledge to barter for material gain. Several characters in *Cinder* are prized because of what they know or what they learn. Prince Kai's android, for example, becomes a contested commodity because she has been researching the identity of the missing Lunar princess. After Kai learns that Queen Levana has planted a communication chip in the same android, he understands the value of this knowledge as a commodity: now the Queen "knows everything that android knows, everything she'd been researching," including information about the identity of the missing Lunar princess (322).

Cinder withstands a confrontation with Queen Levana precisely because the girl's bioelectrical knowledge is finally unlocked, giving Cinder the intellectual energy to weather Levana's attack. Once Cinder realizes that *she* is the missing princess—and that she is of the Lunar "race," and not Earthen—she has a "thought" that "both sickened and frightened her": she can transform the material world through the tool of her own knowledge (387). Her knowledge of her own race as Lunar forces her out of the privilege of ignoring race; she now has a double-consciousness, even though she does not acknowledge that fact. Nevertheless, because of her epistemological power, she will be the superspecial individual who transcends the rest of her community and its vague notions of race. She will save her neoliberal world, but without having the self-awareness to critique the social stratification that results from its market forces. *Cinder* thus relies on knowledge production as a commodity to ultimately erase the concept of race.

While reading this novel, readers themselves are restricted in the process of knowledge production: they usually know only what Cinder knows. Sherri L. Smith's *Orleans*, on the other hand, employs three shifting narrative levels, which enables readers to view events in the story from multiple perspectives and which helps to create what Alice Crary calls "resistant logics"—in this case, resistance to neoliberalism and its related forces, especially those that privilege individualism and erase racism (134). *Orleans*'s narrative structure demonstrates the importance of multiple ways of knowing. For example, on one level, the text relies on a third-person limited narrator to describe the events that Daniel, the military scientist who travels to Orleans in search of a cure for Delta Fever, experiences. These chapters initially reflect a privileged, patriarchal faith in neoliberal-technoscience, but this bias gradually erodes as the story unfolds. On a second level, the teenager Fen narrates events in a patois variant of African American Vernacular English as she experiences them in the first-person and in the present tense. These chapters indicate an epistemology that focuses more on knowledge as an embodied and collective process than as a commodity. On yet a third level, Fen recounts events from her childhood in the first-person and in the past tense. These chapters take the form of flashbacks and are distinguished by Fen's use of Standard (American) English, a register that she acquired growing up with parents who were academics. In those passages, Fen experiences the importance of intergenerational knowledge sharing.

In this storyworld organized according to ideologies associated with abuses of free enterprise and technoscience, Smith uses the three narrative levels described above to examine competing perspectives on neoliberalism, tribalism, and privilege. Throughout much of the story, Daniel—whose status as a white, male, college-educated scientist working for the US military places him in a socially empowered position—is confident in his ability "to save the world" (109). He has the perspective of a neoliberal technocrat who values individual ingenuity and whose faith in rationality and technology assures him that all problems can be solved. Smith uses an objective third-person narrator to mediate Daniel's experiences, thereby permitting the reader to perceive shortcomings in his character and individualistic worldview that he is not cognizant of himself.

As one example, like Cinder, Daniel is oblivious to the role that social systems play in privileging him. He is financially secure, as evidenced by the fact that he has the personal means to fund an expensive research expedition to Orleans, and he naïvely assumes that his access to high-end technology will give him the epistemological power to safely navigate the city. So strong is his faith in technology that he never even considers the possibility that it might fail him, which it does repeatedly. When he finally reaches the Institute for Post-Separation Studies, where he expects to find data he can use to transmute the virus he created into a cure for Delta Fever, Daniel entertains the possibility that he might "signal the States for help, call in the cavalry" (197). Because he is a presumably white male American citizen, he trusts that he has access to a military that will respond if he beckons. Never acknowledging the extent to which his social positioning and privilege empower him, Daniel, like Cinder, effectively assumes the role of the neoliberal "hero" with "a world to save" (*Orleans* 197, 200). Cut off from the institutions that privilege his race and gender and empower his knowledge production, however, he is ultimately forced to concede that though he had expected to "save this unsalvageable place . . . he had failed" (243).

In contrast, Fen articulates clearly the ideological divide between knowledge as a process of collective sharing and neoliberalism's emphasis on knowledge as an individually owned commodity that can be traded on for profit tied to racial exploitation. Acting as narrator, she distinguishes between the competing moral codes that guide the Ursuline Sisters and the researchers at the Institute for Post-Separation Studies: "Everyone is supposed to help everyone. That's what Sister Mary Margaret says. It's called the Golden Rule. It's not the same as Dr. Warren's Rules of Blood. Those are different. Those say everyone has to stay apart from everyone else" (187). Later, when she and Daniel are preparing to leave the Institute, Daniel wonders whether they ought to help Dr. Warren and his colleagues, who, in the absence of a vaccine for Delta Fever, are dependent on biopolitical computers and machinery to keep them alive. "They ain't tribe," Fen responds, leading Daniel to exclaim, "That's insane" (207). In a response that is notable for its condemnation of neoliberalism's destructiveness, Fen insightfully replies, "That the world they made" (207). Worlds that cannot respect racial difference, and in which people cannot (or will not) collectively share knowledge, are doomed to fail.

CONCLUSION

Like *Orleans*, *Dig* and *Cinderella Is Dead* also imagine knowledge, knowledge production, and knowledge sharing as processes of immaterial production that serve to bring people together in the groups they need to survive. Fen and Baby Girl need Daniel. The five Hemmings cousins need each other. Sophia and Constance need each other. Even more important, all of these characters grow stronger as they share knowledge and as they learn from others. Knowledge itself becomes the catalyst for all of these characters' improved lives.

In the next chapter, the last in this volume, we examine how YA literature plays an active role in encouraging teenagers to improve the lives of themselves and other people. Specifically, we address teen social activism and the many forms it takes, but as we do so, we also connect that activism to our discussion in previous chapters of this book concerning the ways in which neoliberalism intersects with environmentalism, structural racism, gender imbalance, biopolitics, and knowledge production itself. This final chapter also has a pedagogical focus, since we believe that when students are aware of neoliberalism and knowledgeable about how it structures their relationships with other people, they are better prepared to address the profound inequalities this economic and social ideology exacerbates.

Chapter 8

YOUTH ACTIVISM AS A RESPONSE TO NEOLIBERALISM

> We are the change and change is coming.
>
> —Greta Thunberg, *No One Is Too Small to Make a Difference* (106)

In Paola Mendoza and Abby Sher's YA dystopia *Sanctuary*, two of the story's characters—a Filipino teenage boy and a gay Brazilian man—discover that they share a common experience: as undocumented, unhoused immigrants living in New York, they both once found refuge riding the city's subway trains in a series of unending loops. This image of an unending loop strikes us as an appropriate metaphor for neoliberalism, which, as we have argued throughout this book, advocates for a world where individuals only ever compete against others: for education, for jobs, for access to goods such as health insurance and quality medical care, for childcare, for basic necessities like healthy foods and clean air and water, and even for equality.

Despite reassurances to the contrary, the endless competition loop in which many of us are caught does not take place on a level playing field. On the contrary, imbalances that are attributable to systemic racism, classism, ableism, sexism, heterosexism, and so on mean that some groups of people have access to privileges and opportunities denied others. Inequities also exist even within demographic groups. At the same time, rather than "trickling down," wealth in the US has only trickled *up* since the early 1980s, dramatically increasing the income gap between the middle class and the wealthy (Horowitz et al.). As a result, the rich have grown richer, while too many in the middle class have been left struggling to keep their heads above water as they search for new ways to compete in order to provide for themselves and their families. The situation is even more dire for the working class and those living in poverty. Fortunately, people throughout the world have begun to protest against this perpetual state of neoliberally driven inequity.

In *Stay Alive: Surviving Capitalism's Coming Hunger Games*, Michael Harris describes how youth activists protesting reforms to Hong Kong's election system in 2014 adopted the three-finger salute from Suzanne Collins's Hunger Games trilogy as "a symbol of solidarity and defiance" (2). Young protesters in Thailand did the same in 2014, as did protesters in Myanmar in 2021. In the US, Emma Gonzaléz and David Hogg, survivors of the 2018 school shooting in Parkland, Florida, and cofounders of #NeverAgain, a social-media movement committed to gun control, have each connected their activism to the Harry Potter books (Ceron). Another Parkland survivor, fifteen-year-old Anna Crean, provided a rationale for her and her classmates' speaking out when she observed, "We can make a difference because that's what books and movies have told us since we were little" (Trombetta). These youthful protesters have taken a page from the YA novels they have been reading.

They are not alone in connecting YA literature to youth activism. Andrew Slack, cofounder of the Harry Potter Alliance (now known as Fandom Forward), describes how the nonprofit organization aims to redirect the passion that millions of readers feel for the Harry Potter books toward addressing social problems such as poverty, racism, genocide, and environmental destruction. Using money its members raised, the organization has donated more than 400,000 books worldwide, established libraries in underserved communities, and collected signatures for a petition that led the Warner Bros. corporation to ensure that its Harry Potter-licensed chocolate products are Fair Trade certified (Fandom Forward). The organization also sponsored the "Climate Crisis Horcrux" competition, which challenged young people to submit proposals for plans to combat climate change.

As these anecdotes suggest, a growing number of people are turning to YA literature as a road map to address social injustice through activism, suggesting that literary texts are neither apolitical nor static works of art that explore timeless themes. Rather, as Jane Tompkins argues, literary texts represent a writer's efforts to remake the social order. From this perspective, "novels and stories should be studied not because they manage to escape the limitations of their particular time and place, but because they offer powerful examples of the way a culture thinks about itself, articulating and proposing solutions for the problems that shape a particular historical moment" (xi). As with Tompkins, we attend closely to the cultural work that YA literature performs, hence our decision to interrogate different ways books for teenagers reproduce and resist neoliberal ideologies.

In this concluding chapter, we build on our discussion in chapter 1 by examining how what we call *YA protest literature* resists the emphasis that we have suggested neoliberalism places on self-enclosed individualism and competition between and among people. In doing so, we show how YA protest literature can expose adolescents to ideologies that counter neoliberalism by depicting characters who resist this economic, social, and political theory by organizing, taking action, and voicing social criticism. Read through this lens, we believe these texts can model for teen readers what David Harvey, in his book *Spaces of Hope,* calls "optimism of the intellect" (17). Harvey uses the phrase "spaces of hope" to describe how two concepts that initially appear to compete with each other—for example, the study of globalization and the study of personal embodiment—can become conjoined to help intellectuals, activists, and pedagogues reenvision global problems that the laissez-faire liberalism of the nineteenth century created and that its progeny, neoliberalism, has manufactured since the late 1970s. In a clear and very specific example of personal embodiment being a global concern, Kiran Gandi ran the 2015 London Marathon while freebleeding during her menstrual cycle. This young woman's action inspired various other freebleeding protests, bringing international attention to the physical need for menstrual products, their ever-increasing expense, and the environmental consequences of their use (Bobel and Fahs). We use the phrase "spaces of hope" in this chapter to refer to a similar mindset wherein YA protest literature invites readers to imagine more compassionate and more just forms of social organization throughout the world as they endeavor to find ideas and practices—spaces of hope—that counter neoliberalism's emphasis on self-enclosed individualism and competition.

Our foregrounding protest activities, such as organizing, collectivism, and taking action as a response to neoliberalism's emphasis on individualism and competition, reflects Julie Wilson's observation that "organizing asks us to work across difference to find common ground and sense a new future," thus allowing us to reclaim "our capacities for interconnection, equality, imagination, and democracy and open up those new worlds we're all yearning for" (213). As evidenced by our discussion in other chapters of this book, some YA novels—many of them, in particular, written by people of color—emphasize collectivism as an antidote to neoliberalism's emphasis on individualism and competition. For example, in discussing Darcie Little Badger's *A Snake Falls to Earth,* we have shown how the characters model a perspective of intersectional environmentalism for teen readers as they reject oppositional binaries. The characters work together to address climate-related problems that impact humans as well as nonhuman animals, thereby flattening a hierarchy commonly taken for granted. Likewise, in our close reading of *Sanctuary,* we have argued that Vali, Ernie, and Malakas are able to reach California not because of their own exceptionalism, but rather, because of the sacrifices that other people—Vali's mother and father, Volcanoman, Rosa, Malakas's grandmother—make on their behalf. In YA protest literature, however, teenage protagonists go beyond working with others to address common problems. They also learn to take action as they organize (or are organized by) members of their local communities to resist structural oppression and, by extension, neoliberalism's overvaluing of self-enclosed individualism and competition.

In the sections that follow, we examine how two YA protest novels—*The Hate U Give* (2017), a realist novel by Angie Thomas, and *The Marrow Thieves* (2017), a dystopia by Canadian novelist Cherie Dimaline—model organizing, collectivism, and taking action as remedies for neoliberal policies that reproduce systemic oppression. Having done so, we transition from examining how neoliberalism is implicated in literature for teenagers to offering practical suggestions for teachers and teacher educators interested in supporting high school and college students as they interrogate the presence of neoliberal ideologies in YA literature.

THE HATE U GIVE: TAKING ACTION AND SPEAKING OUT TO CREATE "SPACES OF HOPE"

Angie Thomas's *The Hate U Give* is an open critique of structural racism and a renunciation of the self-enclosed individual whose extraordinary talents alone can save the world from itself. Starr Carter is a sixteen-year-old Black girl who lives in a poor African American neighborhood but who attends Williamson, an elite high school in an upper middle-class white community about an hour's drive away. When a party Starr attends in her neighborhood is disrupted by gunfire, her friend Khalil offers to drive her home, but they are delayed when a white police officer stops them and orders Khalil to get out of the car and then not move. After the officer returns to his patrol car with Khalil's identification, the teenager unexpectedly reaches into the driver's side window to grab a brush and check on Starr. The officer subsequently shoots Khalil three times, killing him and leaving Starr as the only witness. A central tension in *The Hate U Give* is attributable to two competing frameworks: the neoliberal value placed on the actions and life of the white police officer (a representative of the state) enforcing structural racism and the concomitant rejection of that valuation in favor of collectivism employed in the name of racial justice. The knowledge production of sharing information collectively for the betterment of all who will listen is the novel's most important contribution to its critique of neoliberalism.

Over the course of the story, Starr's understanding of the role that unjust systems play in producing and perpetuating oppression rooted in race deepens as she learns about her culture and its history from people around her, including her father, Maverick. He is an admirer of the Black Panthers, an activist organization that formed in Oakland, California, in the 1960s to contest police brutality against African Americans. Maverick tells his children stories about the group's cofounder, Huey Newton, and its mission to empower the Black community by educating its members about how to resist social injustice. Maverick also shares stories about other Black activists who fought for social justice. A fan of Tupac Shakur, he teaches Starr about "THUG LIFE," an acronym the rapper is said to have interpreted as meaning, "The Hate U Give Little Infants Fucks Everybody" (16); in other words, the systematic racial oppression of young people harms everyone in a society. Helping his daughter connect that idea to systemic oppression, and unmasking neoliberalism's reliance on the concept of postracialism to obscure the latter, Maverick explains:

> Corporate America don't bring jobs to our communities, and they damn sure ain't quick to hire us. Then, shit, even if you do have a high school diploma, so many of the schools in our neighborhoods don't prepare us well enough. That's why when your momma talked about sending you and your brothers to Williamson, I agreed. Our schools don't get the resources to equip you like Williamson does. It's easier to find some crack than it is to find a good school around here. (169)

Similar to the words of a character in *Firekeeper's Daughter*, Maverick calls the drug-dealing business in their local community "a multibillion-dollar industry," pointing out that the profits don't return to community members, which is not unusual for a neoliberal enterprise: "That shit is flown into our communities, but I don't know anybody with a private jet" (170). He concludes, "That's the hate they're giving us, baby, a system designed against us" (170). Starr responds to her father's efforts to educate her by connecting the protests that have broken out after Khalil's brutal murder by the white police officer to systemic oppression, noting, "Everybody's pissed 'cause . . . he's not the first one to do something like this and get away with it. It's been happening, and people will keep rioting until it changes" (170–71).

Starr consequently concludes that systemic oppression "won't change if we don't *say* something" (171, emphasis added). The attorney representing her pro bono tells Starr, "I'll do whatever I can to make sure you're *heard*. . . . You matter and your *voice* matters" (219, emphasis added). Thus, from listening to her father and this female attorney, Starr internalizes the understanding that her voice is her most precious gift, reasoning, "What's the point of having a voice if you're gonna be silent in those moments you shouldn't be?" (252). Via the knowledge she gains from her parents, her attorney, her uncle, and her friends, Starr takes action to become an advocate for her community. She is not the neoliberal hero who acts alone, however. Far from it, she is part of a collective of people protesting against police brutality. Without the ties to the people she has grown up with, her adult mentors, and her awareness of national sociopolitical conditions for African American peoples, she could not finally speak her truth to the district attorney. When she eventually does, she uses her voice as a "weapon," speaking through a bullhorn (while standing on an empty police officer's car during a protest) to amplify her voice and share Khalil's story to agitate for social justice and inspire other people in her community to do the same (410). Starr tells the police trying to subdue the protestors: "His life mattered. Khalil lived! . . . Khalil lived!" (412). Having taken action by exercising her voice to call for justice, she makes the following promises to her memory of Khalil:

> I'll never forget.
> I'll never give up.
> *I'll never be quiet.* (444, emphasis added)

With these words, Starr demonstrates that she has found her own space of hope. She chooses to be an activist rather than to accept structural racism, but reflecting our critique of neoliberal epistemology in chapter 7, her activism is based on collectively shared knowledge, stories, histories, and conversations. The novel does not depict Starr's decision to speak out against police brutality as single-handedly producing social change: at the book's conclusion, the officer who murdered Khali is exonerated by a grand jury. Instead, *The Hate U Give* argues that the seeds of change are sown when one person is willing to listen to her community and then lend her voice to a chorus of others demanding justice. Starr's activism is not based on material goods, profiteering, or competitive, individualistic entrepreneurship; rather, it is steeped in organizing people to work together and her belief in—and hope for—change.

In direct contrast to Starr, an adult called King—who leads a gang called the King Lords—positions himself as a neoliberal entrepreneur who does not need to follow the conventions of his community. He pimps out his girlfriend, beating her and their children when he is drunk; he commits arson to enact revenge; he is a drug dealer with no sense of obligation to the larger community. Eventually, a member of his own gang, one who is emotionally worn out by King's effect on the community and physically worn out by King beating him, offers to help the police find where King hides the drugs he sells so that the gang leader can be arrested and imprisoned for his many crimes. His self-interest motivates him to believe that he is better than other people and above the law, which causes him to be the most socially isolated individual in the novel. His entrepreneurial competitiveness, his refusal to work with his community, his self-enclosed individualism, and his exploitation of his own family and fellow gang members serve as the object lesson that runs counterpoint to Starr's story: working collectively within a community is more productive than competitively pursuing only one's narrow interests. The novel thus positions collectivism as being especially important for economically and racially oppressed groups, while emphasizing the limitations and pitfalls of self-enclosed individualism.

THE MARROW THIEVES: TAKING ACTION AND COLLABORATING TO CREATE "SPACES OF HOPE"

While *The Hate U Give*, as a realist novel, operates in what theorist of literature for youth Maria Nikolajeva calls "linear time" because it progresses in identifiable time structures (52), Cherie Dimaline's *The Marrow Thieves* is a work of YA dystopian fiction that exists in "mythical time," that is, time which moves in a cyclical pattern and evokes the vagueness of time common to mythology, folklore, and sacred writings (Nikolajeva 1). In this novel, a series of climate-related environmental catastrophes have contaminated the groundwater in North America and unleashed a deadly plague that ravages the population and leaves non-Indigenous people who survive it unable to dream, driving them so insane that some of them commit suicide. In the ensuing fight for the remaining potable water, the majority of which exists on tribal lands, Indigenous peoples are driven from their homes and forced into exile. As one elder explains it:

> And then, even after our way of life was being commoditized, after our lands were filled with water companies and wealthy corporate investors, we were still hopeful. *Because we had each other.* New *communities* started to form, and we were gathering strength. But then the Church and the scientists that were working day and night on the dream problem came up with their solution and everything went to hell. (89, emphasis added)

This so-called "solution" that allows nonnative peoples to dream again requires the extraction of bone marrow from Indigenous peoples, which ultimately kills them. Government operatives known as Recruiters are tasked with hunting Indigenous peoples and interring them in stifling residential schools run by headmistresses and Cardinals—evoking how these same institutions once stripped Indigenous children of their languages and tribal cultures in the Canada and US from the late nineteenth to the mid-twentieth century. In this novel, however, instead of headmistresses and priests stripping them of their culture, the Indigenous people's lifeblood, which emanates within their bone marrow, is sucked from them physically. Indeed, the Cardinals' killing machines extract not only the marrow but also the very cultural soul of their victims in a cycle that replicates historical cycles of white Euro-Canadians and white Euro-Americans surviving at the cost of Indigenous peoples.

After some Recruiters capture the only surviving members of his family, Frenchie—a Métis teenager living in Canada, and the story's protagonist and narrator—escapes into the wilderness and begins to migrate north where he hopes to find remaining tribes and avoid being killed in a residential school. He is eventually taken in by a small band of travelers that consists of Miig, a one-time acquaintance of Frenchie's father and a man whose partner was abducted by Recruiters; Minerva, a female elder versed in the old ways; and other young people, including Rose, a biracial teenager with whom Frenchie becomes romantically involved.

As in *The Hate U Give*, *The Marrow Thieves* depicts communal knowledge production as preparing people to resist neoliberalism's emphasis on self-enclosed individualism and competition. Led by Miig, the band travels north in a cyclical journey that spans five years, while he also tells stories about both the climate-driven catastrophes that displaced Indigenous peoples and the latter's historical oppression at the hands of white colonizers:

> Sometimes [Miig's story] was focused on one area, like the first residential schools: where they were, what happened there, when they closed. Other times he told a hundred years in one long narrative, blunt and without detail. Sometimes we gathered for an hour so he could explain treaties, and others it was ten minutes to list the earthquakes in the sequence that they occurred, peeling the edging off the continents back like diseased gums. (25)

On one occasion, Miig tells the group that "dreams get caught in the webs woven in your bones. That's where they live, in that marrow there. . . . You are born with them. Your DNA weaves them into the marrow like spinners"

(18–19). His motivation to share the group's collective history through story is driven by his desire "to set the memory in perpetuity," as well as his conviction that acquiring knowledge of one's cultural history is "the only way to make the kinds of changes that [are] necessary to really survive" (25).

The Marrow Thieves imagines a future in which neoliberalism's valuing of self-enclosed individualism and competition runs rampant. In this dystopic Canada, individuals compete for water and other life-sustaining resources, so a logic of social Darwinism prevails, with the result being that Indigenous peoples, outnumbered and overwhelmed, are driven from their lands, brutalized, exploited, and stripped of the dreams embedded in their marrow. The novel is clear in its insistence that such an outcome is attributable to a racialized econo-political system that values the lives of some people more than others. As Miig tells Frenchie, Indigenous peoples lost their value to the government after leaders ceased "car[ing] about long-range things like courting votes for the next election and instead cared about things like keeping valued, wealthy community members safe" (88). Later, after scientists discover the medical use of Indigenous people's bone marrow, they are commodified, hunted by Recruiters, and warehoused in processing facilities where they await death.

In this world, collectivism constitutes an antidote to neoliberal racial stratification. After Frenchie is separated from his older brother by Recruiters, the younger boy escapes into the woods and begins to make his way north, afraid and alone. A preadolescent at the time, he nearly perishes but survives because Miig and his companions happen upon him and nurse him back to health. In another example of their collectivism, when they track a deer that holds the promise of nourishment, Miig insists that they hunt individually, not for competition, but rather, because he reasons that "work[ing] separately but together" is for the betterment of the group (45). When the group discovers an abandoned hotel in the forest, they are initially delighted by the prospect of sleeping in their own self-contained rooms. As the night wears on, however, they reject the privacy that arrangement affords them, choosing instead to make their way to Frenchie's room to be together and enjoy the comfort and safety that comes with being members of a group.

While *The Marrow Thieves* associates collectivism with security, it also cautions against overvaluing individual exceptionalism. When the band first reaches the hotel, they notice it is surrounded by an electric fence. Unsure whether the fence holds a current, Miig concludes that the only way to know for certain is for him to touch it. Recognizing Miig's value to the group as both a leader and a keeper of the group's stories, Frenchie intervenes, hurling himself against the fence before the older man is able to do so. Although some of his companions compliment him for his bravery, Miig surprises Frenchie by scolding him for his selfishness, insisting, "No one is more important than anyone else, French.... *No one should be sacrificed for anyone else*" (58, emphasis added). The book is thus clear in its ideological commitment to rejecting any system that holds some lives to be more valuable than others.

In direct contrast, by depicting the persecution of Indigenous peoples at the hands of the Recruiters, who, like the white policeman in *The Hate U Give*, function as a symbol of the state, and hence systemic oppression, the book depicts stratification between races as a direct result of overemphasizing self-enclosed individualism, competition, and white privilege. The end result is a society in which all people not only compete for the resources they need to survive, but in which some groups of people *become resources* that others vampirically consume for their own personal advancement. Precisely because their bone marrow promises to cure non-Indigenous people from the plague, native peoples are hunted and ultimately murdered. As one character tells Frenchie, their nonnative tormentors "don't think of us as humans, just commodities" (203).

At the conclusion of the novel, Frenchie unexpectedly reunites with his father, who has been living in hiding with a small group of resistance fighters since leaving his family and joining with other members of the local council in hopes of persuading their tormentors that Indigenous and non-Indigenous peoples should work together to address the environmental and social challenges that confront them all. Faced with the prospect of remaining with this new community or pursuing the promise of a better life in the north with Rose, Frenchie contemplates leaving. Upon learning that scouts have discovered a group of newcomers in the area, however, he and Rose return to camp. Later, they learn that one of the newcomers is Miig's former partner, a man who was thought to have died in a residential school, but who managed to escape. Moved by the couple's reunion, Frenchie reflects on the power of holding space for other people in one's life. He concludes, "And I understood that as long as there are dreamers left, there will never be want for a dream. I understood just what we would do for each other, just what we would do for the ebb and pull of the dream, the bigger dream that held us all. Anything. Everything" (231). In highlighting the importance of shared dreams as a catalyst for resisting oppression, Frenchie demonstrates the importance of having spaces of hope.

Frenchie has come to understand the power of dreams and hope in part because of Minerva, an elder who proves to have saved the memory of all her dreams in her Indigenous language. When the Cardinals hook her to a machine designed to cull her dreams from her bone marrow, "she called on her blood memory, her teachings, her ancestors.... She sang with volume and pitch and a heartbreaking wail that echoed through her relatives' bones, . . . morphing her singular voice to many, pulling every dream from her own marrow and into her song" (172). With her song, her language, her dreams, and most important, her reliance on her ancestors, Minerva causes the marrow-harvesting machine to explode. As a result, the harvesting system begins to collapse, inspiring the coalition of Indigenous resistance fighters that Frenchie's group has joined to continue their rebellion. Minerva's activism—relying as it does on language, stories, and dreams shared by her ancestors—destroys the competitive, entrepreneurial commodification of the very lifeblood generated in her bone marrow. She is an activist inspired to action against neoliberalism by the very fact of her collectivist ideals.

Whereas Starr's activism in *The Hate U Give* sits comfortably alongside popular understandings of what activism looks like and entails, as when she climbs atop the police car on the frontlines of the Black Lives Matter protest and uses a megaphone to call for an end to systemic oppression, the activism that Minerva and Frenchie practice is distinctly quieter, albeit no less powerful for being so. By choosing to remain and be part of a community of people that organize as a resistance movement committed to preserving their languages and culture in the face of genocidal forces, Frenchie follows in Minerva's path, ultimately becoming an activist himself.

At the novel's conclusion, Frenchie is not a neoliberal self-enclosed individual who overthrows oppressive systems. Rather, he and his companions continue to exist in enforced isolation on the margins of society. The machinations of racism grind on in the form of residential schools; loved ones tragically remain lost and missing; racial stratification remains a reality. Nevertheless, in keeping with the tradition of the critical dystopia, a type of dystopia in which characters reckon with the horrors of their social world while working toward something better (Moylan xii–xiii), *The Marrow Thieves* positions readers to occupy spaces of hope. In the end, Frenchie persists in his activism, fighting for the rights of Indigenous peoples, inspired by the activism of both Miig and Minerva. Like *The Hate U Give*, Dimaline's novel thus identifies unity, collaboration, and shared cultural memories as a potent recipe for activists to follow as they organize and work to annihilate the seeds of discord and destruction that neoliberalism sows.

TEACHABLE MOMENTS

Youth activists have had significant impacts on protest movements throughout the world. In some cases, they have been influenced in their tactics by YA literature, as in the examples we shared in the introduction to this chapter. In one example from "real life," Roberta's doctoral advisor, J. R. LeMaster, told her about a somber day in early June of 1989. Professor LeMaster was teaching American literature at a college in Beijing when, one by one, the students solemnly filed out of class. The oldest and tallest of the young men led the single-file line out of the door, following what seemed to Professor LeMaster to be a preplanned or unspoken pecking order. When he asked the last student, a slight young woman in her teens, "Where are you all going?" she shrugged matter-of-factly, raised her hands up from her waist, and answered, "To start a revolution, of course." He knew this meant they were heading to the protests in Tiananmen Square, where within a week, they risked being killed by Chinese soldiers and police officers. Professor LeMaster and his wife were swiftly evacuated by helicopter out of Beijing on orders from the US Embassy; he never again heard from any of those students, including the young teenager whose calm resolve had touched him so deeply during that troubled and troubling time.

Many more people know the compelling story of fifteen-year-old Malala Yousufzai, who was shot in the head in Pakistan in 2012 for being a girl and still going to school, as she narrates in her memoir *I Am Malala* (2013). She became an activist for universal education rights and was awarded the Nobel Peace Prize in 2014, becoming, at the age of seventeen, the youngest Nobel laureate to date. Still other readers may be familiar with Knud Pedersen, a Danish high school student who, during World War II, organized a small group of friends and classmates that secretly stole and stockpiled Nazi weapons and sabotaged German vehicles after Hitler's army invaded Denmark with virtually no resistance from the country's adult leaders. Known as the Churchill Club, the boys were eventually caught and imprisoned in an adult facility, as Philip Hoose documents in his book, *The Boys Who Challenged Hitler: Knud Pedersen and the Churchill Club* (2015).

Teenagers exhibited similar bravery during the civil rights movement. For example, four freshmen from Agriculture & Technical College of North Carolina led the sit-in that started on February 1, 1960, at the Woolworth's lunch counter in Greensboro. According to Christopher Wilson of the Smithsonian Museums, Jibreel Khazan, Franklin McCain, and Joseph McNeil were all born in 1941—the same year that Emmett Till was born. David Richmond was born in 1942. As McCain later told Wilson, all of them were tired of being humiliated by white-enforced segregation. McCain himself had felt suicidal at times, but "almost instantaneously, after sitting down on a simple, dumb stool, I felt so relieved. I felt so clean, and I felt as though I had gained a little bit of my manhood by that simple act" (Wilson).

In 2015, when Marley Dias was in fifth grade, she was motivated by children's literature in ways that stand in exact opposition to the stories we mentioned at the opening of this chapter. Marley was dismayed by the spate of books they were reading in class about white boys and their dogs. She noticed the "lack of diversity" in those books, so in late 2015, she founded a book drive to collect 1,000 books with Black girl characters. As she later told NPR, "I was frustrated because I was never reading books about black girls or any different type of character" in school (Anderson, "Where's the Color"). By 2023, more than 13,000 books had been donated to her campaign, #1000BlackGirlBooks (Dias).

The UN's Generation Equality held forums in Mexico City and in Paris in 2021 to listen to and learn from youth on topics including "gender-based violence, economic equality, sexual and reproductive health and rights, and climate justice" (UN Women). Many children and teenagers have been involved in leading ecopolitical activism, including Greta Thunberg of Sweden, Licypriya Kangujam and Haaziq Kazi of India, Nkosilathi Nyathi of Zimbabwe, and Autumn Peltier of the Anishinabek Nation in Canada (Ganguly). In 2022 young people began participating in mass protests against politicized misogyny in Iran, chanting "women, life, freedom" and "justice, liberty, no to forced hijab" (Owliaei et al.). Sadly, too many young people have been killed by government action in both Iran and the US.

We, as the authors of this book, have observed that the majority of the social-activist children and teenagers mentioned in this chapter—both the real and the fictional—share two characteristics. First, they do not act alone. Instead, they organize and work within groups to address systemic oppression. Second, their activism takes a variety of forms. Some of them, like Starr, march and participate in traditional protests. Others, like Greta Thunberg, inspire their peers to protest through their own selfless action. Still others act in less obvious ways, either by participating in social-media movements, declining to give their money to discriminatory corporations, or quietly refusing to bend in the face of unjust policies and practices. None of them is a strong, self-reliant hero of the type typically depicted with the arc of self-enclosed individualism that is advanced by neoliberal mythology. As feminist care ethicist Mary Jeanette Moran notes in a different context, "ontological self-sufficiency" can be overcome "only [with] a sense of empathy and ethical responsibility" ("Balance" 260).

Young adult protest novels, such as *The Hate U Give* and *The Marrow Thieves*, reject neoliberalism's valuing of hyperindividualism and competition in favor of collectivity and collaboration. In doing so, these books depict teenage protagonists whose knowledge of systemic oppression deepens as they interact with and learn from other people in their local communities. In turn, they become advocates for their communities. But the activist impulses that we have described in these books are not new. Indeed, they are part of a larger tradition, since adolescent characters have long been embedded in US reform-oriented novels, as we noted in chapter 1. Harriet Beecher Stowe's *Uncle Tom's Cabin* (1852), with its antislavery reform agenda, includes two African American teenagers, Topsy and Emmeline, both of whom are depicted specifically to stir and engage readers' empathy, even though one is portrayed comically and the other pathetically. Subsequently, various bestselling, reform-oriented novels in the nineteenth century portrayed teenage protagonists confronting and responding to oppressive social forces, such as Alcott's *Little Women* (1868, 1869) and Twain's *Adventures of Huckleberry Finn* (1885). As Trites has observed about the foundational authors in the tradition of the US adolescent reform novel, "Whether the reform ideology in a text concerns itself with gender or race or politics or any other social issue, novels for adolescents written in the traditions established by Alcott and Twain communicate that adolescents can make a social difference" (*Twain, Alcott* 143).

We conclude this section with a list of possible questions middle school, high school, and college teachers can explore with students, either as writing or discussion prompts. Although we present the questions as we might use them with our university students, we do so with the understanding that anyone using these suggestions will modify them, as appropriate, for their students' level of achievement and their psychological needs.

- How do characters in the novel you are reading model social activism? What specific tools do they use to overcome the forces that oppress them? Are there specific strategies they use that inspire you to want to make a change in your local community? If so, what changes?
- A scholar named David Harvey has defined *optimism of the intellect* as something that helps create *spaces of hope*. Harvey is especially interested in the relationship between global movements and the experiences people have as they inhabit their own personal embodiment. How does the novel you're reading generate "spaces of hope" for the characters—or for you? In this novel, how are individual bodies affected by larger, global movements?
- What injustices do you see in your own local community, including at your school? What specific steps and subsequent actions does this novel (or movie or video or song lyric, etc.) model that could help you inspire social change?

- *Oppositional binaries* is a term that refers to the way some concepts—like race and gender, for example—are set in opposition to each other, as if there are only two subsets in that categorization and one of them is inherently superior to the other. What oppositional binaries are you aware of in this novel? How do they lead to social injustice? When do characters appear to accept these hierarchical binaries? When do they reject them? And if those oppositional, hierarchical binaries are rejected, how does social change follow?
- Another example of an oppositional binary is "human/nature." Too many people have justified exploiting the Earth and its resources for centuries by creating a false dichotomy between human beings and the natural world. This particular oppositional binary positions humans as more important than animals, plants, or natural resources. To what extent do you think that's the case? How does the novel you're reading depict humans prioritizing themselves over nature? How, if at all, does the story reject that false binary? Can you point to examples of this hierarchy in your own life? Does this story provide you ways to push back against that type of illogic? If so, how? If not, why?
- What other oppositional binaries are you aware of? When have you experienced pressure to conform to an oppositional binary? In what ways do you regard yourself as problematizing or complicating that oppositional binary?
- When you hear the words "activist" or "activism," what comes to mind? Where have you acquired your ideas about activists and activism? Who benefits from depicting activists or activism in a negative—or positive—light, and why? Who is disadvantaged by stereotypical depictions of activists and activism, and why?
- Paola Mendoza, a social activist and one of the authors of the YA novel *Sanctuary*, writes the following in the author's notes at the end of that novel: "Activists believe change is possible even though everything around them tells them it is impossible. Activists fight, against the odds, for years, decades, and centuries. I believe what guides activists in their difficult pursuit of equity is a profound faith in the possibility of a just world and an unconditional love for their communities" (306). What does that quotation means to you? Do you agree with it? Or some parts of it? Or none of it? If so, why? If not, why not?

We suggest that these questions can serve as tools to support students becoming stronger critical thinkers. Moreover, we believe students benefit from becoming aware of oppositional binaries and critiquing them in their own life as one way to learn about—and avoid—logical fallacies, especially those on which neoliberalism relies.

"WELCOME TO ANOTHER EDITION OF THUNDERDOME!"

Throughout this book, we have shown how literature for teenagers can reproduce as well as resist neoliberalism—from its emphasis on self-enclosed individualism and competition to its ruthless exploitation of people and the environment; from its erasure of constructs such as racism and sexism to its reliance on biopolitics that produce and maintain social stratification and the inherent commodification of knowledge as a good on which individuals can trade for profit, as opposed to one that is communally produced and thus shared freely.

As coauthors, we have been involved in interrogating neoliberalism in literature for teenagers for the better part of a decade now, and sadly, the topic is no less relevant today than it was when we first began working together in 2015. While many members of the general public might struggle to name neoliberalism, let alone define this econo-political theory, virtually all of us experience its presence in our lives. Perhaps this explains why, when the two of us invite students in our YA literature classes to critique books they read through a lens of neoliberalism, the topic resonates palpably with them. That this should be the case is not surprising. For most of their lives, our students have been immersed in an educational system that only ever positions them to compete for grades, standardized test scores and class rankings, and for some, college admission and scholarships. We know that when they take YA literature courses with us at the college level, many of our students work two or three jobs to finance their education and make ends meet. In an economy where jobs continue to be exported overseas, students on the precipice of graduating face the prospect of having to compete for fewer jobs with long-term benefits like medical insurance and retirement plans. Instead, they face joining a so-called "gig economy," where short-term, on-demand work is the norm and workers are expected to move between jobs. No wonder a student in Sean's class expressed frustration with a professor who told his students that if they hoped to compete for a small number of seats in coveted graduate programs, they needed to devote themselves to participating in as many university-sponsored extracurricular programs and activities as possible. "If you don't," this professor cautioned, "others will." Sean's student was particularly irritated by what she suggested was the professor's inability to understand how his advice belied his privilege. As she explained, "I'm sure all of us would like to build our resumes, but some of us have to work to put ourselves through school, or care for siblings, or help our parents tend to sick relatives."

The stress and anxiety that many of our students report feeling emerges in part from the economic pressure they experience. Indeed, the stakes they face are arguably higher than those their parents and grandparents confronted. In their book *Deaths of Despair and the Future of Capitalism*, Anne Case and Angus Deaton argue that young people "who do not pass [their] exams and graduate to the cosmopolitan elite do not get to live in the fast-growing, high-tech, and flourishing cities and are assigned jobs threatened by globalization and by robots" (3). The same is true for youth in rural communities who are reluctant to leave their home and family to pursue economic prospects that are increasingly located in urban and suburban areas. Moreover, not only young people are struggling with issues related to mental health. In her research, Anna Zeira cites the psychologist Oliver James as describing a "rapid increase in emotional distress in the United States since the 1980s when the country began to implement neoliberal policies such as eliminating restrictions on the trade market and cutting social services" (205).

By overemphasizing competition at the expense of collaboration, and self-enclosed individualism at the expense of collectivism, neoliberalism diminishes our capacity to build relationships in groups with other people. Julia C. Becker, Lea Hartwich, and S. Alexander Haslam, for example, cite research that suggests "that group memberships and related social identities are the source of a range of health-enhancing social psychological resources—including social connection and social support" (959). By emphasizing self-reliance and positioning us to understand other people as competition for limited opportunities and resources, neoliberalism can leave us feeling isolated and alone, thus limiting our "access to the curative potential of social connections" (949). Equally problematic, "neoliberal politics can also be a direct cause of poor health. This is because under neoliberalism, politicians often support tax cuts for the wealthy while withdrawing support for public services (e.g., in areas of health care and education)" (Becker et al. 960).

Finally, we question the ethical implications of treating all domains of human life as markets in which people compete for goods and services. Online platforms such as DonorsChoose, for example, allow teachers to solicit donations from philanthropists for books and other classroom supplies, but that system positions teachers to compete against other educators for access to basic learning materials they intend to use with and for their students. Should all children not have access to basic learning resources regardless of their teachers' public relations acumen or the earning level of the community into which they are born? Similarly, people increasingly use websites such as GoFundMe to solicit donations to help them cover the cost of surgeries and other medical treatments for loved ones, which raises the following question: should a person's access to life-saving medical procedures depend on their entrepreneurial skills and ability to garner more web page views than their competition? How is it justifiable that anyone would need to become a self-funding entrepreneur inveigling others for medical care or school supplies? We believe that education, like health care, is a basic human right. As UNICEF asserts, all children and adolescents have fundamental and inalienable rights "to protection, education, health care, shelter, and good nutrition" (United Nations, "Global Issues: Children"). Burdening the young with any lower standard is heartless.

CONCLUSION

Throughout this book we have argued that, while YA fiction can potentially reproduce neoliberal ideologies and discourses, it can also resist them, exposing readers to more humane and just ideas about social relations. Specifically, YA protest literature constitutes one example of how this genre can engage in subversive critiques of neoliberalism and other inequitable systems of power, while also advocating for progressive activist causes. Despite—or perhaps because of—the intended age of its reading audience, YA texts are well positioned to engage in radical social critique.

YA literature is often perceived as inferior to literature with a capital "L," and as a result, the latter receives considerably more critical attention. Ageist assumptions that depict the intended teenage audience of the genre as being less sophisticated readers than adults may also contribute to the genre's marginalization, but paradoxically, that very assumption allows books for teenagers to be subversive in ways that often escape the notice of reviewers and academic critics alike.

If traditional academics don't always take YA literature seriously enough, however, many young readers do. As the anecdotes we have shared throughout this chapter attest, a growing number of teenagers are embracing books they grew up reading as if they were blueprints for engaging in activism. When they respond to calls for action, young people are using narratives as road maps for combating social injustice. Representations of youth activism in YA literature can thereby invite young adults to speak out against injustice—as opposed to remaining silent—while also positioning them to understand themselves as agentic people who have the capacity to resist neoliberal discourses, including those that perpetuate systemic oppression by emphasizing self-enclosed individualism and competition at the expense of collectivism and cooperation. In challenging teen readers to imagine more compassionate and just forms of social organization, YA popular culture that rejects neoliberal ideology positions young people to occupy spaces of hope from which they can resist despair.

In many ways, our critical approach to reading and teaching literature establishes for us spaces of hope that we, the authors, find ourselves needing now more than ever. Although we started this project with feelings of moral indignation and no small amount of despair in the face of neoliberalism's cynical machinations, we now have more hope because we've developed strategies for helping young people think critically about how this econopolitical theory circumscribes their futures. This book thus constitutes our own form of social protest.

This is only one small step, however.

For high school and college students to occupy the critical reading position that we have advocated in this book, they need to know what neoliberalism is and how to identify its presence, not only in literary texts, but also in the world more broadly. When students can name "neoliberalism," and when they can explain how it operates on and through them, they are better prepared to ask if it is a belief system they wish to embrace fully or whether they can instead envision other, more inclusive, and compassionate forms of social relations that allow not only them, but all people, to grow and flourish.

In light of the populist triumph of neoliberalism in the 2024 presidential election, we have come to believe that our students—indeed, all of us—deserve nothing less.

NOTES

INTRODUCTION

1. Where possible throughout this volume, we italicize either the first or the defining usage of specialized vocabulary.

2. See, for example, Anna Zeira's 2022 study (205–12).

3. We believe that gender is a social construct and that fictional characters, in particular, are representational constructs. Throughout this volume, we therefore employ the pronouns authors apply to their fictional characters as a matter of respect for authors' choices, even while we condemn those who would discriminate against the trans and gender-nonconforming communities.

4. Sarah Park Dahlen and Ebony Elizabeth Thomas make note of the "Potter franchise's multicultural (some would say neoliberal) view of cultural inclusion in fantastic storytelling" (7). In other words, earlier in the twenty-first century the series was praised for being "multicultural," although most scholars now recognize that the series lacks a true commitment to diversity and equity. We also stand with Dahlen and Thomas in believing that J. K. Rowling "chooses not to see everybody as whole persons" (4).

5. See also Ebony Elizabeth Thomas, "Hermione Is Black" (181–206). Farah Mendelsohn describes the early books in the series as being set in a world of "hierarchy and prejudice" (177). See Jackie Horne for a detailed analysis of the series as interpreted through the lenses of "multicultural antiracism" and "social justice antiracism" (76–104).

6. We borrow here from the subtitle of Jane Tompkins's *Sensational Designs: The Cultural Work of American Fiction*.

7. Jeremy Johnston analyzes how neoliberal economics have led to the explosion of self-reliant protagonists in the YA book industry: "shifting economic conditions within the US since the mid-twentieth century—for instance, the development of neoliberal policies through the 1970s and 1980s—correspond to the emergence and proliferation of YA fiction as a literary field, its prevalent themes, and its narrative tropes. . . . YA literature . . . [has been] an increasingly marketable commodity, but [its] . . . literary features encourage a specific model of young adulthood I term 'productive citizenship.' Productive citizens, who champion self-reliant behaviors in particularly gendered ways, mature as they accept the transformation of systemic problems into individual issues. In

other words, adolescent maturation only occurs through strict adherence to the neoliberal doctrine of personal responsibility" (Johnston 1).

8. Joseph W. Campbell defines dystopias in terms of their ideological functioning: "Dystopian texts perform social critical work ... that allows the reader to question the polyvalent relationships between subjectivity and power. Dystopian authors create texts that show us a worst-case scenario.... The effect is often a chilling warning-by-hyperbole of what might come if we are not careful" (82).

CHAPTER 1: SELF-ENCLOSED INDIVIDUALISM AND THE NEOLIBERAL TRADITION

1. Unless otherwise noted, all literary documents cited in this section are widely available online, including via Gutenberg Press (gutenberg.org).

2. When we teach, both authors of this book prefer to teach conflict in terms of "person vs. person," "person vs. self," and "person vs. environment" (since both "nature" and "society" are part of any character's environs).

3. See Trites, *Disturbing the Universe* (1–3, 37–38).

CHAPTER 2: NEOLIBERALISM'S LOGIC OF EXPLOITATION

1. See, for example, Taylor, *Toxic Communities*, and Washington, *A Terrible Thing to Waste*.

2. The etymology invokes the "fabled fire-breathing monster of Greek mythology, with a lion's head, a goat's body, and a serpent's tail (or according to others, with the heads of a lion, a goat, and a serpent), killed by Bellerophon" ("chimera/chimera, n.").

3. Beck goes on to cite Little Badger thusly: "Both in and outside fiction, we are pushed to the past tense. The reality is, many Indigenous cultures in North America survived an apocalypse. The key word is *survived*. Any future with us in it, triumphant and flourishing, is a hopeful one" (quoted in Beck, emphasis in the original; see also Rebecca Roanhorse, "Decolonizing Science Fiction" and Gracie Dillon's *Walking the Clouds*.)

4. According to Rebecca Roanhorse, convener of an Indigenous Futurisms roundtable, "One aspect of Indigenous Futurism is an awareness and embrace of Indigenous science, which is only radical because Western colonial culture discounts our cultures as primitive." In that article, Roanhorse interviews Little Badger and other authors of Indigenous Futurism. Little Badger says this about her own work: "Whether writing about Future Earth, distant galaxies, or fantasy worlds, I'm mindful that there's no 'right way' to learn about the natural world. Western science is certainly not universal. In my stories, characters—humans, aliens, whales with tentacles, whatever!—pursue knowledge in varied ways, and that's a beautiful thing!" (Roanhorse).

5. For more about ethical caring as an act of resistance, see Mary Jeanette Moran, "The Three Faces of Tally Youngblood" (129–35).

6. The possessive pronoun "nuestra" and the article "una" are standard contextual clues for Spanish speakers to understand the connotation of the word *historia*. In historical

terms, although English speakers shortened the Latinate word from French "*histoire*" to "story" when they were describing a narrative, by the time Middle English was spoken, in French as in Spanish, the words for "story" and "history" still remain the same ("history, n."; "story, n.").

CHAPTER 3: US NEOLIBERALISM AND ITS RACIST ORIGINS

1. Readers can find critiques of MacLean's scholarly argument, both positive and negative, among the following academic book reviews: Geoffrey Brennan; Jennifer Burns; Jean-Baptiste Fleury and Alain Marciano; Robert O. McDonald; Eleni Schirmer and Michael W. Apple. See also Marc Parry, "A New History of the Right Has Become an Intellectual Flashpoint."

2. We offer broad historical context for our discussion in part because of concerns articulated by the Council of Chief State School Officers that K–12 time allocated for social studies education decreased by 44 percent in the years immediately following the implementation of the No Child Left Behind Act ("The Marginalization of Social Studies"). Moreover, according to a 2018 Brookings Institution report: "The overall trend in eighth-grade civics largely mirrors the trend in eighth-grade reading: slow and modest improvements, with perhaps a slight uptick in scores in recent years" (Hansen et al. 3). In May 2023, *Education Week* documented that "history scores have been steadily declining since 2014, while civics scores have remained mostly flat for over a decade before 2022" (Schwartz).

3. See, for example, Antonio Backman et al. (1–22); Sarah Park Dahlen, "We Need Diverse Books" (83–108); Marilisa Jiménez Garcia (230–49); Kenan Metzger and Wendy Kelleher (36–52); and Philip Nel (136–66).

4. The first reason the State of Mississippi offered for seceding from the Union in 1861 is listed as follows in the secession document its legislature ratified: "Our position is thoroughly identified with the institution of slavery—the greatest material interest in the world." See, among other available online copies of this document: https://avalon.law.yale.edu/19th_century/csa_missec.asp.

5. As we have explained in chapter 2, the language of neoliberalism relies on many oppositional binaries that support systems of oppression, including sexism (male/female), anthropocentrism (human/animal), or geography (Global North/Global South). Reading YA literature as a critique of neoliberalism thus entails identifying false dualities that define one concept hierarchically, as if one of the terms were inherently more important than the other term in the binary.

6. We also pledge to donate royalties generated from this book to benefit youth in the Choctaw Nation, the Ojibwe Nation, and the Lipan Apache Tribe of Texas, as well as the NAACP of Jackson, Mississippi.

7. Luther notes that his mother would monetize everything if she possibly could: "If there was a way she could get a tax deduction out of it, I bet she'd've kept track of how many times [a patient in the group home] farted in 2002" (215).

8. Georgetown is the name of the Jackson neighborhood in which Thomas grew up (Bragg). For more on the historical origins of racism, segregation, and urban planning in Jackson, Mississippi, see Joan Marshall Wesley et al. (21–22).

CHAPTER 4: RACISM IN OUR NEOLIBERAL ERA

1. Readers interested in the history of racism and antiracism in children's literature will find the following as helpful as we have: Rudine Sims Bishop, *Free Within Ourselves* (2007); Katharine Capshaw, *Children's Literature of the Harlem Renaissance* (2004); Paula Connolly, *Slavery in American Children's Literature* (2013); Michelle H. Martin, *Brown Gold: Milestones of African American Children's Picture Books* (2004); Phil Nel, *Was the Cat in the Hat Black?* (2017); and Ebony Elizabeth Thomas, *The Dark Fantastic* (2019).

2. Ed Borough appears to be loosely based on Barry Farm, a federal housing project built in southeastern Washington, DC, following World War II as segregated housing for African Americans (see Schoenfeld; see also Perry-Brown).

CHAPTER 5: RESISTING POSTFEMINIST THINKING

1. Chris Holmlund defines the term as follows: "Postfeminism entails a backlash against or a dismissal of the desirability for equality between women and men, in the workforce and in the family" (116).

2. See Derek Bell for more on postracialism (9–14).

3. According to Rosalind Gill (2007), the analysis of postfeminism requires a "sensibility" (148) that examines the "contradictory nature" of many works about the concept and that shows "the entanglement of both feminist and anti-feminist themes within them" (149). Postfeminism advances several consistent themes: "These include the notion that femininity is a bodily property; the shift from objectification to subjectification; the emphasis upon self-surveillance, monitoring, and discipline; *a focus upon individualism, choice and empowerment*; the dominance of a makeover paradigm; a resurgence in ideas of natural sexual difference; a marked sexualization of culture; and *an emphasis upon consumerism and the commodification of difference*. These themes coexist with, and are structured by, stark and continuing inequalities and exclusions that relate to 'race' and ethnicity, class, age, sexuality and disability as well as gender" (149, emphasis added). See also Yaszek, "I'll Be a Postfeminist."

4. "The effects of poverty are pernicious and persistent across generations. Those born to parents in the lowest quintile of the income distribution are twice as likely to end up there as children born to middle-income parents, and the intergenerational correlations in income, educational attainment, female household headship, government assistance receipt, and risky behavior are high" (Barr and Gibbs 3253).

5. According to Rottenberg, "This neoliberal feminism, in turn, is helping to produce a particular kind of feminist subject. Using key liberal terms, such as equality, opportunity, and free choice, while displacing and replacing their content, this recuperated feminism forges a feminist subject who is not only individualized but entrepreneurial in the sense that she is oriented toward optimizing her resources through incessant calculation, personal initiative, and innovation. Indeed, creative individual solutions are presented as feminist and progressive, while calibrating a felicitous work-family balance becomes her main task. Inequality between men and women is thus paradoxically acknowledged only

to be disavowed. And the question of social justice is recast in personal, individualized terms" (59). See Rottenberg also for cogent critiques of the inherently neoliberal workings in Anne-Marie Slaughter's "Why Women Still Can't Have It All" (53–78) and in Cheryl Sandberg's *Lean In* (79–104).

6. "The oil that lay under Biafran earth had a lot to do with that unlikely alliance" of Britain and the USSR in aiding the Muslim northern region of Nigeria to its genocidal destruction of southeastern Biafra (Venter 6–7). See Venter for a full account of the role oil, the UK, and the USSR played in the Nigerian genocide of Biafrans from 1967 to 1970 (114–20).

7. See also Moran on the ethical importance of maternal anger in "Angry Caregiver" (108–12).

8. Mark Dery's "Black to the Future" defines Afrofuturism as follows: "Speculative fiction that treats African-American themes and addresses African-American concerns in the context of twentieth-century technoculture—and, more generally, African-American signification that appropriates images of technology and a prosthetically enhanced future—might, for want of a better term, be called 'Afrofuturism'" (180). He also observes that "African Americans, in a very real sense, are the descendants of alien abductees; they inhabit a sci-fi nightmare in which unseen but no less impassable force fields of intolerance frustrate their movements; official histories undo what has been done; and technology is too often brought to bear on black bodies (branding, forced sterilization, the Tuskegee experiment, and tasers come readily to mind)" (180). Writing as he was in the early 1990s, Dery understandably equates the then marginalized status of science fiction as a genre with "the subaltern position to which blacks have been relegated throughout American history" (180). Ebony Elizabeth Thomas describes Afrofuturism as "both an aesthetic and an activist movement in the arts" (*Dark Fantastic* 9).

CHAPTER 6: BIOPOLITICS AND NEOLIBERAL ERASURE

1. See Melanie A. Marotta's *African American Adolescent Female Heroes* for an insightful interpretation of Smith's *Orleans* as a neo-slave narrative (3–17).

2. See also Clare Jean Kim (105–38).

3. For further analysis of the causes and effects of "The Emergency" in India from 1975 to 1977 that also reflects on the rise of neoliberalism, see Mary E. John (625–37).

CHAPTER 7: KNOWLEDGE PRODUCTION AND NEOLIBERALISM

1. A. S. King confirmed that she used the name "Hemmings" intentionally to evoke Sally Hemings in a personal interview with Sean P. Connors, 11 April 2023.

2. For examinations of how the Cinderella figure influences the female hero in mythopoetic speculative fiction, see both Leah Phillips's *Female Heroes in Young Adult Fantasy Fiction* and Cristina Santos's *Untaming Girlhood*.

WORKS CITED

@TheDailyShow. "'There's Something Liberating about Fighting an Obvious Enemy as Opposed to One You Have to Prove Exists.' Trevor Discusses the Difference Between Racism in America and South Africa." YouTube, 5 Sept. 2022, 11:07 a.m., https://twitter.com/TheDailyShow/status/1566820199256526848.

Aalbers, Manuel B. "Do Maps Make Geography? Part 1: Redlining, Planned Shrinkage, and the Places of Decline." *ACME: An International E-Journal for Critical Geographies*, vol. 13, no. 4, 2014, pp. 525–56, https://acme-journal.org/index.php/acme/article/view/1036/890. Accessed 4 Dec. 2022.

"Abacha, Sani." In *Dictionary of African Biography*, vol. 1, edited by Emmanuel K. Akyeampong and Henry Louis Gates Jr., Oxford UP, 2012, pp. 1–3.

"About WNDB." We Need Diverse Books, https://diversebooks.org/about-wndb/. Accessed 29 Sept. 2022.

Achebe, Chinua. *There Was a Country: A Personal History of Biafra*. Penguin, 2012.

Adams, Glenn, Sara Estrada-Villalta, Daniel Sullivan, and Hazel Rose Markus. "The Psychology of Neoliberalism and the Neoliberalism of Psychology." *Journal of Social Issues*, vol. 75, no. 2, 2019, pp. 189–216.

Adeyemi, Tomi. *Children of Blood and Bone*. Henry Holt and Company, 2018.

Alexander, Michelle. *The New Jim Crow: Mass Incarceration in the Age of Colorblindness*. 2010. The New Press, 2020.

Althusser, Louis. "Ideology and Ideological State Apparatuses." *Lenin and Philosophy and Other Essays*, translated by Ben Brewster, edited by Frederic Jameson. Monthly Review Press, 2001, pp. 85–126.

Ambrosio, John. "Changing the Subject: Neoliberalism and Accountability in Public Education." *Educational Studies*, vol. 49, no. 4, 2013, pp. 316–33.

Anderson, Meg. "Where's the Color in Kids' Lit?" *Morning Edition*, 26 Feb. 2016, https://www.npr.org/sections/ed/2016/02/26/467969663/wheres-the-color-in-kids-lit-ask-the-girl-with-1-000-books-and-counting. Accessed 29 Nov. 2022.

Arizona Rural Policy Institute. "Demographic Analysis of the Navajo Nation Using 2010 Census and 2010 American Community Survey Estimates." Northern Arizona University, Window Rock, AZ, Navajo Nation Planning and Development, n.d., https://gotr.azgovernor.gov/sites/default/files/navajo_nation_0.pdf. Accessed 20 Sept. 2023.

Aronson, Marc. *Race: A History Beyond Black and White*. Simon & Schuster, 2007.

Aschoff, Nicole. *The New Prophets of Capital*. Verso, 2015.

Asher, Jay. *Thirteen Reasons Why*. Razorbill, 2007.
Ashton, J. E. *The Industrial Revolution, 1760–1830*. Oxford UP, 1948.
Azevedo, Flavio, John T. Jost, Tobias Rothmund, and Joanna Sterling. "Neoliberal Ideology and the Justification of Inequality in Capitalist Societies: Why Social and Economic Dimensions of Ideology are Intertwined." *Journal of Social Issues*, vol. 75, no. 1, 2019, pp. 49–88.
Bacevic, Jana. "Knowing Neoliberalism." *Social Epistemology*, vol. 33, no. 4, 2019, pp. 380–92.
Backman, Antonio, Chayse Sundt, and Sarah Park Dahlen. "Asian American Teen Fiction: An Urban Public Library Analysis." *Journal of Research on Libraries and Young Adults*, vol. 9, no. 1, 2018, pp. 1–22.
Barbie. Directed by Greta Gerwig, Warner Bros., 2023.
Barr, Andrew, and Chloe R. Gibbs. "Breaking the Cycle: Intergenerational Effects of an Antipoverty Program in Early Childhood." *Journal of Political Economy*, vol. 130, no. 12, 2022, pp. 3253–85.
Basu, Balaka, Katherine R. Broad, and Carrie Hintz. "Introduction." *Contemporary Dystopian Fiction for Young Adults: Brave New Teenagers*, edited by Balaka Basu, Katherine R. Broad, and Carrie Hintz, Routledge, 2013, pp. 1–18.
Bayron, Kalynn. *Cinderella Is Dead*. Bloomsbury, 2020.
Beck, Abaki. "Indigenous Futurism." *WeRNative*, 2022, https://www.wernative.org/articles/indigenous-futurism. Accessed 13 Oct. 2021.
Becker, Julia C., Lea Hartwich, and S. Alexander Haslam. "Neoliberalism Can Reduce Well-being by Promoting a Sense of Social Disconnection, Competition, and Loneliness." *British Journal of Social Psychology*, vol. 60, no. 3, 2021, pp. 947–65.
Bell, Derek. "After We've Gone: Prudent Speculations on America in a Postracial Epoch." *Critical Race Theory: The Cutting Edge*, 3rd ed., edited by Richard Delgado and Jean Stefancic. Temple UP, 2013, pp. 9–14. Originally published in *St. Louis University Law Journal*, 1990.
Benz, Terressa A. "Toxic Cities: Neoliberalism and Environmental Racism in Flint and Detroit, Michigan." *Critical Sociology*, vol. 45, no. 1, 2019, pp. 49–62.
Berlin, Jonathon, and Kori Rumore. "Twelve Times the President Called in the Military Domestically." *Chicago Tribune*, 1 June 2020, https://www.chicagotribune.com/news/ct-national-guard-deployments-timeline-htmlstory.html. Accessed 12 Nov. 2020.
"Best Sellers List: Children's Chapter Books." *New York Times*, 9 Sept. 2008, nytimes.com/books/best-sellers/2008/09/28/chapter-books/. Accessed 2 Nov. 2022.
Bettache, Karim, and Chi-yue Chiu. "The Invisible Hand Is an Ideology: Toward a Social Psychology of Neoliberalism." *Journal of Social Issues*, vol. 75, no. 1, 2019, pp. 8–19.
Bettache, Karim, Chi-yue Chiu, and Peter Beattie. "The Merciless Mind in a Dog-Eat-Dog Society: Neoliberalism and the Indifference to Social Inequality." *Current Opinion in Behavioral Sciences*, vol. 34, Aug. 2020, pp. 217–22.
Bishop, Rudine Sims. *Free Within Ourselves: The Development of African American Children's Literature*. Greenwood, 2007.
Bishop, Rudine Sims. "Mirrors, Windows, and Sliding Glass Doors." *Perspectives*, vol. 6, no. 3, 1990, pp. ix–xi.
Blake, Aaron. "Obama's 'You Didn't Build That' Problem." *Washington Post*, 18 July 2012, https://www.washingtonpost.com/blogs/the-fix/post/obamas-you-didnt-build-that-problem/2012/07/18/gJQAJxyotW_blog.html. Accessed 17 Oct. 2020.

Bobel, Chris, and Breanne Fahs. "The Messy Politics of Menstrual Activism." *The Palgrave Handbook of Critical Menstruation Studies*, edited by Chris Bobel et al., Palgrave Macmillan, 2020, pp. 1001–18, https://doi.org/10.1007/978-81-15-0614-7_71. Accessed 30 Nov. 2022.

Bothelho, Maria J., and Masha Kabakow Rudman. *Critical Multicultural Analysis of Children's Literature: Mirrors, Windows, and Doors*. Routledge, 2009.

Boulley, Angeline. *Firekeeper's Daughter*. Henry Holt and Company, 2021.

Bradford, Clare, Kerry Mallan, John Stephens, and Robyn McCallum. *New World Orders in Contemporary Children's Literature: Utopian Transformations*. Palgrave Macmillan, 2008.

Braedley, Susan, and Meg Luxton. "Competing Philosophies: Neoliberalism and Challenges of Everyday Life." *Neoliberalism and Everyday Life*, edited by Susan Braedley and Meg Luxton, McGill-Queen's UP, 2010, pp. 3–21.

Bragg, Ko. "Best-Selling Author Angie Thomas Receives Key to Jackson." *Jackson Free Press*, 5 March 2018, https://www.jacksonfreepress.com/news/2018/mar/05/best-selling-author-angie-thomas-receives-key-jack/. Accessed 4 Dec. 2022.

Braidotti, Rosi. "Posthuman Humanities." *European Educational Research Journal*, vol. 12, no. 1, 2013, pp. 1–19.

Brennan, Geoffrey. "*Democracy in Chains: The Deep History of the Radical Right's Stealth Plan for America*." Rev. in *History of Political Economy*, vol. 50, no. 3, 2018, pp. 635–40.

Breu, Christopher. *Insistence of the Material: Literature in the Age of Biopolitics*. U of Minnesota P, 2014.

Brooks, Cleanth, and Robert Penn Warren. *Understanding Fiction*. Appleton Century, 1943.

Brooks, Wanda, Susan Brown, and Gregory Hampton. "'There Ain't No Accounting for What Some Folks See in Their Own Mirrors': Considering Colorism Within a Sharon Flake Narrative." *Journal of Adolescent & Adult Literacy*, vol. 51, no. 8, 2008, pp. 660–69.

Brown, Wendy. *Undoing the Demos: Neoliberalism's Stealth Revolution*. Zone Books, 2015.

Burlingame, Michael. "Abraham Lincoln: Foreign Affairs." UVA Miller Center, https://millercenter.org/president/lincoln/foreign-affairs. Accessed 18 July 2022.

Burns, Jennifer. "*Democracy in Chains: The Deep History of the Radical Right's Stealth Plan for America*." Rev. in *History of Political Economy*, vol. 50, no. 3, 2018, pp. 640–48.

Campbell, Joseph W. *The Order and the Other: Young Adult Dystopian Fiction and Science Fiction*. UP of Mississippi, 2019.

Capshaw, Katharine (Smith). *Children's Literature of the Harlem Renaissance*. Indiana UP, 2004.

Case, Anne, and Angus Deaton. *Deaths of Despair and the Future of Capitalism*. Princeton UP, 2020.

"CDC Museum COVID-19 Timeline." Center for Disease Control and Prevention, https://www.cdc.gov/museum/ timeline/covid19.html#:~:text=March%2015%2C%20 2020,restaurants%20and%20bars%20to%20close. Accessed 20 Sept. 2023.

Cerón, Ella. "Why 'Harry Potter' Means So Much to the Parkland Activists." *Teen Vogue*, 26 March 2018, https://www.teenvogue.com/story/what-harry-potter-means-to-parkland-activists. Accessed 20 Sept. 2023.

Chen, Shi-Wen Sue, and Sin Wen Lau. "Good Chinese Girls and the Model Minority: Race, Education, and Community in *Girl in Translation* and *Front Desk*." *Children's Literature in Education*, vol. 52, no. 3, 2021, pp. 291–306.

Childs, Ann M. M. "The Incompatibility of Female Friendships and Rebellion." *Female Rebellion in Young Adult Dystopian Fiction*, edited by Sara K. Day, Miranda A. Green-Barteet, and Amy L. Montz, Ashgate, 2014, pp. 187–201.

"chimera/chimaera, n." *OED Online*. Oxford UP, Sept. 2022. www.oed.com/view/Entry/31708. Accessed 21 Oct. 2022.

Chishti, Muzaffar, and Jessica Bolter. "Merit-Based Immigration: Trump Proposal Would Dramatically Revamp Immigrant Selection Criteria, But with Modest Effects on Numbers." *Migration Information Source: The Online Journal of the Migration Policy Institute*, 30 May 2019, https://www.migrationpolicy.org/article/merit-based-immigration-trump-proposal-immigrant-selection. Accessed 21 Sept. 2023.

Collins, Suzanne. *Catching Fire*. Scholastic, 2009.

Collins, Suzanne. *The Hunger Games*. Scholastic, 2008.

Collins, Suzanne. *Mockingjay*. Scholastic, 2010.

Connolly, Paula. *Slavery in American Children's Literature, 1790–2010*. U of Iowa P, 2013.

Connors, Sean P. "Becoming Mockingjays: Encouraging Student Activism through the Study of YA Dystopia." *ALAN Review*, vol. 44, no. 1, 2016, pp. 18–29.

Connors, Sean P. "Drawing Back the Curtain on the Human-Animal Relationship: A Conversation with Eliot Schrefer." *SIGNAL, The Journal of the International Reading Association's Special Interest Group Network on Adolescent Literature*, vol. 41, no. 2, 2017, pp. 26–34.

Connors, Sean P. "Interview with Kalynn Bayron." *The Storyteller's Thread*, No. 30 [podcast]. 1 March 2021. https://soundcloud.com/user-438902690/kalynn-bayron.

Connors, Sean P. "Orleans." Email received by Roberta Seelinger Trites, 7 Oct. 2015.

Connors, Sean P. Personal interview with A. S. King, 11 April 2023.

Connors, Sean P., and Roberta Seelinger Trites. "*Legend*, Exceptionalism, and Genocidal Logic: A Framework for Reading Neoliberalism in YA Dystopias." *ALAN Review*, vol. 45, no. 3, 2018, pp. 31–41.

Cormier, Robert. *The Chocolate War*. 1974. Dell Laurel-Leaf, 2000.

Cosgrove, Lisa, and Justin M. Karter. "The Poison in the Cure: Neoliberalism and Contemporary Movements in Mental Health." *Theory & Psychology*, vol. 28, no. 5, 2018, pp. 669–83.

Craft, Jerry. *New Kid*. Harper, 2019.

Crane, Stephen. *The Red Badge of Courage*. 1895. Dover, 1990.

Crary, Alice. "What Do Feminists Want in an Epistemology?" *Feminist Interpretations of Ludwig Wittgenstein*, edited by Naomi Scheman and Peg O'Connor, Pennsylvania State UP, 2002, pp. 97–118.

Crenshaw, Kimberlé W. "Mapping the Margins: Intersectionality, Identity Politics, and Violence Against Women of Color." *Stanford Law Review*, vol. 43, no. 6, 1991, pp. 1241–99.

Curry, Alice. *Environmental Crisis in Young Adult Fiction: A Poetics of Earth*. Palgrave, 2013.

Curtis, Christopher Paul. *Bucking the Sarge*. Random House, 2004.

Dahlen, Sarah Park. "'We Need Diverse Books': Diversity, Activism, and Children's Literature." *Literary Cultures and Twenty-First-Century Childhoods*, edited by Nathalie op de Beeck, Palgrave Macmillan, 2020, pp. 83–108.

Dahlen, Sarah Park, and Ebony Elizabeth Thomas. "Introduction." *Harry Potter and the Other: Race, Justice, and Difference in the Wizarding World*, edited by Sarah Park Dahlen and Ebony Elizabeth Thomas, UP of Mississippi, 2022, pp. 3–16.

Day, Sara K., Miranda A. Green-Barteet, and Amy L. Montz. *Female Rebellion in Young Adult Dystopian Fiction*. Ashgate, 2014.

Delgado, Richard. "Storytelling for Oppositionists and Others: A Plea for Narrative." *Critical Race Theory: The Cutting Edge*, 3rd ed., edited by Richard Delgado and Jean Stefancic, Temple UP, 2013, pp. 71–80.

Delgado, Richard, and Jean Stefancic. "Introduction." *Critical Race Theory: The Cutting Edge*, 3rd ed., edited by Richard Delgado and Jean Stefancic, Temple UP, 2013, pp. 1–5.

Denchak, Melissa. "Flint Water Crisis: Everything You Need to Know." NRDC, National Resources Defense Council, 8 Nov. 2018. nrdc.org/stories/flint-water-crisis-every thing-you-need-know. Accessed 16 Nov. 2022.

Dery, Mark. "Black to the Future: Interviews with Samuel R. Delany, Greg Tate, and Tricia Rose." *Flame Wars: The Discourse of Cyberculture*, edited by Mark Dery, Duke UP, 1994, pp. 179–222.

Desmond, Matthew. "In Order to Understand the Brutality of American Capitalism, You Have to Start on the Plantation." *New York Times Magazine*, 14 Aug. 2019, pp. 30–42, https://pulitzercenter.org/sites/default/files/inline-images/bRWij1TAAhE0DsC4DLX djrXJpTLKjAqgEI91uaOfom7QStnmcw.pdf. Accessed 29 Aug. 2023.

Dhar, P. N. *Indira Gandhi, "The Emergency," and Indian Democracy*. Oxford UP, 2000.

Diary of an Aspiring Loser. "All the Black, Asian, and Wizards and Witches of Color in the Harry Potter Series." https://www.diaryofanaspiringloser.com/all-the-black-asian-and -wizards-and-witches-of-color-in-the-harry-potter-series/. Accessed 23 Oct. 2020.

Dias, Marley. "Marley Dias: About Me." #10,000BlackGirlBooks, 2023, https://www.marley dias.com/about/. Accessed 17 Nov. 2023.

Dillon, Gracie. *Walking the Clouds: An Anthology of Indigenous Science Fiction*. U of Arizona P, 2012.

Dimaline, Cherie. *The Marrow Thieves*. DCB, 2017.

Du Bois, W. E. B. *The Souls of Black Folk*. 1903. Millennium, 2014.

Eley, Latasha N. "Black Body Politics in College: Deconstructing Colorism and Hairism toward Black Women's Healing." *Color Struck: How Race and Complexion Matter in the "Color-Blind" Era*, edited by Lori Latrice Martin et al., Sense Publishers, 2017, pp. 77–122.

Emerson, Ralph Waldo. "Letter to Walt Whitman from Ralph Waldo Emerson." http://mason.gmu.edu/~rnanian/Emerson-Whitmanletter.html. Accessed 2 Dec. 2022.

Fandom Forward. "About." https://fandomforward.org/mission. Accessed 10 Dec. 2022.

Farrow, Anne, Joel Lang, and Jenifer Frank. *Complicity: How the North Promoted, Prolonged, and Profited from Slavery*. Ballantine, 2006.

Fasenfest, David. "A Neoliberal Response to an Urban Crisis: Emergency Management in Flint, MI." *Critical Sociology*, vol. 45, no. 1, 18 Aug. 2017, https://journals.sagepub.com /doi/full/10.1177/0896920517718039. Accessed 31 Aug. 2022.

Flanagan, Victoria. *Technology and Identity in Young Adult Fiction: The Posthuman Subject*. Palgrave Macmillan, 2014.

Fleury, Jean-Baptiste, and Alain Marciano. "The Sound of Silence: A Review Essay of Nancy MacLean's *Democracy in Chains: The Deep History of the Radical Right's Stealth Plan for America*." Rev. in *Journal of Economic Literature*, vol. 56, no. 4, 2018, pp. 1492–1537, https://www.aeaweb.org/articles?id=10.1257/jel.20181502. Accessed 4 Dec. 2022.

"Flint, Michigan Census Data." Infoplease, 2003, last revised 12 Jan. 2007, https://www.infoplease.com/us/census/michigan/flint. Accessed 31 Aug. 2022.

Foucault, Michel. *The Birth of Biopolitics: Lectures at the Collège de France, 1978–79*, translated by Graham Burchell, edited by Michel Senellart, Palgrave, 2008.

Foucault, Michel. *Discipline and Punish: The Birth of the Prison*, translated by Alan Sheridan. 1977. Pantheon, 1978.

Foucault, Michel. *History of Sexuality, Vol. 1*, translated by Robert Hurley. 1978. Vintage Books, 1990.

Foucault, Michel. *The Order of Things: An Archaeology of the Human Sciences*. 1970. Knopf, 1994.

"Four Foods Jefferson Helped Popularize in America." Monticello.org, https://www.monticello.org/site/blog-and-community/4-foods-jefferson-helped-popularize-america. Accessed 17 Jan. 2022.

Frank, Arthur W. *Letting Stories Breathe: A Socio-Narratology*. U of Chicago P, 2010.

Freedom House. "New Report: The Global Decline in Democracy Has Accelerated." 3 March 2021, https://freedomhouse.org/article/new-report-global-decline-democracy-has-accelerated. Accessed 9 Dec. 2022.

Freitas, Donna. "How to Be Bad." *New York Times*, 15 Aug. 2008, https://www.nytimes.com/2008/08/17/books/review/Freitas-t.html. Accessed 24 Sept. 2020.

Friedman, Thomas L. "How We Broke the World: Greed and Globalization Set US up for Disaster." *New York Times*, 31 May 2020, Sunday Review, pp. 4–5, https://www.nytimes.com/2020/05/30/opinion/sunday/coronavirus-globalization.html. Accessed 1 June 2020.

Fritz, Sonya Sawyer. "Girl Power and Girl Activism in the Fiction of Suzanne Collins, Scott Westerfeld, and Moira Young." *Female Rebellion in Young Adult Dystopian Fiction*, edited by Sara K. Day, Miranda A. Green-Barteet, and Amy L. Montz, Ashgate, 2014, pp. 17–31.

Ganguly, Riya. "Inspiring Young Activists Changing the World." Education World, https://www.educationworld.in/inspiring-young-activists-changing-the-world/. Accessed 29 Nov. 2022.

Garcia, Marilisa Jiménez. "En(countering) YA: Young Lords, Shadowshapers, and the Longings and Possibilities of Latinx Young Adult Literature." *Latino Studies*, vol. 16, no. 2, 2018, pp. 230–49.

Gill, Rosalind. "Postfeminist Media Culture: Elements of a Sensibility." *European Journal of Cultural Studies*, vol. 10, no. 2, 2007, pp. 147–66.

Gill, Rosalind, and Christina Scharff. "Introduction." *New Femininities: Postfeminism, Neoliberalism, and Subjectivity*, edited by Rosalind Gill and Christina Scharff, Palgrave, 2011, pp. 1–20.

Giroux, Henry. "Spectacles of Race and Pedagogies of Denial: Anti-Black Racist Pedagogy Under the Reign of Neoliberalism." *Communication Education*, vol. 52, no. 3–4, 2003, pp. 191–211.

Glennerster, Howard, John Hills, David Piachaud, and Jo Webb. *One Hundred Years of Poverty and Policy.* Joseph Rowntree Foundation, 2004, https://eprints.lse.ac.uk/3913/1/One_hundred_years_of_poverty.pdf. Accessed 23 Oct. 2020.

Glennon, Robert. *Water Follies: Groundwater Pumping and the Fate of America's Fresh Waters.* Island Press, 2002.

Goldschlag, William, and Dan Janison. "Trump: Some Will Die for Economy's Restart, But You're 'Warriors.'" *Newsday*, 6 May 2020, https://www.newsday.com/long-island/politics/trump-mask-coronavirus-reopen-bright-fauci-task-force-primary-1.44409243. Accessed 8 June 2020.

Goldstein, Dana. "Little Rock Will Offer A.P. African American Studies Despite State Objections." *New York Times*, 17 Aug. 2023, https://www.nytimes.com/2023/08/17/us/little-rock-ap-african-american-studies.html. Accessed 6 Sept. 2023.

Gondola, Didier. "Threatened." Book review. *Africa Access*, 10 Oct. 2014, http://africaaccessreview.org/2014/10/threatened/. Accessed 10 Nov. 2020.

Goodley, Dan, and Mark Rapley. "Changing the Subject: Postmodernity and People with 'Learning Difficulties.'" *Disability/Postmodernity: Embodying Disability Theory*, edited by Mairian Corker and Tom Shakespeare, Cassell, 2002, pp. 127–42.

Gottdiener, Mark. *The Social Production of Urban Space*, 2nd ed., U of Texas P, 1994.

Green, John. "Scary New World." *New York Times Book Review*, 7 Nov. 2008, https://www.nytimes.com/2008/11/09/books/review/Green-t.html. Accessed 29 Dec. 2022.

Grosz, Elizabeth. *Volatile Bodies: Toward a Corporeal Feminism.* Indiana UP, 1994.

Guerra, Stephanie. "Colonizing Bodies: Corporate Power and Biotechnology in Young Adult Science Fiction." *Children's Literature in Education*, vol. 40, no. 4, 2009, pp. 275–95.

Hansen, Michael, Elizabeth Levesque, Jon Valant, and Diana Quintero. "The 2018 Brown Center Report on American Education: How Well Are American Students Learning?" Brookings, 2018, https://www.brookings.edu/wp-content/uploads/2018/06/2018-Brown-Center-Report-on-American-Education_FINAL1.pdf. Accessed 4 Dec. 2022.

Haraway, Donna J. *When Species Meet.* U of Minnesota P, 2008.

Harris, Anita. *Future Girl: Young Women in the Twenty-First Century.* Routledge, 2004.

Harris, Michael. *Stay Alive: Surviving Capitalism's Coming Hunger Games.* Zero Books, 2021.

Harvey, David A. *A Brief History of Neoliberalism.* Oxford UP, 2005.

Harvey, David A. *Spaces of Hope.* U of California P, 2000.

Hayles, N. Katherine. *How We Became Posthuman.* U of Chicago P, 1999.

Heller, Meredith. "Feminist Media Studies Checklist: The Young Adult Novel Edition." Saucy Scholar, 17 Nov. 2017, https://meredithheller.wordpress.com/2017/11/17/feminist-media-studies-checklist-the-young-adult-novel. Accessed 6 Dec. 2022.

Hemingway, Ernest. *Green Hills of Africa.* 1935. Jonathan Cape, 1936.

Hentges, Sarah. *Girls on Fire: Transformative Heroines in Young Adult Dystopian Literature.* McFarland, 2018.

Herndon, Jaime. "Report: 2019 Diversity in Children's Books." *Book Riot*, 26 June 2020, https://bookriot.com/diversity-in-childrens-and-young-adult-literature/. Accessed 2 Sept. 2022.

Herring, Cedric, and Anthony Hynes. "Race, Skin Tone, and Wealth Inequality in America." *Color Struck: How Race and Complexion Matter in the "Color-Blind" Era*, edited by Lori Latrice Martin et al., Sense Publishers, 2017, pp. 1–17.

Hidier, Tanuja Desai. *Born Confused*. Scholastic, 2002.

Hinton, S. E. *The Outsiders*. 1967. Speak, 2006.

"history, n." *OED Online*. Oxford UP, Sept. 2022, https://www.oed.com/dictionary/history_n#. Accessed 11 Oct. 2022.

Hohle, Randolph. *Race and the Origins of American Neoliberalism*. Routledge, 2015.

Hohle, Randolph. *Racism in the Neoliberal Era: A Meta History of Elite White Power*. Routledge, 2018.

Hollindale, Peter. "Ideology and the Children's Book." *Signal*, vol. 55, 1988, pp. 3–22.

Holmlund, Chris. "Postfeminism from A to G." *Cinema Journal*, vol. 44, no. 2, 2005, pp. 116–21. *JSTOR*, http://www.jstor.org/stable/3661099. Accessed 6 Dec. 2022.

Horne, Jackie C. "Harry and the Other: Answering the Race Question in J. K. Rowling's *Harry Potter*." *The Lion and the Unicorn*, vol. 34, 2010, pp. 76–104.

Hoose, Phillip. *The Boys Who Challenged Hitler: Knud Pedersen and the Churchill Club*. Farrar, Straus and Giroux, 2015.

Horowitz, Juliana Menasce, Ruth Igielnik, and Rakesh Kochhar. "Trends in Wealth and Income Equality." Pew Research Center, 9 Jan. 2020, https://www.pewresearch.org/social-trends/2020/01/09/trends-in-income-and-wealth-inequality. Accessed 10 Dec. 2022.

Howe, Irving. *Politics and the Novel*. 1957. Ivan R. Dee Books, 2002.

Hswen, Yulin, Xiang Xu, Anna Hing, Jared B. Hawkins, John S. Brownstein, and Gilbert C. Gee. "Association of '#covid19' Versus '#chinesevirus' with Anti-Asian Sentiments on Twitter, March 9–23, 2020." *American Journal of Public Health*, vol. 111, 2021, pp. 956–64, https://doi.org/10.2105/AJPH.2021.306154. Accessed 7 Dec. 2022.

Hunter, Margaret L. *Race, Gender, and the Politics of Skin Tone*. Routledge, 2005.

Hursh, David. "Assessing No Child Left Behind and the Rise of Neoliberal Education Policies." *American Educational Research Journal*, vol. 44, no. 3, 2007, pp. 493–518.

"hype, n." *Green's Dictionary of Slang*, by Jonathon Green, 2022, https://greensdictofslang.com/search/basic?q=hype. Accessed 28 Sept. 2022.

Issar, Siddhant. "Listening to Black Lives Matter: Racial Capitalism and the Critique of Neoliberalism." *Contemporary Political Theory*, vol. 20, no. 1, 2021, pp. 48–71.

Jackson, Tiffany D. *Monday's Not Coming*. Katherine Tegen Books, 2018.

James, Oliver. *The Selfish Capitalist: Origins of Affluenza*. Vermilion, 2008.

Jaques, Zoe. *Children's Literature and the Posthuman: Animal, Environment, Cyborg*. Routledge, 2015.

John, Mary E. "The Emergency in India: Some Reflections on the Legibility of the Political." *Inter-Asia Cultural Studies*, vol. 15, no. 4, 2014, pp. 625–36.

Johnston, Jeremy. "Neoliberal Adolescence and the Economic Base of YA Literature." Children's Literature Association Conference, Seattle, WA, 16 June 2023. *Productive Citizenship: Neoliberal Capitalism and the Young Adult Novel*, UP of Mississippi, forthcoming.

Jordan, Winthrop. *White Over Black: American Attitudes toward the Negro, 1550–1812*, 2nd ed. U of North Carolina P, 2012.

Kavka, Misha. "Feminism, Ethics, and History, or What Is the 'Post' in Postfeminism?" *Tulsa Studies in Women's Literature*, vol. 21, no. 1, 2002, pp. 29–44.

Kaw, Eugenia. "Medicalization of Racial Features: Asian-American Women and Cosmetic Surgery." *Medical Anthropology Quarterly*, vol. 7, no. 1, 1993, pp. 74–89.

Keating, AnaLouise. *Transformation Now! Toward a Post-Oppositional Politics of Change*. U of Illinois P, 2013.

Keay, Douglas. "AIDS, Education and the Year 2000: An Interview with Margaret Thatcher." *Margaret Thatcher Foundation*, 23 Sept. 1987, https://www.margaretthatcher.org/document/106689. Accessed 6 Oct. 2020.

Kelly, Deirdre M., and Shauna Pomerantz. "Mean, Wild, and Alienated: Girls and the State of Feminism in Popular Culture." *Girlhood Studies: An Interdisciplinary Journal*, vol. 2, no. 1, 2009, pp. 1–17.

Kendi, Ibram X. *Stamped from the Beginning: The Definitive History of Racist Ideas in America*. Bold Type Books, 2016.

Kennedy, Merrit. "Lead-Laced Water in Flint: A Step-By-Step Look at the Makings of a Crisis." *The Two Way*, 20 April 2016, https://www.npr.org/sections/thetwo-way/2016/04/20/465545378/lead-laced-water-in-flint-a-step-by-step-look-at-the-makings-of-a-crisis. Accessed 31 Aug. 2022.

Keys, Alicia. "Girl on Fire (Official Video)." YouTube, 19 Oct. 2012, https://www.youtube.com/watch?v=J91ti_MpdHA.

Khanna, Nikki. "Introduction." *Asian American Women on Skin Color and Colorism*, edited by Nikki Khanna, New York UP, 2020, pp. 1–35.

Kidd, Kenneth. *Making American Boys: Boyology and the Feral Tale*. U of Minnesota P, 2004.

Kiely, Eugene. "'You Didn't Build That,' Uncut and Unedited." *FactCheck.org*, 23 July 2012, https://www.factcheck.org/2012/07/you-didnt-build-that-uncut-and-unedited/. Accessed 6 Oct. 2020.

Kim, Clare Jean. "The Racial Triangulation of Asian Americans." *Politics & Society*, vol. 27, no. 1, 1999, pp. 105–38.

King, A. S. *Dig*. Dutton Books, 2019.

King, Thomas. *The Truth About Stories: A Native Narrative*. U of Minnesota P, 2005.

King, Ynestra. "The Ecology of Feminism and the Feminism of Ecology." *Healing the Wounds: The Promise of Ecofeminism*, edited by Judith Plant, New Society, 1989, pp. 18–28.

Kings, Amy Elizabeth. "Intersectionality and the Changing Face of Ecofeminism." *Ethics & the Environment*, vol. 22, no. 1, 2017, pp. 63–87.

Klein, Naomi. *This Changes Everything: Capitalism vs. the Climate*. Simon & Schuster, 2014.

Kolata, Gina, and Roni Caryn Rabin. "'Don't be Afraid of Covid,' Trump Says, Undermining Public Health Messages." *New York Times*, 8 Oct. 2020, https://www.nytimes.com/2020/10/05/health/trump-covid-public-health.html. Accessed 12 Nov. 2020.

Krehbiel, Randy. "Ryan Walters Denies Saying Tulsa Race Massacre Was Not About Race." *Tulsa World*, 7 July 2023, updated 14 Aug. 2023, https://tulsaworld.com/news/local

/education/ryan-walters-denies-saying-tulsa-race-massacre-was-not-about-race/article_72a3e2cc-1cf6-11ee-b1b0-5a8ffc83ba6.html. Accessed 6 Sept. 2023.

Latour, Bruno. *We Have Never Been Modern*. Harvard UP, 1993.

Lawrence, Charles R., III. "Who Is the Child Left Behind? The Racial Meaning of the New School Reform." *Suffolk Univ. Law Review*, vol. 39, 2005, pp. 699–718.

Leonhardt, David. "Why Are Republican Presidents So Bad for the Economy?" *New York Times*, Opinion, 8 Feb. 2021, p. 2, https://www.nytimes.com/2021/02/02/opinion/sunday/democrats-economy.html. Accessed 30 Dec. 2022.

Lim, Hong Kai. "Asian Blepharoplasty: A Review of the Ethnocultural Motivations and Ethical Implications." *Journal of the Foundations of Ophthalmology*, 3 Nov. 2021, https://jfophth.com/asian-blepharoplasty-a-review-of-ethnocultural-motivations-and-ethical-implications/. Accessed 28 Sept. 2022.

Little Badger, Darcie. *A Snake Falls to Earth*. Levine Querido, 2021.

Lockhart, E. *The Disreputable History of Frankie Landau-Banks*. Hyperion, 2008.

Lorey, Isabell. *State of Insecurity: Government of the Precarious*, translated by Aileen Derieg. Verso, 2015.

Lu, Marie. *Legend*. 2011. Speak, 2013.

MacLean, Nancy. *Democracy in Chains: The Deep History of the Radical Right's Stealth Plan for America*. Viking, 2017.

Mad Max Beyond Thunderdome. Directed by George Miller and George Ogilvie, Warner Bros., 1985.

Madani, Doha. "Dan Patrick on Coronavirus: 'More Important Things than Living.'" NBC News, 21 April 2020, https://www.nbcnews.com/news/us-news/texas-lt-gov-dan-patrick-Reopening-economy-more-important-things-n1188911. Accessed 8 June 2020.

Marchetti, Adrianna. "Lipstick Feminism, Neoliberalism, and the Undoing of Feminism." *Young Feminist Europe*, 1 April 2020, http://www.youngfeminist.eu/2020/04/lipstick-feminism-neoliberalism-and-the-undoing-of-feminism/. Accessed 5 Nov. 2022.

"The Marginalization of Social Studies." Council of Chief State School Officers, 16 Nov. 2018, https://ccsso.org/resource-library/marginalization-social-studies. Accessed 4 Dec. 2022.

Marotta, Melanie A. *African American Adolescent Female Heroes: The Twenty-First-Century Young Adult Neo-Slave Narrative*. UP of Mississippi, 2023.

Martel, Yann. *The Life of Pi: A Novel*. Harcourt, 2001.

Martin, Michelle H. *Brown Gold: Milestones of African American Children's Picture Books, 1845–2002*. Routledge, 2004.

McDonald, Robert O. "*Democracy in Chains: The Deep History of the Radical Right's Stealth Plan for America* by Nancy MacLean." Rev. in *Journal of Cultural Economy*, vol. 11, no. 4, 2018, pp. 371–75, https://www.tandfonline.com/doi/full/10.1080/17530350.2018.1463277. Accessed 4 Dec. 2022.

McKibben, Bill. *Eaarth*. St. Martin's Griffin, 2011.

McRobbie, Angela. *The Aftermath of Culture: Gender, Culture, and Social Change*. Sage, 2009.

McRobbie, Angela. "Postfeminism and Popular Culture." *Interrogating Postfeminism: Gender and the Politics of Popular Culture*, edited by Yvonne Tasker and Diane Negra, Duke UP, 2007, pp. 27–39.

Mendelsohn, Farah. "Crowning the King: Harry Potter and the Construction of Authority." *The Ivory Tower and Harry Potter: Perspectives on a Literary Phenomenon*, edited by Lana A. Whited, U of Missouri P, 2002, pp. 159–81.

Mendoza, Paola, and Abby Sher. *Sanctuary*. Putnam, 2020.

Merritt, J. E. "The Triangular Trade." *Business History*, vol. 3, no. 2, 1960, pp. 1–7.

Metzger, Kenan, and Wendy Kelleher. "The Dearth of Native Voices in Young Adult Literature." *ALAN Review*, vol. 35, no. 2, 2008, pp. 36–42.

Meyer, Marissa. *Cinder: The Lunar Chronicles*. Square Fish, 2012.

"Michigan Economic Indicators: A Monthly Newsletter on Key Economic Indicators Prepared by the Senate Fiscal Agency," May 2003, https://www.senate.michigan.gov/SFA/Publications/EconInd/MEI_MAY03.pdf. Accessed 31 Aug. 2022.

Mickenberg, Julia. *Learning from the Left: Children's Literature, the Cold War, and Radical Politics in the United States*. Oxford UP, 2006.

Mills, Charles W. *The Racial Contract*. Cornell UP, 1997.

Montz, Amy L. "Rebels in Dresses: Distractions of Competitive Girlhoods in Young Adult Dystopian Fiction." *Female Rebellion in Young Adult Dystopian Fiction*, edited by Sara K. Day, Miranda A. Green-Barteet, and Amy L. Montz, Ashgate, 2014, pp. 107–22.

Morales, Laurel. "Coronavirus Infections Continue to Rise on Navajo Nation." NPR, 11 May 2020, https://www.npr.org/sections/coronavirus-live-updates/ 2020/05/11/854157898/Coronavirus-infections-continue-to-rise-on-navajo-nation. Accessed 8 June 2020.

Moran, Mary Jeanette. "The Angry Caregiver: Gendered Emotion in the Penderwicks series and the *One Crazy Summer* Trilogy." *Emotion in Texts for Children and Young Adults*, edited by Karen Coats and Gretchen Papazian, John Benjamins, 2022, pp. 104–29.

Moran, Mary Jeanette. "'Balance Is the Trick': Feminist Relationality in *The Amazing Maurice* and the Tiffany Aching Series." *The Lion and the Unicorn*, vol. 42, no. 3, 2018, pp. 259–80.

Moran, Mary Jeanette. "The Three Faces of Tally Youngblood: Rebellious Identity-Changing in Scott Westerfeld's 'Uglies' Series." *Female Rebellion in Young Adult Dystopian Fiction*, edited by Sara K. Day, Miranda A. Green-Barteet, and Amy L. Montz, Ashgate, 2014, pp. 123–39.

Morrison, Ewan. "YA Dystopias Teach Children to Submit to the Free Market, Not Fight Authority." *The Guardian*, 1 Sept. 1, 2014, https://www.theguardian.com/books/2014/sep/01/ya-dystopias-children-free-market-hunger-games-the-giver-divergent. Accessed 14 Oct. 2020.

Morrison, Toni. *The Bluest Eye*. 1970. Vintage International, 2007.

Moylan, Tom. *Scraps of the Untainted Sky: Science Fiction, Utopia, Dystopia*. Westview Press, 2000.

Na, An. *The Fold*. Simon and Schuster, 2008.

Nel, Philip. *Was the Cat in the Hat Black? Hidden Racism in Children's Literature and the Need for Diverse Books*. Oxford UP, 2017.

Nikolajeva, Maria. *From Mythic to Linear: Time in Children's Literature*. Scarecrow Press, 2000.

Nikolajeva, Maria. *The Rhetoric of Character in Children's Literature*. Scarecrow Press, 2002.

Niro, Shelley, Keller George, and Alan Brant. "Origin Stories: Skywoman." *Canadian Museum of History*, 1999, 2001, https://www.historymuseum.ca/cmc/exhibitions/aborig/fp/fp2f22e.html. Accessed 11 Nov. 2020.

Norwood, Kimberly Jade, and Violeta Solonova Foreman. "The Ubiquitousness of Colorism: Then and Now." *Color Matters: Skin Tone Bias and the Myth of a Post-Racial America*, edited by Kimberly Jade Norwood, Routledge, 2014, pp. 9–28.

Nwaubani, Adaobi Tricia. "Remembering Nigeria's Biafra Civil War That Many Prefer to Forget." BBC News, 15 Jan. 2020, https://www.bbc.com/news/world-africa-51094093. Accessed 3 Nov. 2022.

"Oil Shock of 1973–74." Federal Reserve History, 2013, https://www.federalreservehistory.org/essays/oil-shock-of-1973-74. Accessed 16 Nov. 2022.

Okorafor, Nnedi. *Akata Warrior*. Speak, 2017.

Okorafor, Nnedi. *Akata Witch*. Speak, 2011.

Okorafor, Nnedi. *Akata Woman*. Speak, 2022.

Olmos, Sergio, Mike Baker, and Zolan Kanno-Youngs. "Federal Agents Unleash Militarized Crackdown on Portland." *New York Times*, 17 July 2020, updated 1 Sept. 2020, https://www.nytimes.com/2020/07/17/us/portland-protests.html. Accessed 12 Nov. 2020.

Owliaei, Negin, Ruby Zamand, and Halla Mohieddeen. "Women, Life, Freedom: The Chants of Iran's Protests." *Al Jazeera*, 28 Sept. 2022, https://www.aljazeera.com/podcasts/2022/9/28/women-life-freedom-the-chants-of-irans-protests. Accessed 13 Sept. 2023.

Oziewicz, Marek, and Lara Saguisag. "Introduction: Children's Literature and Climate Change." *The Lion and the Unicorn*, vol. 45, no. 2, 2021, pp. v–xiv.

Papenfuss, Mary. "Surgeon General Singles Out People of Color to Stop Alcohol, Drugs in Covid-19 Fight." *HuffPost*, 10 April 2020, https://www.huffpost.com/entry/surgeon-general-jerome-adams-minorities-drugs-drinking-tobacco-covid-19_n_5e910917c5b6F7b1ea811195. Accessed 8 June 2020.

Parry, Marc. "A New History of the Right Has Become an Intellectual Flashpoint." *Chronicle Review*, 19 July 2017, https://www.chronicle.com/article/a-new-history-of-the-right-has-become-an-intellectual-flashpoint/. Accessed 4 Dec. 2022.

Pellizzoni, Luigi, and Marja Ylönen. *Neoliberalism and Technoscience*. Ashgate, 2012.

Perry-Brown, Nena. "Barry Farm Redevelopment Illustrates How Far DCHA Still Has to Go." Greater Greater Washington.org, 7 April 2021, https://ggwash.org/view/80939/barry-farm-redevelopment-illustrates-how-far-dcha-still-has-to-go. Accessed 31 Aug. 2022.

Phillips, Leah. *Female Heroes in Young Adult Fantasy Fiction: Reframing Myths of Adolescent Girlhood*. Bloomsbury, 2023.

Pomerantz, Shauna, and Rebecca Raby. "Reading Smart Girls: Post-Nerds in Post-Feminist Popular Culture." *Girls, Texts, Cultures*, edited by Clare Bradford and Mavis Reimer, Wilfred Laurier UP, 2015, pp. 287–311.

Pomerantz, Shauna, and Rebecca Raby. *Smart Girls: Success, School, and the Myth of Post-Feminism*. U of California P, 2017.

Quintero, Isabel. *Gabi: A Girl in Pieces*. Cinco Puntos Press, 2014.

Ratcliffe, Rebecca. "J. K. Rowling Tells of Anger at Attacks on Casting of Black Hermione." *The Guardian*, 5 June 2016, https://www.theguardian.com/stage/2016/jun/05/harry-potter-jk--rowling-black-hermione. Accessed 23 Oct. 2020.

Reece, Robert L. "Color Crit: Critical Race Theory and the History and Future of Colorism in the United States." *Journal of Black Studies*, vol. 50, no. 1, 2019, pp. 3–25, https://journals.sagepub.com/doi/epub/10.1177/0021934718803735. Accessed 21 Sept. 2022.

Reynolds, Jason, and Kendi, Ibram X. *Stamped: Racism, Antiracism, and You*. Little, Brown, 2020.

Ringrose, Jessica. *Postfeminist Education? Girls and the Sexual Politics of Schooling*. Routledge, 2013.

Rivera, Lilliam. *The Education of Margot Sanchez*. Simon & Schuster, 2017.

Roanhorse, Rebecca, Elizabeth Lapensee, Johnnie Jae, and Darcie Little Badger. "Decolonizing Science Fiction and Imagining Futures: An Indigenous Futurisms Roundtable." *Strange Horizons*, 2017, http://strangehorizons.com/non-fiction/articles/decolonizing-science-fiction-and-imagining-futures-an-indigenous-futurisms-roundtable. Accessed 13 Oct. 2022.

Robehmed, Natalie. "At 21, Kylie Jenner Becomes the Youngest Self-Made Billionaire Ever." *Forbes*, 5 Mar. 2019, https://www.forbes.com/sites/natalierobehmed/2019/03/05/at-21-kylie-jenner-becomes-the-youngest-self-made-billionaire-ever/#4c00c0142794. Accessed 4 Oct. 2020.

Robertson, Roland. "Glocalization: Time-Space and Homogeneity-Heterogeneity." *Global Modernities*, edited by Scott Lash, Roland Robertson, and Mike Featherstone, Sage, 1995, pp. 25–44.

Robinson, Cedric J. *Black Marxism: The Making of the Black Radical Tradition*. 1983. U of North Carolina P, 2000.

Rogers, Katie. "Protestors Dispersed with Tear Gas So Trump Could Pose at Church." *New York Times*, 1 June 2020, updated 17 Sept. 2020, https://www.nytimes.com/2020/06/01/us/politics/trump-st-johns-church-bible.html. Accessed 12 Nov. 2020.

Rottenberg, Catherine. *The Rise of Neoliberal Feminism*. Oxford UP, 2018.

Rowling, J. K. *Harry Potter and the Half-Blood Prince*. Scholastic, 2005.

Sadler, John. "Native American Tribe Claims Nuclear Waste Can't Be Stored on Its Lands." *Las Vegas Sun*, 15 Aug. 2019, https://lasvegassun.com/news/2019/aug/15/native-american-tribe-claims-nuclear-waste-cant-be/. Accessed 22 Dec. 2022.

"Sally Hemings." Monticello.org, https://www.monticello.org/sallyhemings/. Accessed 17 Jan. 2022.

Sandberg, Sheryl. *Lean In: Women, Work, and the Will to Lead*. Knopf, 2013.

Sandel, Michael J. "The Tyranny of Merit." *TED2020*, May 2020, https://www.ted.com/talks/michael_sandel_the_tyranny_of_merit?language=en#t-11690. Accessed 5 Oct. 2020.

Sandel, Michael J. *The Tyranny of Merit: What's Become of the Common Good?* Farrar, Straus and Giroux, 2020.

Sanders, Joe Sutliff. *Disciplining Girls: Understanding the Origins of the Classic Orphan Girl Story*. Johns Hopkins UP, 2011.

Santos, Cristina. *Untaming Girlhood: Storytelling Female Adolescence*. Routledge, 2023.

Satrapi, Marjane. *Persepolis: The Story of a Childhood*. Pantheon, 2003.

Sawers, Naarah. "Capitalism's New Handmaiden: The Biotechnical World Negotiated Through Children's Fiction." *Children's Literature in Education*, vol. 40, no. 3, 2009, pp. 169–79.

Sawhill, Isabel V. "2011: The Year that Income Inequality Captured the Public's Attention." Brookings, 19 Dec. 2011, https://www.brookings.edu/blog/up-front/2011/12/19/2011-the-year-that-income-inequality-captured-the-publics-attention/. Accessed 7 Nov. 2022.

Schirmer, Eleni, and Michael W. Apple. "(Un)Chaining Democracy: An Essay Review of Nancy MacLean's *Democracy in Chains*." Rev. in *Education Review*, 31 Jan. 2018, https://edrev.asu.edu/index.php/ER/article/viewFile/2345/708. Accessed 4 Dec. 2022.

Schrefer, Eliot. *Endangered*. Scholastic, 2012.

Schrefer, Eliot, *Orphaned*. Scholastic, 2018.

Schrefer, Eliot. *Rescued*. Scholastic, 2016.

Schrefer, Eliot. *Threatened*. Scholastic, 2014.

Schwartz, Sarah. "Understanding the Sharp Drop in History and Civics NAEP Scores: 4 Things to Know." *Education Week*, 4 May 2023, https://www.edweek.org/teaching-learning/understanding-the-sharp-drop-in-history-and-civics-naep-scores-4-things-to-know/2023/05. Accessed 29 Aug. 2023.

Schwebel, Sara L. *Child-Sized Histories: Fictions of the Past in US Histories*. Vanderbilt UP, 2011.

Shrestha, Sriya. "Threatening Consumption: Managing US Imperial Anxieties in Representations of Skin Lightening in India." *Social Identities*, vol. 19, no. 1, 2013, pp. 104–19.

Silverman, Hollie, et al. "Navajo Nation Surpasses New York State for the Highest Covid-19 Infection Rate in the US." CNN, 18 May 2020, https://www.cnn.com/2020/05/18/us/navajo-nation-infection-rate-trnd/index.html. Accessed 8 June 2020.

Sims, Rudine. *Shadow and Substance: Afro-American Experience in Contemporary Children's Fiction*. NCTE, 1982.

Slack, Andrew. "The Strength of a Story: Andrew Slack at TEDxTransmedia 2011." YouTube, uploaded by TEDx Talks, 11 Oct. 2011, https://www.youtube.com/watch?v=Rq5NbWmyGWk. Accessed 30 Dec. 2022.

Slaughter, Anne-Marie. "Why Women Still Can't Have It All." *The Atlantic*, vol. 310, no. 1, July/Aug. 2012, pp. 85–102, https://www.theatlantic.com/magazine/archive/2012/07/why-women-still-cant-have-it-all/309020/. Accessed 2 Nov. 2022.

Smith, Sherri L. *Orleans*. Penguin, 2013.

Snircova, Sona. "Postfeminist Trends in Contemporary Young Adult Literature: The Reassessment of the Victim/Perpetrator Binary in Helen Cross's *My Summer of Love*." DOI: 10.5937/ZRFFP48-18673, vol. 48, no. 3, Jan. 2018, https://www.researchgate.net/publication/328324681_Postfeminist_trends_in_contemporary_young_adult_literature_The_reassessment_of_the_victimperpetrator_binary_in_Helen_Cross's_my_Summer_of_Love. Accessed 2 Nov. 2022.

Stephens, John. *Language and Ideology in Children's Fiction*. Longman, 1992.

Stone, Nic. *Dear Martin*. Crown, 2017.

Stork, Francisco X. *Marcelo in the Real World*. Scholastic, 2009.

"story, n." *OED Online*. Oxford UP, Sept. 2022, https://www.oed.com/search/dictionary/?q=story. Accessed 11 Oct. 2022.

Tappe, Anneken. "30 Million Americans Have Filed Initial Unemployment Claims Since Mid-March." CNN, 30 April 2020, https://www.cnn.com/2020/04/30/economy/unemployment-benefits-coronavirus/index.html. Accessed 8 June 2020.

Taranto, James. "You Didn't Sweat, He Did: Constructing a Sentence Is Hard Work When You're the World's Greatest Orator." *Wall Street Journal*, 18 July 2012, https://www.wsj.com/articles/SB10000872396390444873204577535053434972374. Accessed 17 Oct. 2020.

Taylor, Dorceta E. *Toxic Communities: Environmental Racism, Industrial Pollution, and Residential Mobility*. New York UP, 2014.

Taylor, Laini. *Daughter of Smoke and Bone*. Little, Brown and Company, 2011.

Taylor, Laini. *Days of Blood and Starlight*. Little, Brown and Company, 2012.

Taylor, Laini. *Dreams of Gods and Monsters*. Little, Brown and Company, 2014.

Taylor, Mildred. *The Land*. Scholastic, 2001.

Taylor, Mildred. *Roll of Thunder, Hear My Cry*. Dial, 1976.

Thomas, Angie. *Concrete Rose*. HarperCollins, 2021.

Thomas, Angie. *The Hate U Give*. HarperCollins, 2017.

Thomas, Angie. *On the Come Up*. HarperCollins, 2019.

Thomas, Ebony Elizabeth. *The Dark Fantastic: Race and the Imagination from Harry Potter to the Hunger Games*. New York UP, 2019.

Thomas, Ebony Elizabeth. "Hermione Is Black: Harry Potter and the Crisis of Infinite Dark Fantastic Worlds." *Harry Potter and the Other: Race, Justice, and Difference in the Wizarding World*, edited by Sarah Park Dahlen and Ebony Elizabeth Thomas, UP of Mississippi, 2022, pp. 181–206.

Thomas, Leah, et al. *Intersectional Environmentalist*, https://www.intersectionalenvironmentalist.com/. Accessed 30 Sept. 2022.

Thunberg, Greta. *No One Is Too Small to Make a Difference*. Penguin Books, 2021.

Tompkins, Jane. *Sensational Designs: The Cultural Work of American Fiction, 1790–1860*. Oxford UP, 1985.

Trimble, Sarah. "(White) Rage: Affect, Neoliberalism, and the Family in *28 Days Later* and *28 Weeks Later*." *Review of Education/Pedagogy/Cultural Studies*, vol. 32, no. 3, 2010, pp. 295–322.

Trites, Roberta Seelinger. *Disturbing the Universe: Power and Repression in Adolescent Literature*. U of Iowa P, 2000.

Trites, Roberta Seelinger. "'Some Walks You Have to Take Alone': Ideology, Intertextuality, and the Fall of the Empire in The Hunger Games Trilogy." *The Politics of Panem: Challenging Genres*, edited by Sean P. Connors, Sense Publishers, 2014, pp. 15–28.

Trites, Roberta Seelinger. *Twain, Alcott, and the Birth of the Adolescent Reform Novel*. U of Iowa P, 2007.

Trombetta, Sadie. "Harry Potter Has Probably Had a Bigger Impact on Student Activists than You Realize." *Bustle*, 27 March 2018, https://www.bustle.com/p/how-harry-potter-inspired-the-parkland-student-activists-what-that-means-for-the-future-of-childrens-literature-8613896. Accessed 30 Dec. 2022.

Tuana, Nancy. "Feminist Epistemology: The Subject of Knowledge." *The Routledge Handbook of Epistemic Injustice*, edited by Ian James Kidd, José Medina, and Gaile Pohlhaus Jr., Routledge, 2017, pp. 125–38.

Twain, Mark. *Adventures of Huckleberry Finn*. 1885. U of California P, 2001.

UN Women. "Through Generation Equality, Young Activists Hold the World Accountable." United Nations, 10 Oct. 2022, https://ethicalmarketingnews.com/through-generation-equality-young-activists-hold-the-world-accountable. Accessed 18 Oct. 2023.

United Nations. "Global Issues: Children." UNICEF, 2022, https://www.un.org/en/global-issues/children. Accessed 9 Dec. 2022.

Vallone, Lynne. *Disciples of Virtue: Girls' Culture in the Eighteenth and Nineteenth Centuries*. Yale UP, 1995.

Vavrus, Michael. *Teaching Anti-Fascism: A Critical Multicultural Pedagogy for Civic Engagement*. Teachers College Press, 2022.

Vazquez, Maegan. "Trump Invokes George Floyd's Name While Taking Economic Victory Lap." CNN, 5 June 2020, https://www.cnn.com/2020/06/05/politics/donald-trump-george-floyd-rose-garden/index.html. Accessed 8 Jun 2020.

Venter, Al J. *Nigeria: Bloodletting and Mass Starvation, 1967–70*. Pen and Sword Books, 2018.

Viswanath, Tharini. "Voice, Choice, and Material Agency: The Sexualized Feminine Body in Young Adult Literature." Diss. Illinois State Univ., Normal, IL, 2020.

Wald, Priscilla. *Contagious: Cultures, Carriers, and the Outbreak Narrative*. Duke UP, 2008.

Walker, Alice. *In Search of Our Mothers' Gardens*. 1983. Harcourt, 2008.

Warren, Karen J. *Ecofeminist Philosophy: A Western Perspective on What It Is and Why It Matters*. Rowman & Littlefield, 2000.

Washington, Harriet A. *A Terrible Thing to Waste: Environmental Racism and Its Assault on the American Mind*. Little, Brown Spark, 2019.

Watson, Renée. *Piecing Me Together*. Bloomsbury, 2017.

Weiler, Hans N. "Whose Knowledge Matters? Development and the Politics of Knowledge." Stanford University, http://web.stanford.edu/~weiler/Texts09/Weiler_Molt_09.pdf. Accessed 16 Jan. 2022.

Wesley, Joan Marshall, Matthew Dalbey, and William H. Harris. "Urban Segregation in the Deep South: Race, Education, and Planning Ethics in Jackson, Mississippi." *Race, Gender & Class*, vol. 12, no. 3–4, 2005, pp. 11–30. *JSTOR*, http://www.jstor.org/stable/41675259. Accessed 6 Dec. 2022.

"WHO Timeline: COVID-19." World Health Organization, 27 April 2020, https://www.who.int/news/item/27-04-2020-who-timeline---covid-19. Accessed 7 Dec. 2022.

"Whose Knowledge Matters? Development and the Politics of Knowledge." *Entwicklung als beruf*. Nomos Verlagsgesellschaft mbH & Co. KG, 2009. Available as "Whose Knowledge Matters? Development and the Politics of Knowledge," Stanford University, pp. 1–12, https://web.stanford.edu/~weiler/Texts09/Weiler_Molt_09.pdf. Accessed 30 Dec. 2022.

Williams, Alicia D. *Genesis Begins Again*. Atheneum, 2019.

Wilson, Christopher. "At the Moment When Four Students Sat Down to Take a Stand." *Smithsonian Magazine*, 31 Jan. 2020, https://www.smithsonianmag.com/smithsonian-institution/lessons-worth-learning-moment-greensboro-four-sat-down-lunch-counter-180974087/. Accessed 29 Nov. 2022.

Wilson, Edmund. *The Triple Thinkers: Twelve Essays on Literary Subjects.* 1938. Farrar, 1976.
Wilson, Julie A. *Neoliberalism.* Routledge, 2018.
Wilson, Julie A. "Star Testing: The Emerging Politics of Celebrity Gossip." *Velvet Light Trap*, no. 65, 2010, pp. 25–38.
Wise, Justin. "Kudlow Says US Will Have to Make 'Difficult Tradeoffs' on Coronavirus: 'Cure Can't be Worse than Disease.'" *The Hill*, 23 March 2020, https://thehill.com/homenews/administration/489064-kudlow-says-us-will-have-to-make-difficult-trade-offs-on-coronavirus. Accessed 8 June 2020.
Wong, Kristine. "How to Be Stewards of the Land: Nicole Horseherder Champions Sustainability on Tribal Lands." Sierra Club, 2 Nov. 2019, https://www.sierraclub.org/sierra/2019-6-november-december/faces-clean-energy/how-be-stewards-land. Accessed 5 Nov. 2020.
Wui, Sui-Lee, and Vivian Wang. "Two Women Fell Sick from the Coronavirus. One Survived." *New York Times*, 13 March 2020, https://www.nytimes.com/interactive/2020/03/13/world/asia/coronavirus-death-life.html. Accessed 7 Dec. 2022.
Wyne, Ali. "Foreign Policy Lessons from Brown v. Board of Education." Inkstick, 2 June 2021, https://inkstickmedia.com/foreign-policy-lessons-from-brown-v-board-of-education/. Accessed 18 July 2022.
Yaszek, Lisa. "I'll Be a Postfeminist in a Postpatriarchy, or Can We Really Imagine Life after Feminism?" *Electronic Book Review*, 29 Jan. 2005, https://electronicbookreview.com/essay/ill-be-a-postfeminist-in-a-postpatriarchy-or-can-we-really-imagine-life-after-feminism/. Accessed 14 Sept. 2020.
Yoong, Melissa. *Professional Discourses, Gender and Identity in Women's Media.* SpringerLink, 2020, https://link.springer.com/book/10.1007/978-3-030-55544-3. Accessed 2 Nov. 2022.
Yousufzai, Malala. *I Am Malala.* Hatchette, 2013.
Zeira, Anna. "Mental Health Challenges Related to Neoliberalism in the United States." *Community Mental Health Journal*, vol. 58, no. 2, 2022, pp. 205–12.
Zhao, Christina. "GOP Congressman Says US Will Always Choose 'Loss of American Lives' Over 'Loss of Our Way of Life.'" *Newsweek*, 14 April 2020, https://www.newsweek.com/gop-congressman-says-us-will-always-choose-loss-american-lives-over-loss-our-way-life-1497913. Accessed 8 June 2020.
Zipes, Jack. *Sticks and Stones: The Troublesome Success of Children's Literature from Slovenly Peter to Harry Potter.* Routledge, 2001.
Zoboi, Ibi. *American Street.* HarperCollins, 2018.

INDEX

Abacha, Sani, 149
ability, xi, 44, 47, 57, 60, 137, 152, 153, 163, 185, 205
ableism, 29, 35, 39, 43, 157, 160, 188, 209
abortion, 130, 158–59, 163. *See also* reproductive health
activism, 32, 107, 172, 213, 226. *See also* youth activism
Adams, Jerome, 5
Adeyemi, Tomi, *The Children of Blood and Bone*, 12
Advanced Placement (AP) African American studies, 106
Adventures of Huckleberry Finn (Twain), 29, 222
affirmative action, 9
Africa, 122. *See also* Democratic Republic of the Congo (DRC); Nigeria; South Africa; Zimbabwe
African American Vernacular English (AAVE), 206
African Americans, 5, 9, 11, 12, 15, 56, 83–104, 105–27, 156, 162, 163, 170, 191, 192, 194, 195, 197, 199–204, 205, 221, 222, 232n, 233n. *See also* BIPOC; Civil Rights Act; civil rights movement; Civil War; colonialism; Emancipation Proclamation; enslavement; exploitation; racism
Afrofuturism, 158; defined, 233n
age, 60, 159, 226, 232n
agency (personal), 19, 33, 134, 135, 138, 146, 154, 164, 204. *See also* subjectivity
albinism, 147, 149, 151, 152, 155, 156

Alcott, Louisa May, 11, 222; *Little Women*, 222
Althusser, Louis, 11, 38, 174, 199. *See also* Ideological State Apparatus; Repressive State Apparatus
American Library Association, 116, 128
American literature, 27–31, 116
American Street (Zoboi), 104
André, Claudine, 67
Anishinaabe, 101, 102, 103, 125
Anishinabek Nation, 221
anthropocentrism, x, 70, 75–76, 81, 158, 231n
anti-Asian expressions, 162
anti-feminism, 130, 232n
antigovernment sentiment, 49, 52
anti-immigration, 172
antiracism, 96, 171, 194, 199, 229n, 232n
anti-Semitism, xii, 29, 139, 163, 194
Ape Quartet, 67. *See also* Schrefer, Eliot
Apple Inc., 13, 34–35
Arab-Israeli War of 1973, 180
Arbury, Ahmaud, 7
Aristotle, 86; *Poetics*, 86
Arizona Rural Policy Institute, 55
Aronson, Marc, xii; *Race*, xii
Asher, Jay, *Thirteen Reasons Why*, 12
Asian Americans, 120, 126, 162, 171
Asian Britons, 17
Asians, 120, 121, 122, 126, 161–62
Asperger syndrome, 44
Astor, John Jacob, 87
austerity, x, 89, 99, 108, 111, 119. *See also* neoliberalism

INDEX

authoritarianism, 3, 38, 48, 164, 172, 189
autobiography, 28
Autobiography of Benjamin Franklin (Franklin), 28

Banks, Lynne Reid, 107; *The Indian in the Cupboard*, 107
Bannerman, Helen, 107; *Little Black Sambo*, 107
Barbie (film), 129
Bayron, Kalynn, 188, 189, 199, 202–3, 205; *Cinderella Is Dead*, 188, 189, 199–204, 205, 208
Beyoncé, 131; "Run the World," 131
Biafran War, 148–49, 233n. *See also* Nigeria
Bible (KJV), 60, 61
biocapital, 165
bioethics, 164
biopolitics, xii, 15, 21, 41–43, 160, 161–85, 188, 208, 224, 233n; defined, 162
biotechnology, 164. *See also* cyborg
Bishop, Claire Hutchet, 107; *Five Chinese Brothers*, 107
BIPOC, 85, 88, 103, 107. *See also* African Americans; Asian Americans; Latinx peoples; people of color; Native Americans; racial identity
Black Lives Matter movement, 82, 219
Black Panther (film franchise), 129
Black Panthers, 213
Black peoples. *See* African Americans; people of color
Blackwater, 8
blepharoplasty, 126
Bluest Eye, The (Morrison), 122
Born Confused (Hidier), 126
Boulley, Angeline, 86, 100, 183; *Firekeeper's Daughter*, 86, 100–103, 108, 125, 183, 213
boyology, 11
Bridget Jones's Diary (film), 133
Brookings Institute, 128, 231n
Brooks, Cleanth, 29
Brown, Michael, 7
Brown v. Board of Education, 83, 88
Buchanan, James McGill, 83, 84, 85, 89–90

Bucking the Sarge. *See* Curtis, Christopher Paul
Buffy the Vampire Slayer, 131
Bush, George H. W., 6
Bush, George W., 112

Caddo Nation, 91. *See also* Native Americans
Canada, 61, 180, 212, 215–19, 221
capitalism, 9, 35, 40, 41, 72, 81, 85–88, 90, 91, 92–93, 95, 96, 104, 138, 150, 158, 166, 168–69, 173, 181, 191, 206
carbon economy, 82, 172–73, 181. *See also* fossil fuels
Card, Orson Scott, 30, 31; *Ender's Game*, 30, 31
Carlson, Tucker, 4
Carter, Jimmy, 181
caste, 42, 64, 167, 174, 182. *See also* social class; social stratification
Castile, Philando, 7
Caucasians. *See* Euro-Americans
Center for Disease Control and Prevention, US, 161
Chackchiuma, 91. *See also* Native Americans
charter schools, 8, 111, 113–14
Chauvin, Derek, 6
Cherokee Nation, 61. *See also* Native Americans
Chickasaw Nation, 91. *See also* Native Americans
Children of Blood and Bone, The (Adeyemi), 12
China, 161–62, 167, 169, 220. *See also* Tiananmen Square revolution
Chocolate War, The (Cormier), 32
Choctaw Nation, 91, 231n. *See also* Native Americans
Christianity, 27, 86, 140, 166, 191. *See also* religion
Churchill Club, 220
Cinder. *See* Meyer, Marissa
Cinderella, 143, 199–204, 233n
Cinderella Is Dead. *See* Bayron, Kaylee

INDEX

cis gender, ix, 58, 158, 188, 200, 201, 202, 203

Civil Rights Act, 25, 105

civil rights movement, 32, 84, 88–89, 111, 121, 220

Civil War, 86–87, 88, 92, 94, 108, 231n. *See also* Confederate States of America; Lincoln, Abraham

class. *See* social class

classism, x, 9, 16, 18, 59, 68, 70, 81, 82, 89, 93, 112, 119–21, 136, 139, 155, 156, 157, 187, 188, 198, 200, 201, 209. *See also* entitlement; privilege; social class

Clemens, Samuel. *See* Twain, Mark

climate change, ix–x, xii, 3, 20, 37, 52, 61, 62, 79, 81, 82, 172, 210, 211, 215, 216. *See also* global warming

Clinton, William J., 89, 94

collective bargaining, x, 84. *See also* unions

collective character, 147, 148

collectivism, 10, 17–18, 19, 21, 22, 27, 30, 31, 36–37, 43, 44, 46, 52, 53, 61, 62, 72, 74, 82, 90, 99, 108, 135, 144, 145, 146, 149–50, 151, 160, 166, 167, 171, 177–78, 179, 185, 190, 193, 199, 204, 207, 211, 212, 214, 215, 217, 218–19, 221, 225, 227. *See also* communalism

Collins, Suzanne, ix, 48, 129; *Catching Fire*, ix, 50, 52, 189; *The Hunger Games*, 48–52, 53, 128–29, 189; *Mockingjay*, 49, 50, 53, 189. *See also* Hunger Games trilogy

Colombian Americans, 172–79

colonialism, 63, 67, 68, 69, 75, 78, 86, 91, 121, 126, 172, 187, 195, 197, 216, 230n

colorism, 104, 119–27, 152, 156–57; defined, 119–20. *See also* racism, internalized

commercialism, 122, 124, 183, 187. *See also* commodification; consumerism

commodification, 13, 43, 67, 76, 77, 96, 107, 143, 173, 179, 183, 229n, 232n; of African Americans, 98; of children, 13; of human life, 173, 175–76, 215, 217, 219; of knowledge, 185, 187, 188–99, 205–6, 207, 224; of racism, 104, 108; of women, 175; of young people, 35, 52, 148, 173, 175, 188. *See also* objectification of female body

Common Sense (Paine), 28

communalism, 44, 78, 101, 143, 145. *See also* collectivism

Communism, 88

competition, xi, xii, 7, 8–9, 10, 12, 13–14, 16, 18, 19, 20, 21, 23–54, 72, 76, 85, 90, 112, 113, 114, 119, 123–24, 129, 130, 131, 132–34, 135, 142, 144, 147, 159–60, 167, 178, 186, 188–89, 193, 194, 198, 199, 209–19, 221, 224–25, 226, 227. *See also* competitive femininity; epistemologies of competition

competitive femininity, 143, 160, 184–85

Concrete Rose (Thomas), 104

Confederate States of America, 88

conflict, as literary term, 19, 29–30, 43, 230n

Congo. *See* Democratic Republic of the Congo

Constitution, US, 27, 33, 36, 43–44, 84, 85, 92, 159

Consumer Product Safety Commission, 25

consumerism, 23, 62, 108, 120, 131–32, 134, 135, 150, 198–99, 200, 232n. *See also* commercialism; commodification; consumption

consumption, 42, 65, 152, 158, 180, 200. *See also* consumerism

contagion. *See* disease

Cooper, James Fenimore, 28; *The Leatherstocking Tales*, 28

Cormier, Robert, 32; *The Chocolate War*, 32

COVID-19, x, 3, 4–7, 9, 35, 36, 161–62. *See also* pandemic

Council of Chief State School Officers, 231n

counterstory, 202. *See also* critical race theory

Craft, Jerry, 108, 116; *New Kid*, 108, 116–19

Crane, Stephen, 29; *The Red Badge of Courage*, 29

Crean, Anna, 210

Creek Nation, 91

critical dystopia, 219

critical multicultural analysis (CMA), 58, 68, 81, 106

critical race theory (CRT), 85–86, 87–88, 90, 91, 105–6, 160, 202

Cross, Helen, 135; *My Summer of Love*, 135

Cult of Self, 33–37, 52. *See also* individualism
Curtis, Christopher Paul, 86, 94, 96, 107, 110, 183; *Bucking the Sarge*, 86, 94, 96–100, 107, 110, 183
cyborg, 167, 169. *See also* biotechnology; posthumanism
Cyrus, Miley Ray, 131

Daily Show, The, 105
Daughter of Smoke and Bone trilogy, 62–67, 73, 181. *See also* Taylor, Laini
Dear Martin (Stone), 103
Declaration of Independence, 27, 92, 196
Declaration of the Rights of Man (Paine), 28
Democratic Republic of the Congo (DRC), 67, 68–69, 70, 72, 81, 182
Democratic Socialist Party, 30
democracy, 3, 27, 36, 55, 84, 85, 87, 88, 211
Deng, Danjing, 161–62
Denmark, 220
Department of Justice, US, 88
deracialization, 205
deregulation, 7, 25, 48. *See also* neoliberalism
desegregation: of public schools, 25, 83–84, 89; of US Armed Forces, 25
Desert Shield. *See* Gulf Wars
Desert Storm. *See* Gulf Wars
Dias, Marley, 221
Dig. *See* King, A. S.
Dimaline, Cherie, 212, 215, 219; *The Marrow Thieves*, 212, 215–19, 221
disability, 44, 57, 58, 96, 121, 152, 153, 156, 187, 232n. *See also* ability
discipline (of children), 11–12, 153
discourse(s), 3, 20, 106, 109, 111, 121, 134, 159, 186. *See also* postfeminist discourse; postrace discourse
discrimination, x, 17, 35, 57, 88, 90, 119–21, 134, 137, 146, 159, 160, 163, 171, 176. *See also* ableism; ageism; anti-Semitism; homophobia; Islamophobia; queerphobia; racism; sexism; transphobia; xenophobia

disease, 5, 38, 41, 42, 77, 161–62, 165, 167, 168, 169, 170, 181–82, 189, 192–93, 195, 215, 218. *See also* COVID-19; pandemic
disempowerment, 44. *See also* repression
Disney, 13, 107, 129, 202
disposability (of human life), 9, 27, 47, 51, 52, 121, 216, 218–19
Disreputable History of Frankie Landau-Banks, The. *See* Lockhart, E.
Divergent (Roth), 32
diversity, 116, 117–18, 132, 158, 221, 229n. *See also* ability; BIPOC; desegregation; gay; gender identity; Islam; Judaism; lesbianism; multiculturalism; people of color; trans gender
"Divinity School Address" (Emerson), 28
Dobbs v. Jackson Women's Health Organization, 158. *See also* abortion; reproductive health; *Roe v. Wade*
Doctrine of Discovery, 95–96
double consciousness, 204, 206
Du Bois, W. E. B., 204
Dumezweni, Noma, 17
dystopia, ix–x, xi, 19–20, 32–33, 37, 42, 48, 53, 61, 129, 163, 164–65, 166, 171–72, 175–79, 181, 209, 212, 215–19, 230n. *See also* critical dystopia

ecocriticism, xi, 55–82, 149, 158, 188. *See also* ecofeminism
ecofeminism, 20, 57, 59, 60, 61, 70, 131, 156, 157–58, 160
econo-politics, x, 22, 104, 181, 185, 186, 187, 199, 217, 222, 224, 227. *See also* neoliberalism
economy, US, 3, 4–5, 9, 21, 85, 88, 194
education, x, 7–8, 9, 11, 13, 18, 25, 89, 104, 105–6, 108–19, 130, 132, 146, 186, 209, 220, 224, 225–26, 231n; public education, x, 8, 83, 84, 111, 119. *See also* charter schools; public schools; school privatization
Education of Margot Sanchez, The (Rivera), 126
Edwards, Jonathan, 28; "Sinners in the Hands of an Angry God," 28

Efik, 156
Eliot, T. S., 29; "Tradition and the Individual Talent," 29
Emancipation Proclamation, 88
embodiment, xi, 73, 88, 126, 133, 136, 138, 140–43, 151–55, 158, 159, 169, 175, 183, 184–85, 206, 211, 222, 233n
Emergency, the, 180, 233n. *See also* India
Emerson, Ralph Waldo, 28; "Divinity School Address," 28
empowerment, 14, 39, 43, 44, 45, 77, 84, 88–89, 129, 132–36, 142, 144, 145, 151, 152, 160, 162, 187, 189, 190, 198, 206, 207, 213, 232n
Encanto, 129
Endangered (Schrefer), 67–72, 73, 182
England. *See* United Kingdom
Enlightenment, the, 27, 34
Enron, 48
enslavement, 6, 12, 15, 17, 85, 86–88, 92, 94, 108, 109, 119, 155, 166, 169, 176, 179, 192, 194, 195, 196, 197, 231n, 233n. *See also* Civil War; colonialism; Confederate States of America; Emancipation Proclamation; Triangle Trade
entitlement, 29, 140, 195. *See also* classism; privilege; racism; sexism
entrepreneurship, 13, 15, 16, 17, 23, 26, 50–51, 85, 86, 90, 94, 96–97, 99, 100, 119, 133, 135, 146, 155, 165, 166, 169, 175, 176, 179, 192, 194, 195, 197, 214–15, 219, 226, 231n
environmental justice, 56, 59, 66, 71, 72, 81, 157
Environmental Protection Agency, 25
environmentalism, x, xi, 5, 14–15, 20, 21, 42, 54, 55–82, 131, 149, 157, 158, 160, 171, 182–83, 208, 211, 218, 224. *See also* ecocriticism; ecofeminism; environmental justice; intersectional environmentalism; neoliberal environmentalism
epistemologies of competition, 188–89
epistemology, 21, 186–88, 199, 189–99, 202, 204–7, 214. *See also* epistemologies of competition; liberatory epistemologies; neoliberal epistemologies
equal opportunity, 9

equality, 19, 22, 32, 24, 85, 112, 130, 136, 161, 209, 211, 221, 232n. *See also* gender equality; race, equality
erasure, xi, 15, 22, 61, 117, 134, 143–46, 165, 168, 187, 224. *See also* race, erasure
ethics, 71, 126, 221, 225
ethics of care, 52, 57, 72–80, 154–55, 221, 230n, 233n
ethnicity, 17, 60, 168, 169, 170, 171, 185, 232n. *See also* people of color
eugenics, 42
Euro-Americans, 15, 69, 96, 116, 117, 119, 126, 127, 150, 155, 156, 168, 170, 197, 216
Euro-Canadians, 216
Euro-white, 58, 90, 187
exceptionalism, xi, 12, 13–15, 18, 19–20, 21, 22, 25, 26, 27, 30–61, 76, 102, 107, 113, 121, 132, 133, 135, 138, 139, 140, 144, 146, 149, 150, 151, 155, 171, 176, 179, 185, 204, 206, 211–12, 217; defined, 26. *See also* individualism; Me-Consciousness
exploitation, x, xi, xii, 6, 7, 14–15, 16, 20, 21, 22, 54, 55–82, 85, 107, 152, 158, 164, 168–69, 172–73, 176, 185, 199, 201, 207, 215, 222, 223; of African American women, 146; of African Americans, 6, 85, 98–100, 127, 146, 192, 212–15; of animals, x, 3, 14, 20, 42, 57, 60, 62, 65, 66, 223; of children, 100, 101, 148, 172–73; of Earth, x, xi, 6, 57, 62, 127, 131, 146, 158, 181, 223; of economics, 6, 86, 107, 200, 215; of environment, x, 6, 14, 20, 42, 54, 57, 61, 63, 65, 86, 157, 158, 182–83, 223, 224; of females, 127, 131, 146, 158, 179, 198, 199, 200; of immigrants, 6, 172–73; of Indigenous peoples, 5, 215–19; of land, 20, 91; of Latinx peoples, 172–73; of natural resources, 20, 65, 95, 146, 148, 149, 157, 162, 168, 173, 181, 182, 223; of peoples, x, xi, 14, 20, 42, 43, 54, 57, 62, 63, 65, 66, 96, 100, 107–8, 127, 146, 168–69, 182–83, 224; of plants and vegetation, x, 3, 57, 223; of racialized peoples, 107, 131, 168–69, 207, 215; of workers, 168. *See also* oppression; systemic oppression

Facebook, 13, 23
Fandom Forward, 210
fantasy, as genre, xi, 12, 20, 229n, 230n
Federal Housing Authority, 93
Federal Indian Removal, 78
female friendship, 143–46, 160
femininity, ix, 11, 49, 120, 130, 132, 135, 138, 141, 142, 143, 155, 160, 184, 200, 202, 232n. *See also* competitive femininity; lipstick feminism
feminism, ix, 15, 20, 33, 57, 60, 143, 128–55, 159, 184–85, 199, 221, 232n. *See also* anti-feminism; ecofeminism; feminist movement; neoliberal feminism; postfeminism; second wave feminism; third wave feminism; #WomenAgainstFeminism
feminist movement, 129, 132, 137–38, 144, 184. *See also* second wave feminism; third wave feminism
Firekeeper's Daughter. See Boulley, Angeline
First Nations peoples, 56, 91, 215–19. *See also* Native Americans; people of color
Five Chinese Brothers (Bishop), 107
Flaubert, Gustave, 29–30
Floyd, George, x, 6, 7, 108
Fold, The (Na), 126
Ford, Henry, 34
Ford Motors, 34–35
fossil fuels, 3, 7, 55–56, 82, 158, 179. *See also* carbon economy; petroleum
Foucault, Michel, 15, 162, 163–64, 184, 186–88, 201
Fox Nation, 91. *See also* Native Americans
France, 196, 221
Franklin, Benjamin, 28; *Autobiography of Benjamin Franklin*, 28
free market economy, 7, 72, 90, 162, 165, 166, 167, 168, 171, 181. *See also* market solutions; neoliberalism
Friedman, Milton, 83
Fulani, 149. *See also* Nigeria
futurity, as aspect of sexism, 142–43

Gabi: A Girl in Pieces (Quintero), 126–27
Gandhi, Indira, 180
Gandi, Kiran, 210
gay, 178, 194, 202–3, 209. *See also* lesbianism; queerness
gender, 9, 11, 20, 51, 56, 57, 58, 59, 60, 85, 90, 126, 127, 128–60, 168, 170, 183–85, 188, 201, 202, 205, 206–7, 208, 221, 222, 223, 229n, 232n. *See also* feminism; gender discrimination; gender equality; gender identity; gender inequality; gender oppression; gender roles; sexism
gender discrimination, 134, 137, 146, 159, 160. *See also* sexism
gender equality, 130, 133, 232n
gender identity, xi. *See also* cis gender; LGBTQ+; trans gender
gender inequality, 143–46, 232n. *See also* sexism
gender oppression, 47, 131, 132, 134, 136, 139, 144, 146, 187, 199–204. *See also* sexism
gender roles, 133, 153. *See also* gender
Genesis Begins Again (Williams), 107, 119–25
genocidal logic, 21, 42–43, 171–75, 178, 182
genocide, 15, 31, 37, 42, 43, 63, 95, 168, 179, 182, 210, 233n
genre, x, 20, 32, 163, 181, 226. *See also* autobiography; critical dystopia; dystopia; gothic; historical realism; magic realism; memoir; nonfiction; postapocalyptic fiction; realism; science fiction; speculative fiction; spiritual realism
Germany, 180, 182, 220
Gerwig, Greta, 129
"Girl on Fire" (song) (Keys), 131
girl power, 131, 138
Global North, 60, 231n
Global South, 60, 61, 231n
global warming, ix, 62, 72, 82, 178. *See also* climate change
globalization, 24, 164, 168–69, 179, 204, 211, 224, 225
glocalization, 169
González, Emma, 210

Google, 13
gothic, 108. *See also* genre
government, as institution, 38–39, 40, 42, 43, 61–62, 146
government, US, 84, 108, 109, 163
government regulation. *See* regulation, government
Gracie, Archibald, 87
graphic novels, 116
Great Depression, 9, 18, 128, 181
Great Recession of 2008, 9, 35, 48, 128
Green, John, 128
Green Hills of Africa (Hemingway), 29
Grrl Power movement, 131, 138
Gulf War(s), 8, 180, 181

Harlem Renaissance, 11
Haroun and the Sea of Stories (Rushdie), 181
Harris, Kamala, 159
Harry Potter (series), xi, 12–18, 42, 129, 131, 150, 151, 155, 210, 229n
Harry Potter Alliance. *See* Fandom Forward
Harry Potter and the Cursed Child (Rowling), 17
Harry Potter and the Half-Blood Prince (Rowling), 14
Hate U Give, The. See Thomas, Angie
Hausa, 149. *See also* Nigeria
Hawthorne, Nathaniel, *The Scarlet Letter*, 28
health, x, 4–7, 15, 21, 45, 56, 58, 59, 61, 74, 78, 100, 183, 209, 217, 221, 225–26. *See also* mental health; reproductive health
Health and Human Services, US, 94
health care, 5, 7, 9, 16, 25, 26, 35, 36, 146, 161, 209, 221, 225–26. *See also* health; mental health; reproductive health
hegemonic knowledge, 199–204. *See also* knowledge
Heinlein, Robert A., 30; *Methuselah's Children*, 31; *Stranger in a Strange Land*, 31
Hemings, Sally, 196, 233n
Hemingway, Ernest, 29; *The Green Hills of Africa*, 29
heteronormativity, 153–54

heterosexism, 45, 59, 81, 160, 187, 188, 201, 204, 209. *See also* transphobia
heterosexuality, ix, 49, 56, 119, 132, 133, 143, 153, 158, 160, 187, 188, 200, 201, 202, 203. *See also* sexual orientation
Hidier, Tanuja Desai, 126; *Born Confused*, 126
Hinton, S. E., 31; *The Outsiders*, 31–32
historical realism, 11, 94–96. *See also* genre
Hogg, David, 210
Hollingsworth, Trey, 4, 5
Holocaust, 15, 42, 182. *See also* genocide
home ownership, 101, 104
homelessness, 8, 70, 80, 152, 209
homo oeconomicus, 142
homogenization, 169
homophobia, 29, 134, 178, 194. *See also* queerphobia
homosexuality. *See* gay; homophobia; lesbianism; LGBTQ+; queerphobia; sexual orientation
housing, 48, 89, 91–94, 98–99, 103–4, 107, 108–9, 111, 232n. *See also* Federal Housing Authority; home ownership; Housing and Urban Development (HUD); housing project; public housing
Housing and Urban Development (HUD), 101
housing project. *See* Federal Housing Authority; public housing
Howe, Irving, 30
human capital, 43, 142, 163–64, 166, 175–79, 184–85; defined, 164
human rights, 95, 113, 172, 226. *See also* education; health care; immigration; social services
Hunger Games trilogy, ix, xi, 12, 27, 32, 48–52, 53, 131, 183, 188–89, 205, 209, 210. *See also* Collins, Suzanne
hurricanes, as North American climate catastrophes, 56, 113

I Am Malala (Yousufzai), 220
I Am Not Your Perfect Mexican Daughter (Sánchez), 125–26

identity politics, 46, 163, 176
Ideological State Apparatus (ISA), x, 11
ideology, x, xi, xii, 3, 11, 12, 15, 17, 18, 29, 30, 32–33, 38–39, 42–43, 46, 53, 57, 58, 59, 64, 67, 70, 71, 72, 85, 89–90, 91, 96, 102, 104, 106, 107, 108, 113, 125, 130–32, 136, 145, 150, 152, 158–60, 165–66, 176, 185, 188, 194, 201, 206, 207, 210–11, 212, 218, 222, 226–27, 230n
Igbo, 147, 148, 155, 156
Illini, 91. *See also* Native Americans
immaterial production, 13, 16, 21, 163–64, 167, 181, 185, 205, 208; defined, 164. *See also* material production
immigration, 6, 21, 121, 163, 169, 171–79, 209
Immigration and Customs Enforcement, US (ICE), 6, 172, 174
incarceration, US, 163
independence, 10, 23, 27, 36, 37, 48, 49, 57, 81, 131, 132, 136. *See also* individualism
India, 122, 126, 169, 180, 221, 233n. *See also* Emergency, the
Indian in the Cupboard, The (Banks), 107
Indigenous futurism, 72, 230n
Indigenous peoples, 5, 9, 56, 57, 61, 72, 75, 78, 85, 91, 92, 94–95, 107, 161, 215–19, 230n. *See also* BIPOC; First Nations peoples; Native Americans; people of color
individualism, ix, xi, xii, 8, 10, 12, 13, 17, 18, 19–20, 23–54, 78–82, 88, 90, 100, 110, 132, 134, 138, 143, 149–50, 158, 159, 165, 166, 171, 188, 206–7, 210, 211, 214, 229–30n, 232–33n; extreme individualism, 27, 33, 199; hyperindividualism, xi, 31, 33, 57, 81, 221; rugged individualism, 24, 25, 26, 31, 50, 52, 62; self-enclosed individualism, 10, 19, 23–54, 61, 76, 100, 110, 150, 171, 176, 179, 210, 211, 212, 215–19, 221, 224, 227; US, history of, 29–31; within US literature, 29–31; YA literature and historical tradition of, 31–33, 38–54. *See also* Cult of Self; self-reliance
indoctrination, 11, 106
industrialization, 25, 77, 87, 158, 164
Instagram, 8

Institutional State Apparatus, x, 38
integration. *See* desegregation
interdependence, 37, 44, 46, 48, 50, 75, 79, 81, 136; defined, 10, 36. *See also* collectivism; communalism
intersectional environmentalism, 56–59, 60, 61, 67–72, 81, 82, 157–58, 160, 171, 182, 211; defined, 57
intersectionality, 57, 59, 156, 157–58, 160. *See also* intersectional environmentalism
Ioway Nation, 91. *See also* Native Americans
Iran, 180–81, 221
Iranian hostage crisis, 181
Iranian Revolution, 180–81
Iraq, 8, 186
Iroquois Confederacy, 61. *See also* Native Americans
Islam, 81, 163, 180, 194, 233n. *See also* Islamophobia; Muslim Americans; religion; Shiites; Sunnis
Islamophobia, 194
Israel, 180. *See also* Arab-Israeli War

Jackson, Tiffany D., 107, 108–10, 113–15; *Monday's Not Coming*, 107
Jamaica, 122, 192, 193, 195
James, Henry, 29
Japan, 180
Jefferson, Thomas, 27, 196
Jenner, Kylie, 23–24, 26
Jim Crow (segregation laws), 88, 105, 163
Jobs, Steve, 34
John Newbery Medal, 116
Judaism, 182, 194. *See also* anti-Semitism; religion

Kangujam, Licypriya, 221
Kanien'kehaka, 61. *See also* Native Americans
Kardashian, Khloé, 23
Kardashian, Kim, 23
Kardashian, Kourtney, 23
Kardashian-Jenner family, 23–24, 35
Kazi, Haaziq, 221

Keats, Ezra Jack, 106; *Snowy Day*, 106
Keeping Up with the Kardashians, 23
Kendi, Ibram X., xii, 86, 87, 92, 108; *Stamped* (with Reynolds), xii; *Stamped from the Beginning*, 92
Keynesian economics, 89. *See also* neoliberalism
Keys, Alicia, 131; "Girl on Fire" (song), 131
Khazan, Jibreel, 220
Khomeini, Ruhollah (Ayatollah), 180
Kickapoo Nation, 91. *See also* Native Americans
King, A. S., 188, 189; *Dig*, 188, 189–99, 205, 208
King, Martin Luther, Jr., 6
knowledge, 8, 78, 150–51, 156, 185, 186–208, 230n; hoarding, 190, 192, 194; production, 21, 186–208, 216; sharing, 194, 195, 196–97, 198, 199–204, 206–8, 216, 217, 224. *See also* epistemology; hegemonic knowledge; liberatory epistemologies; neoliberal epistemologies
Koch, Charles, 84
Koch brothers, 84
Korea, 122
Korean Americans, 126. *See also* Asian Americans
Kudlow, Larry, 4
Kylie Cosmetics, 24

laissez-faire, 7, 25, 32, 91, 169, 211
Land, The (Taylor), 86, 94–96
land ownership. *See* property ownership
Latinx peoples, 5, 6, 9, 56, 119, 120, 126–27, 172–75. *See also* BIPOC; Colombian Americans; exploitation; Mexican Americans; people of color; Puerto Rico; racism
lead contamination, 99, 100, 162, 183. *See also* pollution
Leatherstocking Tales, The (Cooper), 28
Lefebvre, Henri, 92
Legend. *See* Lu, Marie
Legend of Zelda, The, 131
Lehman brothers, 87

LeMaster, J. R., 220
lesbianism, 73, 199–204
LGBTQ+, 199, 229n. *See also* gay; gender identity; lesbianism; queerness; sexual orientation; trans gender
liberalism (classical), 7, 25, 88–89, 90, 91, 109; defined, 25
liberatory epistemologies, 189–99
libertarianism, 9, 31, 84
Life of Pi (Martel), 180, 181
Lincoln, Abraham, 88, 92
linear time, as concept, 215
LinkedIn, 8
Lipan, as language, 73–74, 78
Lipan Apache Tribe of Texas, 91, 231n. *See also* Native Americans
lipstick feminism, 132, 137, 153, 232n. *See also* neoliberal feminism; postfeminism; third wave feminism
Little Badger, Darcie, 72, 77, 80, 161, 211, 230n; *A Snake Falls to Earth*, xii, 72–80, 161, 183, 211
Little Black Sambo (Bannerman), 107
Little Golden Books, 107
Little Women (Alcott), 222
Locke, John, 28, 92; *Second Treatise on Government*, 28
Lockhart, E., 129, 130; *The Disreputable History of Frankie Landau-Banks*, xi, 128–29, 130–31, 136–46
logic of exploitation, 55–82
Lowry, Lois, 32; *The Giver*, 32
Lu, Marie, 27, 37; *Legend*, 27, 37–43, 45, 53, 179, 181–82, 189, 205

Mad Max Beyond Thunderdome, 224
magic realism, 103, 183
Marcelo in the Real World. *See* Stork, Francisco X.
market solutions, 90, 107–8. *See also* neoliberalism
marketplace, as economic concept, 100, 126, 169. *See also* market solutions
Marrow Thieves, The (Dimaline), 212, 215–19, 221

Martel, Yann, 181; *Life of Pi*, 180, 181
Marvel, 129
Mascouten Nation, 91. See also Native Americans
material production, 13. See also immaterial production
materialism, 41, 201, 214. See also consumerism
McCain, Franklin, 220
McNeil, Joseph, 220
Meat Inspection Act, 25
Me-Consciousness, 53. See also exceptionalism; individualism
Medicaid, 10
Medicare, 10, 25
Melville, Herman, 28; *Moby-Dick*, 28
memoir, xi, 149, 220. See also nonfiction
Mendoza, Paola, 223; as coauthor with Sher, 163, 164–65, 171, 175, 185; *Sanctuary*, 163, 164–65, 171–79, 185, 209, 211–12, 223
mental health, 90, 110, 156, 192, 193, 194, 225. See also health
meritocracy, 9, 20, 23–24, 26, 31, 34, 36, 46, 53, 56, 62, 121, 130, 131, 132, 138, 139, 146, 171–79. See also tyranny of merit
Methuselah's Children (Heinlein), 31
Métis, 216–19
#MeToo movement, 130, 158. See also feminism
Mexican Americans, 44, 46, 120, 125–26, 127–28, 194. See also Latinx peoples
Mexico, 6, 172, 221
Meyer, Marissa, 163, 165, 166, 167, 205; *Cinder*, xi, 163, 165, 166–67, 176, 179, 181, 185, 205–7
middle class, 8, 24, 59, 169, 209, 212, 232n
Middle East, 3, 120, 173. See also Arab-Israeli War of 1973; Gulf Wars; Israel; Iran; Iraq; petroleum; Saudi Arabia
Middle Passage, 87
Milton, John, 62; *Paradise Lost*, 62
minority rule, 85
miscegenation, 15
Moby-Dick (Melville), 28
model minority myth, 171

Monday's Not Coming (Jackson), 107
Morgan, J. P., 87
Morrison, Toni, 122; *The Bluest Eye*, 122
Moynihan, Daniel, 93
multiculturalism, 203, 229n. See also BIPOC; critical multicultural analysis (CMA); people of color
Muscogee (Creek) Nation, 91. See also Native Americans
Muslim Americans, 163. See also Islam
Muslims. See Islam; Muslim Americans; Shiites; Sunnis
My Summer of Love (Cross), 135
Myaamia, 91. See also Native Americans
mythic time, as concept, 215

Na, An, 126; *The Fold*, 126
NAACP of Jackson, MS, 231n
narrative levels, 204–7
Natchez, 91. See also Native Americans
National Book Award for Young People's Literature, 67
National Mall, 109
Native Americans, 61, 91. See also BIPOC; exploitation; First Nations peoples; Indigenous peoples; people of color; racism; Trail of Tears; *and specific tribes and nations*
Navajo Nation, 5, 55–56, 58. See also Native Americans
neoconservativism, 112–13, 132. See also neoliberalism
neoliberal environmentalism, xi, xii, 54, 57, 62, 82
neoliberal epistemologies, 189–99, 214
neoliberal erasure, 161–85
neoliberal exploitation, 62–67. See also exploitation
neoliberal feminism, 135, 142, 232n. See also competitive feminism; lipstick feminism; third wave feminism
neoliberalism, defined, 7–10, 25–27, 33–34. See also austerity; commercialism; deregulation; economy, US; econopolitics; free market economy; Keynes-

ian economics; liberalism (classical); market solutions; marketplace; privatization; Reaganomics; Thatcherism; trickle-down economics
Netherlands, 180
#NeverAgain, 210
New Criticism, 29
New Kid (Craft), 108, 116–19
New York Times Best Sellers list, 128–29
New York Times Book Review, 128–29, 138
Newton, Huey, 213. *See also* Black Panthers
Nigeria, 146, 147, 148, 149, 150, 155, 157, 233n
Nixon, Richard, 6, 105
No Child Left Behind Act (NCLB), 12, 112, 113, 231n. *See also* privatization, school; standardized testing
Noah, Trevor, 105
Nobel Peace Prize, 220
nonfiction, xi, xii, 107. *See also* autobiography; genre; memoir
Nsibidi Script trilogy (Okorafor), 131, 146–58
Nyathi, Nkosilathi, 221

Obama, Barack, 34, 35, 121
objectification of female body, 133, 136, 137, 141–42, 143, 232n. *See also* sexism
objectivism, 30
Occupy Movement, 128
Ofo, 91. *See also* Native Americans
oil production. *See* petroleum
Ojibwe Nation, 100–103, 108, 125, 183–84, 231n. *See also* Native Americans
Okorafor, Nnedi, 131, 146; *Akata Warrior*, 146, 148–49, 153, 155–58; *Akata Witch*, 146, 147–48, 150–53, 154, 155; *Akata Woman*, 146, 148–49, 154–56
On the Come Up (Thomas), 104
100, The (television program), 129
one percent, 16, 128, 129. *See also* upper class
Oneida, 61. *See also* Native Americans
ontology, 73, 204, 205, 221
oppositional binaries, 59–61, 63–82, 127, 135, 160, 211, 222, 223, 231n; defined, 59–60, 223, 231n

oppression, ix, 14, 28, 43, 57, 59–64, 67–71, 82, 129, 187, 189, 199–204, 212, 218, 231n; of animals, 67, 70 (*see also* exploitation, of animals); of Earth, 57, 67 (*see also* exploitation, of Earth); of environment (*see* exploitation, of environment); gender (*see* exploitation, of African American women; exploitation, of females; gender oppression; sexism; subjugation, gender); of nature, 70 (*see also* exploitation, of environment; exploitation, of natural resources; exploitation, of plants and vegetation); of peoples, 67, 70, 71, 174, 179 (*see also* oppression, racial); racial, 46, 57, 69, 116, 213, 215, 216 (*see also* exploitation, of African American women; exploitation, of African Americans; exploitation, of Latinx peoples; exploitation, of Native Americans; exploitation, of racialized peoples; racism); by social class, 40, 46, 49, 53, 57, 68, 129, 215 (*see also* classism; exploitation, of workers; social class). *See also* ableism; ageism; anthropocentrism; anti-Semitism; colonialism; heterosexism; homophobia; Islamophobia; queerphobia; transphobia; systemic oppression; xenophobia
Organization of Arab Petroleum Exporting Countries (OAPEC), 180. *See also* Middle East; petroleum
orientation. *See* sexual orientation
Orleans. *See* Smith, Sherri L.
Osage Nation, 91. *See also* Native Americans
Outsiders, The (Hinton), 31–32
ownership. *See* home ownership; land ownership; property ownership

Pahlavi, Mohammad Reza (Shah), 180
Pahlavi, Reza (Shah), 180
Paine, Thomas, 28; *Common Sense*, 28; *Declaration of the Rights of Man*, 28
Pakistan, 220
pandemic, x, 3, 6, 10, 35, 36, 53, 82, 83, 161–62, 167. *See also* COVID-19; disease

264 INDEX

Papa John's International, Inc., 34–35
Paradise Lost (Milton), 62
patriarchy, 60, 128, 131, 133, 134, 135, 138, 144, 145, 152, 154, 169, 184, 188, 199, 200–201, 206
Patrick, Daniel, 4
Peabody Energy, 55–56
pedagogy, 208, 211, 212, 219–27
Pedersen, Knud, 220
Peltier, Autumn, 221
people of color, x, 3, 5, 9, 17, 20, 57, 61, 69, 85, 107, 116, 120, 158, 163, 187, 211. *See also* African Americans; Asian Americans; Asians; BIPOC; Latinx peoples; Native Americans; race; racism
Peoria, 91. *See also* Native Americans
Perry, Katy, 131; "Roar" (song), 131
Persepolis (Satrapi), 180–81
petroleum, 147–48, 149, 152, 157–58, 163, 179–81, 233n. *See also* fossil fuels
Philippines, 175, 178, 209
Piankashaw Nation, 91. *See also* Native Americans
Piecing Me Together (Watson), 104, 125
plague. *See* disease
police brutality, 212–15, 219
pollution, x, 181, 183; of air, 56, 179, 181; of water, 56, 58–59, 100, 179, 181, 183, 215. *See also* climate change; environmentalism; exploitation
postapocalyptic fiction, 163, 164, 166, 181. *See also* genre
postcolonialism, 63, 64, 90
postfeminism, xi, 45, 128–60, 200; defined, 9, 20, 131, 232n
postfeminist discourse, 20, 134, 159
posthumanism, 58, 59–60 73, 74, 164, 165
post-nerd smart girl, 45
postrace discourse, 20, 121–25
postracialism, xi, xii, 9, 17, 20, 21, 45, 130, 145, 155–57, 158, 160, 165, 170, 213, 232n
Potawatomi Nation, 91. *See also* Native Americans
poverty, 5, 9, 18, 21, 29, 32, 35, 37, 38, 40, 41, 42, 46, 50, 53, 55–56, 57, 59, 61, 68–69, 71, 81, 87, 89, 91–94, 97, 104, 107, 112, 124, 127, 129, 134, 158, 182, 185, 190, 192, 193, 195, 209, 210, 212, 232n. *See also* classism; public assistance; social class
power. *See* empowerment
power feminism, 135. *See also* third wave feminism
Powerpuff Girls, The, 131
Pride (Zoboi), 104
Printz Award, 128
private property, 84, 92, 99. *See also* home ownership; land ownership; property ownership
privatization, x, 7–8, 83, 89, 90; of debt, 187; of prisons, 8; of schools, 7, 8, 107, 111–13, 114, 186; of social safety net programs, 8, 83. *See also* neoliberalism
privilege, 9, 60, 66–67, 134, 145, 187–88, 209; ability privilege, 188 (*see also* ableism); class privilege, 16, 40, 41, 46, 56, 58, 64, 67, 68, 88, 98, 116, 129, 187, 188, 199, 225 (*see also* classism); colonialist privilege, 187; color privilege, 120, 125 (*see also* colorism); epistemological privilege, 77, 188, 206, 207 (*see also* epistemology; technoscience); heterosexual privilege, 56, 143, 187, 200, 201 (*see also* heterosexuality); human privilege, 63, 188 (*see also* anthropocentrism); individualism, 16, 28, 58, 187, 206, 218 (*see also* self-enclosed individualism; self-reliance); male privilege, 58, 140, 144, 187–88, 200, 206, 207 (*see also* sexism); white privilege, 56, 58, 70, 80, 88, 98, 105, 116, 125, 146, 187–88, 194, 195, 199, 204, 205, 206, 207, 218 (*see also* racism). *See also* exploitation; oppositional binaries; oppression
productive citizenship, 229n
progressiveness, 25, 64, 84, 129, 130–31, 133, 226, 232n
property ownership, 91–104, 108, 154
public assistance, 232n. *See also* welfare
public housing, 101, 108–10, 232n
public schools, 8, 25, 89, 104, 106, 112–15, 118, 119, 122, 134 (*see also* education;

schooling); funding of, 104, 112, 113, 114–15, 118–19, 186, 122 (*see also* No Child Left Behind Act)
Puerto Rico, 56
Puritan work ethic. *See* work ethic

Quapaw Nation, 91. *See also* Native Americans
queering, 63, 73–74
queerness, 56, 184, 187, 200–203. *See also* gay; lesbianism; LGBTQ+; sexual orientation
queerphobia, 188, 194. *See also* homophobia; transphobia
Quintero, Isabel, 126; *Gabi: A Girl in Pieces*, 126–27

race, xi, 5, 9, 12, 15, 17, 20, 51, 59, 60, 68, 83–104, 105–27, 146, 152, 156, 165, 168–69, 170, 171, 185, 206–7, 222, 223, 232n; equality, 88; erasure, 163, 165–68; 187; inequality, 82, 90; relations, US, 86, 104. *See also* people of color
racial capitalism, 85–88, 91, 96
racial discrimination. *See* racism
racial history, US, 83–94; 105–8, 191, 233n
racial identity, 92, 94, 107. *See also* BIPOC
racial oppression. *See* oppression, racial
racial stratification, 9, 69, 105, 120–21, 163, 169, 171, 172–74, 217, 218, 219
racialism, 85
racism, ix, x, xii, 3, 5, 9, 15, 17, 18, 57, 64, 70, 81, 82, 83–104, 105–27, 134, 136, 145, 146, 156–57, 160, 165, 168, 171, 174–75, 179, 188, 189–99, 205–7, 209, 219, 224, 231n, 232n; internalized, 107, 108, 123, 125, 191 (*see also* colorism); intraracial, 123, 155–56 (*see also* colorism); South Africa, 105; structural racism, 6, 20, 29, 85, 86, 88–91, 105–6, 208, 209, 212–13, 214. *See also* enslavement; entitlement; privilege; race; racial stratification; racialism; structural racism; white supremacy; xenophobia
Rand, Ayn, 30

rape. *See* sexual violence
realism, as genre, x, xi, 20, 129, 163, 182, 212. *See also* genre; historical realism
Reagan, Ronald, 25, 26, 31, 84, 89, 126, 181. *See also* Reaganism; Reaganomics
Reaganism, 129. *See also* neoliberalism
Reaganomics, 98. *See also* neoliberalism
recession, 181. *See also* Great Recession of 2008
Red Badge of Courage, The (Crane), 29
regulation, government, x, 7, 15, 25, 35, 48, 91, 134, 162–63, 165, 169, 171. *See also* deregulation
religion, 60, 146, 167, 168, 187. *See also* anti-Semitism; Christianity; Islam; Islamophobia; Judaism; Sikh
repression, of power, 162, 174. *See also* oppression; Repressive State Apparatus
Repressive State Apparatus (RSA), 174, 212, 218
reproductive health, 61, 85, 159, 221. *See also* abortion
Republicans, 84
resistant logics, 205, 206
Reynolds, Jason, as coauthor with Kendi, 12; *Stamped*, 12
Rice, Tamir, 7
Richmond, David, 220
Riot Grrl movement, 131. *See also* third wave feminism
Rivera, Lilliam, 126; *The Education of Margot Sanchez*, 126
"Roar" (song) (Perry), 131
Roe v. Wade, 159. *See also* abortion; *Dobbs v. Jackson Women's Health Organization*; reproductive health
Romney, Mitt, 34
Roosevelt, Franklin D., 93
Roth, Veronica, 32; *Divergent*, 32
Rowling, J. K., 16, 17, 18; *Harry Potter and the Cursed Child*, 17; *Harry Potter and the Half-Blood Prince*, 14. *See also* Harry Potter (series)
"Run the World" (Beyoncé), 131

Rushdie, Salman, 181; *Haroun and the Sea of Stories*, 181
Russia, 180. *See also* USSR

Sánchez, Erika L., 125; *I Am Not Your Perfect Mexican Daughter*, 125–26
Sanctuary (Mendoza and Sher), 163, 164–65, 171–79, 185, 209, 211–12, 223
Sandel, Michael J., 23, 36
Satrapi, Marjane, 180, 181; *Persepolis*, 180–81
Saudi Arabia, 129
Sauk Nation, 91. *See also* Native Americans
Scarlet Letter, The (Hawthorne), 28
Schnatter, John, 34
school, as institution, 38, 39, 40, 44, 45, 146, 186
school privatization. *See* privatization
schooling, 36, 117. *See also* education
Schrefer, Eliot, 57, 80–81, 182; *Endangered*, 67–72, 73, 182; *Orphaned*, 67; *Rescued*, 67; *Threatened*, 67
science fiction, 233n. *See also* genre
Second Treatise on Government (Locke), 28
second wave feminism, 135. *See also* feminism; third wave feminism
segregation, 89, 104, 111, 163, 169, 220, 231n. *See also* desegregation; Jim Crow (segregation laws)
self-enclosed individualism. *See* individualism, self-enclosed
self-regulation, 90, 159, 184
self-reliance, 26, 27, 28, 31, 36, 49, 50, 52, 89, 190, 221, 225, 229n. *See also* individualism
Seminole Nation, 91. *See also* Native Americans
Sex in the City, 133
sexism, ix, 9, 15, 18, 29, 57, 81, 82, 133, 134, 136, 139, 146, 151, 152, 154, 157, 158, 159, 160, 163, 183–85, 187, 188, 199–204, 209, 224, 231n. *See also* entitlement; exploitation, of women; gender oppression; patriarchy; privilege, male; subjugation, gender; systemic gender imbalance

sexual orientation, xi, 60, 73, 146, 158, 178, 202. *See also* gay; lesbianism; LGBTQ+; queerness
sexual violence, 176, 177–78, 179, 192, 196, 198. *See also* homophobia; subjugation, gender
sexuality, 106, 129, 132, 135, 136, 153, 205, 221, 232n. *See also* gay; heterosexuality; lesbianism; LGBTQ+; queerness; sexual orientation
Shah of Iran, 180
Shakur, Tupac, 213
Shalala, Donna, 93–94
Shaw, George Bernard, 29–30
Shawnee Nation, 91. *See also* Native Americans
Shell Oil, 149
Sher, Abby: as coauthor with Mendoza, 163, 164–65, 171, 175, 185; *Sanctuary*, 163, 164–65, 171–79, 185, 209, 211–12, 223
Sherman Anti-Trust Act, 25
Shiites, 180. *See also* Islam; religion
Sikh, 194. *See also* religion
"Sinners in the Hands of an Angry God" (Edwards), 28
Skywoman, 60
Slack, Andrew, 210. *See also* Fandom Forward
slavery. *See* enslavement
Smith, Sherri L., ix, 163, 171, 185, 186, 205, 206; *Orleans*, ix, xi, 163, 165–66, 167–68, 169–71, 179, 181, 185, 186, 188, 205, 206–7, 208, 233n
Smithsonian, 109, 220
Snake Falls to Earth, A. *See* Little Badger, Darcie
Snowy Day (Keats), 106
social barriers, 35. *See also* ableism; anti-Semitism; classism; gender identity; homophobia, Islamophobia; poverty; racism; sexism; transphobia
social class, 9, 20, 40–41, 51–52, 59, 60, 68, 90, 119–20, 123–25, 127, 129, 134, 139, 140, 146, 165, 168, 170–71, 202, 205, 207, 226, 232n. *See also* middle class; poverty;

social stratification; upper class; wealth, inequality; working class
social Darwinism, 100, 217
social hierarchy. *See* social class; social stratification
social justice, xii, 19, 56, 59, 66, 71, 72, 81, 82, 145, 157, 188, 213, 214, 226–27, 229n, 233n
social media, 7, 8, 24, 25, 62, 76, 77, 105, 130, 162, 210, 221, 232–33n. *See also* Instagram; LinkedIn; X (formerly Twitter)
social mobility, 15, 20, 107, 116, 123. *See also* social class
social progress, 130. *See also* progressiveness
Social Security, 10, 25. *See also* social services
social services, 93, 225. *See also* Medicaid; Medicare; public assistance; Social Security; welfare
social stratification, 42, 160, 163–68, 170, 172–74, 205, 206, 224, 229n. *See also* caste; classism; social class
socialism, 15–16, 18, 30
solipsism, 7–10, 52. *See also* individualism
"Song of Myself" (Whitman), 28
South Africa, 105
spaces of hope, 21, 211, 212–19, 222, 227
Spears, Britney, 131
speciesism. *See* anthropocentrism; privilege, human
speculative fiction, as genre, 30–31; 57, 62, 163, 233n. *See also* critical dystopia; dystopia; genre; gothic; magic realism; postapocalyptic fiction; science fiction; spiritual realism
Spice Girls, 138
spiritual realism, 103. *See also* genre
Stamped (Reynolds and Kendi), 12
Standard (American) English (SAE), 206
standardized testing, 12, 14, 37, 112, 114, 224
Star Wars franchise, 129
Stone, Nic, 103; *Dear Martin*, 103
Stork, Francisco X., 27, 43; *Marcelo in the Real World*, xi, 27, 43–48, 53

Stowe, Harriet Beecher, 28; *Uncle Tom's Cabin*, 28, 222
Stranger in a Strange Land (Heinlein), 31
structural inequalities, 35, 134, 145. *See also* ableism; classism; poverty; racism; sexism; structural racism
structural racism, 6, 29, 85–87, 88–91, 106, 108, 119–21, 208, 212, 214. *See also* racism
Students for Fair Admission v. Harvard and UNC, 9
#StudentsStrike4Climate movement, 62
subaltern, 182, 233n
subjectivity, as subject position, 60, 131, 106, 132, 164, 230n, 232n. *See also* agency
subjugation, gender, 158, 201. *See also* exploitation, of females; sexism
Sunnis, 180. *See also* Islam; religion
superspecial character, 32–33, 40, 48, 53, 76, 145, 179, 206. *See also* exceptionalism
Supreme Court, US, 9, 88, 158–59, 163
Sweden, 221
systemic gender imbalance, 185, 208. *See also* sexism
systemic oppression, 59, 62, 73, 77, 78, 107, 116, 118, 134, 139, 154, 155, 160, 163, 212, 213, 218, 219, 221–22, 227, 231n. *See also* homophobia; queerphobia; racism; sexism; transphobia
systemic racism, ix, 3, 20, 85–86, 114, 116, 209. *See also* racism; structural racism
systemic sexism, 29, 134. *See also* gender; sexism

Taylor, Breonna, 71
Taylor, Laini, 55, 62, 182; *Daughter of Smoke and Bone*, 55, 62–67; *Days of Blood and Starlight*, 63–65; *Dreams of Gods and Monsters*, 65–66
Taylor, Mildred, 86, 94, 96; *The Land*, 86, 94–96; *Roll of Thunder, Hear My Cry*, 94
technology, 40, 58, 77, 78, 143, 158, 164, 184, 206–7, 233n. *See also* posthumanism
technoscience, 164, 206. *See also* technology

teen social activism. *See* youth activism
#10,000BlackGirlBooks, 221
Thatcher, Margaret, 25, 26, 84, 181. *See also* Thatcherism
Thatcherism, 18. *See also* neoliberalism
theology, 27–28. *See also* religion
third wave feminism, 132, 135. *See also* competitive feminism; lipstick feminism; neoliberal feminism
Thirteen Reasons Why (Asher), 12
Thomas, Angie, 83, 104, 212; *Concrete Rose*, 104; *The Hate U Give*, xii, 12, 83, 104, 212–15, 216, 219, 221; *On the Come Up*, 104
Thoreau, Henry David, 28; *Walden*, 28
Thunberg, Greta, 209, 221
Tiananmen Square revolution, 220
Tiffany, Charles, 87
Till, Emmett, 220
Tioux, 91. *See also* Native Americans
"Tradition and the Individual Talent" (Eliot), 29
trans gender, 57, 184, 229n. *See also* gender identity; LGBTQ+
transphobia, 57, 229n, 232n. *See also* queerphobia
Triangle Trade, 87
tribalism, 156–57, 206. *See also* caste; social stratification
tribe(s), 61, 91, 94, 101–2, 103, 125, 152, 156, 165, 166–68, 170, 207, 216, 231n. *See also* caste; Native Americans; social stratification
trickle-down economics, 128, 129, 181, 209. *See also* neoliberalism
Trilling, Lionel, 29
Trump, Donald J., x, 4–5, 108, 159, 162, 172, 198
Tulsa Race Massacre of 1921, 106
Tunica-Biloxi, 91. *See also* Native Americans
Tuskegee Syphilis Experiment, 162, 170, 233n
Twain, Mark, 11, 28–29; *Adventures of Huckleberry Finn*, 29, 222
Tyendinaga, 61. *See also* Native Americans
tyranny of merit, 44, 46. *See also* meritocracy

Ukraine, 3
Ulta Beauty, 23–24
Uncle Tom's Cabin (Stowe), 28, 222
unemployment, 4, 5, 6, 7, 9, 26, 97
UNICEF, 226
unions, x, 8. *See also* collective bargaining
United Kingdom (UK), 16, 18, 25, 84, 86, 87, 88, 179, 180, 181, 211, 233n
United Nations (UN), 61, 182; Generation Equality, 221
United States (US), 16, 25, 27–33, 83–104, 105, 106–7, 108, 128, 162, 169, 179, 180, 181, 191, 194, 196, 204, 209, 216, 222
Universal Studios, 13
upper class, 38, 40, 46, 188, 209, 217, 225. *See also* wealth
urban renewal, 93–94
US Constitution. *See* Constitution, US
USSR (Union of Soviet Socialist Republics), 233n. *See also* Russia

vampirism, 100, 170, 200, 218
Vietnam, 31
Vietnam War, 31
voter rights laws, 84
Voting Rights Act, 25

Walden (Thoreau), 28
Walker, Alice, 119
Walker, Madame C. J., 107
Wall Street Journal, 34
Walt Disney company. *See* Disney
Walt Disney Presents Uncle Remus, 106
Walters, Ryan, 106
Warner Bros., 210
Warren, Earl, 88
Warren, Robert Penn, 29
water pollution, 61. *See also* lead contamination
Watson, Renée, 104; *Piecing Me Together*, 104, 125

Wea Nation, 91. *See also* Native Americans
wealth, 16–17, 23, 24, 35, 38, 51, 65, 68, 72, 77, 80, 83, 84, 86, 87, 92, 98, 104, 109, 111, 118, 128, 129, 134, 150, 152, 154, 173, 181, 189, 199, 209, 215, 217, 225; inequality, 3, 51, 68–69, 129, 134, 151, 152. *See also* classism; social class; social stratification; upper class
welfare, as social safety-net, 26, 32, 89, 101, 121, 191. *See also* public assistance; social services
#WeNeedDiverseBooks, 103, 107
Western Shoshone Nation, 56. *See also* Native Americans
white (race), 12, 57, 58, 59, 67, 69, 70, 78, 84, 87–88, 90, 92, 93, 95, 96, 105, 106, 111, 116, 117, 118, 158, 172, 173–74, 174–75, 188, 194–96, 197, 202, 206, 212, 213, 216, 220, 221. *See also* Euro-Americans; Euro-Canadians
White House, 109
white privilege, 70, 98, 194, 195, 199, 204, 218
white rage, 169
white supremacy, 12, 90, 92, 116, 171, 176, 188, 194, 195, 198
whiteness, 88, 120, 145, 169, 170, 188, 199
Whitman, Walt, 28; "Song of Myself," 28
Williams, Alicia D., 107, 119; *Genesis Begins Again*, 107, 119–25
Wilson, Edmund, 29–30

Winnebago Nation, 91. *See also* Native Americans
women. *See* gender
#WomenAgainstFeminism, 130
women's suffrage, 25
Wood, Fernando, 87
work ethic, 100, 158
working class, 7, 32, 42, 59, 93, 112, 125, 129, 209. *See also* social class; social stratification
World Health Organization, 161–62
World War I, 180
World War II, 18, 109, 180, 220, 232n

xenophobia, 29. *See also* immigration; racism
Xia, Sisi, 161–62

YA protest literature, 209–24. *See also* youth activism
Yazoo, 91. *See also* Native Americans
young adult (YA) literature (defined), 10–11, 12
youth activism, xii, 21, 32–33, 49, 208, 209–24, 226–27. *See also* activism
Yousafzai, Malala, 220; *I Am Malala*, 220

Zelda, 131
Zimbabwe, 221
Zoboi, Ibi, 104; *American Street*, 104; *Pride*, 104
Zuckerberg, Mark, 23

ABOUT THE AUTHORS

Sean P. Connors is an associate professor of English education at the University of Arkansas. His scholarship and teaching focuses on the application of diverse critical perspectives to young adult literature. He is the editor of *The Politics of Panem: Challenging Genres*, a collection of critical essays about the Hunger Games series, and coeditor of *Teaching Girls on Fire: Essays on Dystopian Young Adult Literature in the Classroom*.

Roberta Seelinger Trites holds the rank of Distinguished Professor of English Emerita at Illinois State University, where she taught children's and YA literature from 1991 to 2022. She is the author of, among other works, *Waking Sleeping Beauty: Feminist Voices in Children's Literature* (1997), *Disturbing the Universe: Power and Repression in Adolescent Literature* (2000), *Twain, Alcott, and the Birth of the Adolescent Reform Novel* (2007), *Literary Conceptualizations of Growth: Metaphors and Cognition in Adolescent Literature* (2014), and *Twenty-First-Century Feminisms in Children's and Adolescent Literature* (2018).

www.ingramcontent.com/pod-product-compliance
Lightning Source LLC
Chambersburg PA
CBHW030612230426
43661CB00053B/1950